3ds Max® 9

Accelerated

Y.

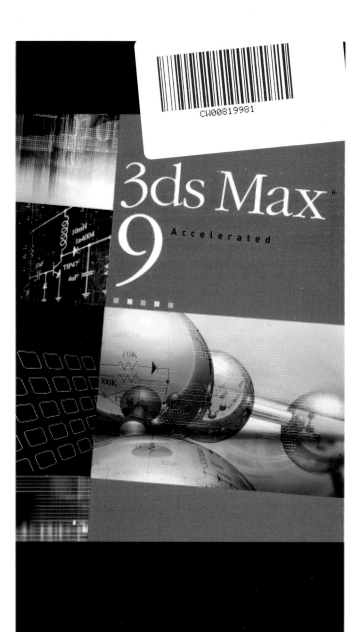

3ds Max® 9 Accelerated

ISBN: 978-89-314-3371-5

Printed and bound in the Republic of Korea.

How to contact us:

support@youngjin.com

feedback@youngjin.com

Address: YoungJin.com

3F Mapo Tower Bldg, 418-1 Mapo-dong,
Mapo-gu, Seoul 121-734, Korea

Fax: 82-2-2105-2206

Credits

Author: James Yeon

Production Manager: Suzie Lee

Editorial Service: Publication Service, Inc.

Developmental Editor: Rachel Lake, Publication Service, Inc.

Editorial Manager: Lorie Donovan, Publication Service, Inc.

Book Designer: Design Chang

Cover Designer: Litmus

Production Control: Woong Ki, SangJun Nam

3ds Max® 9

Accelerated

Installing 3ds Max 9 >>>

Autodesk® 3ds Max® 9 software is available in a high–capacity DVD format. The contents—previously divided into three CDs—are now all in one package for greater convenience and easier management.

Installing 3ds Max 9

Let's find out the stages of installing 3ds Max 9.

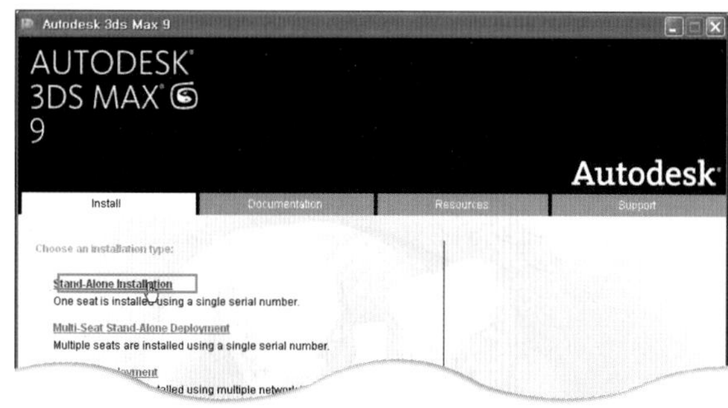

01 When you insert the program DVD, an installation screen will appear. Click [Stand–Alone Installation] to start the installation. The other installation options can be selected if you have a multiple–user license.

System Requirements

Note >>>

The program is available in different versions to fit 32–bit and 64–bit specifications. You must have the minimum system capacity for normal usage of the product. The 64–bit option requires Windows XP Professional 64–bit or Windows Vista operating systems, which require high–performance hardware.

Item	Requirements for 32 bit	Requirements for 64 bit
O/S	Windows 2000 (ServicePack 4), Windows XP Professional (SP2)	Windows XP Professional 64 Bit
Direct X	DirectX 9.0C	DirectX 9.0C
CPU	Intel Pentium IV or AMD Athlon XP or higher	Intel EM64T, AMD Athlon 64, AMD Opteron
Memory	512 MB or higher (1 GB recommended)	1 GB or higher (4 GB recommended)
Free Space	500 MB or higher (2 GB recommended)	2 GB or higher (2 GB recommended)
Graphic Card	Hardware Accelerated OpenGL and Direct3D compatible card	Hardware Accelerated OpenGL and Direct3D compatible card
Pointing Device	Windows compatible mouse	Windows compatible mouse
CD ROM	DVD	DVD
Optional	soundcard, speaker, video I/O device, joystick, MIDI device, 3 button mouse	

02 To install 3ds Max 9, select either 32–bit or 64–bit as compatible with your hardware and operating system specifications. The following example will demonstrate the installation of the 64–bit version on a Windows XP Professional system.

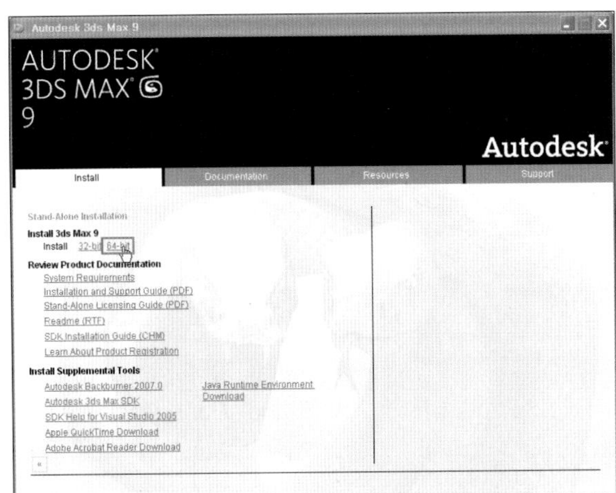

03 Next, a screen will appear for upgrading Windows' .Net environment to reinforce the system's performance. This process may take several minutes.

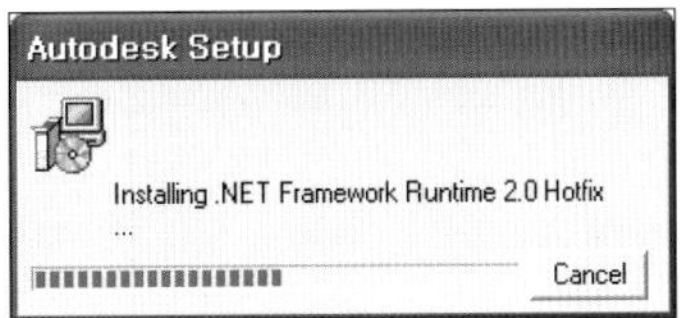

04 When the .Net installation is completed, Autodesk® DWF™ Viewer 7 is automatically installed.

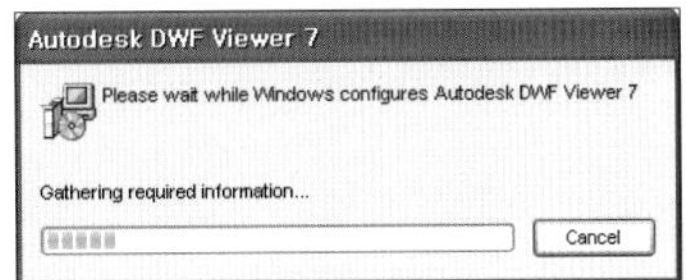

05 When the basic components are installed, a welcome screen will appear. Click [Next].

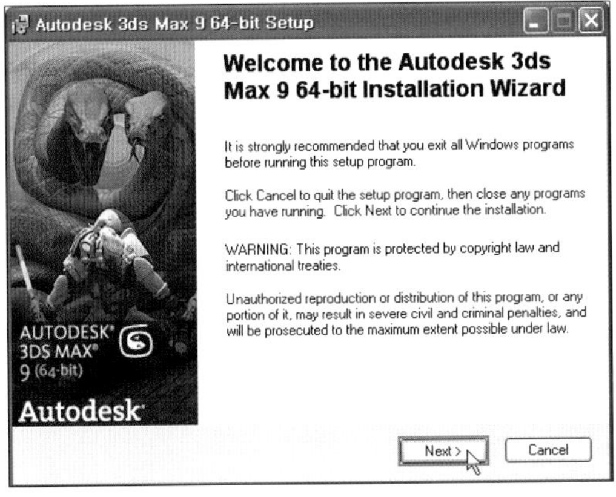

06 When the copyright agreement screen appears, accept the license agreement and click [Next].

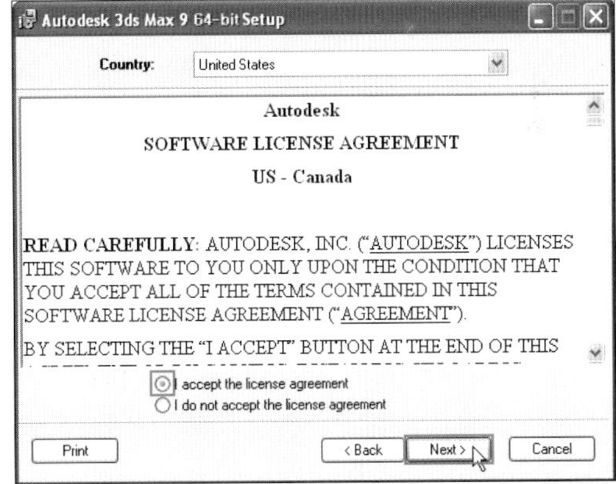

07 Type in your name or company when the user information screen appears, then click [Next].

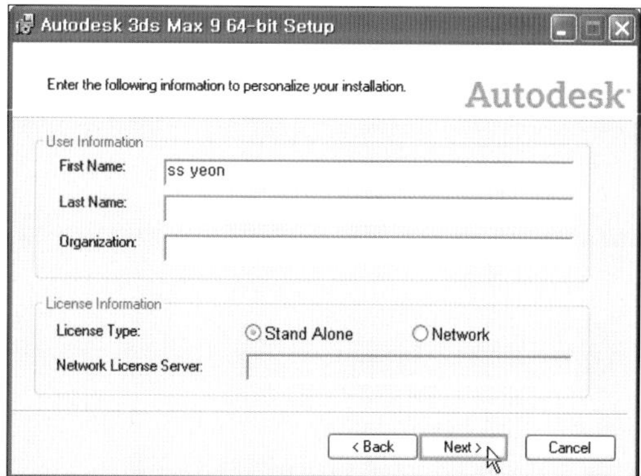

08 The next screen lists the elements to be installed for 3ds Max 9. Keep the default settings and click [Next].

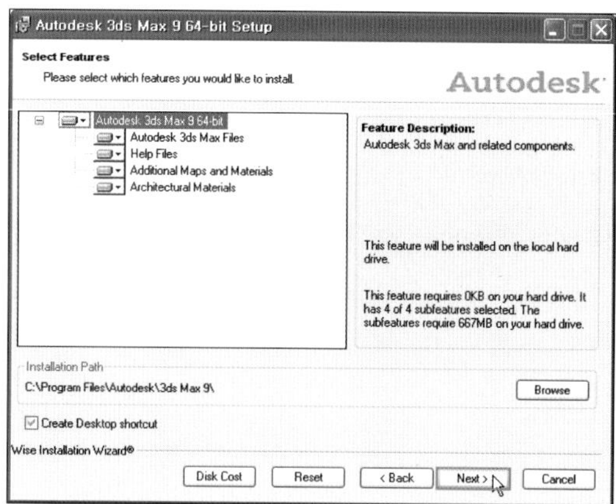

09 The next screen will ask you to set the network port for the Mental Ray renderer and to adjust the installation location of the Backburner. Click [Next] to proceed.

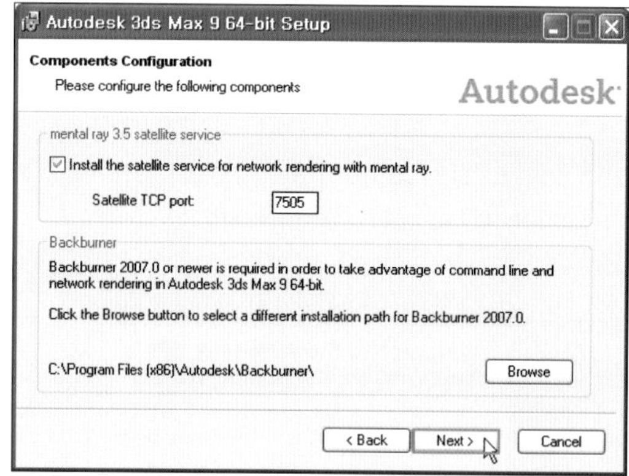

10 Confirm the user information and the installation path and click [Next].

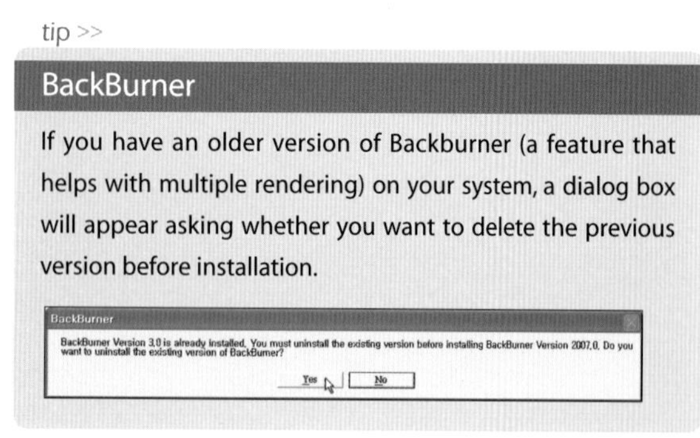
tip >>

BackBurner

If you have an older version of Backburner (a feature that helps with multiple rendering) on your system, a dialog box will appear asking whether you want to delete the previous version before installation.

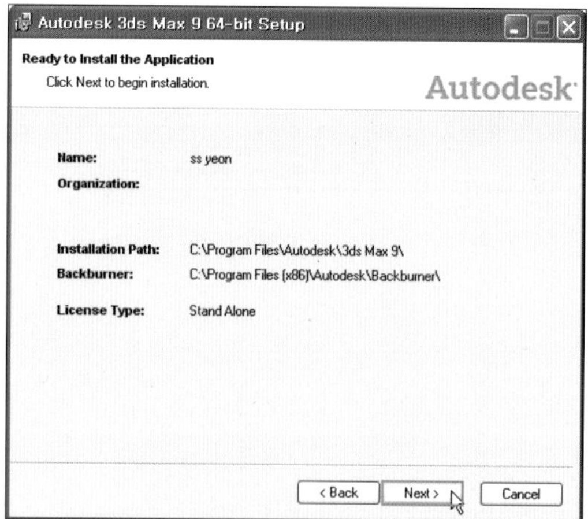

11 3ds Max 9 will install according to the settings indicated.

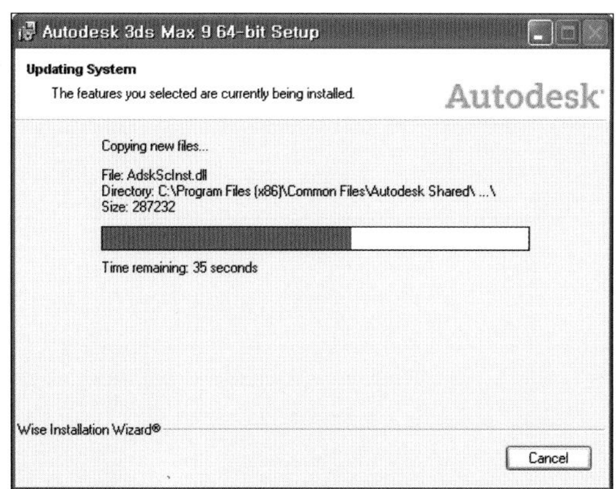

12 When the installation is complete, a final verification screen appears. Click [Finish] to finish the installation.

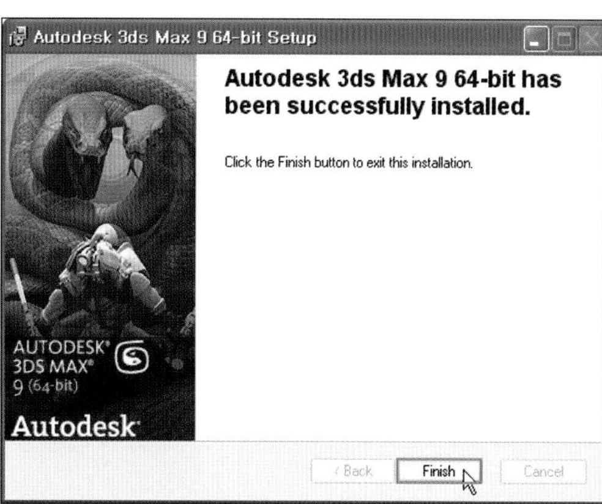

Product Activation >>>

After installing 3ds Max 9, you must authorize the product. The authorization process is automatically activated when the program is opened for the first time after installation.

Product Activation, Startup, and Exit

After installation, a program icon should appear on the desktop.

01 Double–click the Autodesk 3dsMax 9 icon on the desktop, or go to [Start]–[All Programs]–[Autodesk]–[Autodesk 3ds Max 9], and double–click [3ds Max 9]. The icon will indicate either 32–bit or 64–bit.

02 Before the program loads, a window for product authorization appears. Check [Activate the Product] and click [Next] to input the activation code. After inputting the activation code, the program will load.
You may also choose to run 3ds Max 9 for 30 days before authorizing the program.

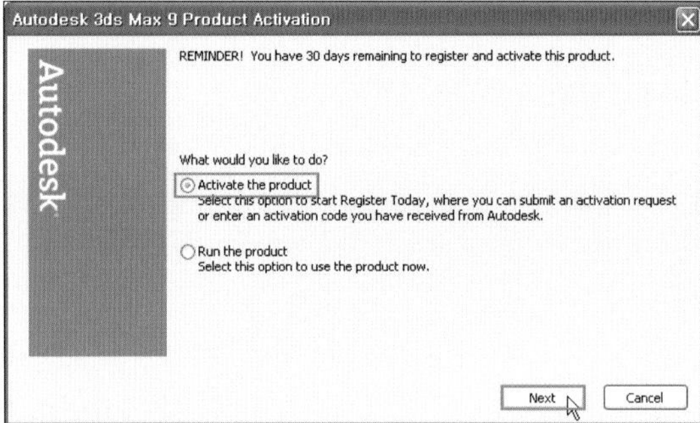

03 After obtaining an activation code from Autodesk, click [Enter an activation code], and the [Next] button.

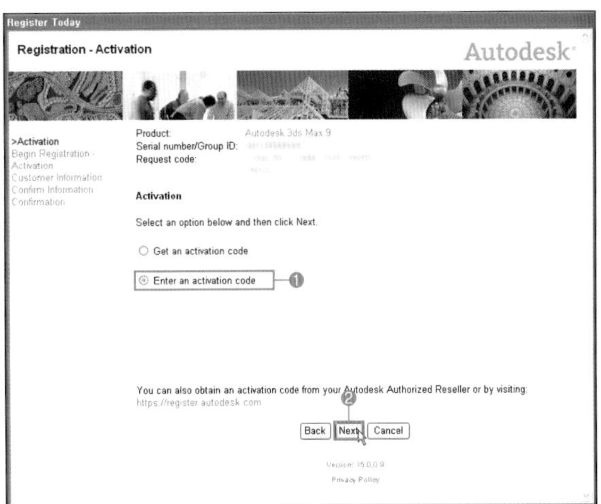

04 First, select the country, and input the authorized activation code at the bottom. Select [Next].

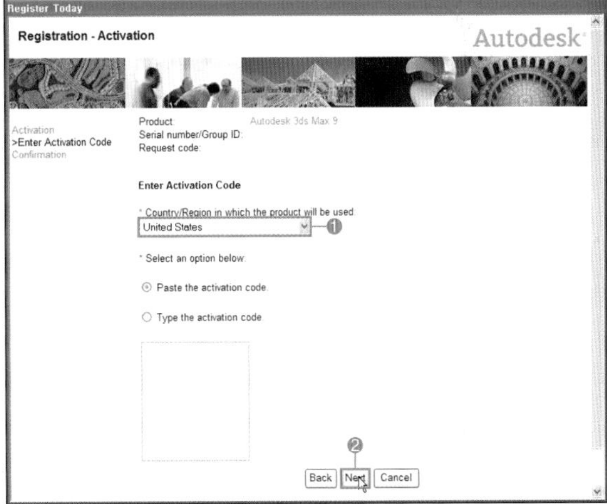

tip >>

Activation Codes

The activation code is issued by Autodesk; this code authorizes the use of the product when a genuine 3ds Max product has been purchased. Normally, the code can be obtained online or through another communication device such as a fax machine. After sending a request code, the user should receive an activation code from Autodesk.

05 A dialog box confirms the activation. Click [Finish].

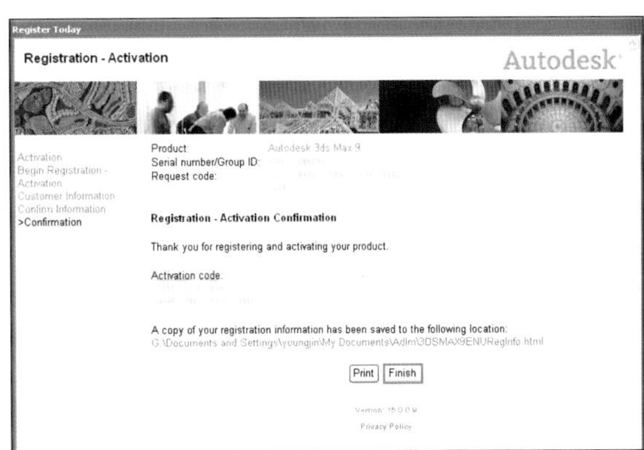

Chapter 1

Challenging 3ds Max 9

As 3D based movies and TV programs today are becoming more common, it's not a surprise that 3ds Max is playing a significant role in this trend. 3ds Max has surpassed all competition and has come to be the ultimate program since the introduction of 3ds Max 1.0 in 1995. Today, 3D design is not possible without using the 3ds Max program. We shall first take a quick look at the basics and basic applications of the ultimate 3D graphic tool, the 3ds Max 9.

SECTION 01

Understanding the User Interface

When using 3ds Max 9 for the first time, the program's many functions may seem confusing at first. Because almost all of the functions are displayed in one screen, the interface may look complicated. However, this integrated interface enables the user to work very speedily once the functions are properly identified and understood. This chapter will examine the basic screen interface and major functions of 3ds Max 9.

The Screen Structure

Within the single workspace, the user can see all of the program's functions, including modeling and animation.

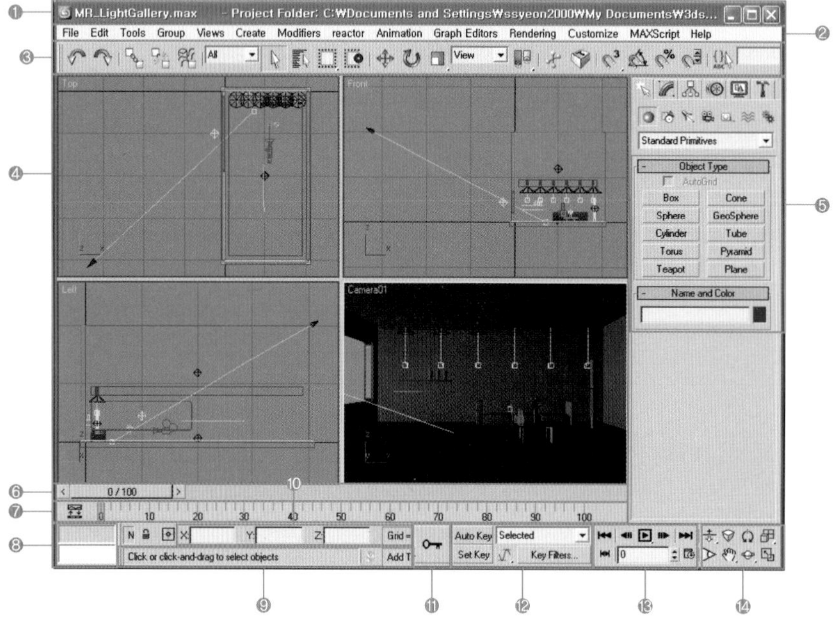

❶ Title Bar

This indicates the name of the file that is currently active.

❷ Menu Bar

The menu shows functions regardir.g the input and output of files, editing, special tools, and animation-related functions. Most of the functions overlap with the Command panel, shown in the right-hand panel. The interface was designed to facilitate easy operation in professional mode, in which only the menu function appears.

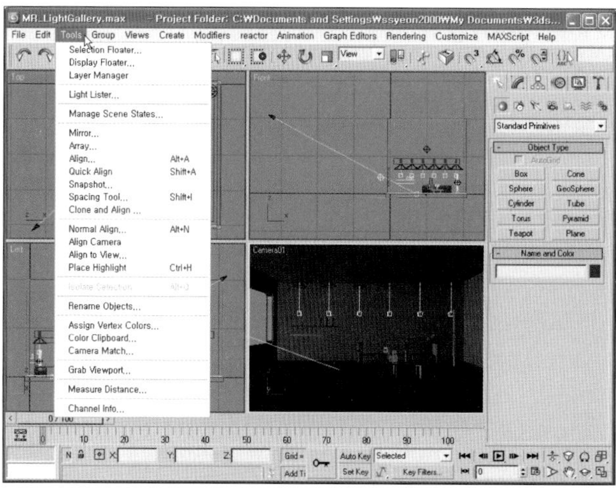

Once the menu is clicked

❸ Main Toolbar

The most frequently used tools--related to modeling, editing and rendering--are organized here. This is the most commonly used feature of 3ds Max 9.

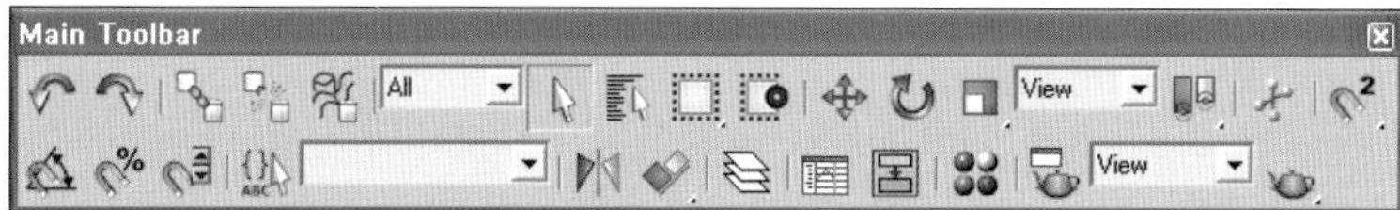

❹ Viewport

In the Viewport you can observe a 3D object from various perspectives. Toggle between top, front, left, and "perspective" views by right-clicking the Viewport icons.

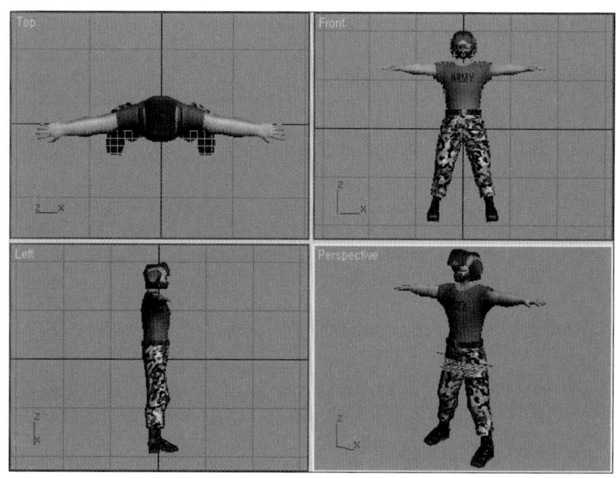

Multiple views of a 3D object

⑤ Command Panel

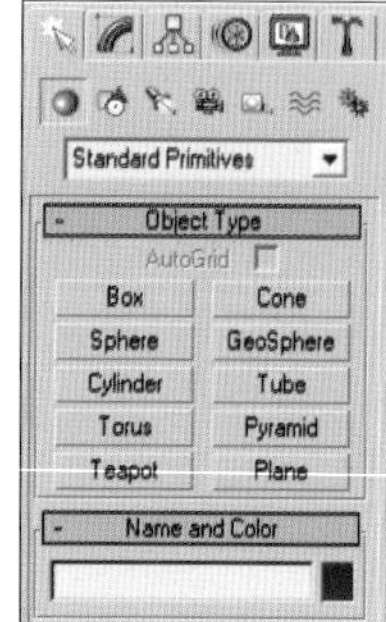

This is where you can find all the editing and basic tools for object design, including those related to figures, cameras, lines, and lights. The tools are categorized as Create, Modify, Hierarchy, Motion, Display, and Utility panels.

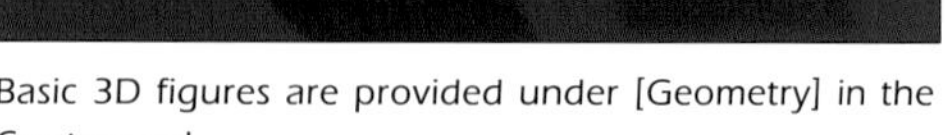

Basic 3D figures are provided under [Geometry] in the Create panel.

Basic 2D curved figures are provided under [Shapes] in the Create panel.

⑥ Time Slider

The Time Slider enables scene–by–scene search of animations. You can observe the flow of the animation precisely frame by frame, which is the minimum unit for animations. One hundred frame sections are set as the basic default, but you can change the animation time under [Time Configuration].

⑦ Track Bar

Here you can instantly observe changes in the animation caused by the object in the Viewport. Changes in the animation's motions are classified using keys, giving the user detailed control over the motions.

⑧ Mini Scripts Listener

3ds Max work is primarily done with a mouse, but for professional modeling or animations the work is processed with Scripts, a programming language. Mini Script Listener enables swift input of the script and observation of the results.

```
create box 0,0,0
```

⑨ Prompt Line and Status Line

This line shows the contents that are currently in progress, as well as usage guidelines for each tool.

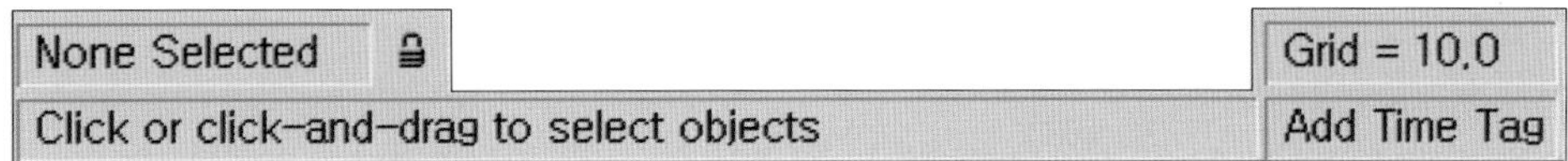

⑩ Transform Type-in

This indicates the location of the object on the Viewport, which can be changed using precise values with the Move, Rotate, and Scale functions. Objects may be moved using absolute coordinates to identify a designated location in the 3D space, or using values relative to the current location of the object.

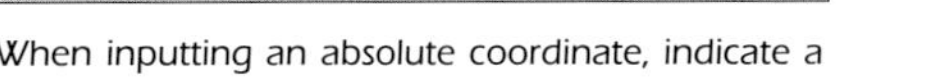

When inputting an absolute coordinate, indicate a location on each axis.

When inputting a relative coordinate, indicate the degree of change from an object's current position.

⑪ Animate Button

The animate button is a tool that registers the moment of change when producing an animation in which the object moves. Select the animation button that you wish to use.

⑫ AutoKey/SetKey

3ds Max 9 provides two methods of animation: the Auto Key and the Set Key methods. When using the Auto Key method, the middle process is automatically created by moving the object frame by frame. When using the Set Key method, the animation is registered by clicking the "Animate" button at the location you choose after the movement has occurred in each frame.

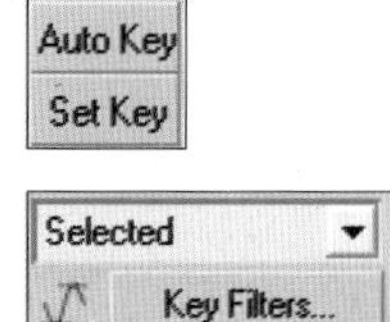

⑬ Animation Time Control

Just as with a video player, you can play or stop the animation created on the Viewport, or even rewind or fast forward. Also, you can change the settings for the animation section by clicking Time Configuration.

⑭ Viewport Navigation Control

Here, you can rotate each Viewport or use functions such as zoom. The object is not changed, but the Viewport is moved. Also, if the Viewport is changed to camera or light view, the control is changed to Viewport navigation control for camera or light.

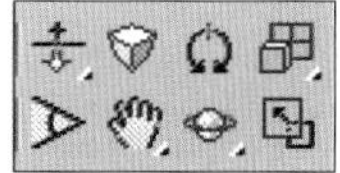

Understanding the Command Panel

For places that require realistic lighting effects, other than the Standard Light, the user can use the Photometric Light. This is mostly used for renderings for buildings. The directions for use is similar to that for the Standard Light, but for precise lighting effects, click [Rendering]–[Advanced Lighting]–[Radiosity] on the menu bar for the Radiosity Solution calculation process.

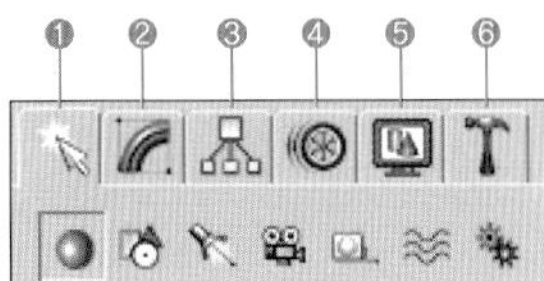

① Create Panel

This feature provides tools such as 2D, 3D, lights, and cameras for creating various objects. More than 80 percent of your 3ds Max 9 work will be conducted here, so it is important to understand the interface options.

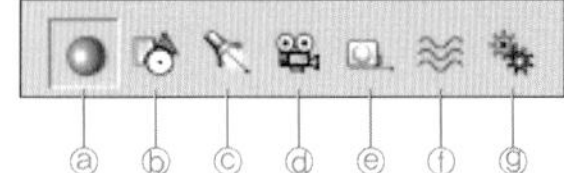

ⓐ Geometry––provides the basic 3D object tools used in 3ds Max 9
ⓑ Shapes––provides object tools to create 2D objects
ⓒ Lights––provides lighting tools
ⓓ Cameras––provides tools for creating a camera
ⓔ Helpers––provides tools that help in creating objects
ⓕ Spacewarps––provides tools that can transform objects or create special effects
ⓖ Systems––provides tools that can be specially used for 3ds Max 9 modeling

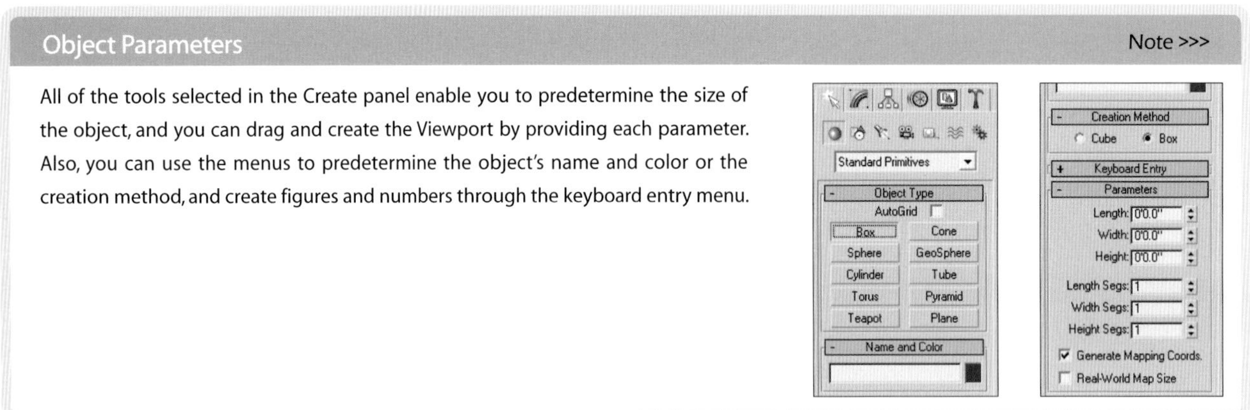

All of the tools selected in the Create panel enable you to predetermine the size of the object, and you can drag and create the Viewport by providing each parameter. Also, you can use the menus to predetermine the object's name and color or the creation method, and create figures and numbers through the keyboard entry menu.

❷ Modify Panel

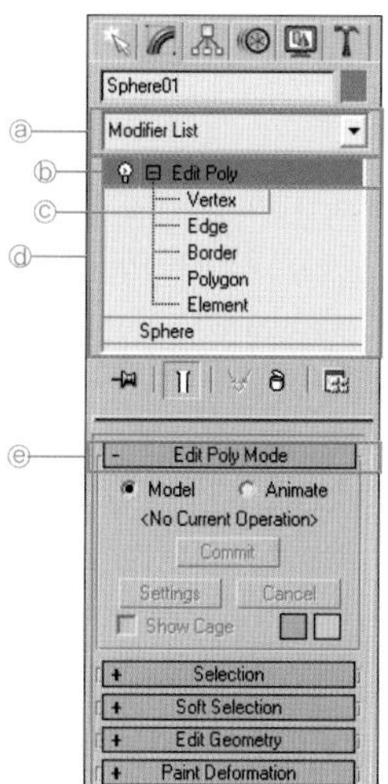

Here, you can modify the parameters of the object created on the Viewport or add a modifier to modify the object. The modifier can be added by clicking the [Modifier List] combo box; up to 80 Modifiers can be added, and they accumulate in a hierarchical order. Modifiers, applied in order to the object, can be confirmed at the Modifier Stack, and each of the Modifier's functions can be activated or deactivated.

ⓐ Modifier List: Select modifiers for editing the object.

ⓑ Activates or deactivates the function

ⓒ Displays Sub–Objects

ⓓ Modifier Stack

Confirm the hierarchy of the Modifier applied to the object, and change the order by dragging the mouse. Each of the Modifiers has a sub–object inside it that can also be manipulated.

ⓔ Parameters

Change the parameters of modifiers applied to an object. The user can show parameters by dragging them until they appear.

❸ Hierarchy Panel

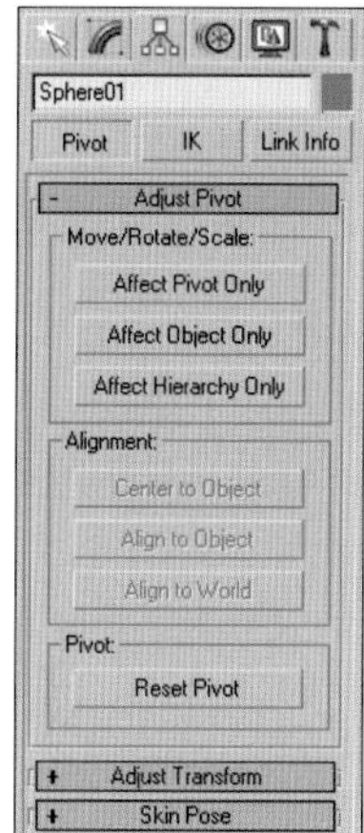

You can modify the pivot in each of the objects during the animation work process or adjust the status of a connected object. Also, you can modify the information of each of the connection stages in conducting IK animation work.

❹ Motion Panel

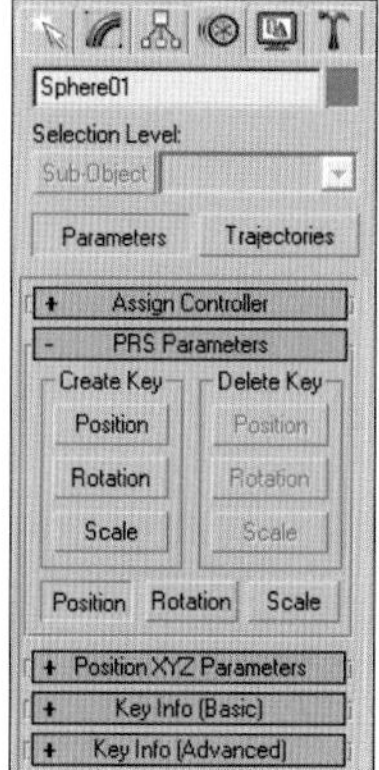

In the Motion panel, you can change the information value for the movement, rotation, or size change within each of the key frames registered in the animation, and you also have detailed control over the flow of the entrance and exit among the key frames.

⑤ Display Panel

Show or hide an object on the Viewport, or use the Freeze function to show the object as fixed.

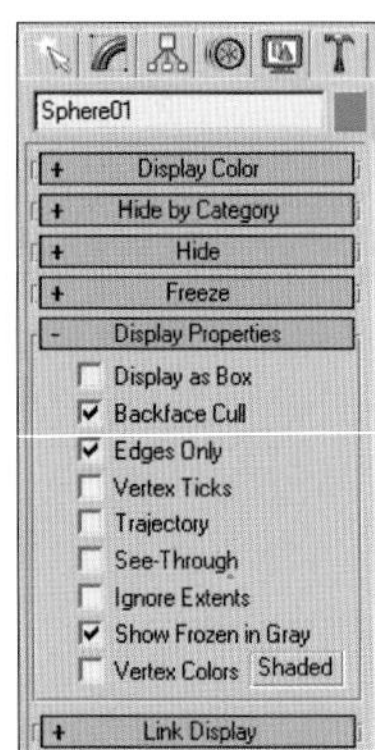

⑥ Utilities Panel

Additional functions that are useful for 3D work are available here, although these are not basic tools. To access the additional tools, click More... and make a selection from the dialog box.

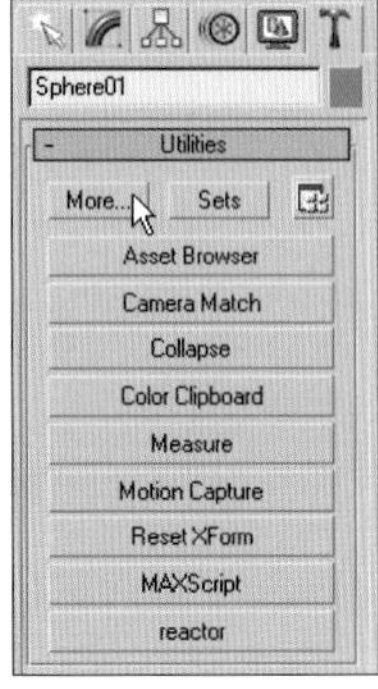

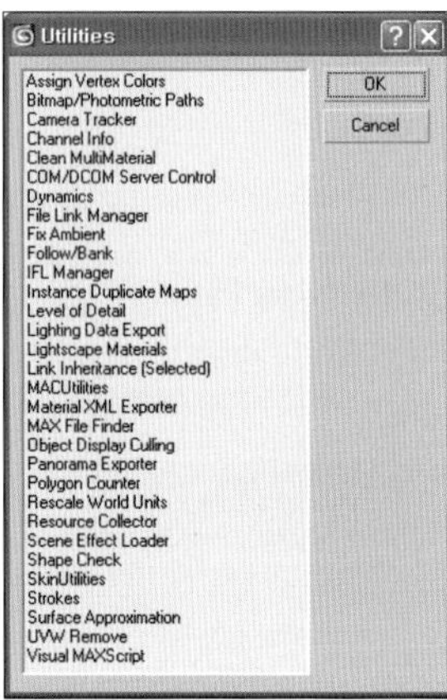

Let's Go Pro!

Viewport

A Viewport is an area in the work space where the user can cutomize such functions as view option and size control to his/her liking. Let's find out some Viewport management methods to make working with 3ds Max more comfortable.

① Active Viewport

Among the various Viewports, the one currently being used is indicated with a yellow border and is called the Active Viewport. If you wish to change the Viewport during modeling or working on the animation, click on the Viewport to be used with the right mouse button.

② Viewport Resizing

While using various Viewports, you may have to magnify one that you wish to focus on.

Magnify the Viewport by clicking [Maximize Viewport] on the Viewport navigation control.

Or you can change the size by dragging the border with the mouse without expanding the Viewport.

③ Viewport Menu

Each of the Viewport characters has a separate menu. This can be used to change to the desired view.

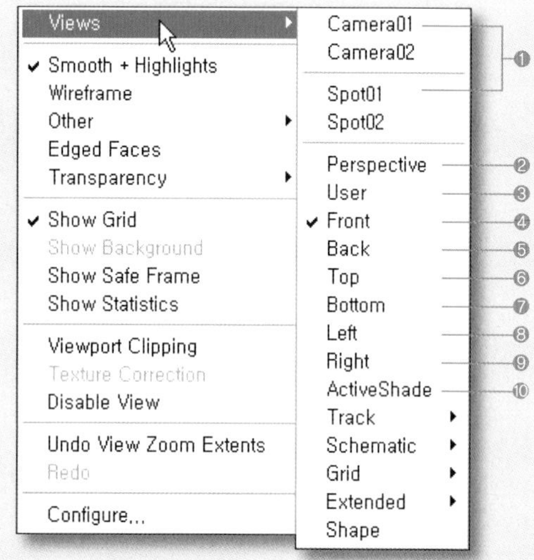

❶ If camera or light is installed in the Viewport, the user can change over to camera view or light view.
❷ View from upper angle
❸ View direction set by user
❹ View from the front of the object
❺ View from the back of the object
❻ View from the top of the object
❼ View from the bottom of the object
❽ View from the left of the object
❾ View from the right of the object
❿ View used for real–time rendering

④ F3 and F4 Keys

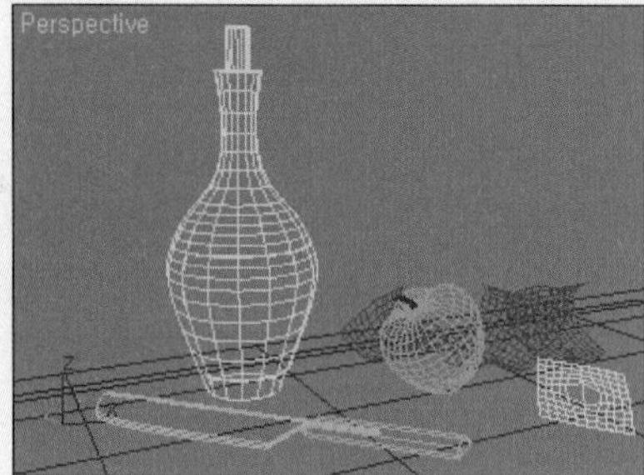

While conducting modeling work in the Viewport, you may need to look not only at an internal segment of the object but also at its color or texture.

In this case, press F3 to see and manipulate the color and mapping of the object (shown here with Smooth + Highlights).

When pressed at the same time as F3, F4 enables the user to turn the internal segment on or off (shown here with Smooth + Highlights + Edges Face).

Exercise 01

Startup and File Management

This exercise will discuss how to launch and exit 3ds Max 9, as well as methods for opening, saving, and converting files.

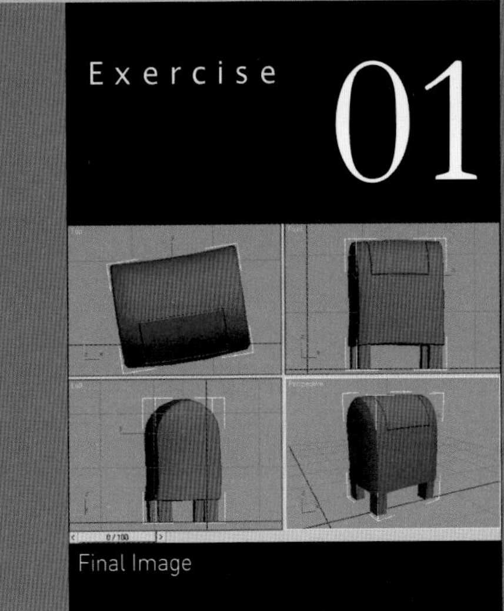

Final Image

3ds Max 9 Startup

Let's take a look at the work space that appears once the 3ds Max 9 has been launched.

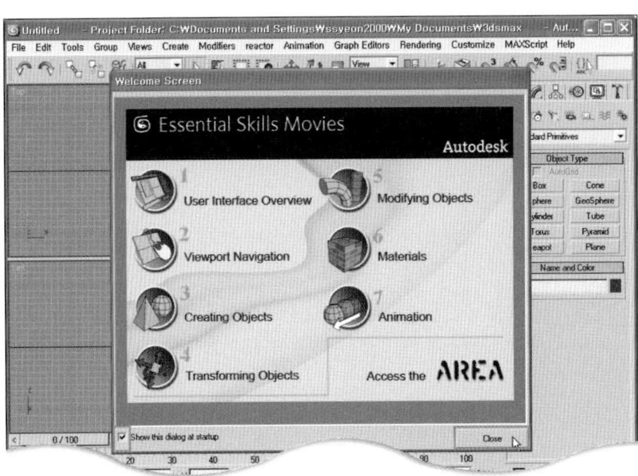

01 As the program loads, a Welcome Screen appears. This screen provides video demonstrations of the program' s basic functions. This feature is helpful for users who are new to the program. This screen will appear every time the program is executed, unless you deactivate it by unchecking [Show this dialog at startup] and clicking [Close].

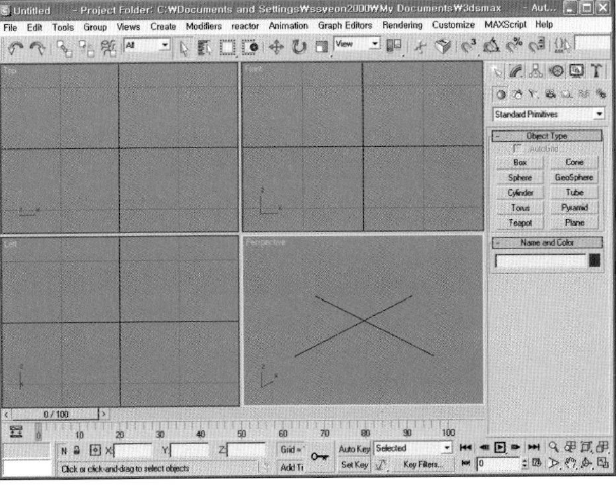

02 As you enter the workspace, key tools will appear, including the upper menu bar, main toolbar, Viewport, Command panel, Time Slider, Time Control, and Viewport Control.

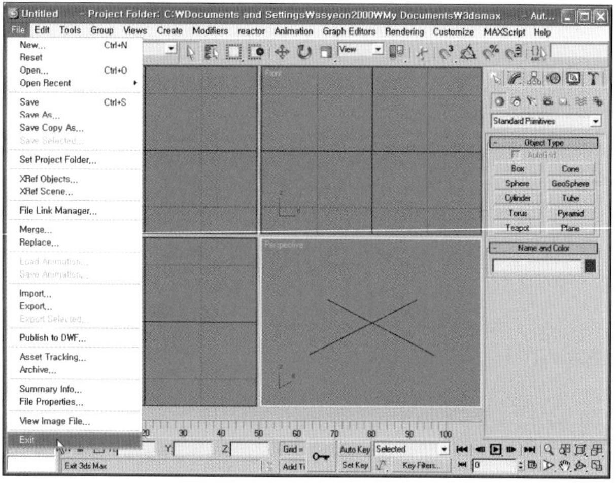

03 When you are ready to close the program, click [File]–[Exit] on the menu bar.

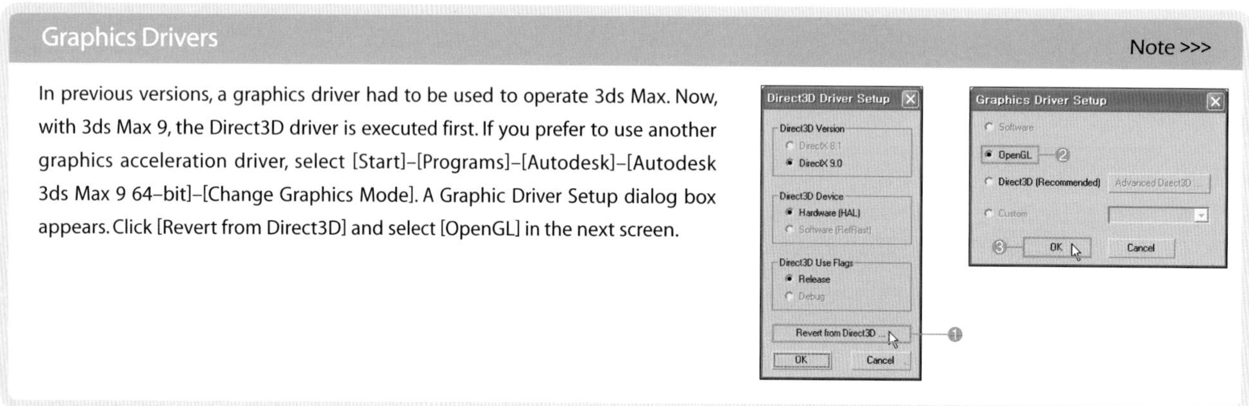

Graphics Drivers

Note >>>

In previous versions, a graphics driver had to be used to operate 3ds Max. Now, with 3ds Max 9, the Direct3D driver is executed first. If you prefer to use another graphics acceleration driver, select [Start]–[Programs]–[Autodesk]–[Autodesk 3ds Max 9 64-bit]–[Change Graphics Mode]. A Graphic Driver Setup dialog box appears. Click [Revert from Direct3D] and select [OpenGL] in the next screen.

Managing 3ds Max 9 Files 

3ds Max 9 uses (.max) as the basic file extension, and you can open files by using the [Open] command. Also, you can export objects created with 3ds Max 9 to other programs or import files from other programs.

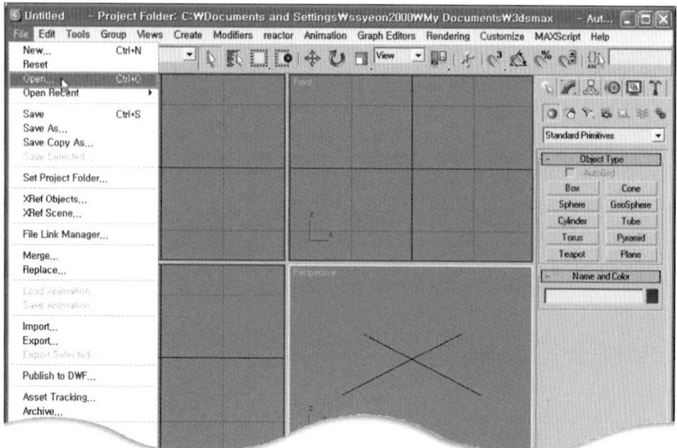

01 To open 3ds Max 9 files, click [File]–[Open] on the menu bar.

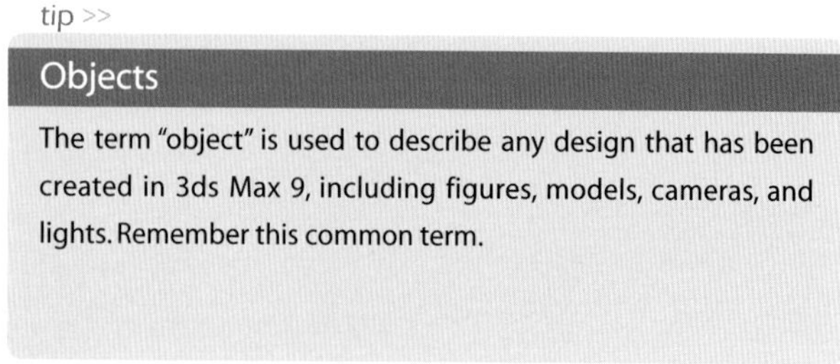

tip >>

Objects

The term "object" is used to describe any design that has been created in 3ds Max 9, including figures, models, cameras, and lights. Remember this common term.

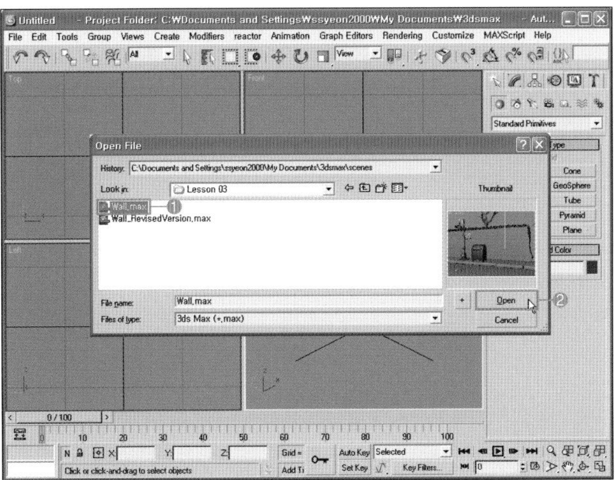

02 When the [Open File] dialog box appears, select the "Wall.max" file from the supplementary CD and click [Open].

Supplementary CD\Sample\Chapter 1\Exercise 1\Wall.max

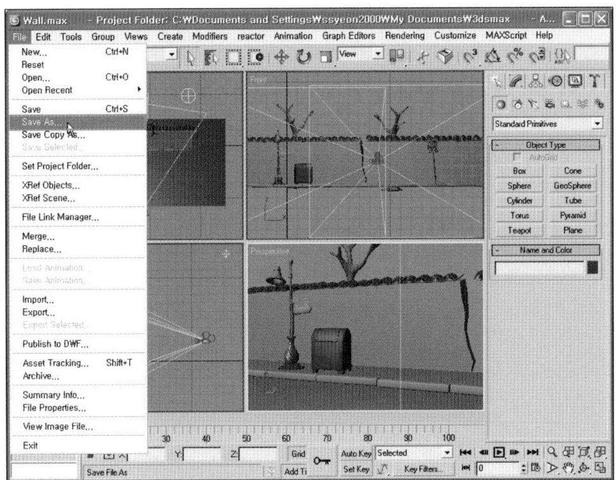

03 Objects that have been already created on the Viewport, such as walls and mailboxes, appear. Click [File]–[Save As] on the menu bar to save the file under a different name.

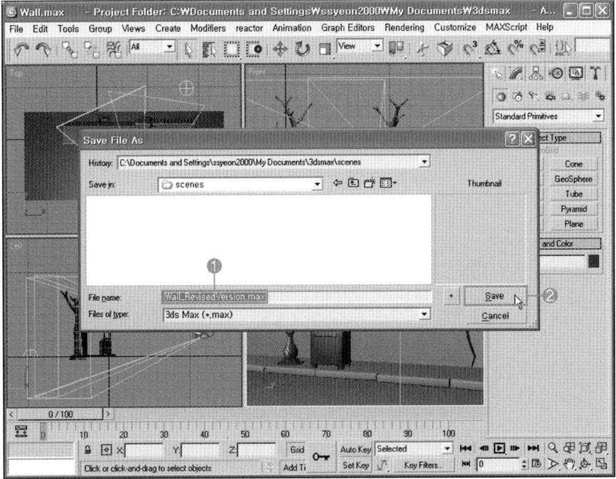

04 When the [Save File As] dialog box appears, select a folder where you want to save the file, name the file "Wall_RevisedVersion.max" and click [Save].

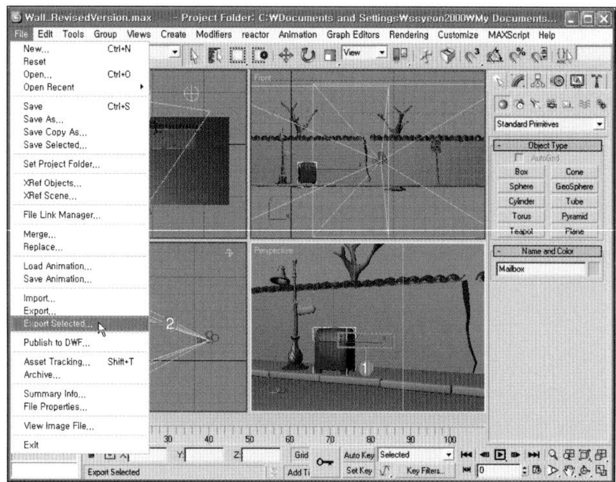

05 To enable the use of a specific object of the current file in a different program, select the mailbox in the Viewport and click [File]–[Export Selected] on the menu bar.

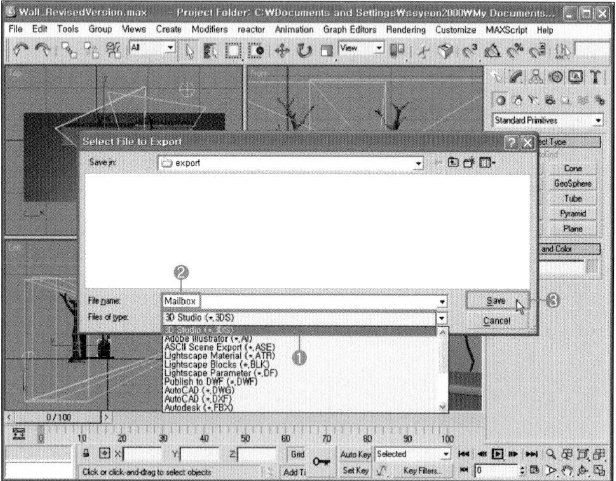

06 When the Select File to Export dialog box "appears, select 3D Studio (.3DS) as the file format, then type in the file name as "Mailbox.3DS" and click [Save].

tip >>

Preserve MAX's Texture Coordinate

When exporting in the 3DS file format for 3D Studio, which is the previous version of 3ds Max, a dialog box appears asking whether to save the Texture Coordinate used for the current object. Click [OK].

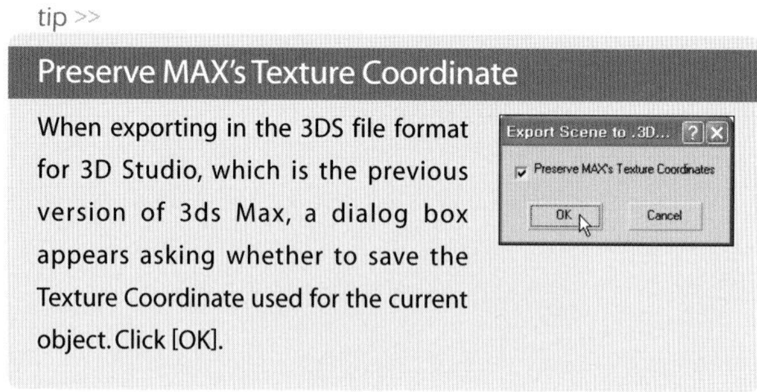

07 To close the current file and return to the initial screen, click [File]–[Reset] on the menu bar.

tip >>

Saving Changes

If you have changed or modified the objects in the Viewport, a dialog box will appear asking whether to save the file before [Reset] appears. Click [No].

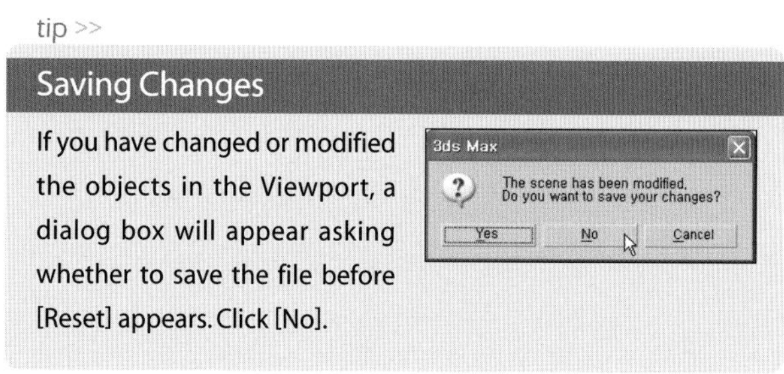

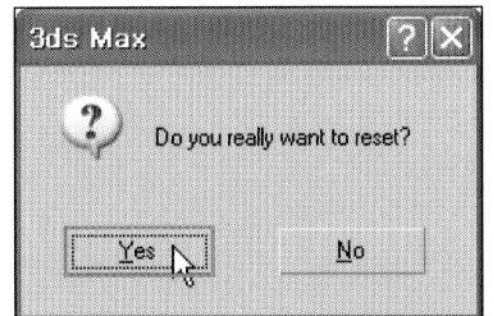

08 A dialog box appears asking whether you really wish to return to the initial screen. Click [Yes]. Initialization will not occur if you click [No].

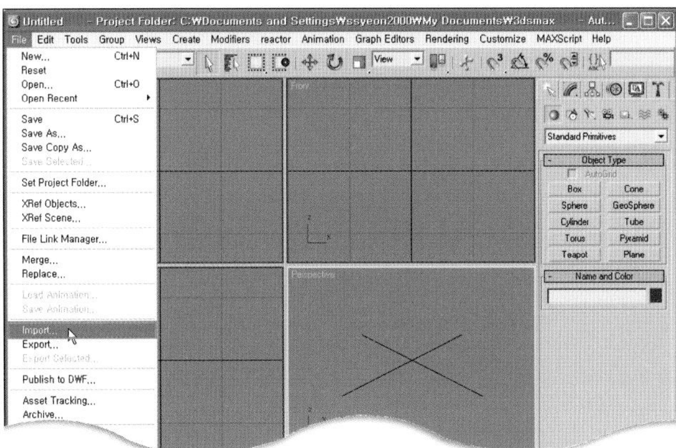
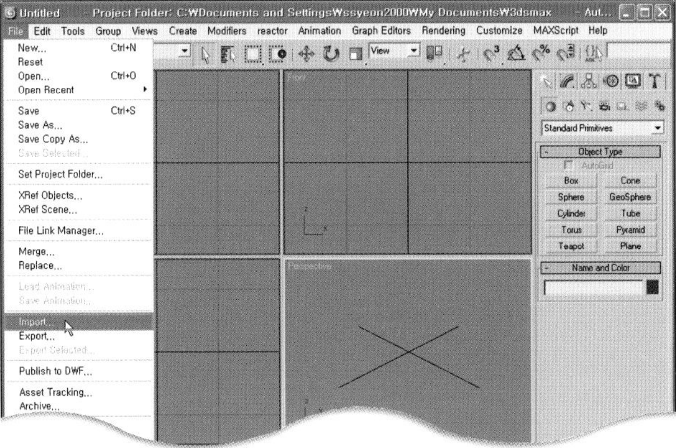

09 To import the “Mailbox” which was exported as a 3D Studio file, click [File]–[Import] on the menu bar.

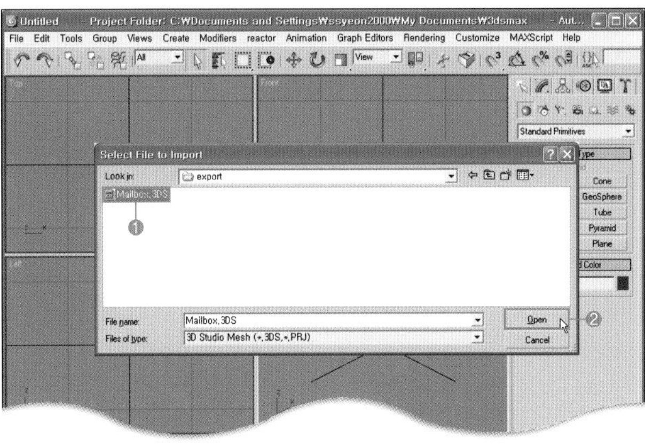

10 A Select File to Import dialog box appears. Select “Mailbox.3DS” from the saved folder and click [Open].

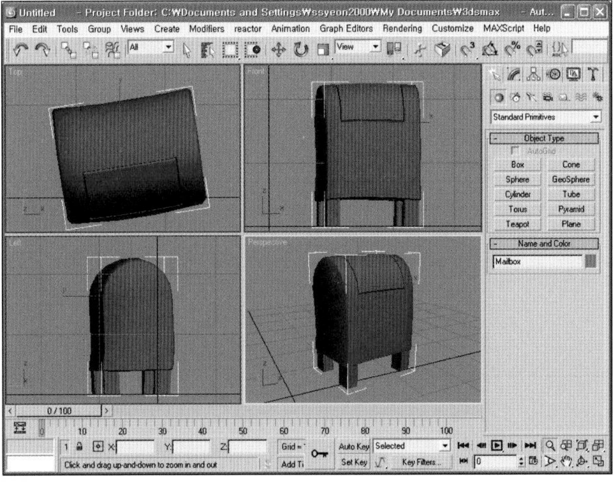

11 The “Mailbox” object, saved for 3D Studio, reappears on the Viewport. However, the material of the “Mailbox” image that was showing on the screen is not saved when being exported. The user must conduct the mapping process of reading the material.

tip >>

Mapping for exporting an object

In previous versions of the program, when a user attempted to export an object, the object was imported in the grey mapped state, even if the object had not been mapped. In the current version, 3ds Max 9, the object is imported as it is in the export state, which makes the work process much easier.

Exercise 02

Basic Skills in 3ds Max 9

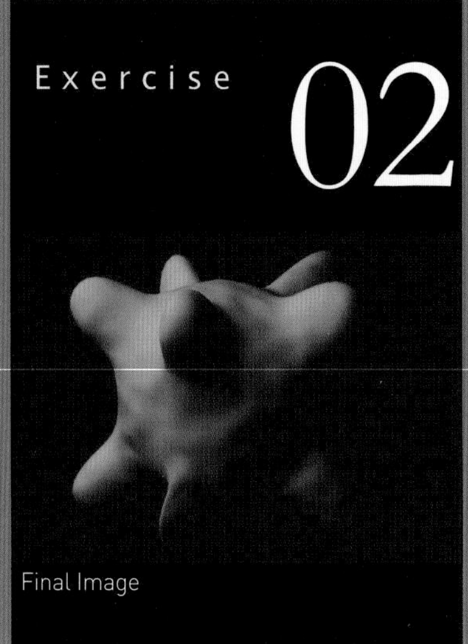
Final Image

For beginners, 3ds Max 9 may seem daunting or difficult to learn. However, learning a few key processes can make the program simple and fun to use. In this section, we will explain some of the basic processes: modeling objects, creating and editing basic figures, finishing and softening the model, and mapping to color the model.

Creating a Shape

One of the first steps in using 3ds Max 9 is to manipulate the basic figures. You can create the desired figures and change their shapes at will.

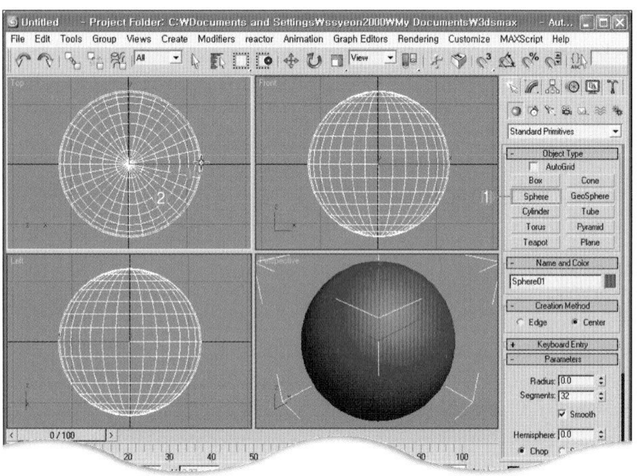

01 On the Create panel, under [Geometry]–[Standard Primitives], click [Sphere]. Drag from the center of the absolute axis (where the black lines cross at the Top Viewport) and create a spherical object.

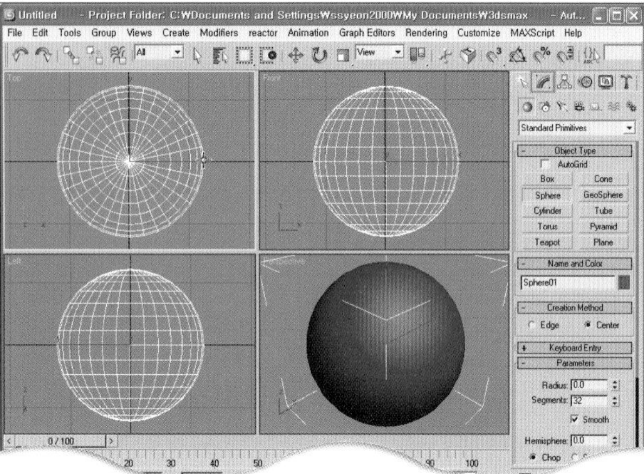

02 Select the sphere just created and click [Modify] to move to the Modify panel.

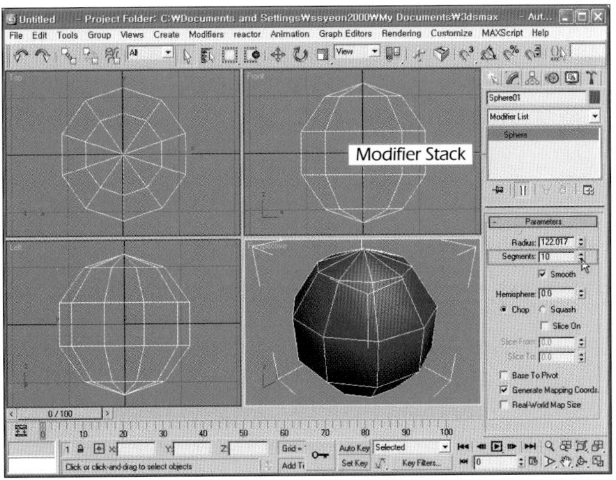

03 On the Modify panel, the currently selected "Sphere01" is listed on the Modifier Stack, and various parameters can be seen below. Input [10] in the parameter [Segment] to change the shape into an angular form.

tip >>

Segment

A segment is a horizontal or vertical grid that underlies the figure. The basic sphere above is composed of numerous crisscrossing lines, which make the shape look round. Generally, shapes that are too round are difficult to change; therefore, users generally reduce the number of segments to make modification easier.

Manipulating a Shape

Because it is difficult to create a variety of shapes with a sphere, we will use the Edit Poly Modifier, which allows greater adjustments. The Edit Poly Modifier is widely used for the modification of 3D figures such as spheres.

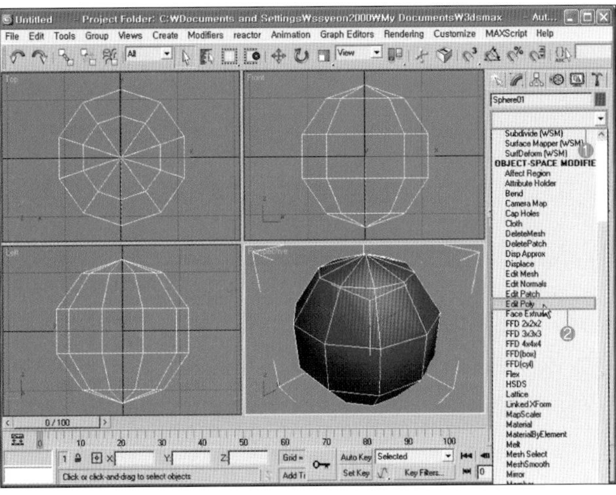

01 Click the [Modifier List] combo box to add a modifier, and select [Edit Poly] Modifier.

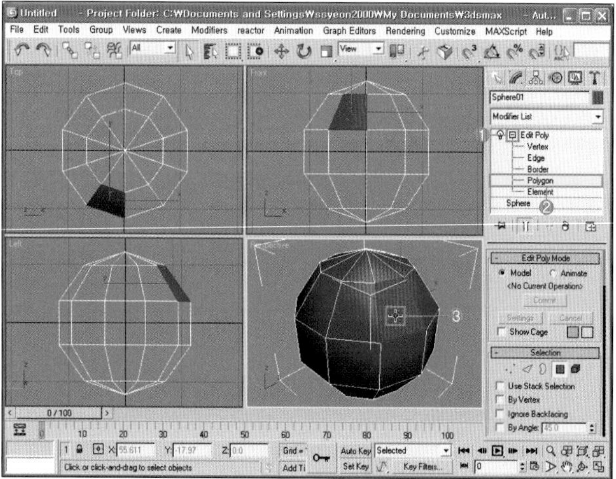

02 On the Modifier Stack, the Edit Poly Modifier is listed above the sphere; this means that the Edit Poly Modifier monitors and modifies the sphere object. In the submenu under Edit Poly, select the sub–object [Polygon], and then select a polygon on the Viewport.

tip >>

Sub–Objects

A sub–object is an internal component that makes up each object. In the case of a sphere, for example, the figure includes Vertexes, Edges, Borders, Polygons, and Elements.

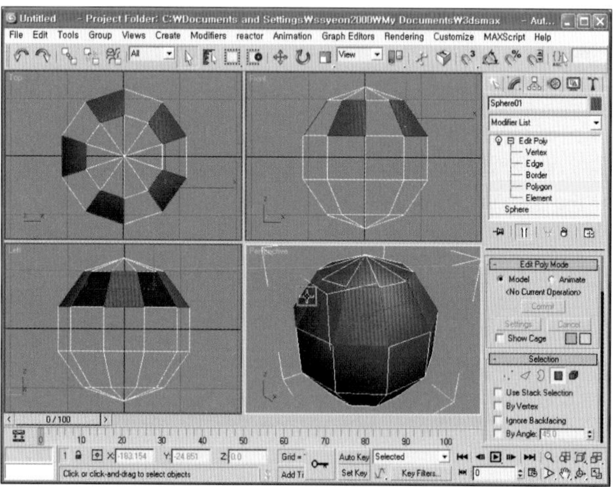

03 By holding down the [Ctrl] key, you can select more than one polygon to create an overlap.

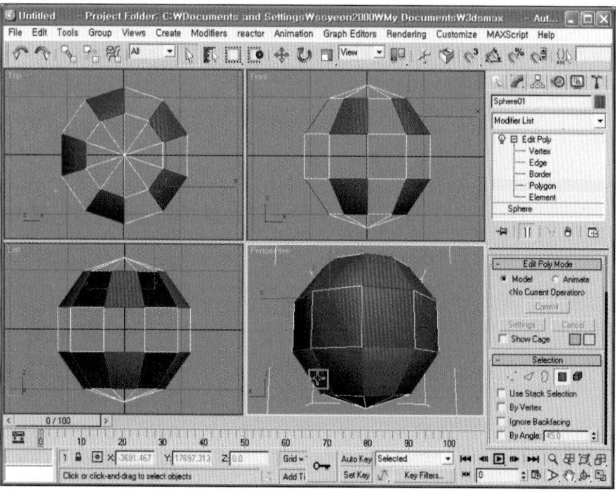

04 By rotating the Perspective Viewport, while holding down [Ctrl], select additional polygons on the sphere.

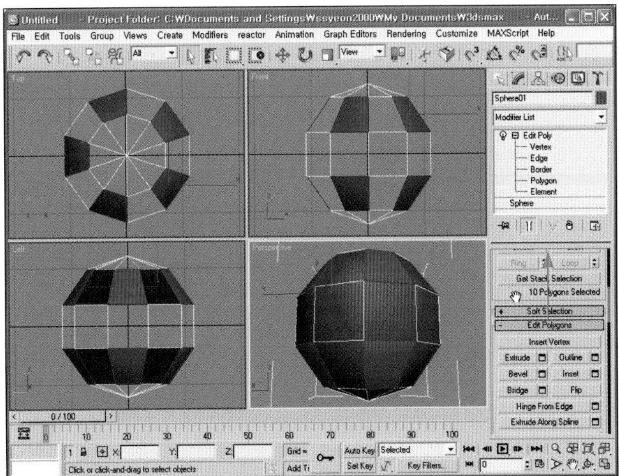

05 When the icon appears in the Modify panel's parameter section, drag it upward to view the additional parameters below.

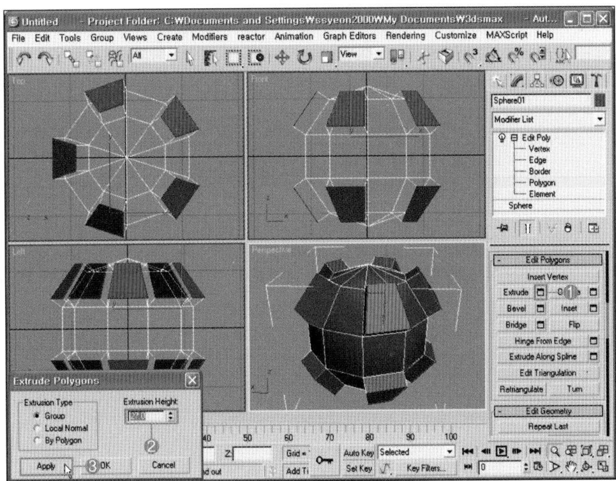

06 Click [Extrude] under the Edit Poly parameter. When the Extrude Polygons dialog box appears, input [27] into [Extrusion Height] and click [Apply]. The selected polygon extrudes to the designated size.

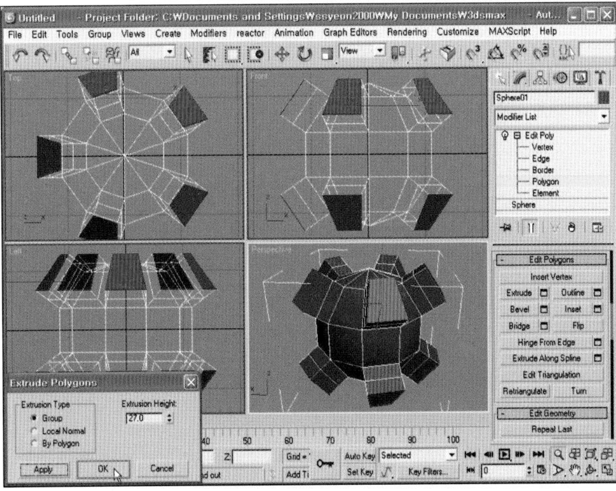

07 To make the selected polygons extrude again, maintain the Extrusion Height and click [OK]. The selected polygons then extrude a second time.

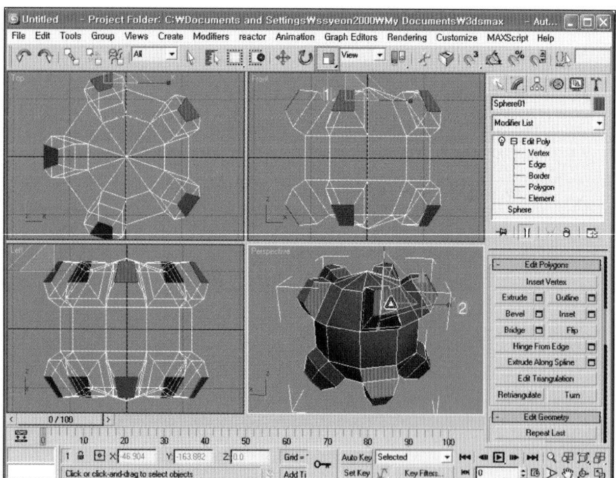

08 Click [Select and Scale] on the main toolbar and drag to reduce the size of each of the extruded polygons.

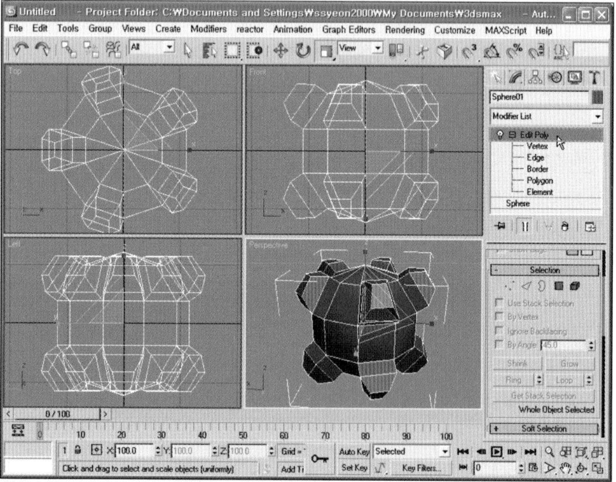

09 Click the [Edit Poly] Modifier character to exit the sub-object mode. The mode must be exited in order to select a different object.

tip >>

Why deselect ?

The sub-object mode must be deselected in order to select another object.

Finishing a Shape

Generally the user finalizes an object using the MeshSmooth Modifier, which smoothes the overall angular polygon when the modeling is completed.

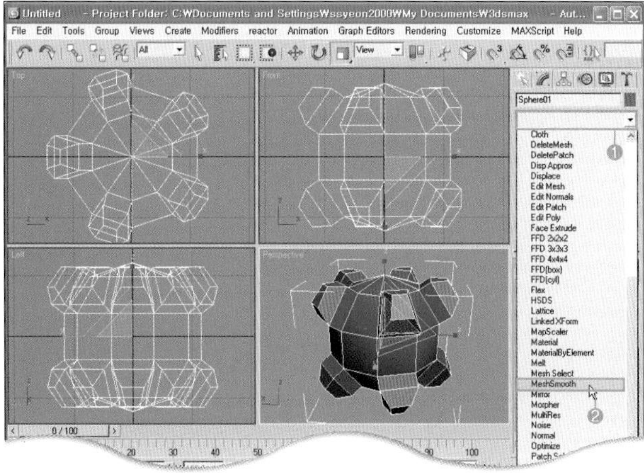

01 Click the [Modifier List] combo box and select the [MeshSmooth] Modifier.

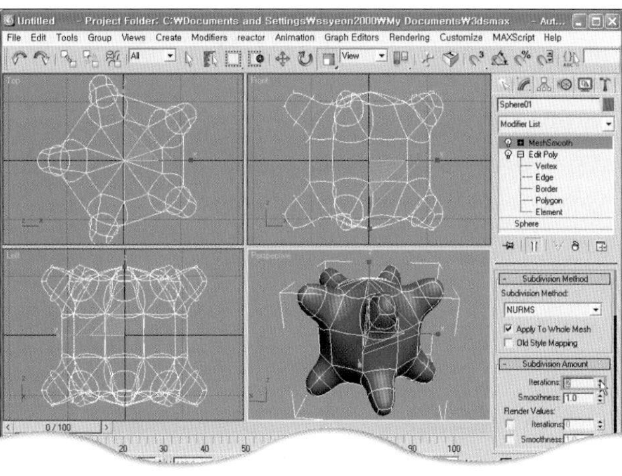

02 On the Modifier Stack, the MeshSmooth Modifier is now listed above the Edit Poly Modifier and the sphere object. Under the modifier's [Subdivision Amount] menu, change [Iterations] to [2].

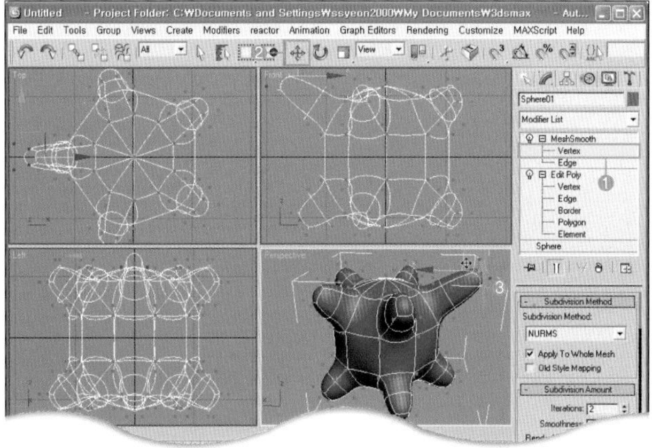

03 Select the [Vertex] sub-object of the MeshSmooth Modifier, click [Select and Move] at the main toolbar, and change the shape by dragging the vertex.

tip >>

The Modifier Stack

When you change shapes using the MeshSmooth Modifier, the change is not applied to the Edit Poly Modifier below. By contrast, changes in the Edit Poly Modifier are immediately reflected to the MeshSmooth Modifier.

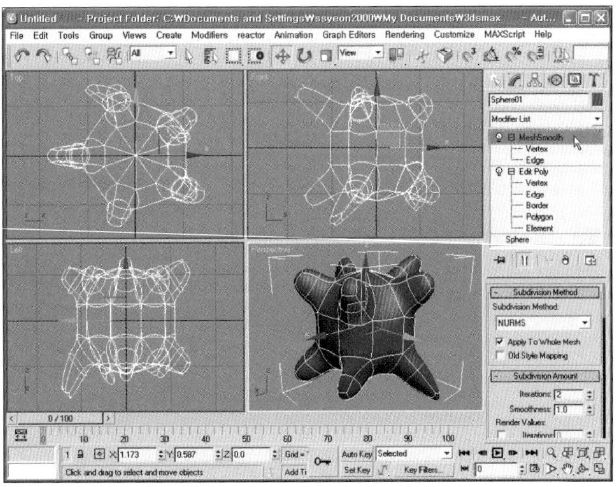

04 Click the character part of the MeshSmooth Modifier to exit the sub–object mode.

Applying Materials 

When the modeling is finished, use the Material Editor to apply materials to the model. "Materials" are the colors, light, reflection, and transparency of the object. In 3ds Max 9, many characteristics can be added to the object.

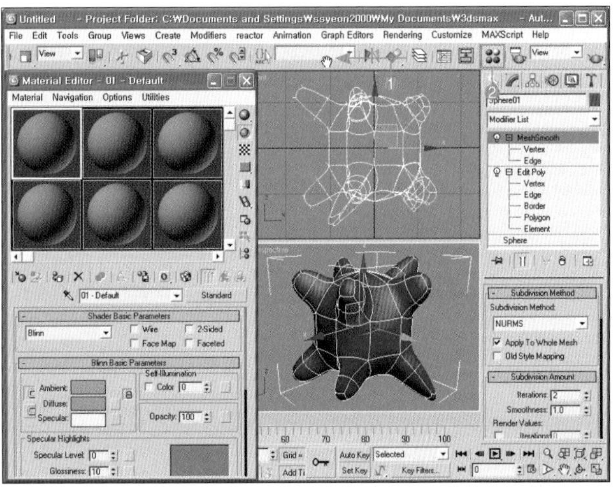

01 When [hand icon] shows on the main toolbar, drag to the left side to view hidden tools. Click [Material Editor [icon]] on the main toolbar to open the Material Editor.

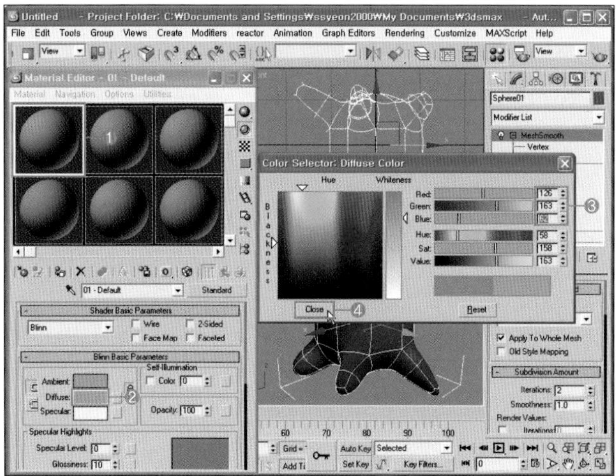

02 Click the first sample shape in the material editor, then click the [Color Selector] icon. Under [Diffuse], modify to green (RGB: 126, 163, 62) in the dialog box, and close the dialog box by clicking [Close].

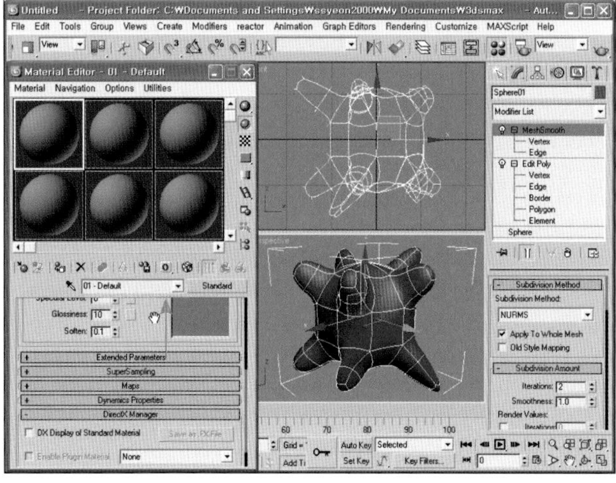

03 When the hand icon appears in the blank space by the parameters, drag it inward to view the hidden parameters.

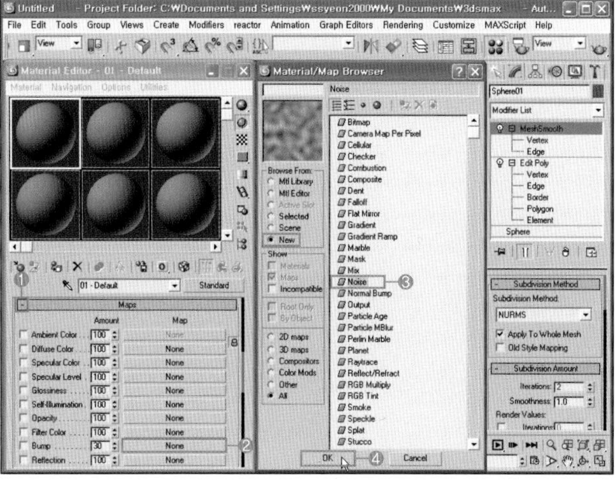

04 Under [Maps], click [+] to expand the parameter, and next to [Bump] click [None] to open the Material/Map Browser. Select the [Noise] map in the Material/Map Browser, and click [OK].

tip >>

Material/Map Browser

When using the Material/Map Browser, you can call up and open pre-produced materials when intending to create a map for materials in a new style; you can also see the status of the objects on the Viewport.

Bump Map

The Bump map creates an effect of unevenness on the object's surface by organizing the distribution and density of the colors. This map can express rough surfaces without dividing the polygons into small sections.

Noise Map

This map is often used to create a rough, uneven effect on the surface. The user can mix two colors from the options given.

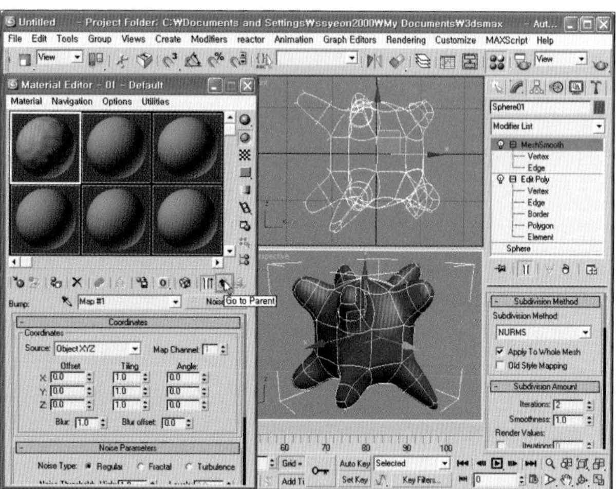

05 To change over to the Noise map parameter screen, click [Go to Parent] while maintaining the setting, and navigate up to the initial screen.

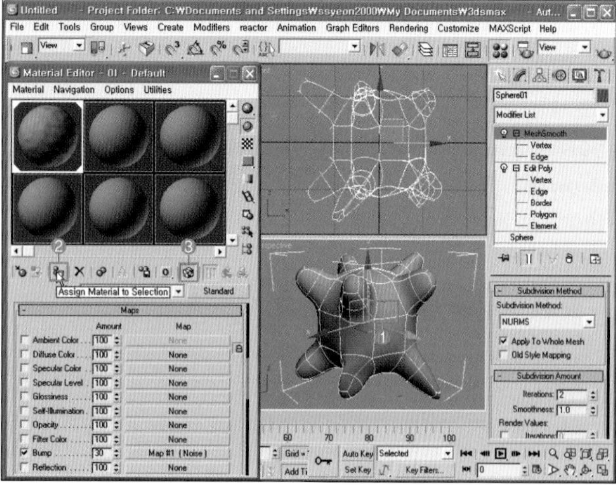

06 To view the material on the object on the Viewport, click [Show Map in Viewport] and then [Assign Material to Selection] to apply the material to the sphere object.

Installing and Rendering Target Spot Lights

When the modeling and mapping are finished, you can install lights and cameras to give a sense of reality. We will discuss only lights here. Then we will show rendering methods to calculate the final image.

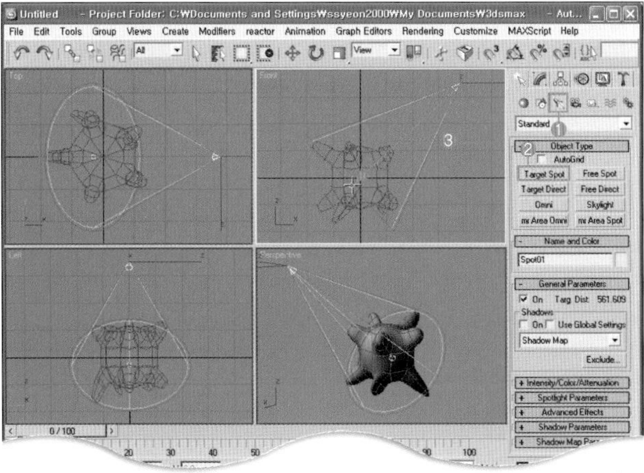

01 On the Create panel, under [Lights]–[Standard], click [Target Spot]. Drag from top to bottom on the Front Viewport to install the target spotlight.

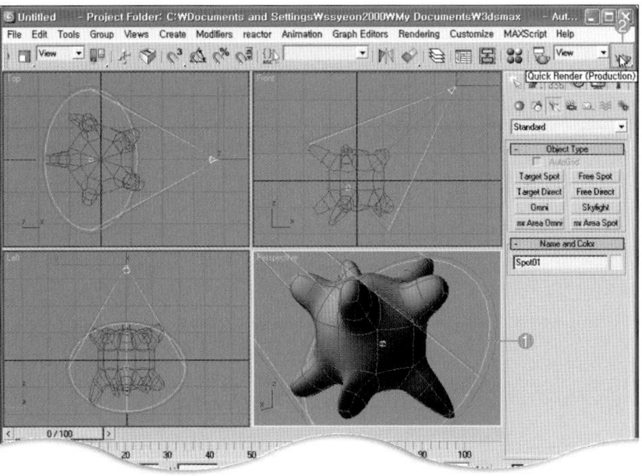

02 Select the Perspective Viewport with the right mouse button, and confirm the rendered shape by clicking [Quick Render] on the main toolbar.

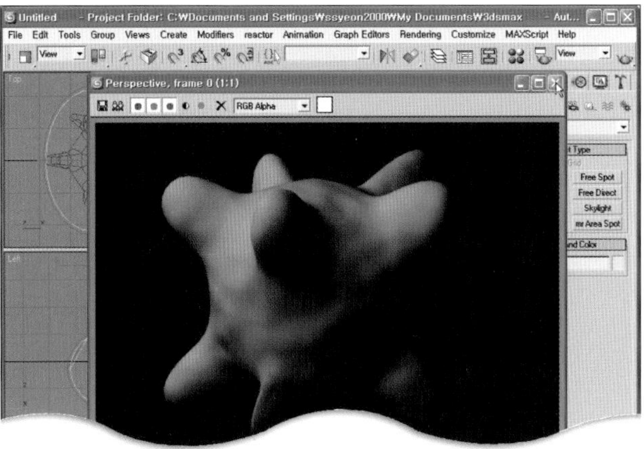

03 Confirm the rendered image, which has a unique green color, and click to close the image window.

Saving an Object

Follow these simple steps to save and store your modeling objects.

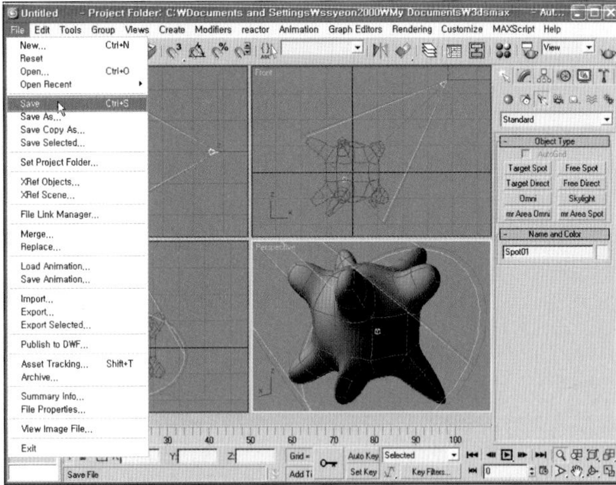

01 To save as a 3ds Max file, click [File]–[Save] on the menu bar.

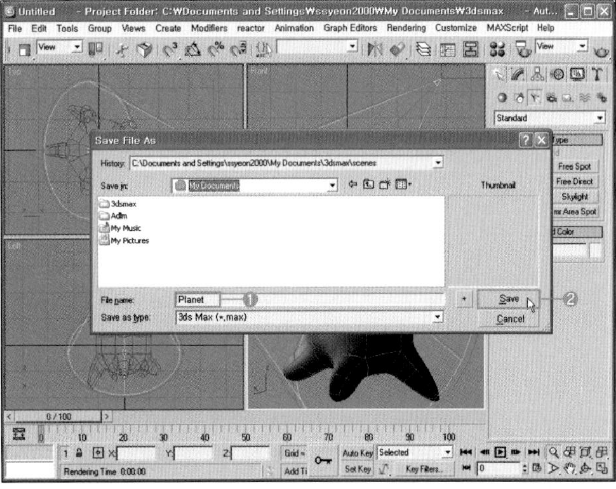

02 When the [Save File As] dialog box appears on screen, name your file and click [Save].

Supplementary CD\Sample\Chapter 1\Exercise 2\Planet.max

Expert Mode

As you become more acclimatized with the working environment of 3ds Max 9, it is possible that you will find the main toolbar, command panel, and etc to be a distraction because it makes the screen that much smaller. The work space can be increased to almost the size of your monitor by working in the expert mode, which hides the toolbar, command panel, and etc. Therefore, users who mostly the Hotkey and Quad Menu can work at a much quicker pace by not having to spend time in navigating through the work window. Before we learn how to change the setting to Expert Mode, let's learn how to change the color of the work environment to black, which will cause less fatigue on your eyes.

① To change the environment setting, click on the [Customized]-[Customize UI and Defaults Switchers] from the menu bar.

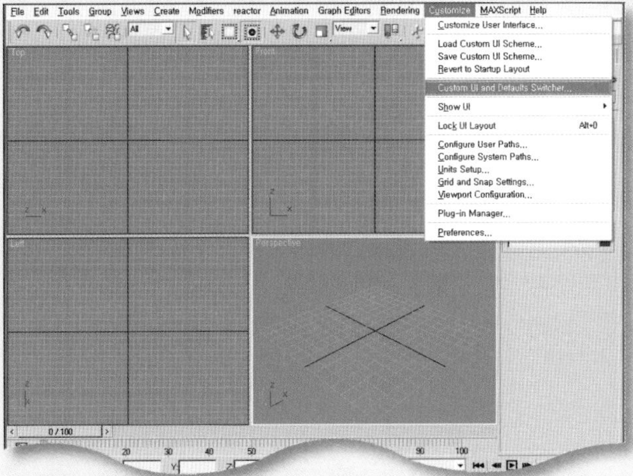

② Once the [Choose initial settings for tool options and UI Layout] dialog box appears, select 'ame-dark' then click on the [Set] button.

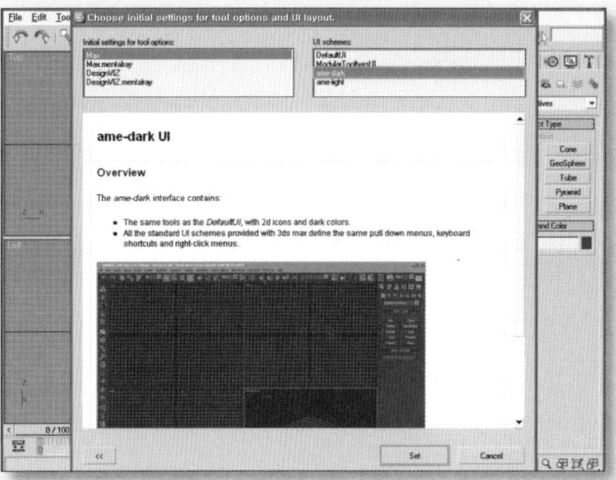

③ Now that the color of the work environment has been changed to a black tone, click on [Views]-[Expert Mode] from the menu bar to set the Expert Mode. As mentioned previously, this will change the work environment to cover most of your monitor.

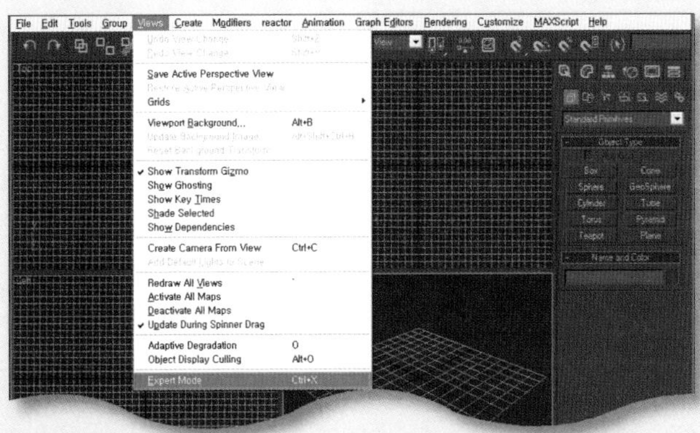

④ The work environment has been changed to the Expert Mode where the toolbar and command menu are hidden.

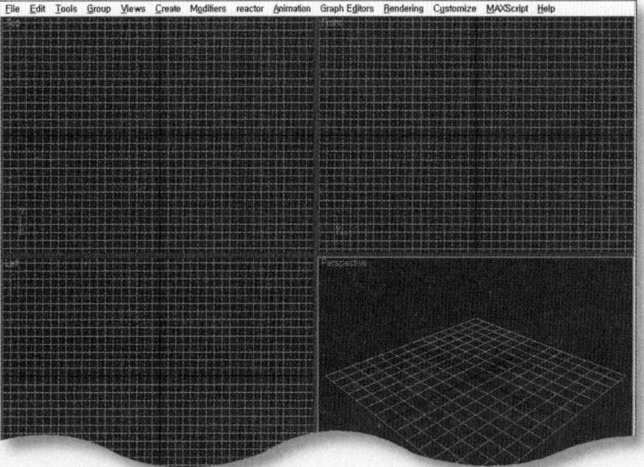

Chapter 2

A Detailed Look at 3ds Max 9

Chapter 1 showed basic skills for conducting 3D work in 3ds Max 9. This chapter will discuss more complex features of 3ds Max 9. First, we will examine the basic figures, then learn methods for editing objects, and finally examine advanced functions such as alignment and arrangement.

SECTION 01

Basic Figures

The success of a 3D object depends on the accurate selection of basic underlying figures. A round figure can be created from a box, cylinder, or even a sphere, but the most efficient method for completing the final model is to select the round figure. Let's look at the basic figures provided by 3ds Max 9 and the basic flow for editing the figures, and then create a sample object.

Basic Figures and the Key Modifier

There are a large number of basic figures built into 3ds Max 9. The program also offers figures for expansion that can be swiftly produced as desired. Let's learn about them, as well as the key modifiers that enable the user to edit the figures.

Polygons as Basic Figures

The Create panel offers the [Geometry] menu, which enables the creation of basic figures.

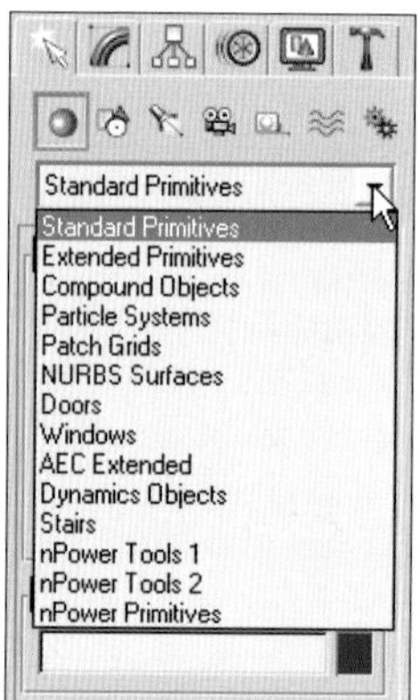

Standard Primitives

Standard Primitives are the most basic figures and are used as the foundations from which all other objects are created. Some figures can be created with one click–and–drag of the mouse, and some are created with two or three click–and–drags.

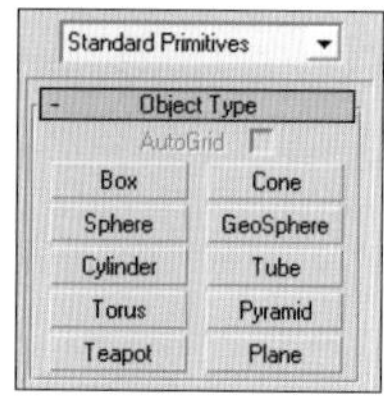

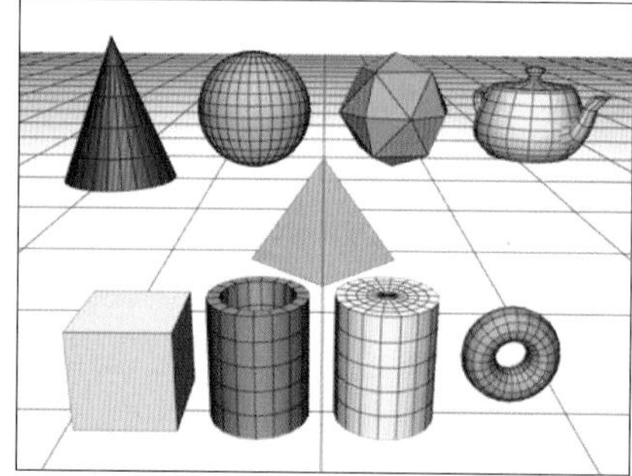

Extended Primitives

Extended Primitives are advanced figures created from the basic figures. They are not used as basic objects, but instead as surrounding or background objects.

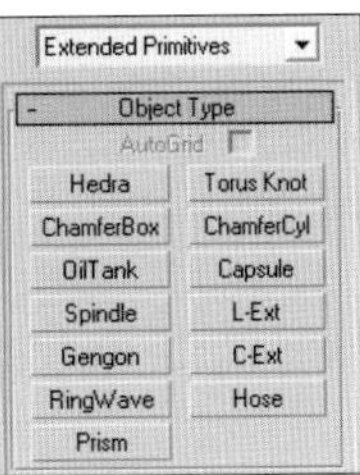

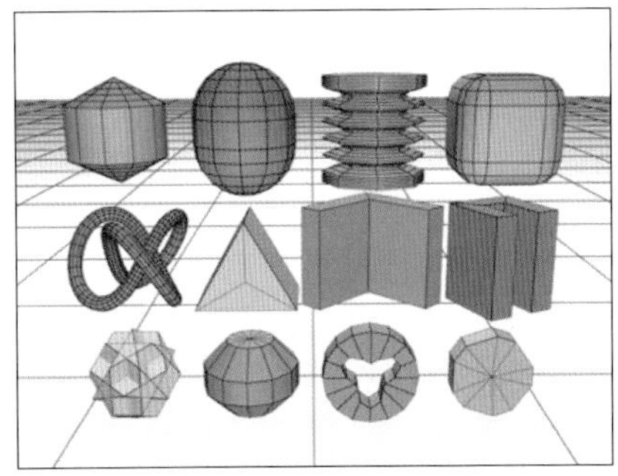

Door, Windows, AEC Extended, and Stairs

Figures that require precise dimensions are included in [Geometry], such as doors, windows, and stairs. The [Geometry] figure group AEC Extended is used for creating foliage, railings, and walls.

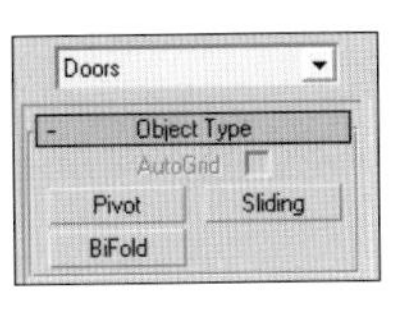

Doors

Windows

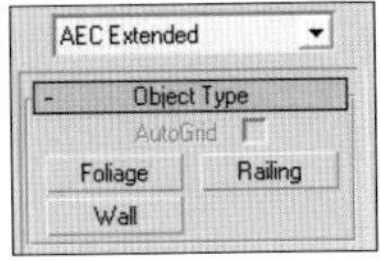

AEC Extended

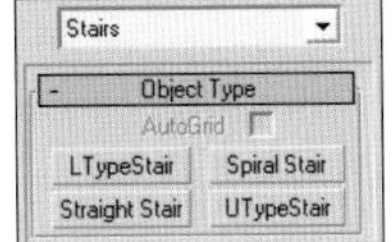

Stairs

Edit Poly Modifiers

The Edit Poly Modifier is the modifier most widely used to edit 3D figures. The user installs this on the prototype object and changes the object's shape with each sub-object to complete the overall shape. The Edit Poly Modifier provides numerous parameters to make the editing of objects easier and offers different functions for each sub-object.

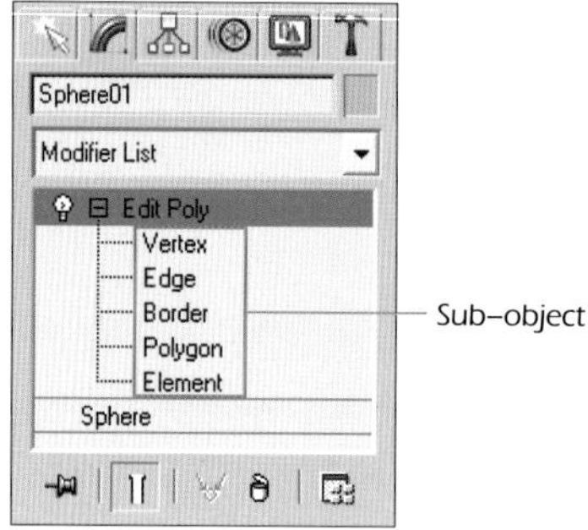

Edit Poly Mode

This mode can be used to model objects or for animations; the [Animate] item is used for animations of the sub-objects, not the parent objects themselves.

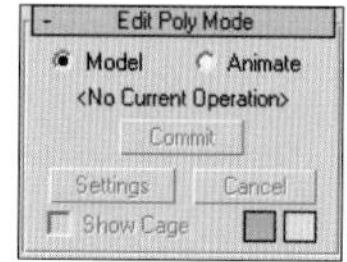

Selection

This provides the Ignore Backfacing option, as well as Shrinking, Growing, Ringing, or Looping functions of the selected area when selecting the sub-object. The sub-objects are selectable.

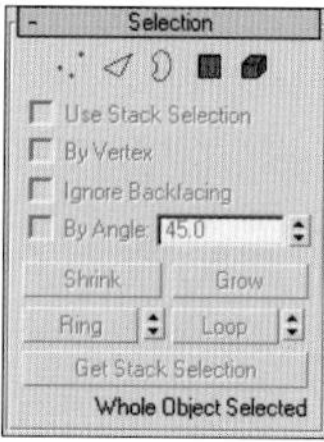

Soft Selection

This advanced function selects all objects within a designated distance from the object the user directly selects.

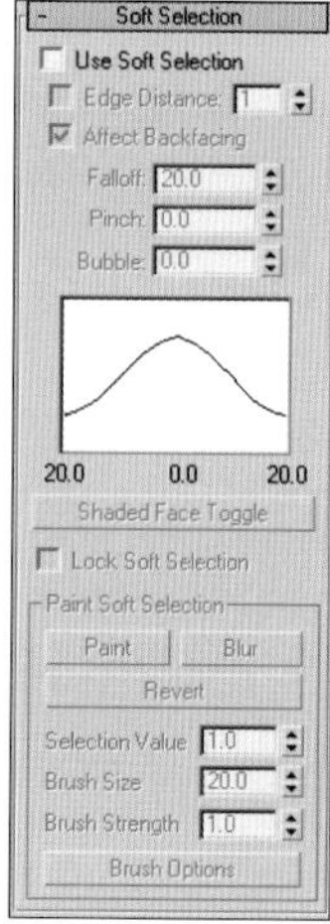

Edit Geometry

These are functions that can be used regardless of the sub-object; they can separate the selected sub-object or import objects that were created externally. Also offered are functions that divide the polygons—Slice Plane, Cut, Quick Slice—and smoothly divide the selected parts—MSmooth, Tesselate.

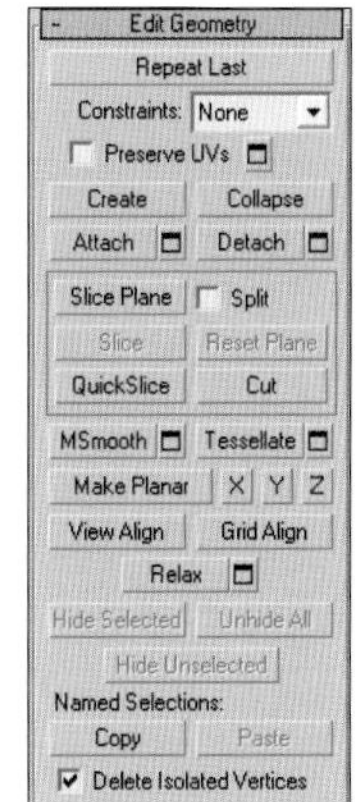

Paint Deformation

These functions enable the user to change the convexity and concavity of an object with many polygons as if using a brush. First, click Push/Pull, and click-and-drag the cursor over the object's surface to make the surface convex. Press <Alt> while click-and-dragging to make the surface concave. The strength and size of the brush can be adjusted with [Push/Pull Value], [Brush Size], and [Brush Strength].

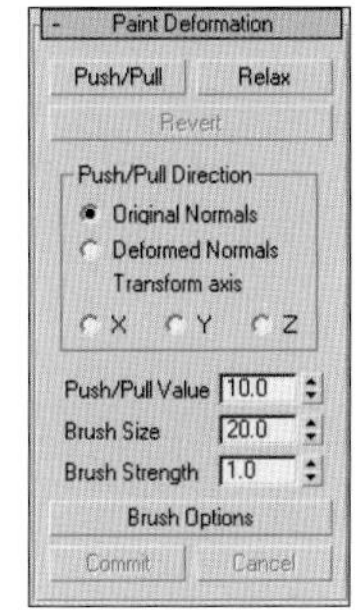

Edit Vertices, Edges, Borders, Polygons, Elements

These are parameters that show up when the sub-object is changed. Various tools that can modify and change each of the sub-objects are provided.

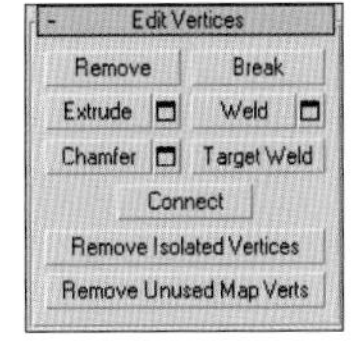

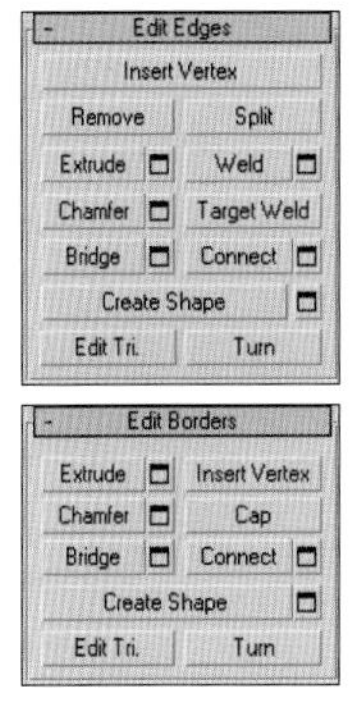

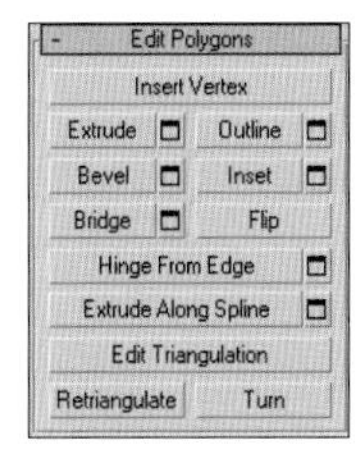

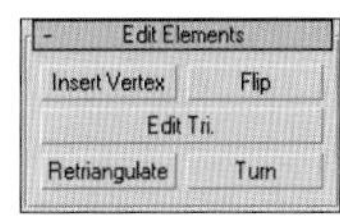

Polygon Properties

This is a parameter that appears when changing over to a [Polygon] or [Element] sub-object. This helps the user give different Material IDs to selected polygons or figures for management purposes.

Overview of Modifiers

3ds Max 9 provides numerous modifiers for polygons, but let's first take a look at the key modifiers that are most widely used.

Modifier	Function
Poly Select	Used to select a special part of the object and apply a different modifier function to that specific part; it may be a little difficult for beginners, but this modifier is very frequently used
Symmetry	Used when the user models half of a symmetrical object and then wishes to automatically model the remaining half
Shell	Fills in the inside automatically after modeling, making the creation of the inside easier
Noise	Makes the surface of the object uneven and rough
MeshSmooth	Smoothes out the overall surface of the object and is often used for finishing works
Unwrap UVW	Helps the user to easily map the object by spreading out the polygons that compose the object on one sheet
UVW Map	Changes the mapping materials applied to the object into various forms, turning it into a normal shape

SECTION 02

2D Figures

Among the various 3D modeling methods, there is a standard classification system for curved lines. Curved polygon lines can be classified as NURBS Curves, Splines, and Extended Splines. First, NURBS Curves can express free curves, but this process delays the system so they are not often used. Splines curves are the most common, and you can view Extended Splines for more options to construct simple figures. Let's deomonstrate how to create figures through basic lines.

Tools for Creating Lines

Let's explore the program's tools for creating basic section lines and learn about the Edit Spline Modifier, which helps to edit them.

Basic Line Tools of 3ds Max 9

The Create panel provides tools for creating the basic section lines. The section lines are classified into Splines (simplest), NURBS Curves (advanced), and Extended Splines. The Extended Splines, a recently added menu, are used for composite type section lines in figure construction.

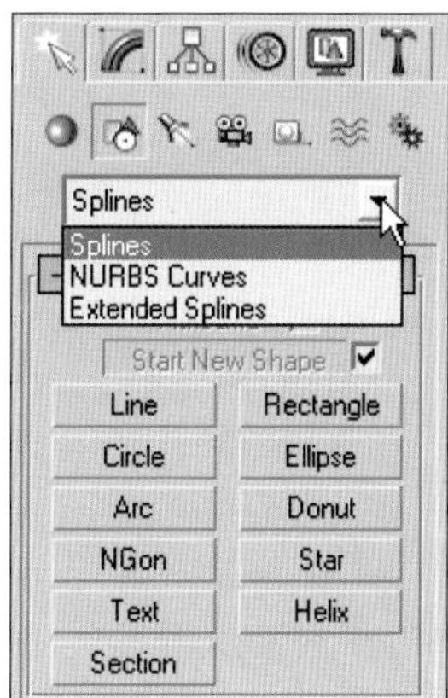

Edit Spline Modifier

While the Edit Poly Modifier is widely used to modify the basic figures, the Edit Spline Modifier is often used to edit 2D section lines. However, in the case of [Line], which has the basic functions of an Edit Spline Modifier, the Edit Spline Modifier is not used.

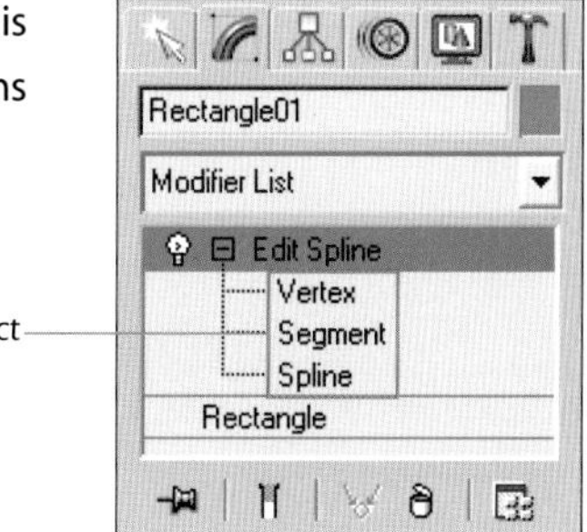

Rendering

Rendering modifies the invisible lines produced when rendering into line forms of appropriate thickness.

❶ Check this box to show lines when rendering.

❷ Check this box to show lines in the image of the rendering on the Viewport.

❸ The user can change the section of the line into Radial or Rectangular shapes.

Interpolation

The Interpolation option allows the user to set the number of the internal dots comprising the lines created in the Viewport. Smaller numbers produce rough lines, whereas higher interpolation values produce smooth lines.

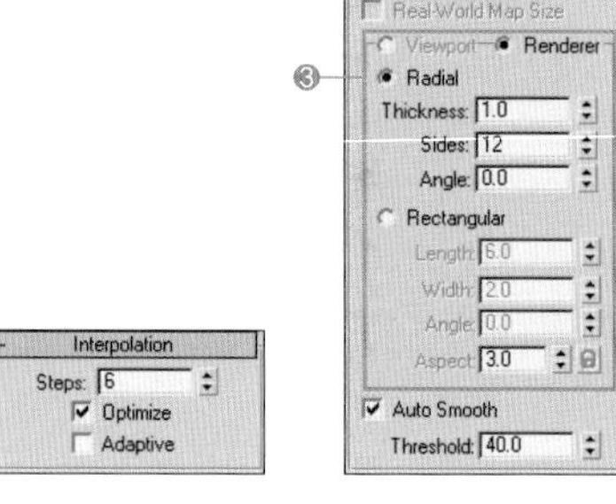

Selection

Under the [Selection] menu, the user can select the sub-object on the [Line] or the [Edit Spline Modifier], control the [Lock Handles], or mark the [Vertex Numbers].

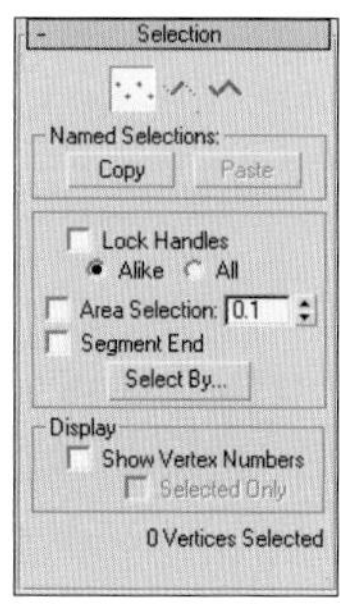

Soft Selection

This advanced function enables the user to smoothly select the sub-objects that are near the directly selected parts.

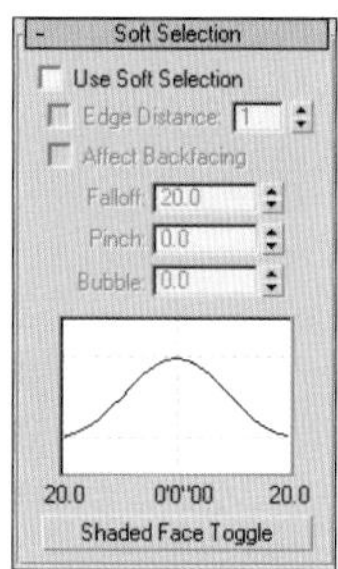

Geometry

The program provides various tools to modify the sub-objects. The user can choose to hide or detach the selected sub-objects, or attach the created objects externally. Also, the user can add a new line with [Create Line], or add a new vertex with [Refine]. The user can weld the nearby vertices, and may also unite (Boolean-Union), subtract (Boolean-Subtract), or intersect (Boolean-Intersection) the lines.

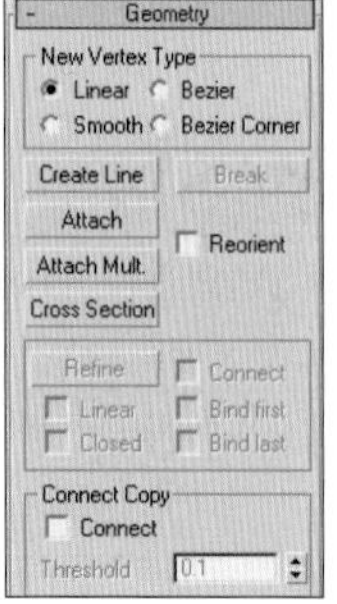

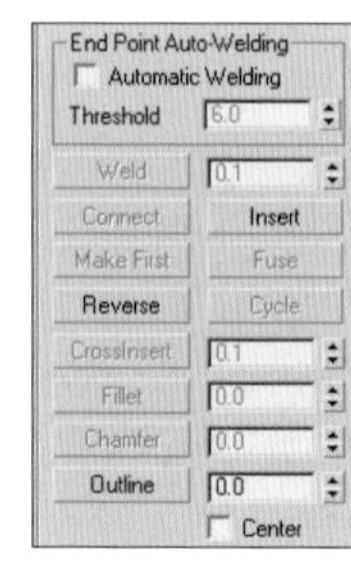

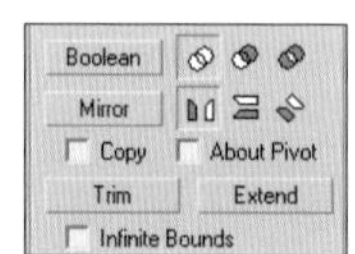

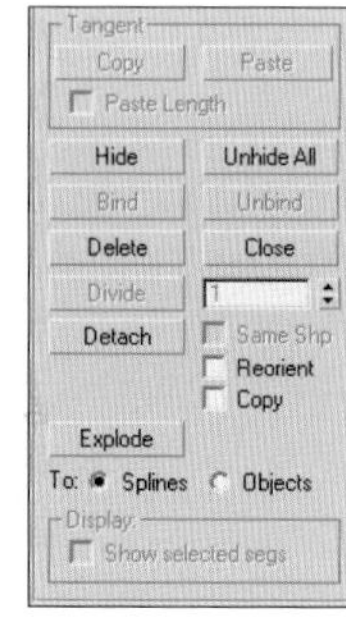

Surface Properties

The [Surface Properties] parameter appears when selecting [Segment] and [Spline] sub-objects, and it allows the user to assign different [Material IDs] to the desired sub-objects for ease of management.

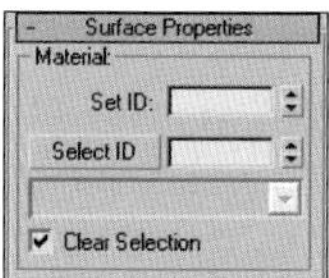

Other Key Modifiers

Let's look at the key modifiers for modifying 2D section lines. Modifiers for 2D lines transform the sections into a 3D format. Therefore, the user must again add modifiers for polygons such as the Edit Poly Modifier for an object that has been made 3D.

Modifier	Function
Bevel	Makes layered polygons protrude, with a section line as the standard
Extrude	Makes the section line protrude in a straight direction
Lathe	Rotates the line
Symmetry	Automatically creates the opposite side or the other half of the line
Hair and Fur	Creates hair or fur using lines
Garment Maker	Creates clothes by attaching section lines
Cloth	Simulates clothes created with the [Garment Maker]

SECTION 03

Editing Tools

The tools for editing objects in the Viewport are concentrated on the main toolbar. Object editing entails mostly the usage of the mouse in combination with the <Ctrl> and <Alt> keys. Let's learn details about the various ways to select, modify, and hide objects. The Freeze tool, which fixes objects so that they cannot be edited, will also be discussed.

Editing Tools Used in 3ds Max 9

The basics of 3D work begin with learning the editing tools for modifying objects. This section provides an overview of the basic editing tools in 3ds Max 9.

Selection Tools

The main toolbar contains key tools for selecting the objects in the Viewport.

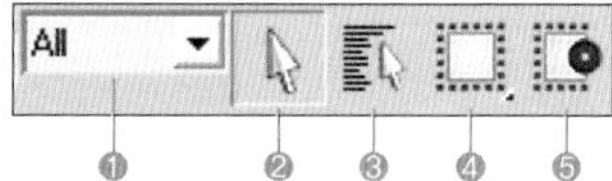

❶ **Selection Filter**: This helps the user to select objects in the Viewport according to their characteristics.

❷ **Select Object**: Manually select the object in the Viewport.

❸ **Select by Name**: The user can select objects by their names.

❹ **Selection Region**: The user can choose the shape of the region with which to select objects: Rectanglular, Circlular, Fence, Lasso, or Paint.

❺ **Window/Crossing**: By toggling, the user decides whether to select objects that are either entirely or at least partly within the selection region.

Transform Tools and Gizmos

The basic methods for modifying objects include Move, Rotate, and Scale. These tools can be found near the center of the main toolbar. When one of these tools is selected, a Gizmo appears in the Viewport for the click-and-drag manipulation of any and all objects selected.

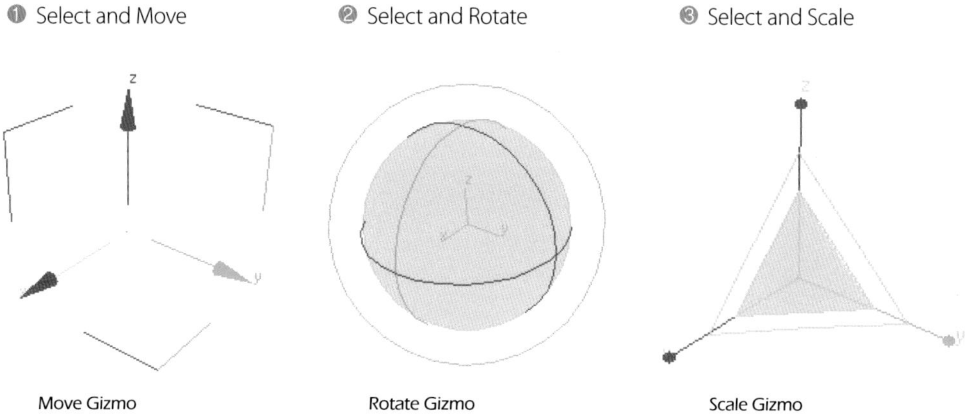

Move Gizmo　Rotate Gizmo　Scale Gizmo

Edit Tools

The Edit menu shows the selection tools in the main toolbar, as well as some other tools that can be used as needed.

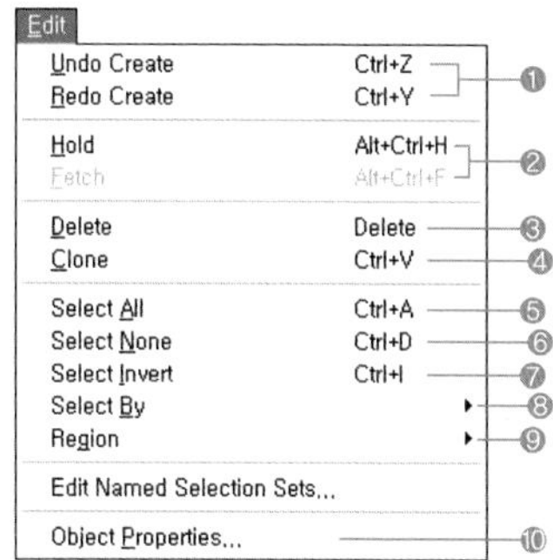

❶ **Undo/Redo**: The user can cancel or execute the previous commands in order.

❷ **Hold/Fetch**: The user can save the current state of the viewport and resore it the state in which it had been saved.

❸ **Delete**: Deletes the selected object.

❹ **Clone**: The user can create an identical copy of the selected object.

❺ **Select All** : The user can select all the objects in the viewport, deselect objects.

❻ **Select None**: The user can deselect any all selected objects in the viewport.

❼ **Select Invert**: The user can deselect the selected and select the non-selected items at once.

❽ **Select By**: The user can select one or more objects by color or name.The user can also choose they type of Selection Region.

❾ **Region**: The user can separately manage the selected objects by giving them representative names.

❿ **Object Properies**: The user can change the internal properties and characteristics of the selected objects.

Exercise 01

Basic Figure Modeling

This section will teach you how to use the basic figure modifier through a simple modeling exercise.

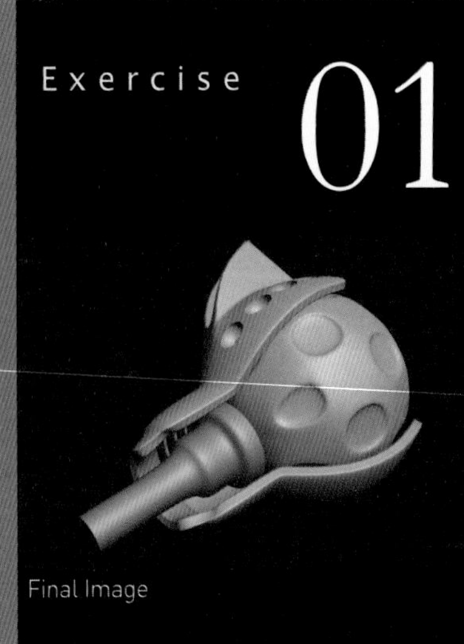

Final Image

Final File
\Sample\Chapter 2\Exercise 1\Machine.max

Setting Parameters

Modeling starts with selecting the basic figure that will eventually become the final object. Also, it is very important to determine the form by changing the internal parameter of the figure after creating it.

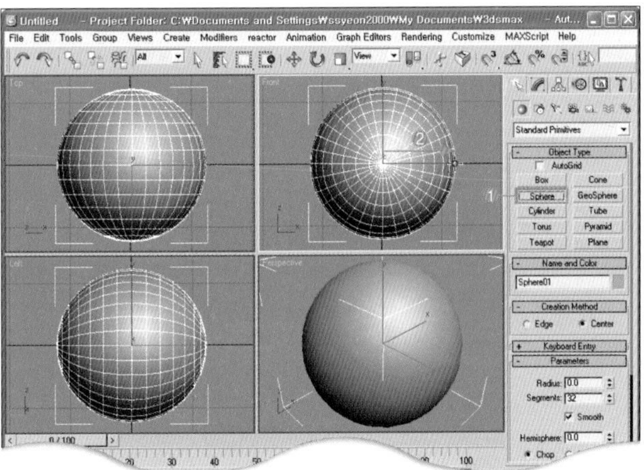

01 Click Sphere in [Geometry]–[Standard Primitives] on the Create panel. Create a Sphere with the absolute axis as the standard on the Front Viewport.

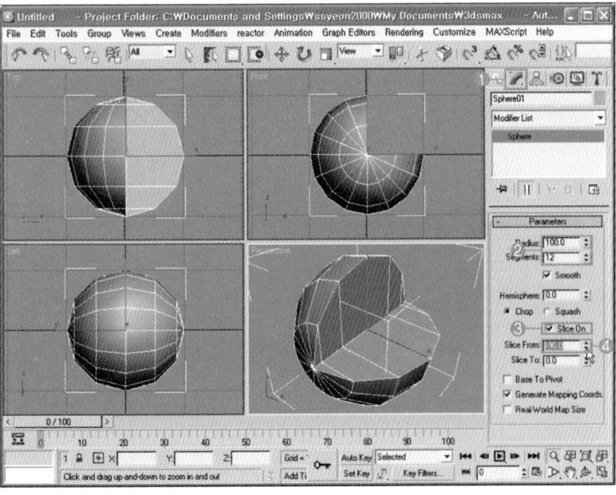

02 With the "Sphere01" object in the Viewport selected, click [Modify], and move to the Modify panel. In the [Parameters], enter [100] for [Radius] and [12] for [Segments] to give angles to the shape. Check the box for [Slice On], and enter [–90] for [Slice From] to fragment the shape.

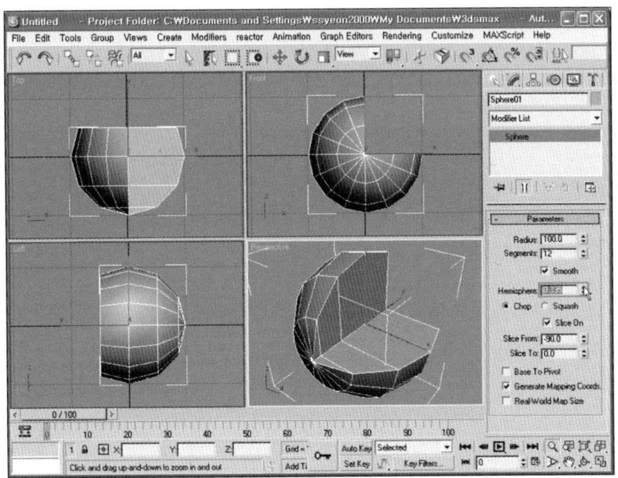

03 Enter [0.335] for [Hemisphere] to cut the fragments.

tip >>

Sphere Parameters

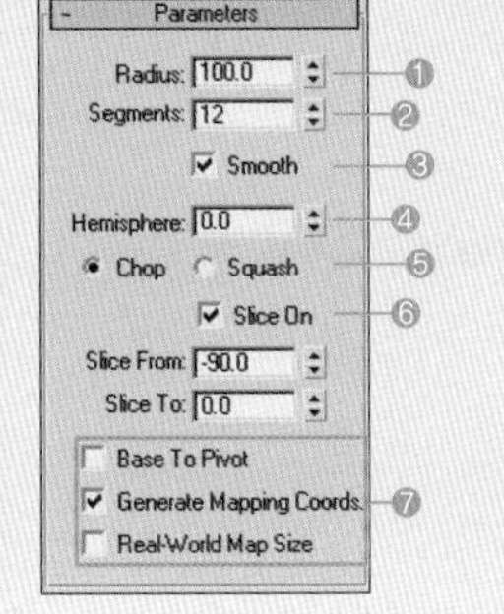

① **Radius:** Set the radius in the sphere
② **Segments:** Set the number of vertical lines that compose the sphere
③ **Smooth:** Make the polygon of the sphere look smooth automatically
④ **Hemisphere:** Change the sphere into a hemisphere
⑤ **Chop/Squash:** When using a hemisphere, you can squash the structure of the horizontal lines
⑥ **Slice On:** Cut the sphere towards the opposite axis of the hemisphere
⑦ **Bese To Pivot/Generate Mapping Cords/Real-World Map Size:** These options are related to mapping

Completing the Forms 

When the basic form is completed, users normally have to add the Edit Poly Modifier to change it into various shapes. The user can create almost any form through this process.

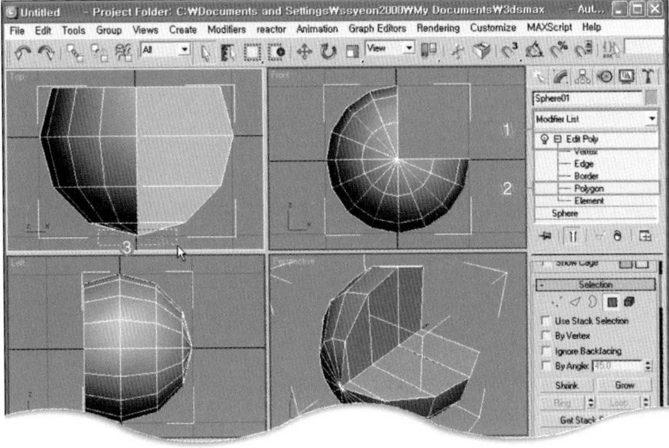

01 Click the [Modifier List] combo box, and select [Edit Poly]. Select the [Polygon] sub-object in the Edit Poly Modifier, and, in the Top Viewport, select the lowest horizontal set of polygons by click-and-dragging.

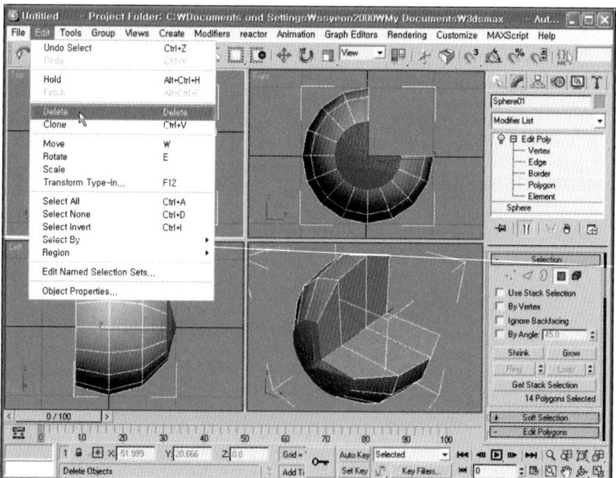

02 Click [Edit]–[Delete] on the menu bar to delete the selected polygons.

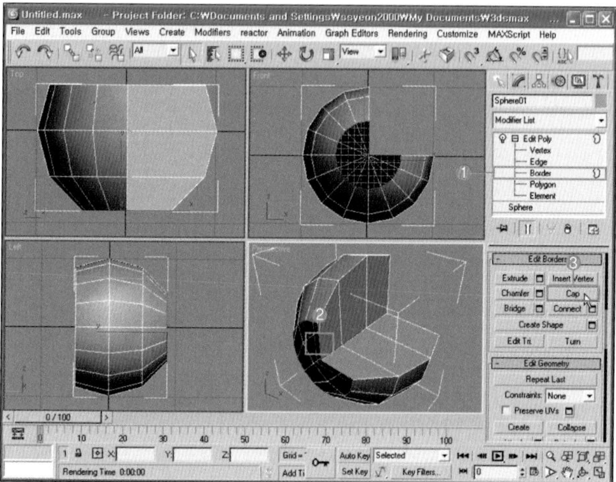

03 Select the [Border] sub–object under [Edit Poly]. In the Front Viewport, select the outline of the polygons that were just deleted, and close the hole by clicking [Edit Borders]–[Cap].

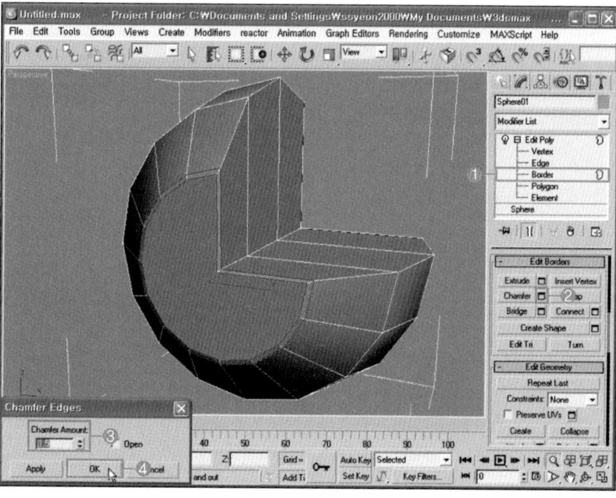

04 Select the [Border] sub–object under [Edit Poly], and select the borderline as shown in the picture. Click [Chamfer Settings ▣], and when the [Chamfer Edges] dialog box appears, enter [1.5] in [Chamfer Edge], and click [OK].

tip >>

Chamfer Edges

The Chamfer Edge feature divides the selected edges in two, according to the set distance. In the case of a polygon, the division into two is not very effective, but when applying the MeshSmooth Modifier, which is used for final finishing, the use of this function sharpens the edges.

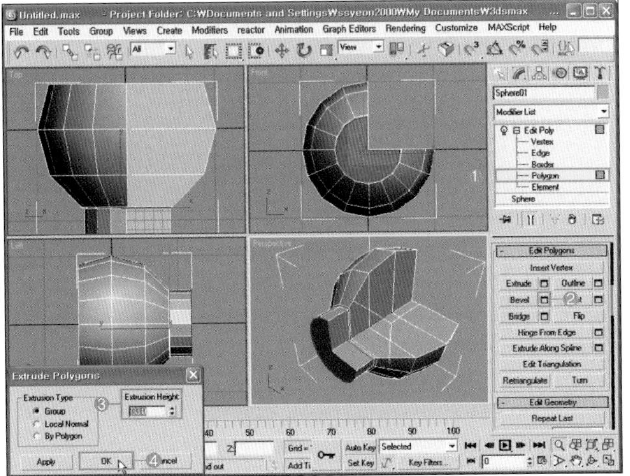

05 Select the [Polygon] sub–object under [Edit Poly], click on the polygon on the front, and then click [Extrude Settings ▣]. Enter [33] in the [Extrude Polygons]–[Extrusion Height] dialog box, and click [OK]. The selected polygon is extruded by the designated amount.

tip >>

[Extrude Polygons] Dialog Box

The selected polygon can be extruded by the value entered for [Extrusion Height]. The user can change the extrusion direction by selecting [Group], [Local Normal], or [By Polygon].

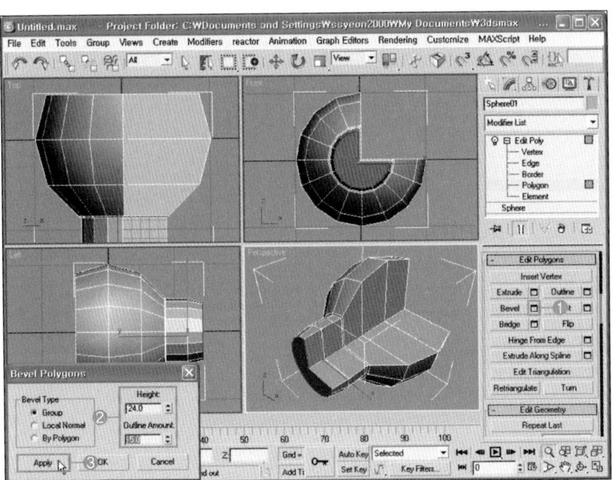

06 In [Edit Polygons], click [Bevel Settings ▣]. In the [Bevel Polygons] dialog box, enter [24] for [Height] and [–5] for [Outline Amount], and click [OK].

tip >>

[Bevel Polygon] Dialog Box

Magnify or reduce the selected polygon with the [Height] and/or [Outline Amount] values.

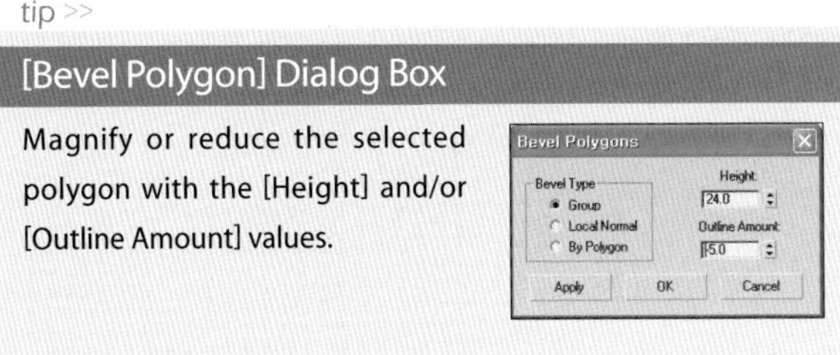

07 In [Edit Polygons], click [Inset Settings ▣]. In the [Inset Polygons] dialog box, enter [4] for [Inset Amount], and click [OK]. The selected polygon is reduced in size, and polygons have been automatically generated to keep the polygon connected to the parent object.

tip >>

[Inset Polygon] Dialog Box

Reduce the size of the selected polygon, while keeping it connected to the parent object.

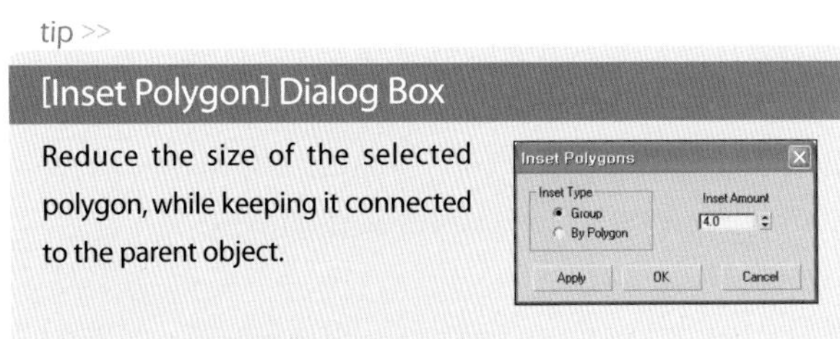

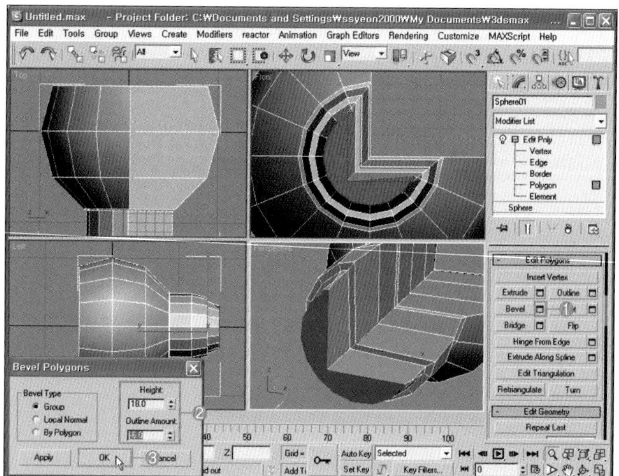

08 In [Edit Polygons], click [Bevel Settings]. In the [Bevel Polygons] dialog box, enter [18] for [Height] and [–6] for [Outline Amount], and click [OK].

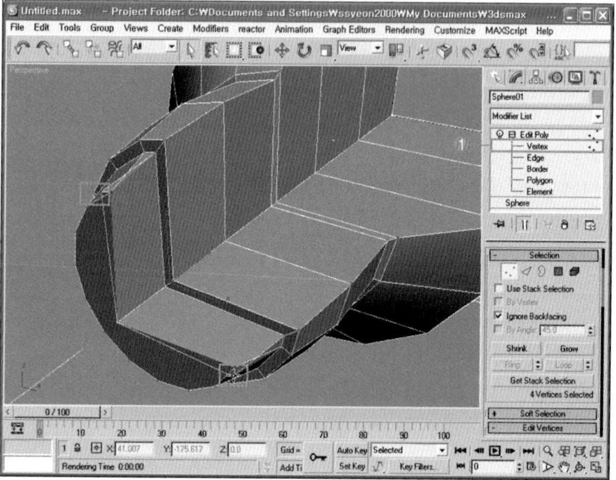

09 Select the [Vertex] sub–object under [Edit Poly], and select all of the vertices that are overlapping.

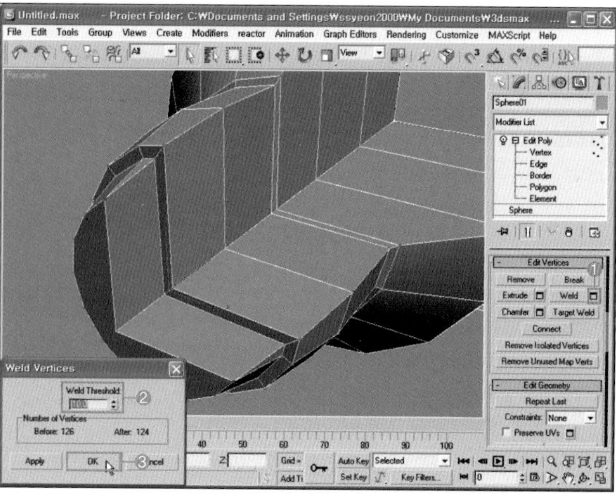

10 In [Edit Vertices], click [Weld Settings]. In the [Weld Vertices] dialog box, enter [10] for [Weld Threshold], and click [OK]. Each selected vertex will merge with any other selected vertices that are within a range equal to the [Weld Vertices] value.

Using the Shell Modifier

In the case of machines that require inner expression, delete the inner polygon and fill it in with the Shell Modifier. Then extrude the external polygons.

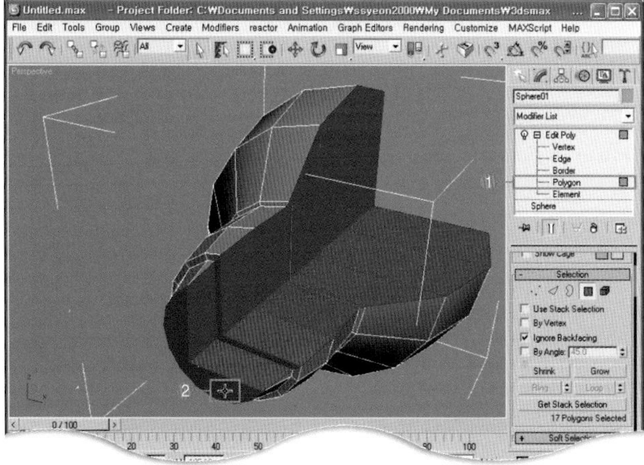

01 Under [Edit Poly], select the [Polygon] sub–object, and select the inner polygons while pressing <Ctrl>.

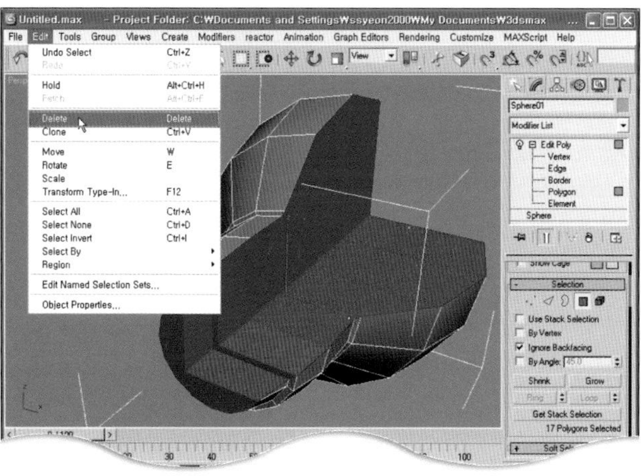

02 Confirm the selected polygons, and delete them by selecting [Edit]–[Delete] on the menu bar.

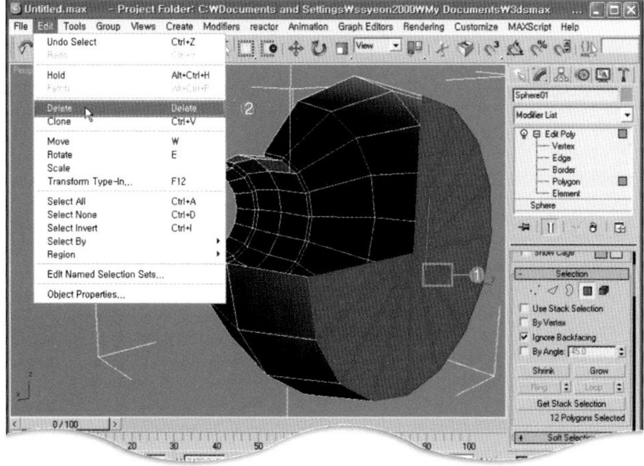

03 Manipulate the viewing angle of the Perspective Viewport in order to select the rear polygons, and delete them by selecting [Edit]–[Delete] on the menu bar.

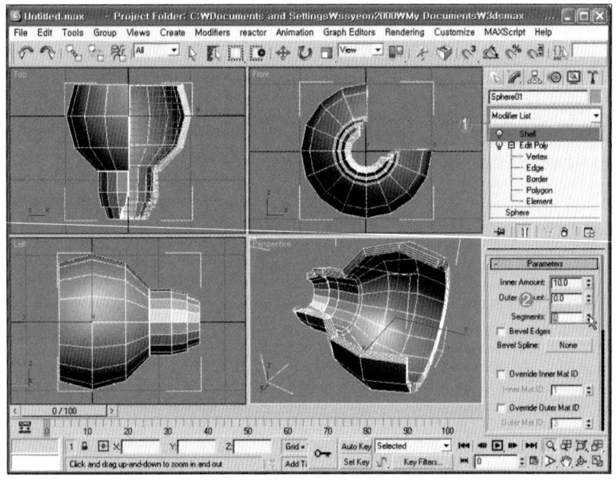

04 Click the [Modifier List] combo box, and select the [Shell] modifier. In [Parameters], enter [10] for [Inner Amount], [0] for [Outer Amount], and [4] for [Segments] to create an inner polygon.

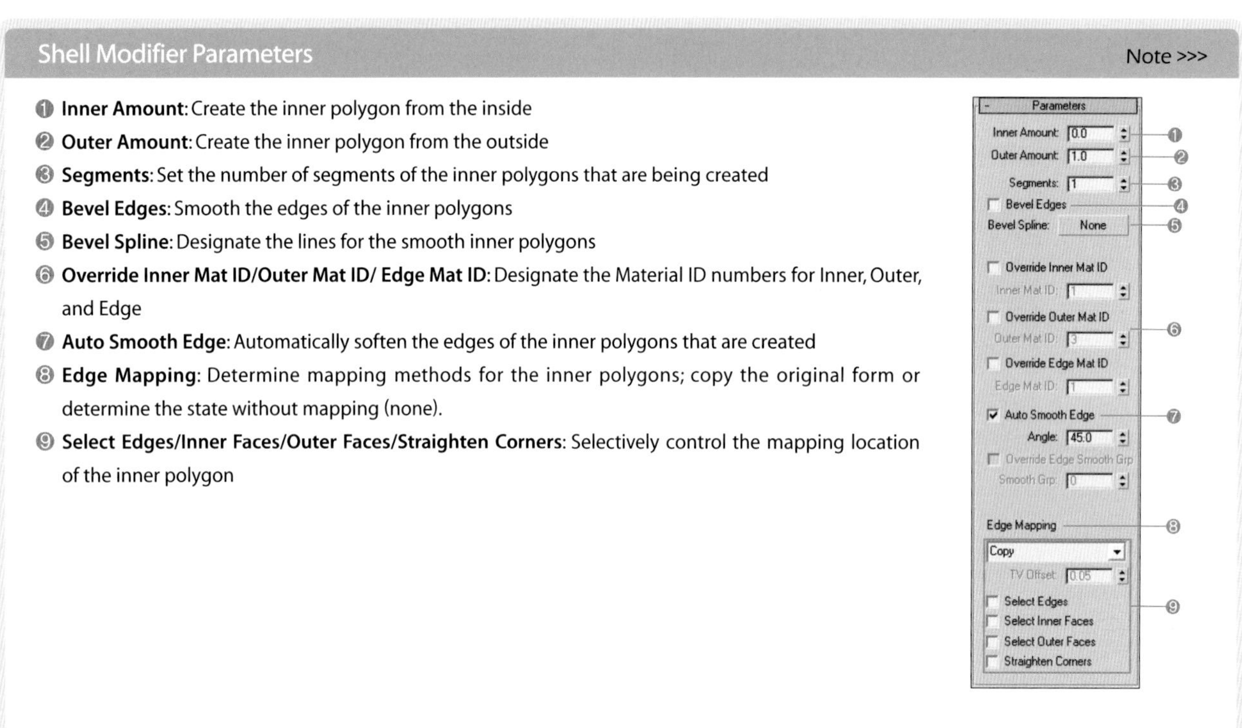

Shell Modifier Parameters

Note >>>

❶ **Inner Amount:** Create the inner polygon from the inside

❷ **Outer Amount:** Create the inner polygon from the outside

❸ **Segments:** Set the number of segments of the inner polygons that are being created

❹ **Bevel Edges:** Smooth the edges of the inner polygons

❺ **Bevel Spline:** Designate the lines for the smooth inner polygons

❻ **Override Inner Mat ID/Outer Mat ID/ Edge Mat ID:** Designate the Material ID numbers for Inner, Outer, and Edge

❼ **Auto Smooth Edge:** Automatically soften the edges of the inner polygons that are created

❽ **Edge Mapping:** Determine mapping methods for the inner polygons; copy the original form or determine the state without mapping (none).

❾ **Select Edges/Inner Faces/Outer Faces/Straighten Corners:** Selectively control the mapping location of the inner polygon

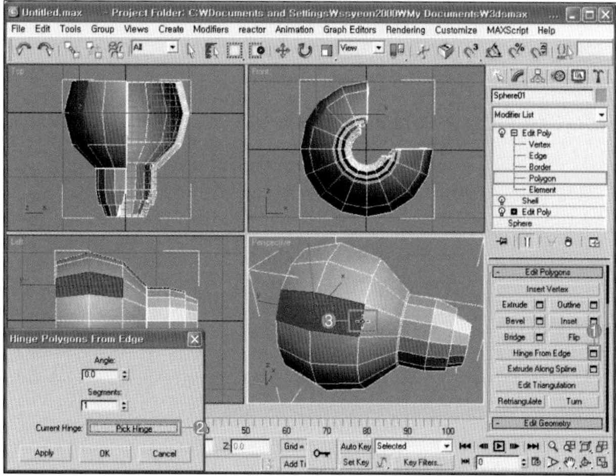

05 Under [Edit Poly], select the [Polygon] sub–object. In [Edit Polygons], click [Hinge From Edge Settings ▣].
In the [Hinge Polygons From Edge] dialog box, click [Pick Hinge], and select the edge that will become the standard line.

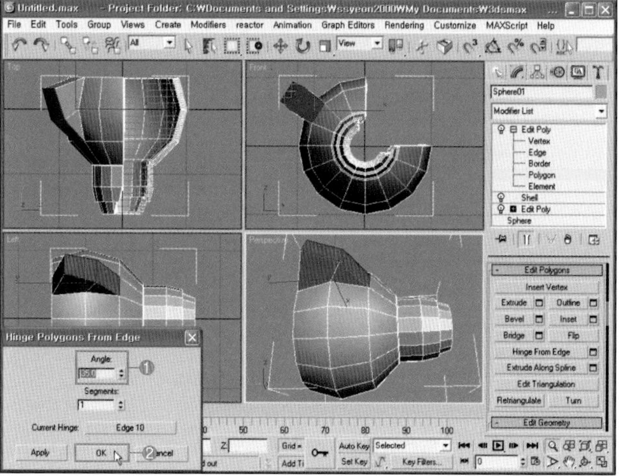

06 In the [Hinge Polygons From Edge] dialog box, enter [35] for [Angle], check the protruding polygon with the edge as the standard, and click [OK].

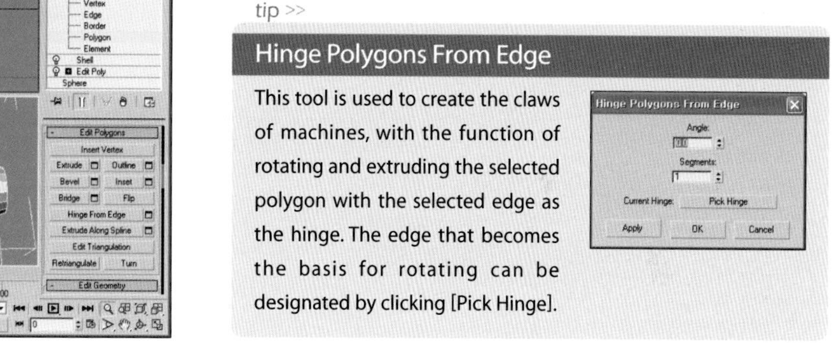

tip >>

Hinge Polygons From Edge

This tool is used to create the claws of machines, with the function of rotating and extruding the selected polygon with the selected edge as the hinge. The edge that becomes the basis for rotating can be designated by clicking [Pick Hinge].

07 Using [Inset] and [Bevel] (see Steps 6–8 above), add an internal polygon as shown in the picture.

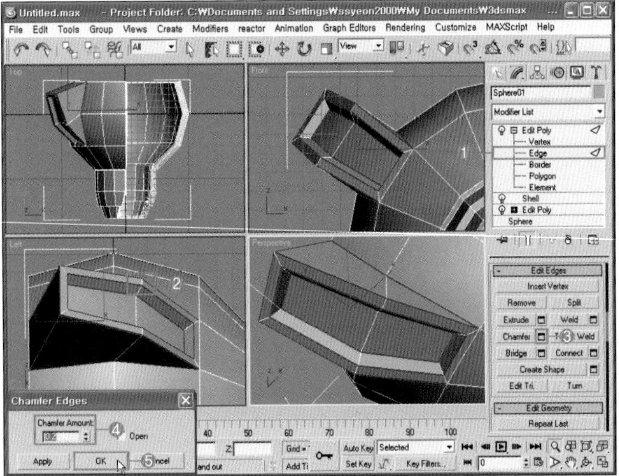

08 Select the [Edge] sub–object, select the edges as shown in the picture, and in [Edit Edges], click [Chamfer Settings ▣]. In the [Chamfer Edges] dialog box, enter [0.2] for [Chamfer Amount], and click [OK].

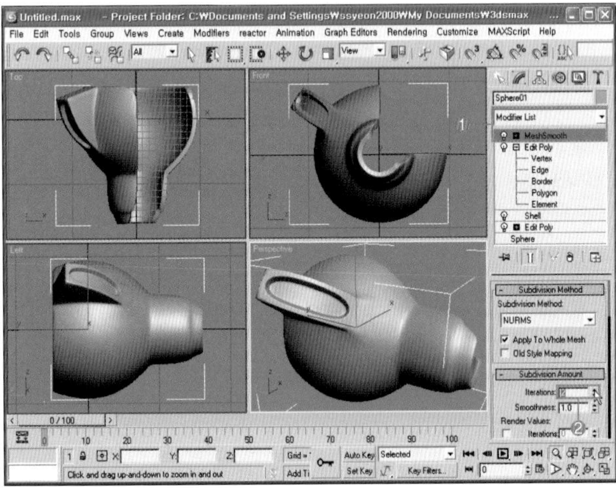

09 Click the [Modifier List] combo box, and select the [MeshSmooth] modifier. In [Subdivision Amount], enter [2] for [Iterations] to complete the shape of the machine.

Creating Precise Holes with Pro Boolean

Let's learn how to drill holes in the completed object using [Pro Boolean], newly added to 3ds Max 9.

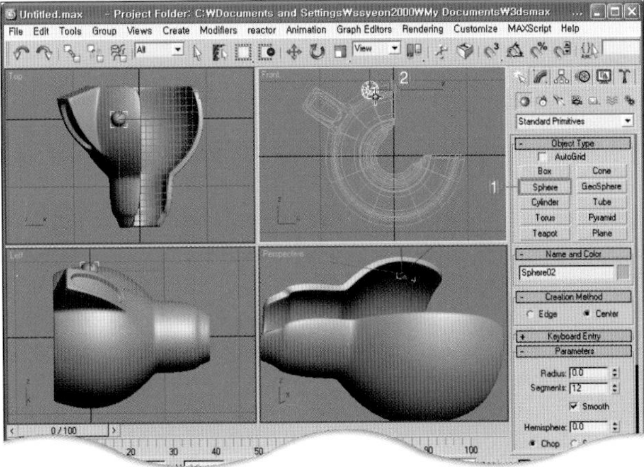

01 In the Create panel, click [Geometry]–[Standard Primitives]–Sphere. Add a new sphere object that intersects with the "Sphere01" object on the Front Viewport.

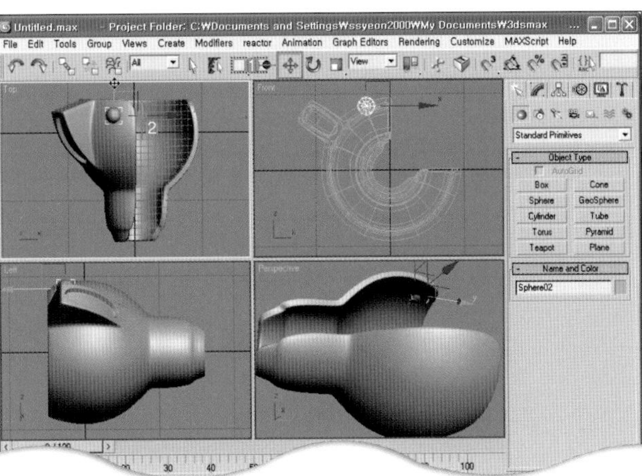

02 Click [Select and Move] on the main tool bar, and move the new sphere to the location in the Top Viewport as shown in the picture.

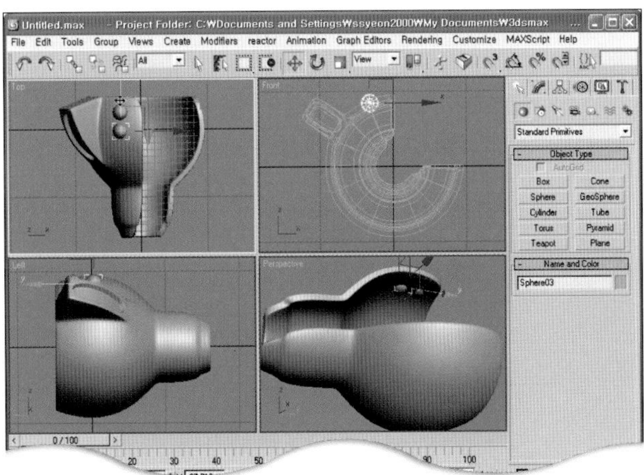

03 Click–and–drag downwards in the Top Viewport while pressing <Shift> to copy the new sphere.

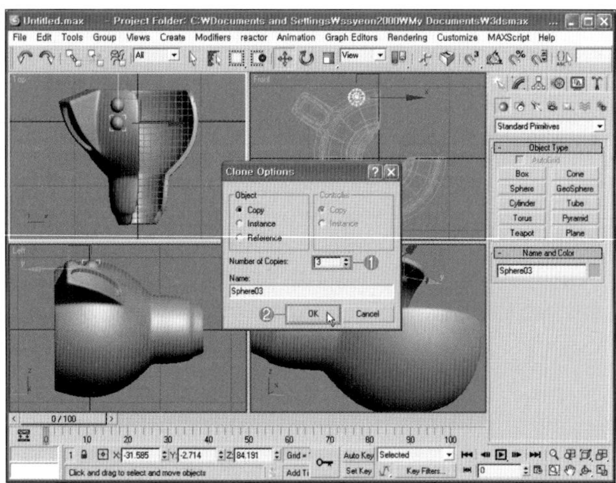

04 When the [Clone Options] dialog box appears, enter [3] for [Number of Copies], and click [OK].

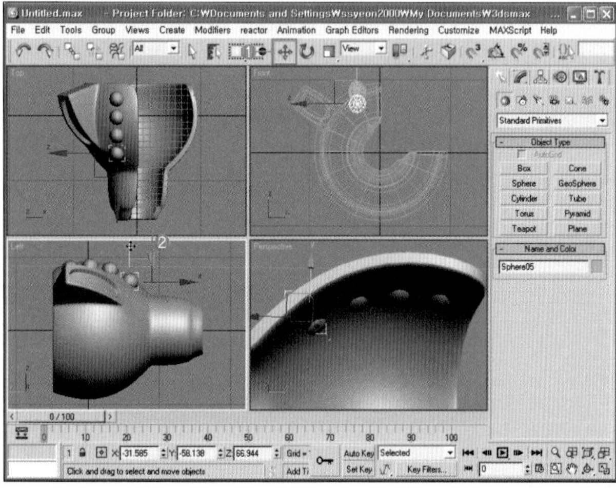

05 Align each of the sphere copies in the location that penetrates the "Sphere01" object as shown in the picture.

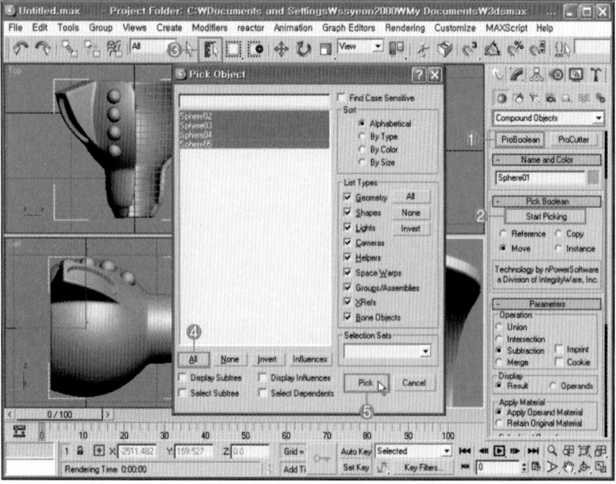

06 Select the "Sphere01" object, and, in the Create panel, click [Geometry]–[Compound Objects]–[ProBoolean]. Check if [Parameters]–[Operation]–[Subtraction] is selected, and click [Start Picking]. Click [Select by Name] on the main tool bar. In the [Pick Objects] dialog box, click [All], and then click [Pick].

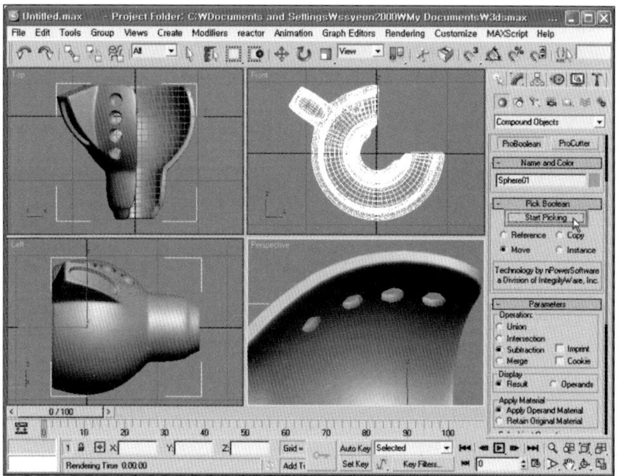

07 Check if a hole has been drilled by [Pro Boolean] that is as big as the Sphere itself, and click [Start Picking] to exit the mode.

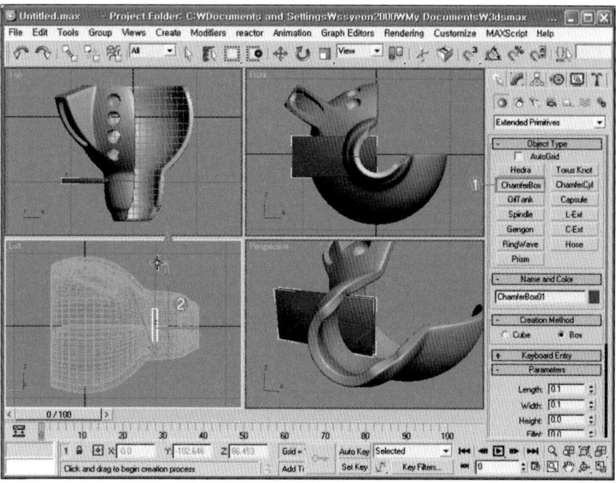

08 In the Create panel, click [Geometry]–[Extended Primitives]–[ChamferBox]. In the Left Viewport, click–and–drag as shown in the picture to create new Chamfer Box that penetrates the "Sphere01" object.

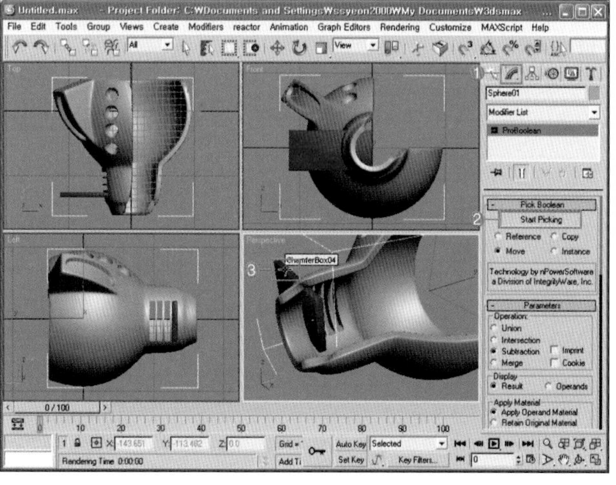

09 Make three more copies of the "ChamferBox01" object by click–and–dragging while pressing <Shift>. Select the "Sphere01" object, and move to the Modify panel by clicking [Modify]. Confirm that [Parameters]–[Operation]–[Subtraction] is selected, and delete the Chamfer Box part by clicking [Start Picking].

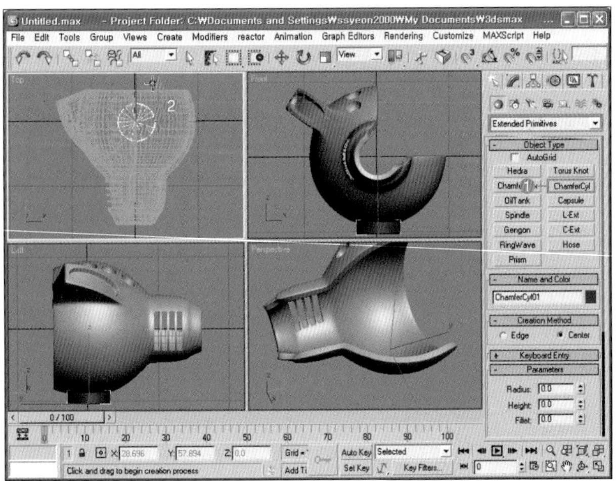

10 In the Create panel, click [Geometry]–[Extended Primitives]–[Chamfer Cylinder ChamferCyl]. Click–and–drag in the Top Viewport to create a new Chamfer Cylinder object below the "Sphere01" object.

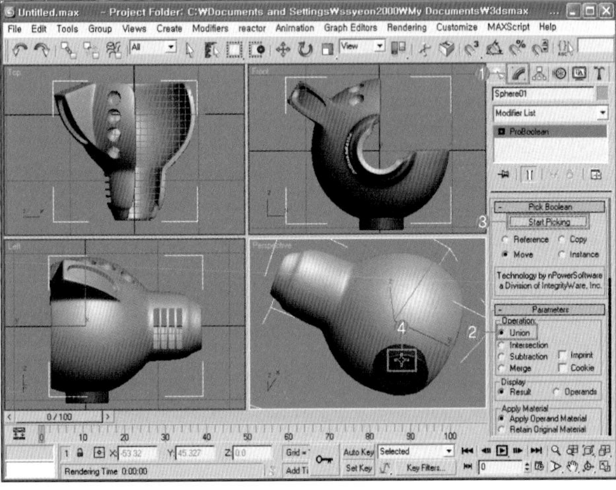

11 Select the "Sphere01" object, and move to the Modify panel. Select [Parameters]–[Operation]–[Union], and click Start Picking to converge the Chamfer Cylinder part.

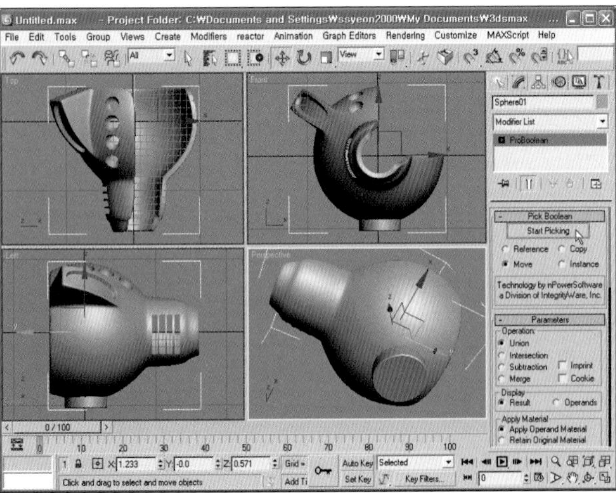

12 Click Start Picking to exit the mode and observe the completed shape.

Adding to the Object Using Sphere and Cylinder

Now let's place a simple object inside the machine to represent a bearing.

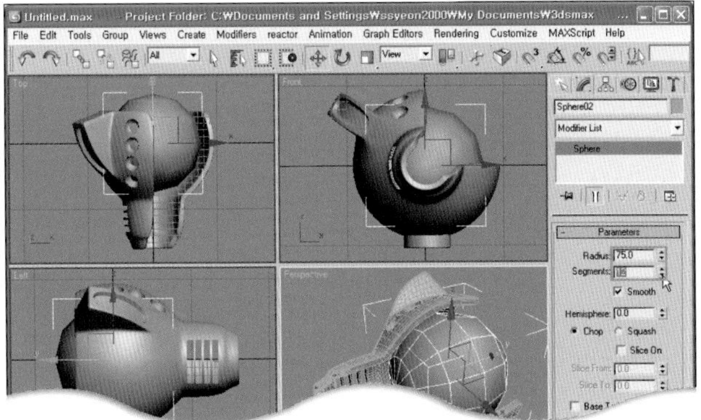

01 In the Create panel, click [Geometry]–[Standard Primitives]–[Sphere]. Click–and–drag the new sphere in the Top Viewport. Move to the Modify panel, and enter [75] for [Radius] and [12] for [Segments].

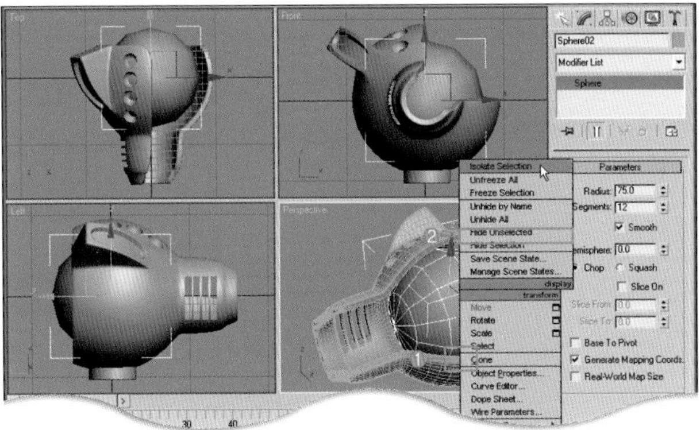

02 Right–click on the newly added "Sphere02" object to open the quad menu. Select [Isolate Selection] to hide everything except the sphere.

tip >>

Isolate Selection

If there are numerous objects in the Viewport, it may be difficult to modify the target object. If this is the case, speed up the job by temporarily hiding the rest of the objects using [Isolate Selection].

Quad Menu

Note >>>

The quad menu is a function that shows a four–directional menu. This menu appears when you click the right button of the mouse over the object or on a blank space of the Viewport. The contents of the quad menu differ when used with the <Alt>, <Ctrl>, and <Shift> keys. An <Alt>+right–click shows an animation–specific quad menu, <Ctrl>+right–click opens one on figures, and <Shift>+right–click shows object snapping.

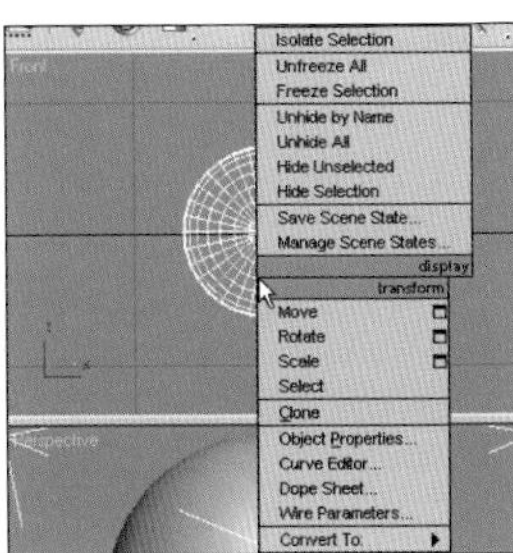

Right–click

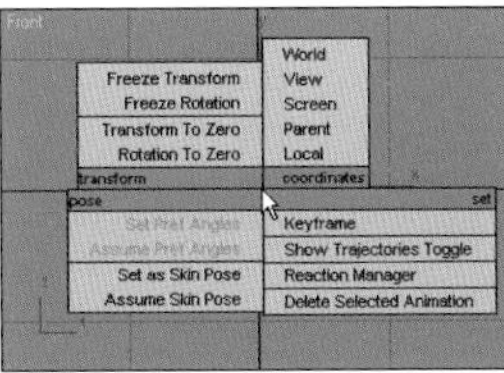

<Alt>+right–click

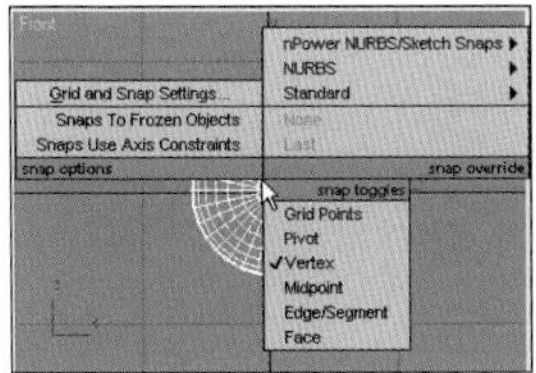

<Shift>+right–click

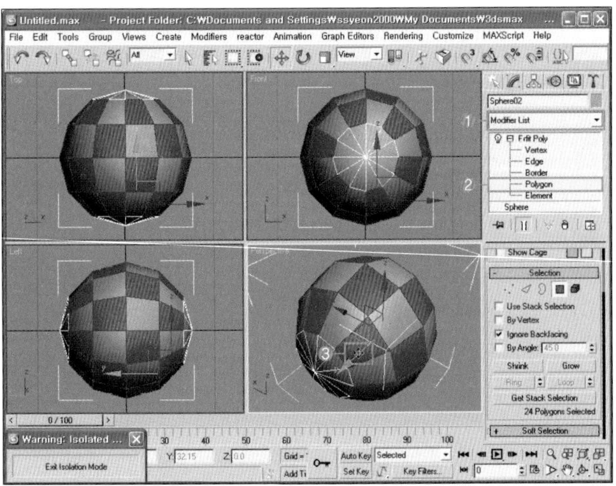

03 Click the [Modifier List] combo box, and select the [Edit Poly] Modifier. Select the [Polygon] sub–object, and, while holding down <Ctrl>, select the polygons shown in the picture.

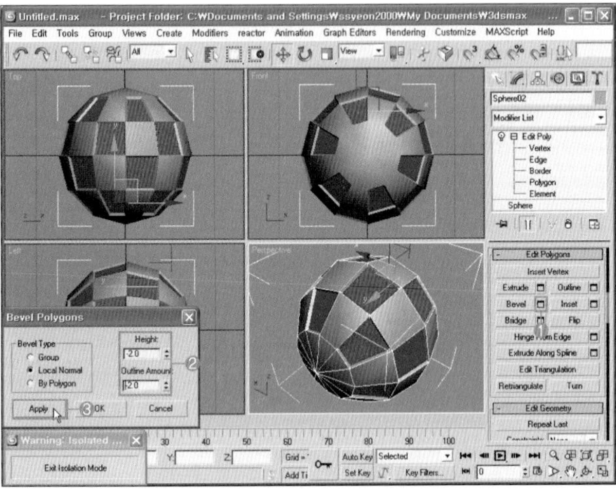

04 Click [Edit Polygons]–[Bevel Settings]. In the [Bevel Polygons] dialog box, enter [–2] for [Height], [–2] for [Outline Amount], and click [Apply].

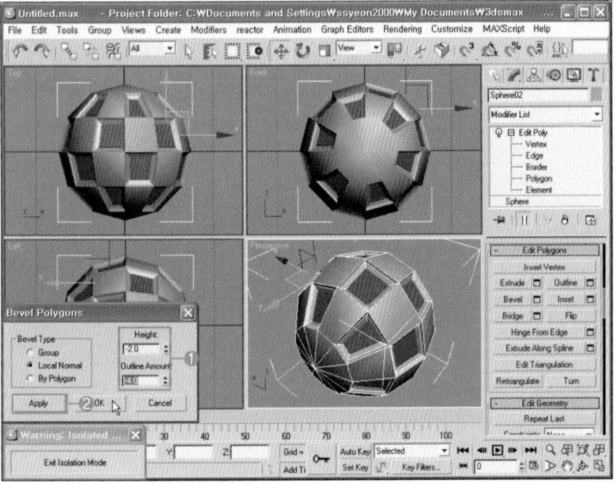

05 With the [Bevel Polygons] dialog box still open, enter [–4] for [Outline Amount], and click [OK].

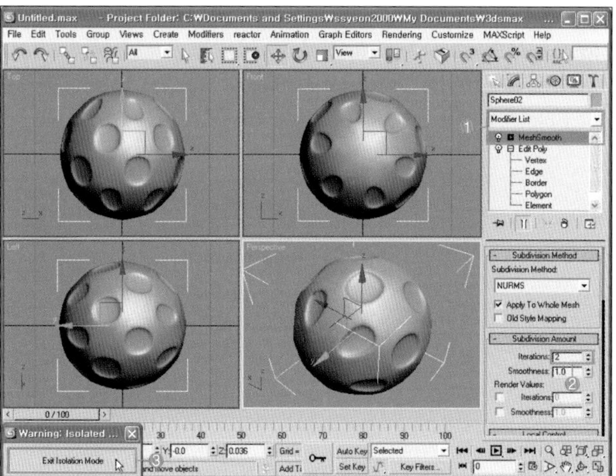

06 After finishing the work, click the [Modifier List] combo box, and select the MeshSmooth Modifier. Enter [2] for [Subdivisions Amount]–[Iterations]. Click [Exit Isolation Mode] to exit the Isolation mode.

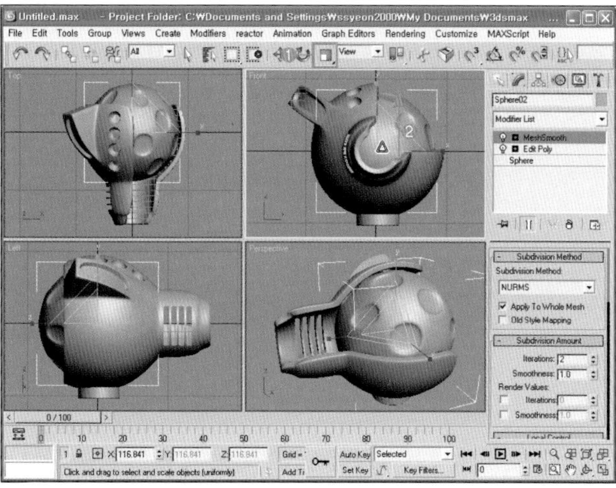

07 Click [Select and Scale] on the main tool bar, and, using the picture as a reference, adjust the size of “Sphere02” in relation to “Sphere01”.

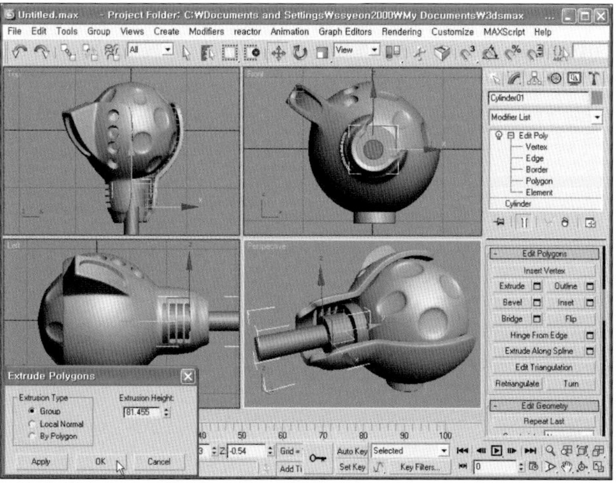

08 In the Create panel, click [Geometry]–[Standard Primitives]–[Cylinder], and create a small Cylinder at the inlet of the machine in the Front Viewport. Click the [Modifier List] combo box, and select the [Edit Poly] Modifier. Select the [Polygon] sub–object, select the front polygon, and create the form shown in the picture using [Inset] and [Extrude].

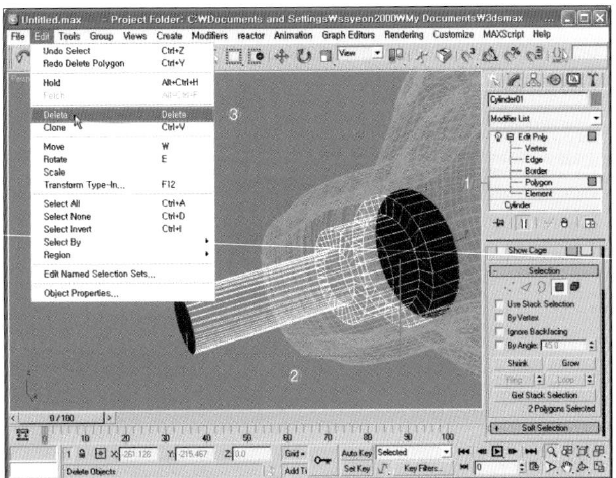

09 Select the [Polygon] sub–object [Edit Poly], select the front and back polygons of the cylinder object, and delete by selecting [Edit]–[Delete] on the menu bar.

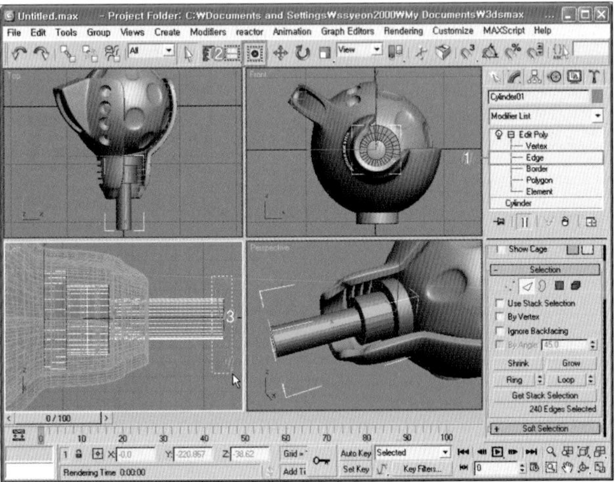

10 Select the [Edge] sub–object in [Edit Poly], and select the edges that should have sharp borderlines by click–and–dragging while pressing <Ctrl>.

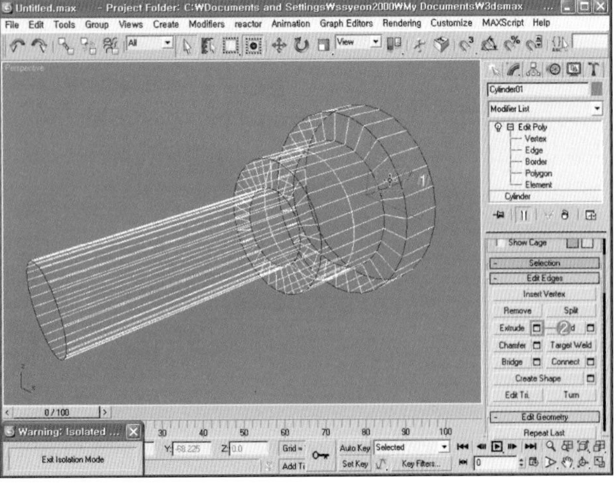

11 Right–click on the "Cylinder01" object to open the quad menu, and select [Isolate Selection]. Press <Alt> to deselect any unnecessary edges accidentally selected. Then divide the edges in two using [Chamfer].

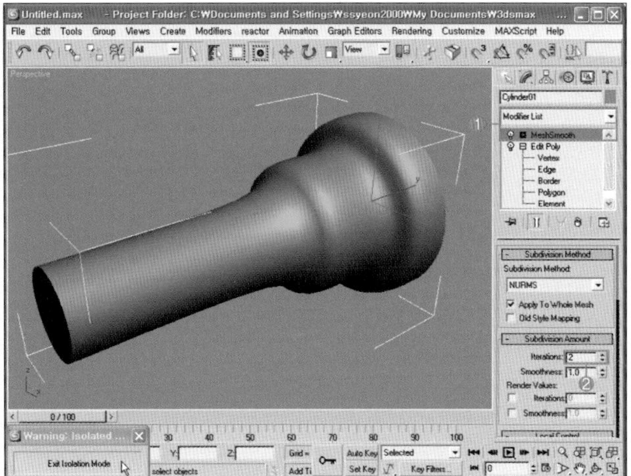

12 Click the [Modifier List] combo box, select the [MeshSmooth] Modifier, and enter [2] for [Iterations]. Click [Exit Isolation Mode] to exit the Isolation mode.

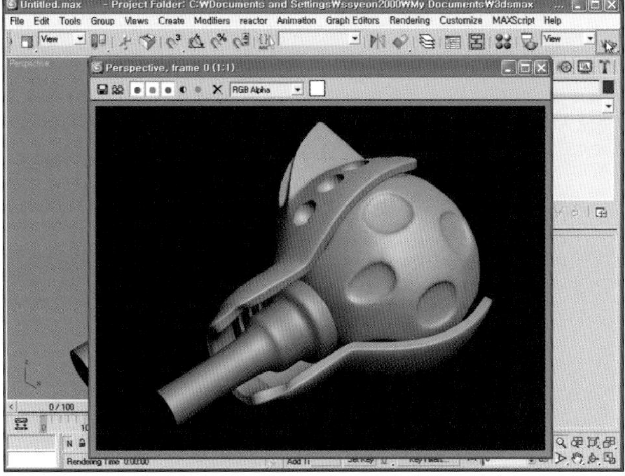

13 Select the Perspective Viewport, and click [Quick Render] on the main tool bar to check the rendered form.

Supplementary CD\Sample\Chapter 2\Exercise 1\Machine.max

Exercise 02

2D Figure Modeling

Let's demonstrate how to create figures through basic lines.

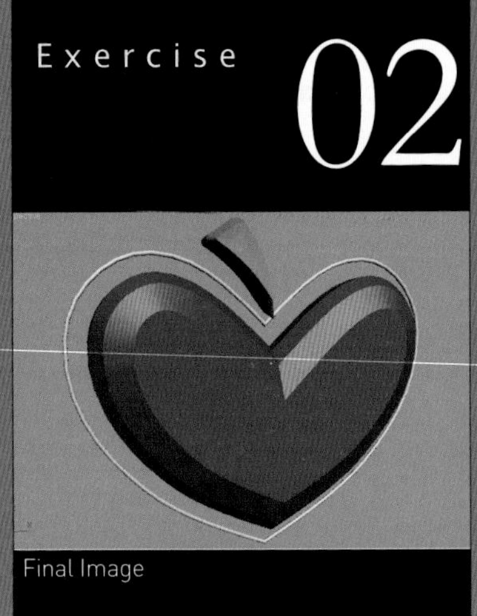

Final Image

Final File
\Sample\Chapter 2\Exercise 2\Heart.max

Handling a Line Sub–Object 

Now, experiment with creating character forms using lines that produce basic 2D forms.

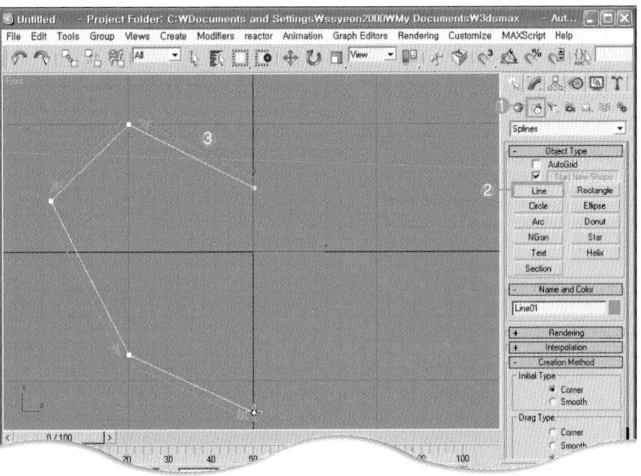

01 On the Create panel, click 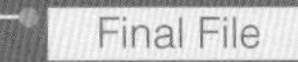 under [Shapes]–[Splines]. Magnify the Front Viewport, click to draw a half–heart shape, and finish by clicking the right mouse button.

tip >>

Magnify the Viewport

To magnify the Viewport, click the right button of the mouse on the desired Viewport and click [Maximize Viewport Toggle] on the Viewport control.

02 Click [Modify] with the "Line01" selected, and move to the Modify panel. Select the [Vertex] sub–object, and select the left vertices, as shown, by dragging.

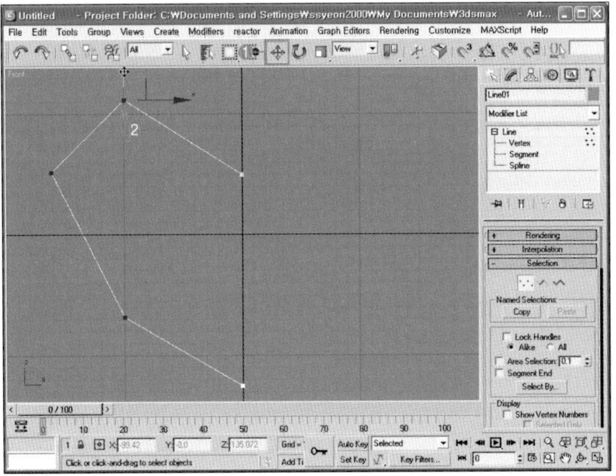

03 Click [Select and Move] on the main toolbar, and move the selected vertices up to modify the shape of the heart.

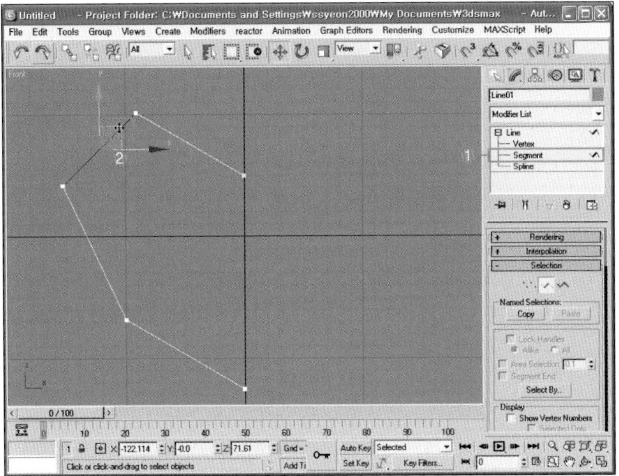

04 Select the [Segment] sub–object under [Line], then select the segment as shown in the picture, and move to [Select and Move].

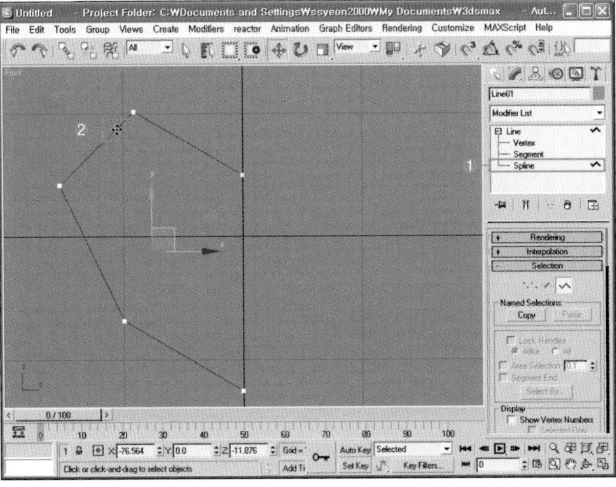

05 Select the [Spline] sub–object, and select the entire line.

Key Parameters 

There are many parameters that regulate lines, but only a few of these functions are commonly used. Let's examine the key parameter controls.

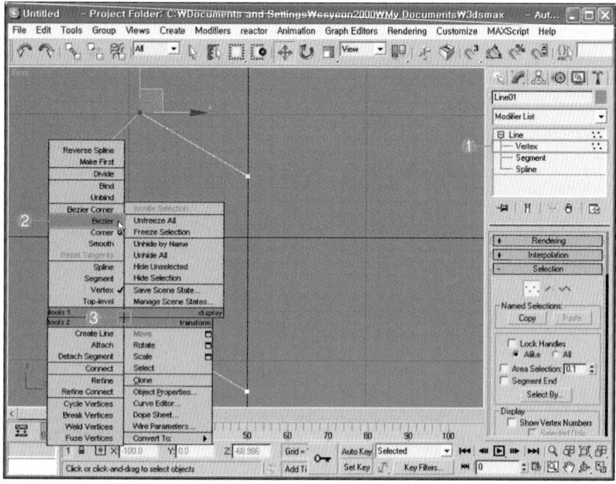

01 Select the [Vertex] sub–object under [Line], and open the quad menu by clicking the right button of the mouse on the selected vertex. Select [Bezier] to change the straight line into a curve.

tip >>

Bezier Curve

A Bezier curve is one of the methods used to add curve to a basic straight line. The methods for changing the curvature include [Bezier Corner], [Bezier], [Corner], and [Smooth]. A Bezier curve provides handlebars at both sides of the vertices, enabling the user to change the curvature. [Bezier Corner] creates a Bezier curve, but the handlebars can each move, and although [Smooth] cannot be controlled, it automatically modifies the line to make it smooth.

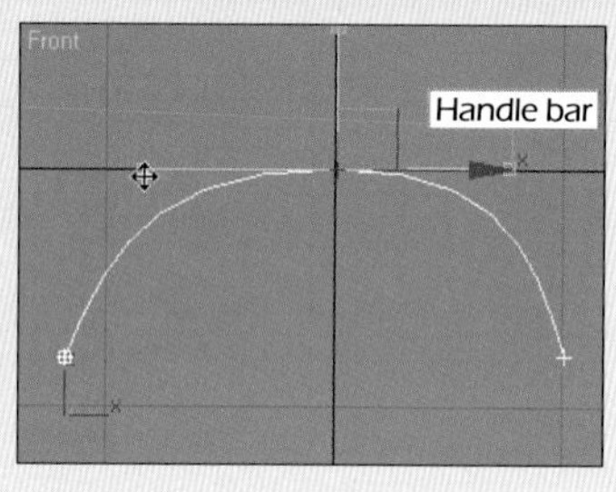

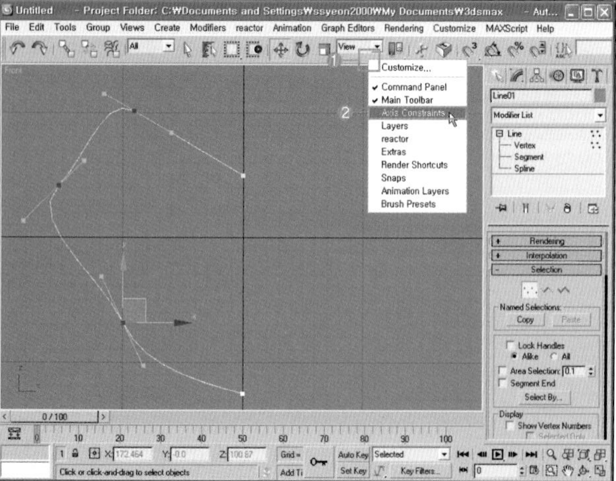

02 Click the right button of the mouse on the blank space of the main toolbar to select [Axis Constraints].

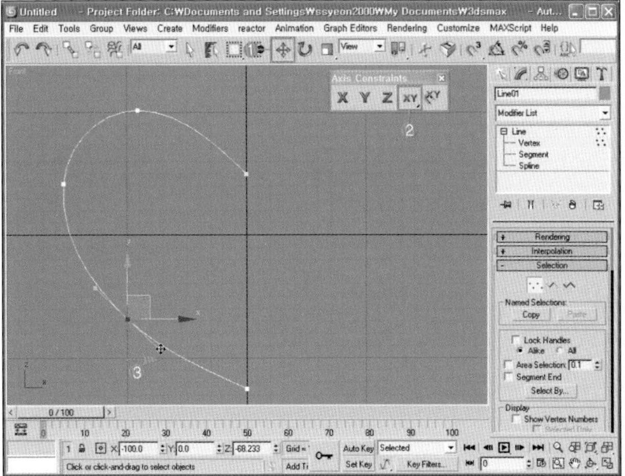

03 Click [Select and Move] on the main toolbar, click [XY] on the [Axis Constraints] dialog box, and modify to the shape as shown in the picture by dragging the handlebar of each vertex.

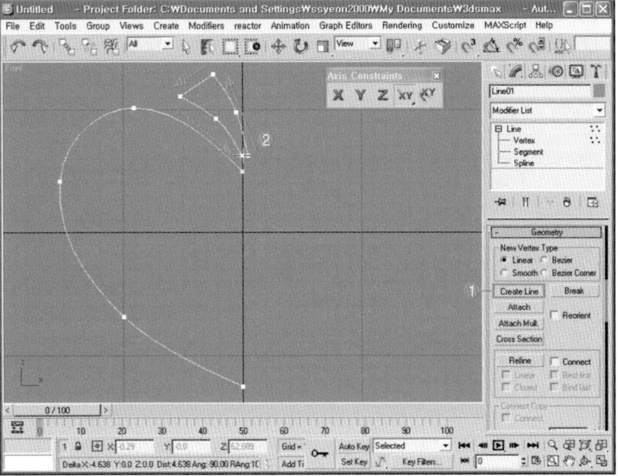

04 Click [Create Line] in [Geometry], and draw a new line the shape of an apple stem.

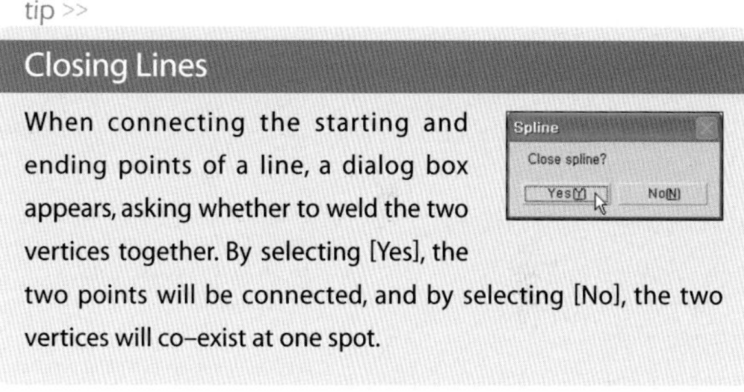

tip >>

Closing Lines

When connecting the starting and ending points of a line, a dialog box appears, asking whether to weld the two vertices together. By selecting [Yes], the two points will be connected, and by selecting [No], the two vertices will co–exist at one spot.

05 Select the [Spline] sub–object under [Line], and select and check the added line.

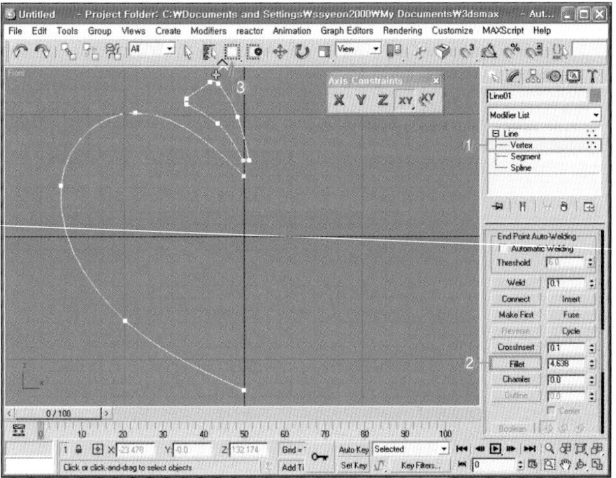

06 Select the [Vertex] sub-object under [Line], click [Fillet], and divide each of the vertices in two by dragging the two vertices of the stalk, as shown.

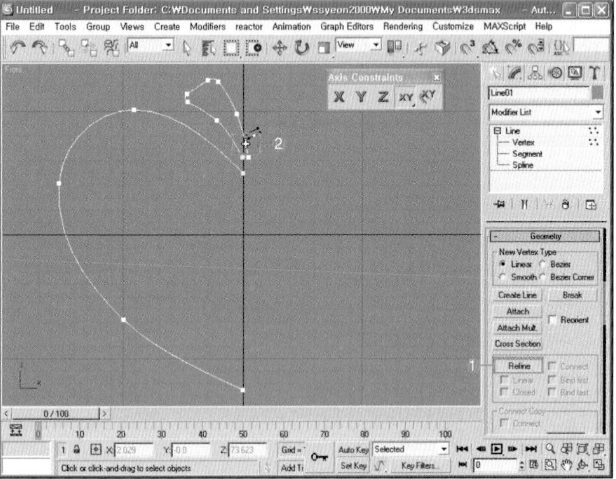

07 Click [Refine] in [Geometry], and click on the location as shown to add a new vertex.

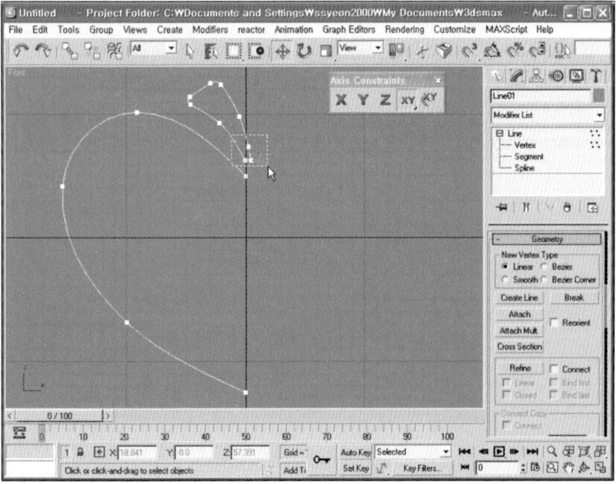

08 Drag with the mouse to select the added vertex.

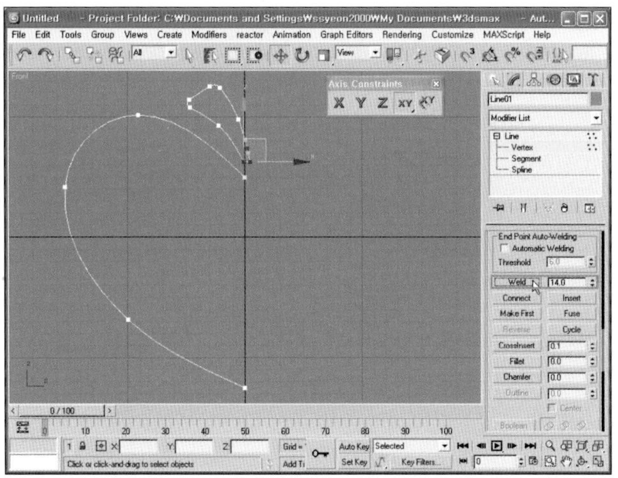

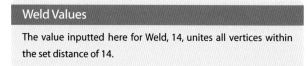

09 Input [14] in [Weld], and click  to combine the selected vertices.

tip >>

Weld Values

The value inputted here for Weld, 14, unites all vertices within the set distance of 14.

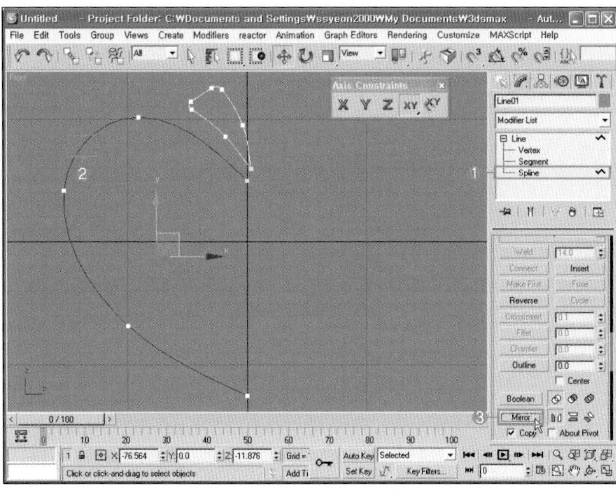

10 Select the [Spline] sub–object of [Line], and then the heart–shaped curve, and click [Mirror] at the [Parameter] menu to conduct symmetrical copying.

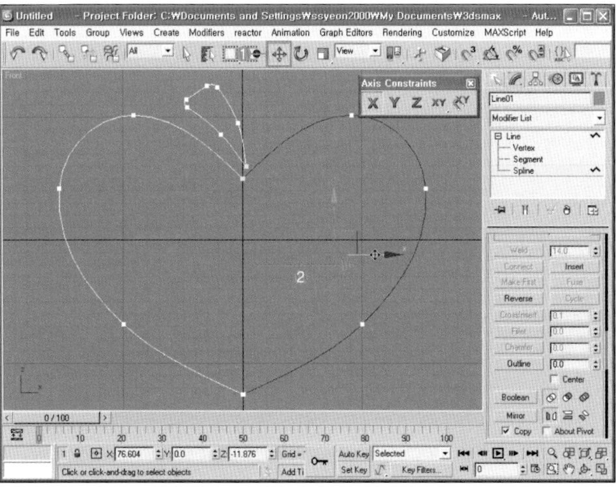

11 Move the copied curve to the opposite side using [Select and Move].

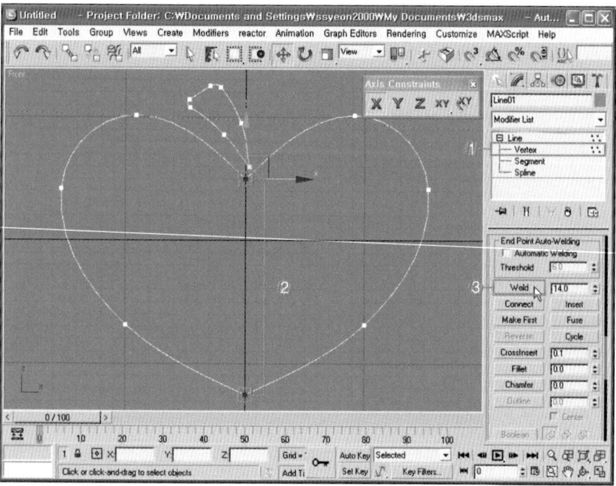

12 Select the [Vertex] sub–object of [Line], select the adjacent vertices by dragging with <Ctrl> pressed, and unite them by clicking [Weld].

Advanced Line Work

Because 3D objects cannot be created just with lines, this section will discuss how to convert lines to sections with the Outline feature and how to use the Bevel Modifier.

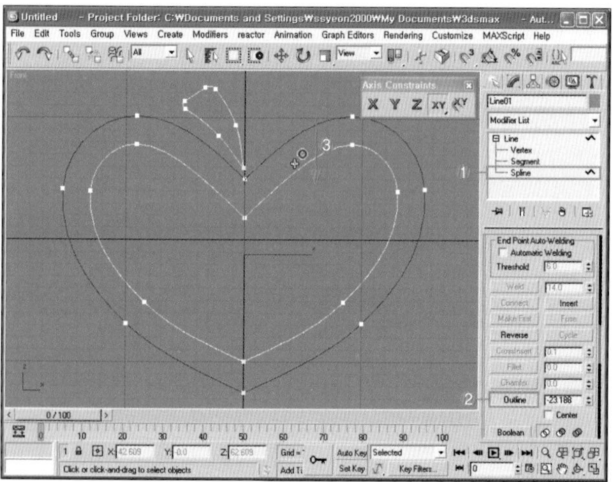

01 Select the [Spline] sub–object under [Line]. Click [Outline], and create the outline by dragging the heart–shaped curve downwards.

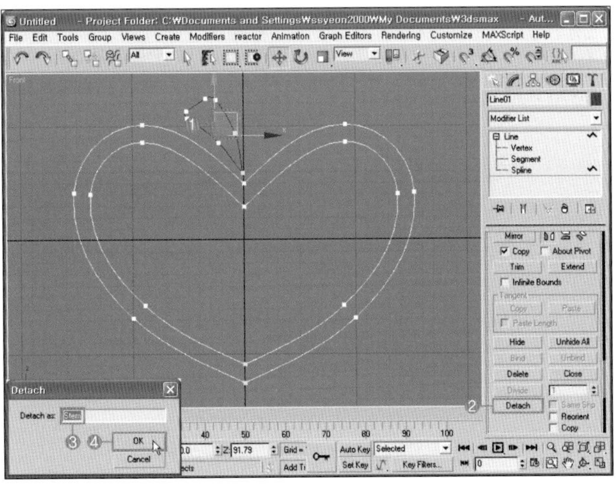

02 Select the stem–shaped curve above, and click . Input the name "stem" when the [Detach] dialog box appears, and click [OK].

tip >>

Detach Feature

Detach provides functions to divide united sub-objects and change them into separate objects. Whereas Detach separates objects, the Attach function unites separated objects.

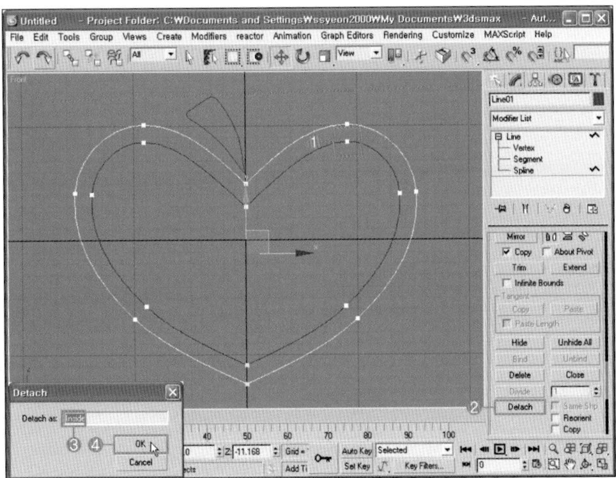

03 Follow the same step to divide the curve inside the heart into "inside." Click on [Line] to exit the sub–object mode.

04 Select the divided "inside" object, click the [Modifier List] combo box, and select the [Bevel] Modifier. Under [Bevel Values], enter [13, 1.4] in [Height] and [Outline] of Level 1, enter [10.5, –7.8] in [Height] and [Outline] of Level 2, and enter [10.5, –18.2] in [Height] and [Outline] of Level 3, respectively.

05 Select the "Line01" object, check [Enable In Renderer] and [Enable In Viewport], check [Radial] in [Rendering], and input [3] in [Thickness].

06 Apply the Bevel Modifier to the "stem" object in the same way, and select colors for each of the objects.

Supplementary CD\Sample\Chapter 2\Exercise 2\Heart.max

Creating Text Characters

By using , the user can create sections with input texts and finish the section with the Bevel Modifier.

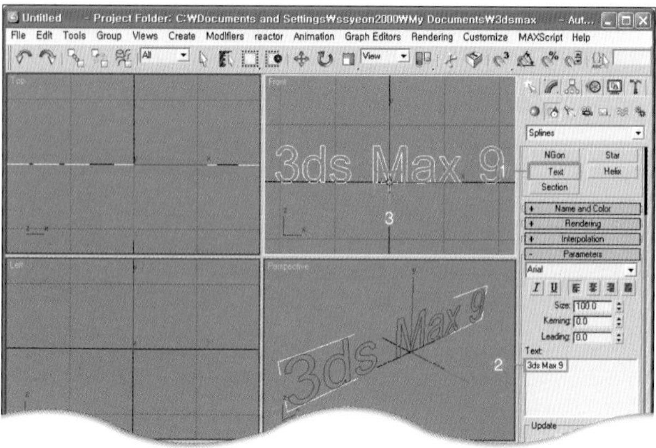

01 Open a new file, and on the Create panel, click Text under [Shapes]–[Splines]. Input [3ds Max 9] in the [Text] section of the [Parameters], and click the Front Viewport to create text type line objects.

tip >>

Text Parameters

The text panel provides parameters that enable settings of fonts and slants installed in the system.

1. Select from available fonts
2. Modify the text alignment
3. Set the size of the text
4. Adjust the distance between letters
5. Adjust the distance between the letters
6. Input the text
7. Modify the appearance of the input text to be shown on the Viewport

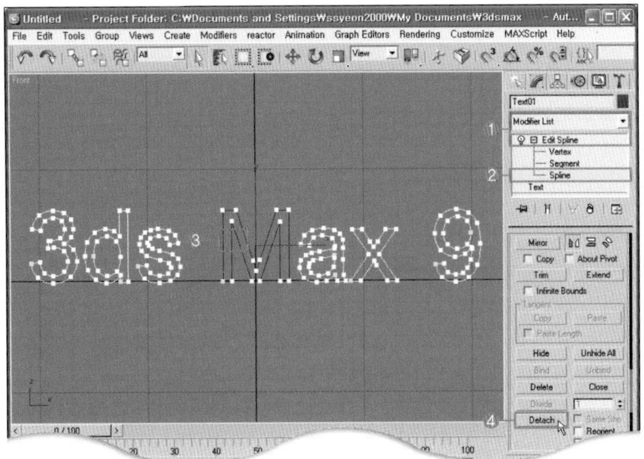

02 Move to the Modify panel with the "Text01" object selected. Click the [Modifier List] combo box, select the [Edit Spline] Modifier, select the [Spline] object, and then "M". Click Detach to divide the selected line.

03 Select each of the objects, click the [Modifier List] combo box, and convert it to 3D using the Bevel Modifier.

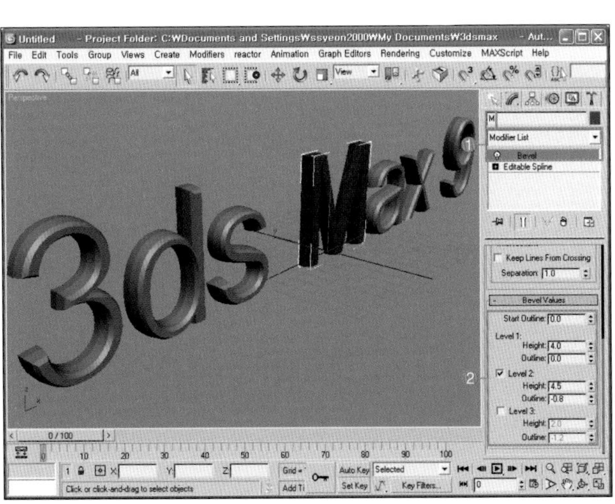

tip >>

Changing Object Colors

By clicking the [Color] button of the Modify panel, the [Color Setting] dialog box appears, where you can select the desired color here. The colors of objects are useful merely for differentiation in the Viewport; they are different from the mapping materials that show in the final rendering. Of course, the objects' colors are rendered during the rendering process, but since light reflection and the surface materials do not show, they are not fit for the final rendering image. Therefore the user must also conduct material rendering for the objects.

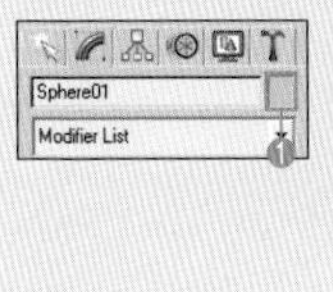

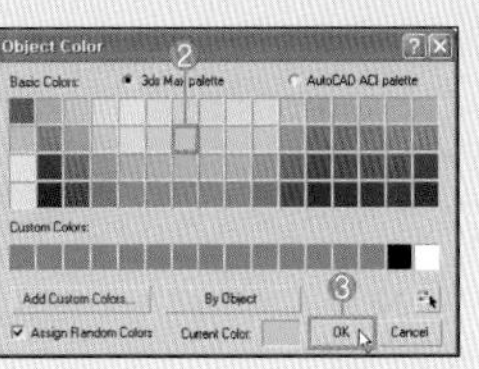

Exercise 03

Object Selection Method

Final Image

The first step in modeling an object is to select the object. This section will not only cover the many ways in which an object can be selected, but also how to hide, freeze, rotate, move, and resize the selected object.

Start Files
\Sample\Chapter 2\Exercise 3\Select.max

Various Methods for Object Selection

Let's learn the various ways to select objects in the Viewport.

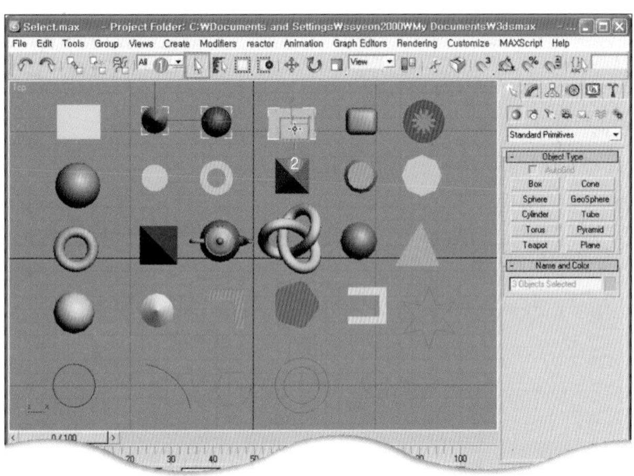

01 On the supplementary CD, open the Sample\Chapter 2\Exercise 3\Select.max file. Once opened, click either [Select Object], [Select and Move], [Select and Rotate], or [Select and Scale] on the main toolbar. Click and select the desired objects in the Viewport while pressing the <Ctrl> key.

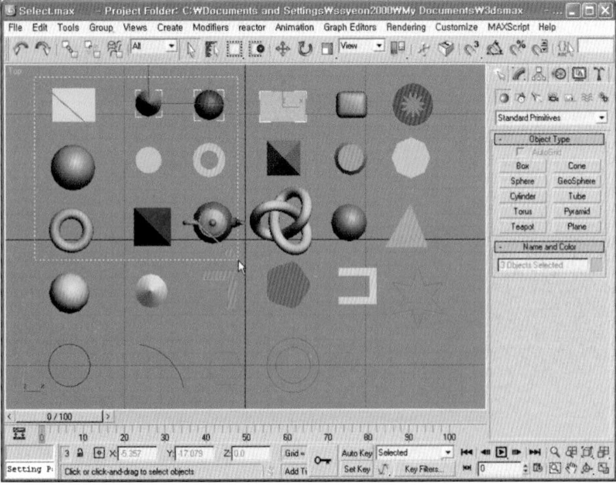

02 Starting from a blank spot in the Viewport, click–and–drag to select multiple objects.

03 To deselect objects, use the <Alt> key in combination with any of the selection methods available. For example, to deselect individual objects, click on them while pressing the <Alt> key.

04 Click [Window/Crossing] on the main toolbar; only the objects that are entirely within the drawn Selection Region will be selected.

tip >>

Selecting Objects that Cross the Drag Area

If [Window/Crossing] is active on the main toolbar, any objects that are even partly within the Selection Region will be selected.

05 To change the square selection method into a circular one, click [Circular Selection Region] on the main toolbar.

06 By click–and–dragging in the Viewport, a circular selection area appears.

07 To use a polygon–shaped selection area, click [Fence Selection Region] on the main toolbar, click–and–drag the first line of the polygon in the Viewport, then click any number of points to create the polygon. To finish the selection region, be sure to click on the shape's starting point.

08 To use a free–hand selection area, click [Lasso Selection Region] on the main toolbar, and click–and–drag the perimeter of the selection region desired.

09 To select as if using a brush, click [Paint Selection Region] on the main toolbar, and select by click–and–dragging in the Viewport.

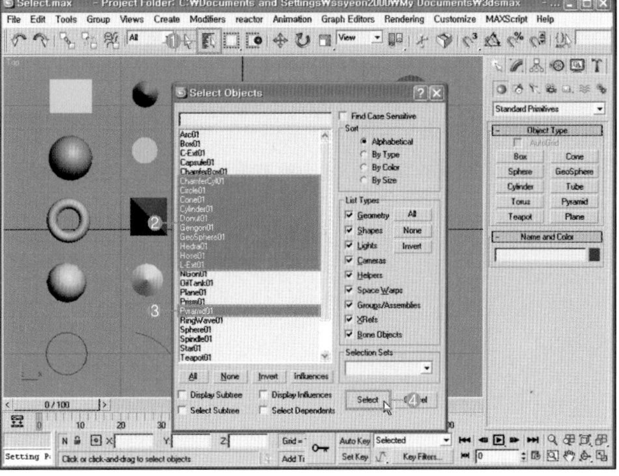

10 Click [Select by Name] on the main toolbar. Click the objects while pressing the <Ctrl> and <Shift> keys in the [Select Objects] dialog box, and click the [Select] button.

tip >>

Selecting Serial Objects

In order to quickly select multiple objects in the [Select Objects] dialog box, hold down either the <Ctrl> or the <Shift> key. Using only the <Ctrl> key will add to the selected object(s) on an individual basis. Using only the <Shift> key will select the object clicked on, plus the object last clicked on, plus all objects in the list between them, and will deselect any objects not within that range. Using both the <Ctrl> and <Shift> keys will act as with the <Shift>, but without deselecting any other objects.

11 To select according to the characteristics of the objects in the Viewport, select [Shape] first. Shape filters enable only the selection of objects that were created with the 2D figure tool.

12 Click [Rectangular Selection Region] on the main toolbar, and click–and–drag in the Viewport. Only 2D figures are selected, leaving out 3D figures.

Hiding Objects and Freezing

In some cases, the user has to hide objects showing in the Viewport.

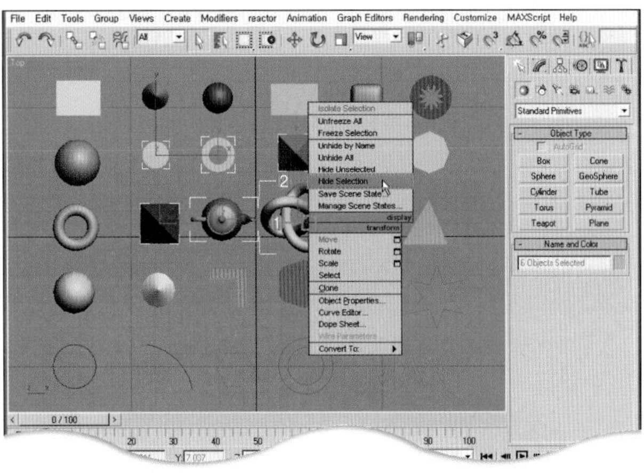

01 Right–click on a selected object to open the quad menu. Choose [Hide Selection] on the menu to hide the selected object(s).

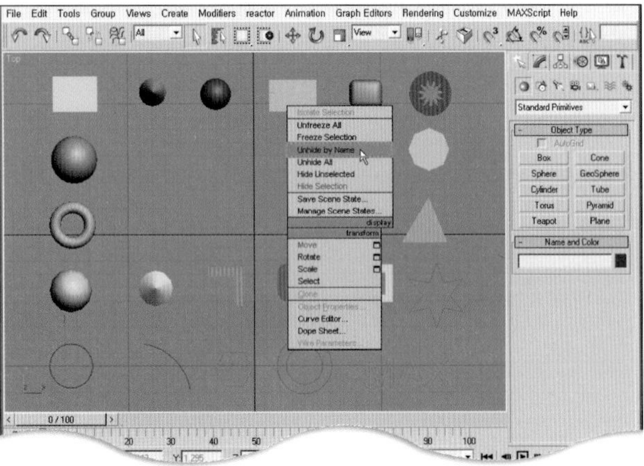

02 To show the hidden objects again, open the quad menu and click [Unhide by Name] on the menu.

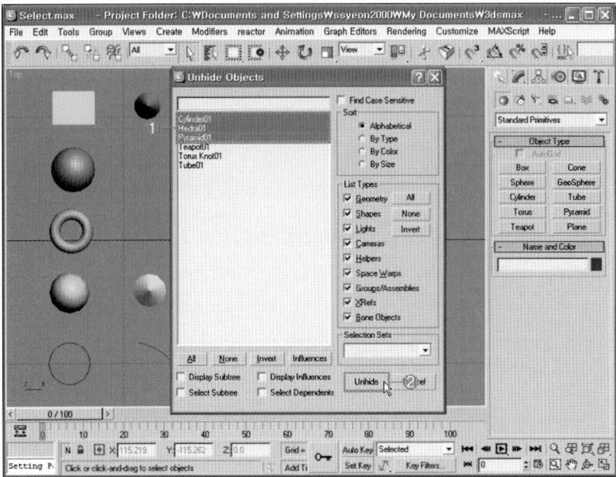

03 When the [Unhide Objects] dialog box appears, click any object(s) desired and select [Unhide].

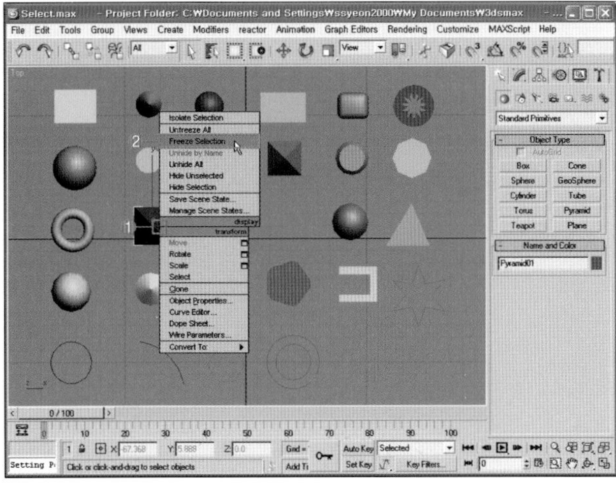

04 Click an object in the Viewport, and right–click on it to open the quad menu. Select [Freeze Selection] in the Viewport to freeze the object.

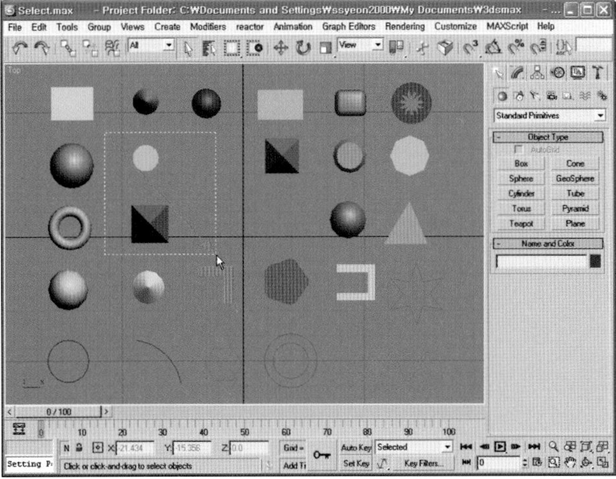

05 The frozen objects can be seen in the Viewport, but cannot be selected or edited.

tip >>

Restoring Frozen Objects

To make frozen objects editable again, select [Unfreeze All] from the quad menu.

Modification Tools 

Let's practice with the basic modification tools on the main toolbar.

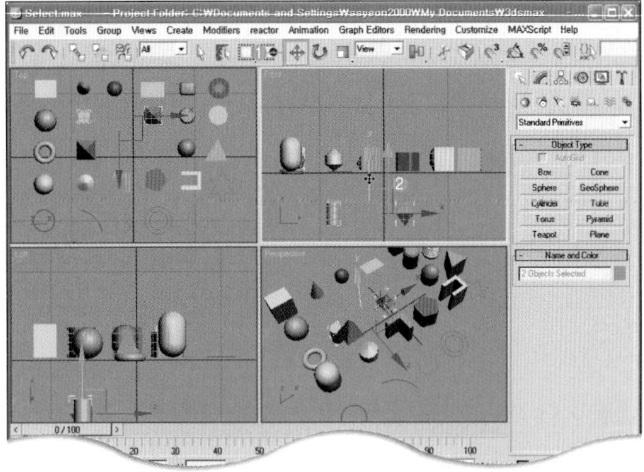

01 Click [Select and Move] on the main toolbar, and move a selection of objects by click–and–dragging. By click–and–dragging on one of the Gizmo's axes, the user can restrict the movement to that axis only.

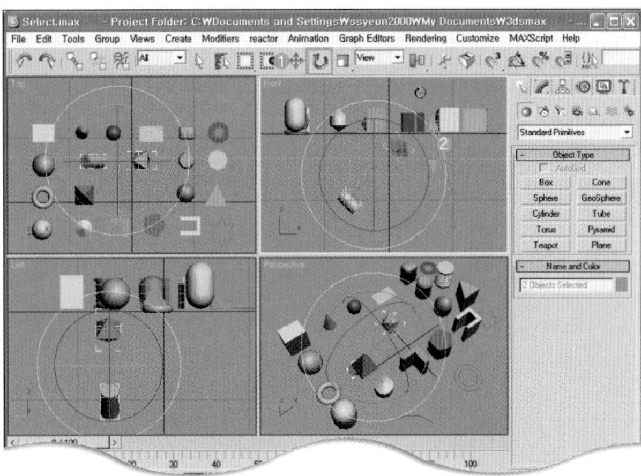

02 Click [Select and Rotate] on the main toolbar and rotate the chosen object(s). By click–and–dragging on one of the Gizmo's axes, the user can restrict the rotation to that axis only.

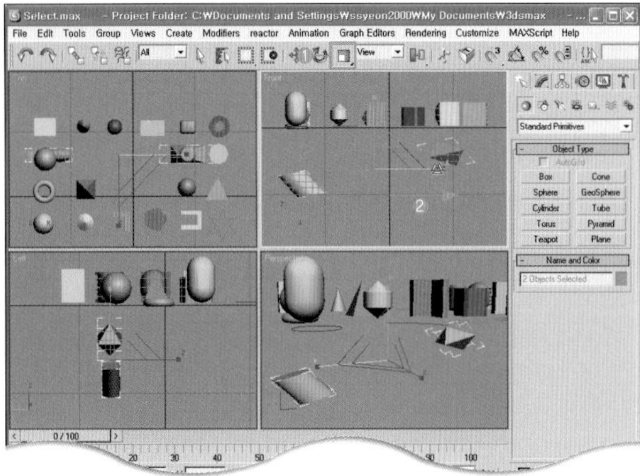

03 Click [Select and Scale] on the main toolbar, and change the size of the chosen object(s). By click–and–dragging on one of the Gizmo's axes, the user can restrict the scaling to that axis only.

Exercise 04

Copying Multiple Objects

The user may need to copy the same object several times in 3D works. This process can be accelerated by using the Array tool. The Mirror tool is useful for symmetric copying. The Align function can copy numerous objects centered on a desired object.

Final Image

Final File
\Sample\Chapter 2\Exercise 4\Array and Mirror_final.max
\Sample\Chapter 2\Exercise 4\Align_final.max

Creating Multi–Dimension Copies Using Array

To copy the same object in many directions at different angles, be sure to use the Array tool. The Array tool enables flat copying as well as vertical or multi–dimension copying, making this a very useful function.

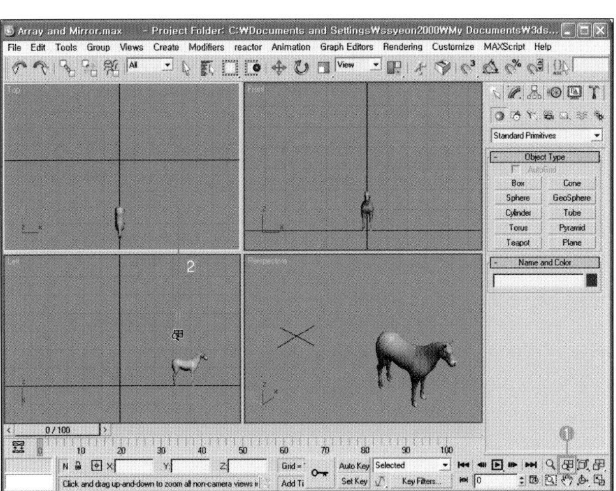

01 Open the "Array and Mirror.max" file on the supplementary CD, click [Zoom All] on the Viewport control, and click–and–drag downward in any Viewport to zoom out in all of the Viewports.

Supplementary CD\Sample\Chapter 2\Exercise 4\Array and Mirror.max

02 Before using Array, to set the absolute axis of the alignment as the center, set the [Reference Coordinate System] drop–down menu on the main toolbar to [World]. Then, click [Use Transform Coordinate Center] to move the Gizmo to the location of the absolute axis.

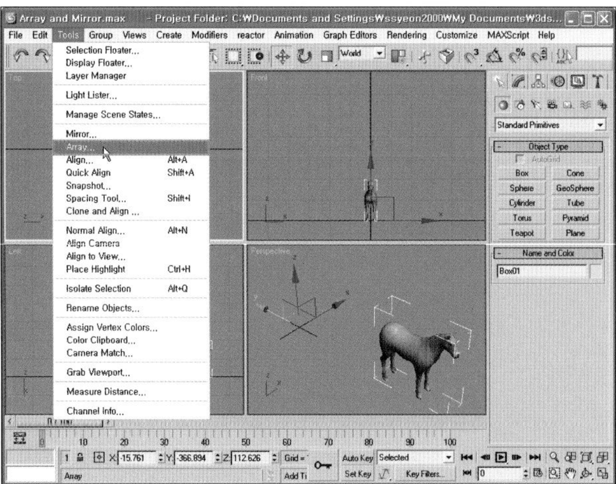

03 Select the horse, and click [Tools]–[Array] on the menu bar to rotate it around the absolute axis.

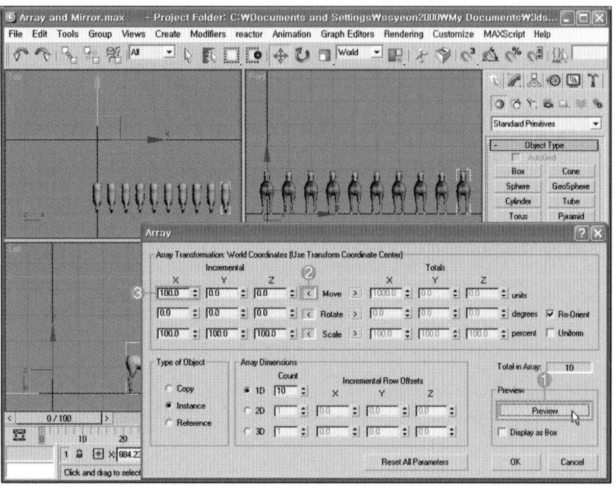

04 When the [Array] dialog box appears, click Preview first to observe the following changes in real–time. In [Array Transformation], click [Move Left <], and enter [100] under [Incremental]–[X] inline with [Move]. The selected horse object is aligned and copied along the X–axis at intervals of 100.

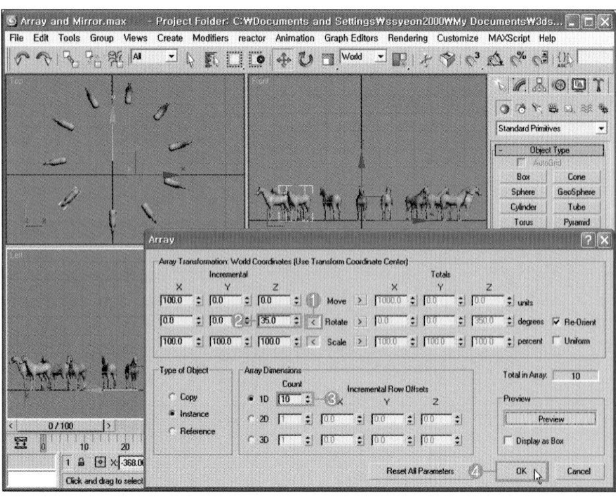

05 With the [Array] dialog box still open, in [Array Transformation], click [Rotate Left <], and enter [35] for [Incremental]–[Z]. Finally, click [Array Dimensions]–[1D] and enter [10]. When 10 horses appear aligned at 35–degree intervals around the absolute axis, click [OK].

Array Dialog Box

Note >>>

Array, which helps the user copy selected objects in multiple directions, also enables alignment in one, two, and three dimensions. A straight–line copying is the result of the 1D Array, and 2D Array means a layered alignment. 3D Array is more complicated; the user must consider the depth direction (Z–axis), which may be difficult to understand. Let's first examine the 2D Array, created by modifying the value of [Array Dimensions]–[2D].

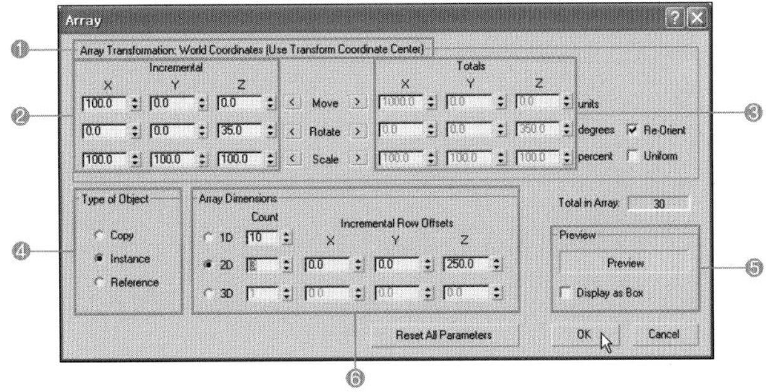

❶ **Array Transformaiton:** Marking the center axis set at the main toolbar

❷ **Incremental XYZ:** Movement, rotation, and size change of objects each in the X, Y, and Z–axis directions

❸ **Total XYZ:** Move, rotation, and size change values of the total number of objects in the X, Y, and Z–axis directions

❹ **Type of Object:** Characteristics of the copied objects (copy, copying multiple copies, symmetric copy)

❺ **Preview:** Preview of Array results

❻ **Array Dimensions:** [1D], [2D], and [3D] determine 1D, 2D, and 3D Arrays

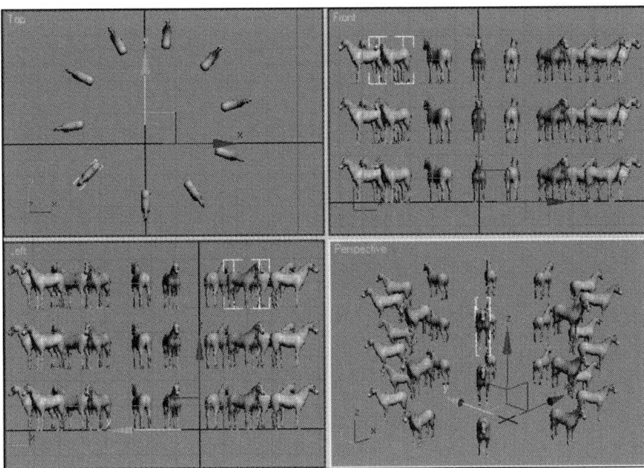

3D Array results

Copying Symmetric Objects Using Mirror

Now, let's explore the [Mirror] function, which copies the objects in symmetric positions.

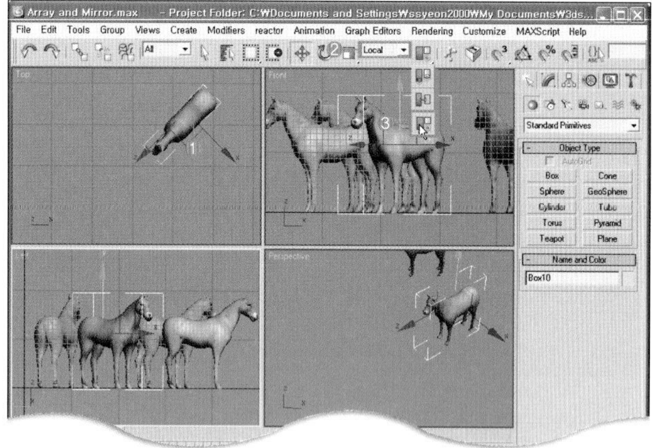

01 Select a horse in the Top Viewport, and, in the [Reference Coordinate System] drop–down menu on the main toolbar, select [Local] to change to the individual local axis of the horse, and click [Use Transform Coordinate Center].

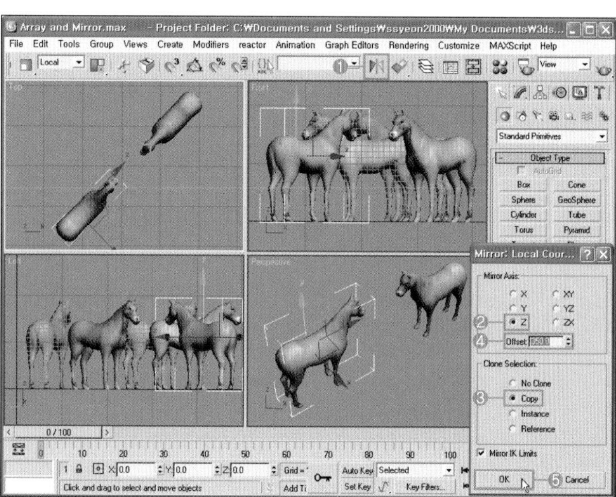

02 Click [Mirror] on the main toolbar to copy the selected horses in a symmetric position. In the [Mirror: Local Coordinates] dialog box, select [Z] and [Copy], then enter [350] for [Offset], and click [OK].

03 Select all of the other objects, and copy similarly.

Using the Clone and Align Function

Unlike the Array or Mirror tools, [Clone and Align] and [Align] can align the objects as well as copy them.

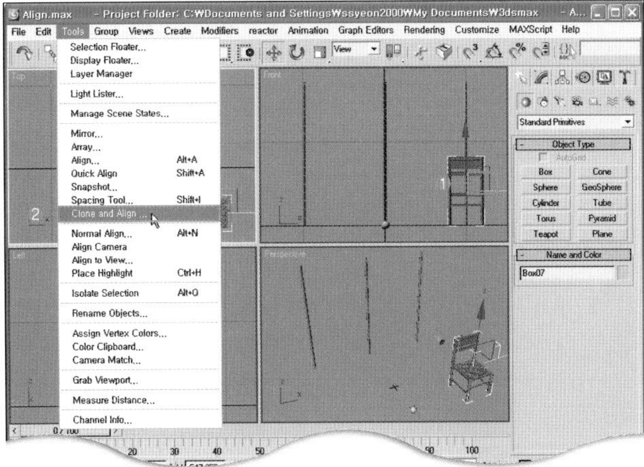

01 Open the "Align.max" file on the supplementary CD, and confirm the three cylinders and spheres that are already modeled. Select the chair, and click [Tools]–[Clone and Align] on the menu bar.

Supplementary CD\Sample\Chapter 2\Exercise 4\Align.max

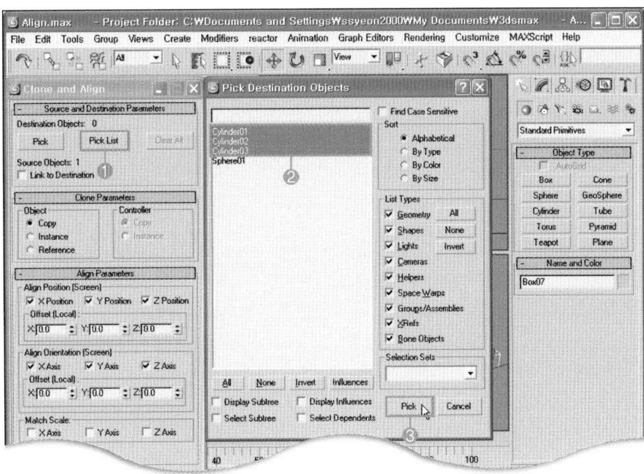

02 In the [Clone and Align] dialog box, click [Pick List], and select all of the Cylinders when the [Pick Destination Objects] dialog box appears. Once selected, click [Pick].

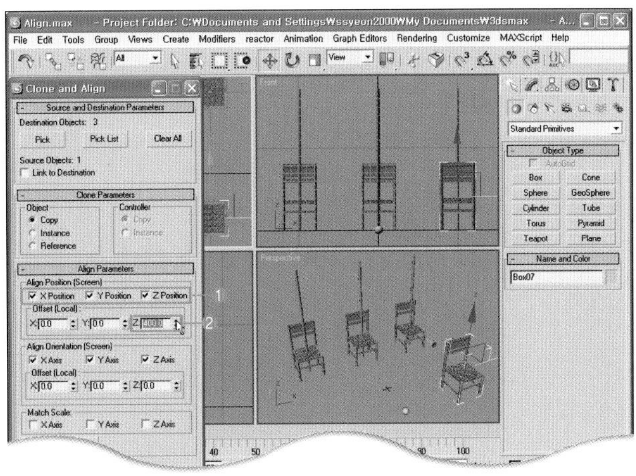

03 Set the [Reference Coordinate System] drop–down menu on the main toolbar to [World]. In the [Clone and Align] dialog box, in [Align Position (World)], check the boxes for [X Position], [Y Position], and [Z Position], and enter [400] for [Offset (Local)]–[Z:] to copy and align with the cylinder in the center.

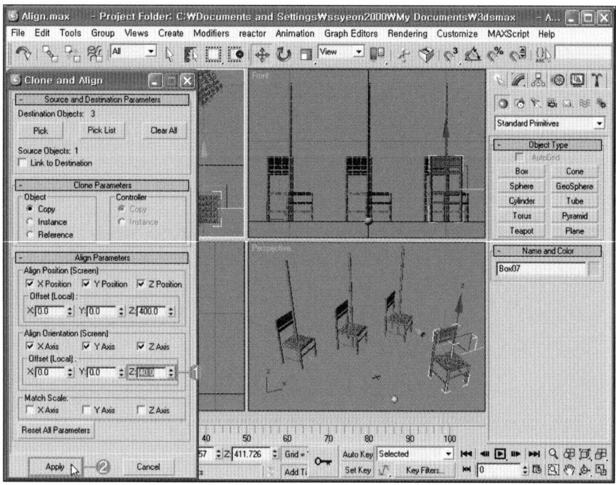

04 In [Align Orientation (World)], check the boxes for [X Axis], [Y Axis], and [Z Axis], and enter [40] for [Offset (Local)]–[Z:] to rotate all of the chairs that have been copied with the cylinder in the center by 40 degrees, and click [Apply].

05 With the original chair selected, click [Align] on the main toolbar, and select [Sphere].

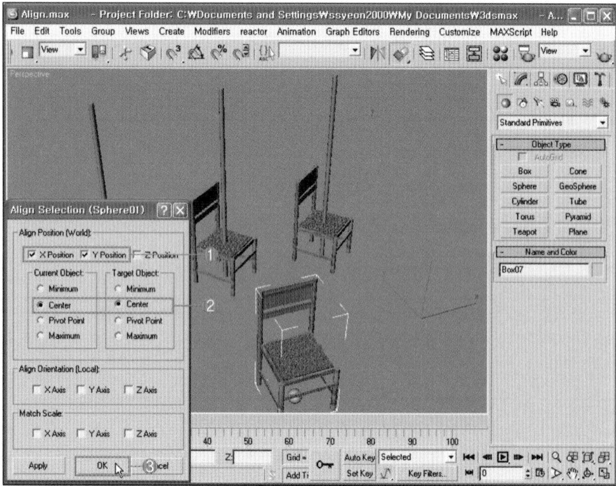

06 When the [Align Selection (Sphere01)] dialog box appears, check only the boxes for [X Position] and [Y Position], select [Current Object]–[Center] and [Target Object]–[Center], and click [OK].

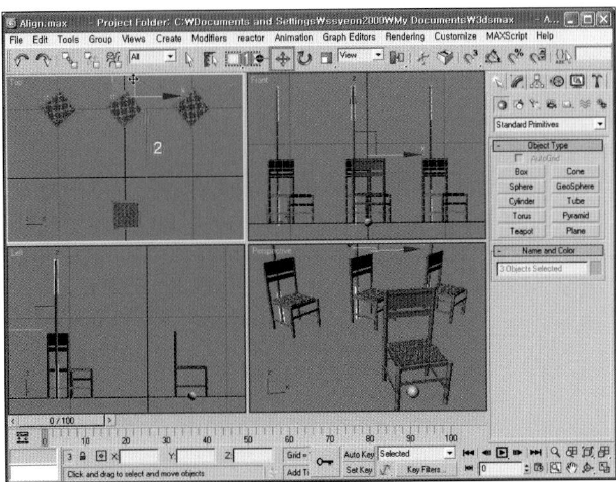

07 Click [Select and Move] on the main toolbar, and move the front cylinders behind the copied chair in the Viewport.

Align Selection Dialog Box

Note >>>

Using the [Align Selection] dialog box, the user can determine how the current object will align with the target object in regard to different reference points on each object.

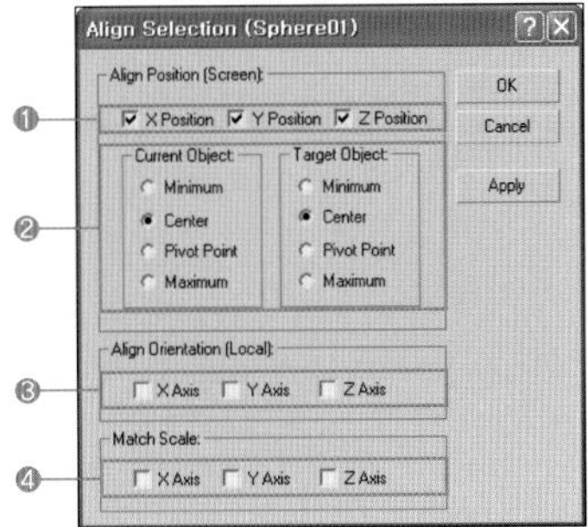

1. **X, Y, Z Position:** Marking the center axis set at the main toolbar
2. **Curent/Target Object:** Set the internal location of the selected object (Current Object) and the object that is the standard for the alignment (Target Object); the user can select [Maximum], [Center], [Pivot Point], or [Minimum] for the internal location
3. **Align Orientation[Local]:** Set the standard axis for the arrangement
4. **Match Scale:** Set the standard axis for the size arrangement between the objects

Chapter 3

Basic Modeling

3D work starts with modeling, which is basically the making of an object. Modeling can be done for anything from a simple diagram to an aircraft carrier, but its success depends on how realistic the completed model looks, regardless of size. This means that an object can be recognized only when it is designed in a highly sophisticated way, no matter how simple it is. In this chapter, various techniques will be taught for refining models, both simple or complex.

Exercise 01

Making Pottery

Final Image

One of the 3D modeling techniques is based on the Line object type. An object made up of lines is generally made by rotating a cutaway segment, and the Line and Lathe Modifier is a simple yet very basic method utilized in this process. This section will also show how to polish the overall object face with the MeshSmooth Modifier and how to cut holes easily with Pro Cutter.

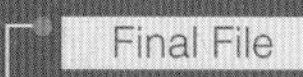

\Sample\Chapter 3\Exercise 1\Pottery–final.max

Outlining a Vase Using Line

First, a cutaway segment of a revolving object can be made using Line, as described in the following steps.

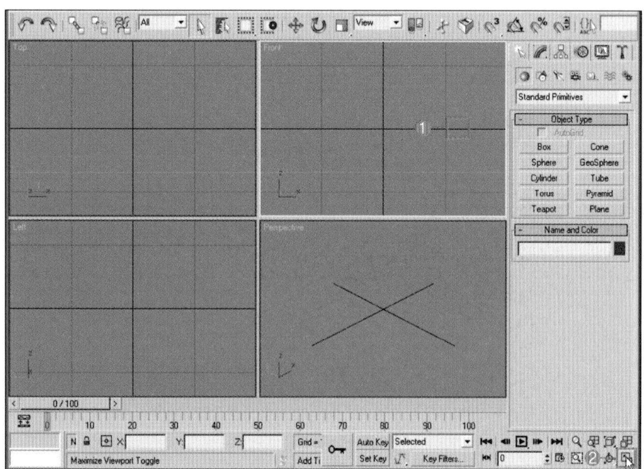

01 Open a new file and click in the Front Viewport to select it. Then enlarge the Viewport by clicking [Maximize Viewport Toggle] in Viewport Control.

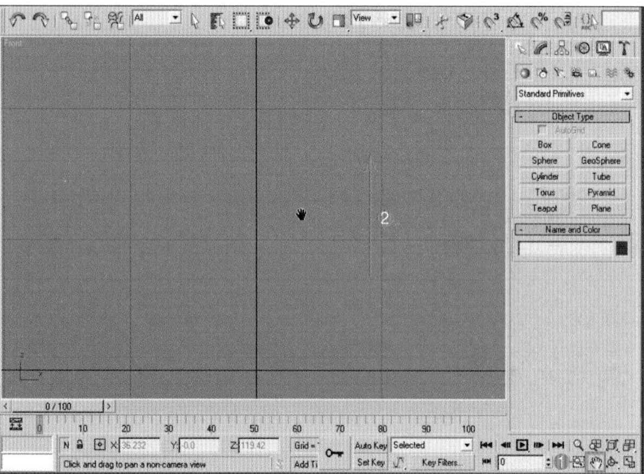

02 Click [Pan View] in Viewport Control and click–and–drag it down to position the absolute axis at the bottom of the Viewport.

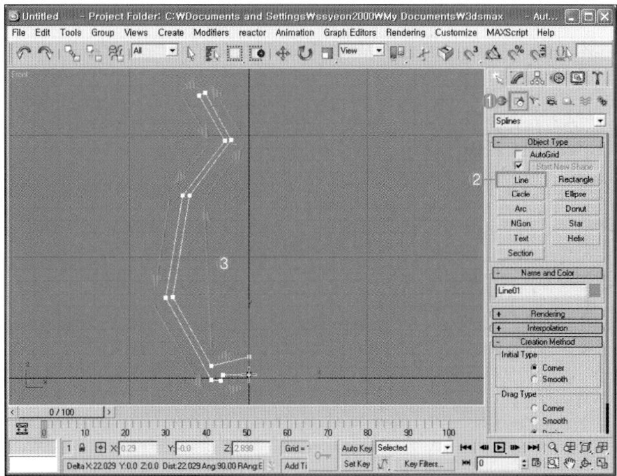

03 In the Create panel, under [Shapes]–[Splines]–[Object Type], click [Line]. Draw the lateral line of the pottery, as shown in the illustration, on the left side of the Y–axis.

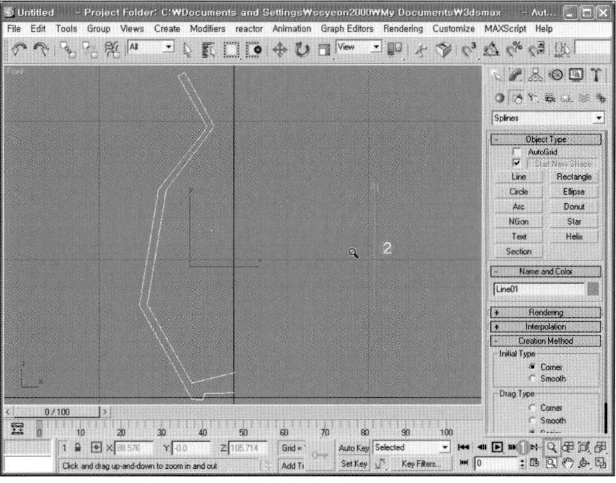

04 Click [Zoom] in Viewport Control and click–and–drag the Viewport upward to enlarge the object "Line01."

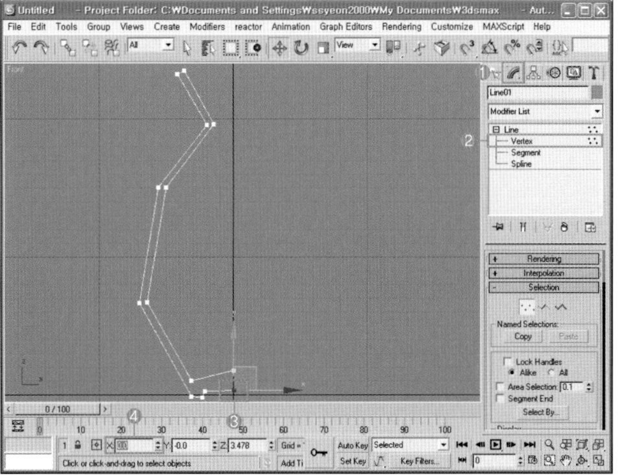

05 With "Line01" selected, move to the Modify panel. Select the sub–object [Vertex]–[Line], select the lower vertex on the Y–axis and enter [0] for the [X] value on the coordinate entry line.

tip >>

The Y-Axis

The Y-axis is not necessarily the center for drawing a segment. In the above explanation, however, the Y-axis is used as the center in order to help a beginner understand the concept of the absolute axis. When the user understands how to model an object based on the absolute axis, it becomes much easier to understand the Array feature, which will be dealt with later.

tip >>

Sub–Objects

Each object present in the Viewport is referred to as an Object, and the designation can mean a Line, Box, Camera, or Light. The internal components of each object are called sub–objects. For example, a Line is composed of sub–objects, such as Vertices, Segments and Splines.

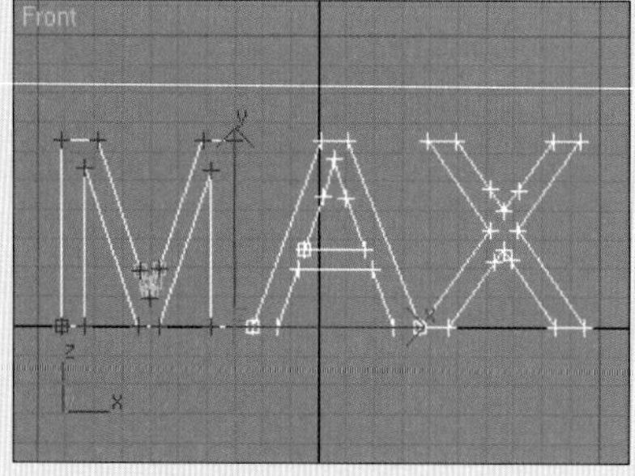

Vertex Sub–Object

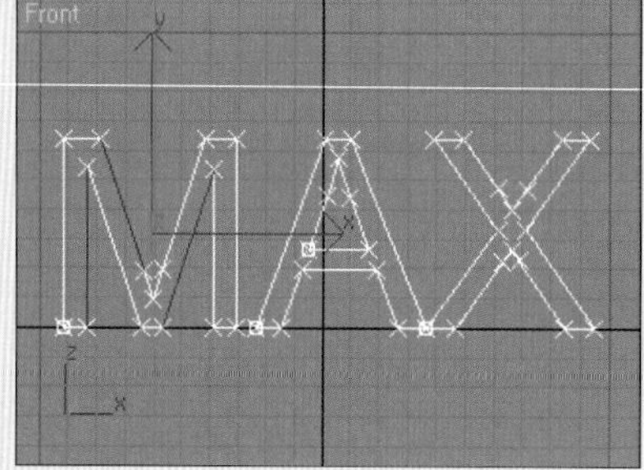

Segment Sub–Object

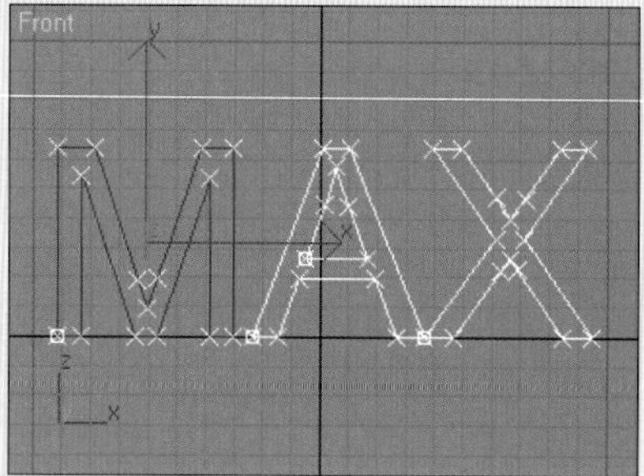

Spline Sub–Object

Polishing the Outline with the Lathe Modifier

As each vertex on the angular segment line looks a bit jagged, it needs to be converted into a soft Bezier curve. This section will demonstrate how to do this and how to apply the Lathe Modifier to the completed segment line.

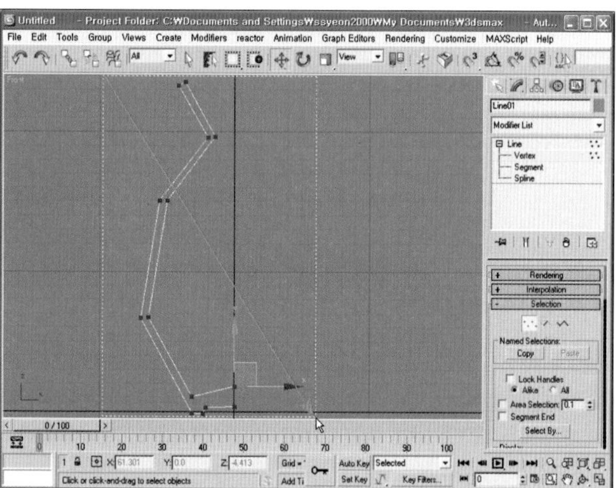

01 Click–and–drag in the Viewport from the upper left to the bottom right to select all the vertices.

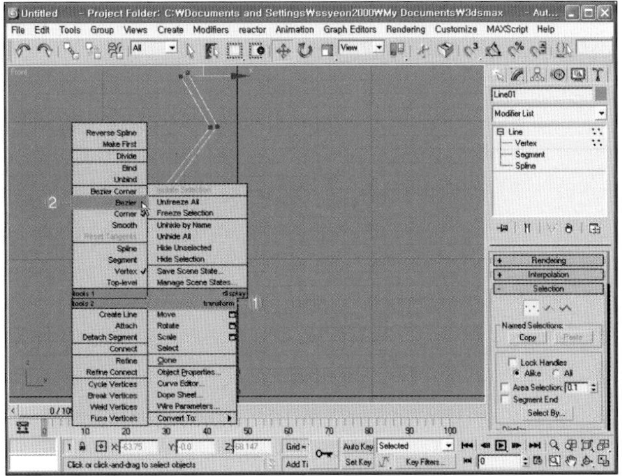

02 Right–click on any vertex, and a quad menu will appear. By selecting [Bezier] on that menu, a straight line can be converted to a curve.

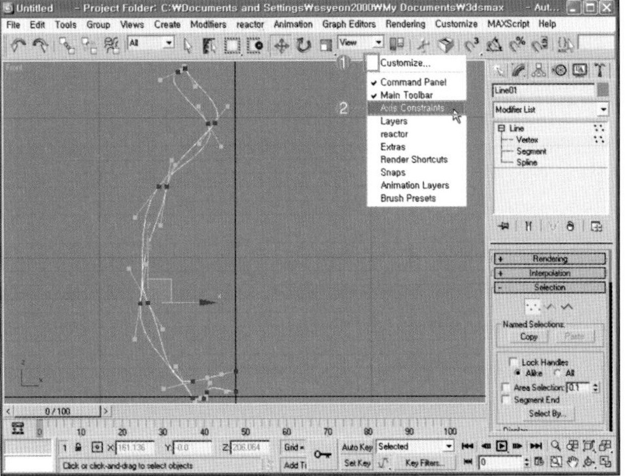

03 Right–click on an empty spot on the main toolbar; another menu will appear. Then select [Axis Constraints].

tip >>

Axis Constraints

Axis Constraints is an axis–constraining tool, helping the user to move only in the direction desired by using the handlebar.

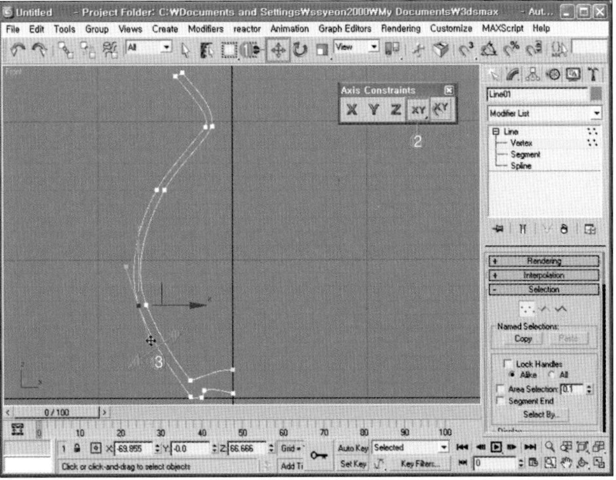

04 Click [Select and Move] in the main toolbar and XY in the [Axis Constraints] dialog box, then click–and–drag the handlebars of each vertex to match the illustration.

tip >>

Changing the Axis

In order to change the axis without the use of the [Axis Constraints] dialog box, press the F8 key as many times as needed.

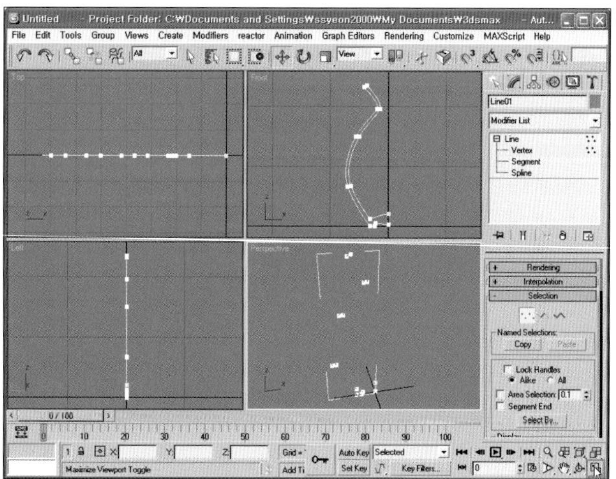

05 Shrink the Viewport by clicking [Maximize Viewport Toggle] in the Viewport Control.

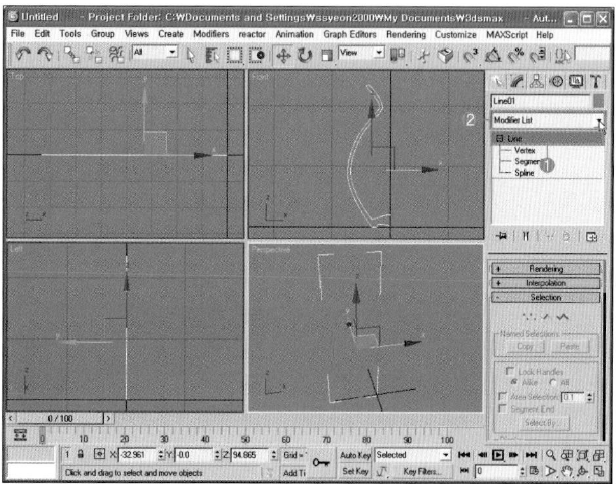

06 Manipulate the lines to complete adjustment of sub–object [Vertex], and click on the [Modifier List] combo box to add another modifier.

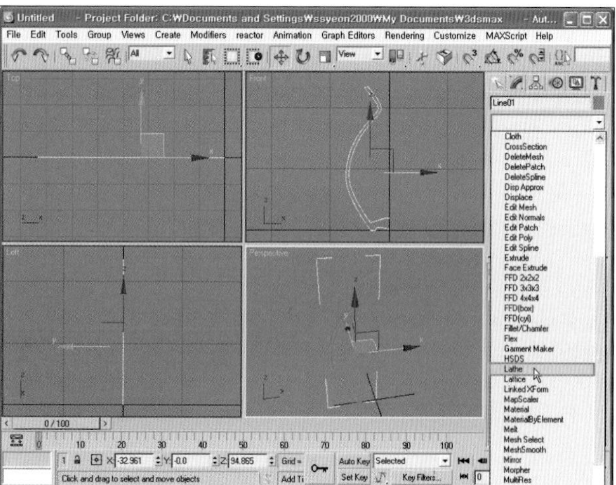

07 When the Modifier List menu appears, select [Lathe].

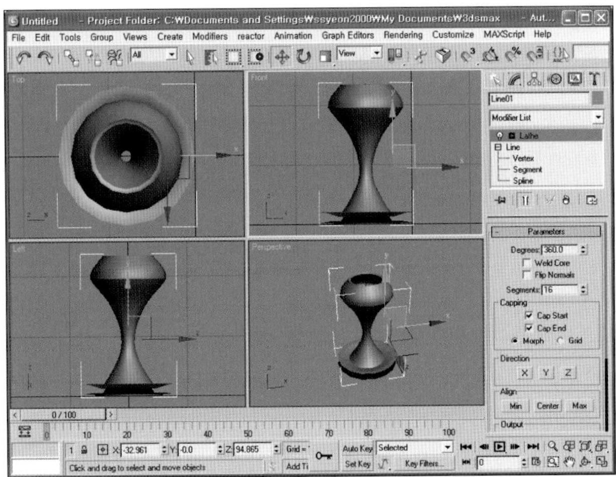

08 When the Lathe Modifier is applied, object “Line01” will rotate to form an irregular shape as shown.

The Lathe Modifier

Note >>>

The Lathe Modifier is a tool used to generate a 3D object from a 2D object made up of lines by rotating it around a chosen axis. The degree to which the object is rotated can be changed arbitrarily, thus making it easy to create a 3D object even if the object is not a 360-degree rotated body.

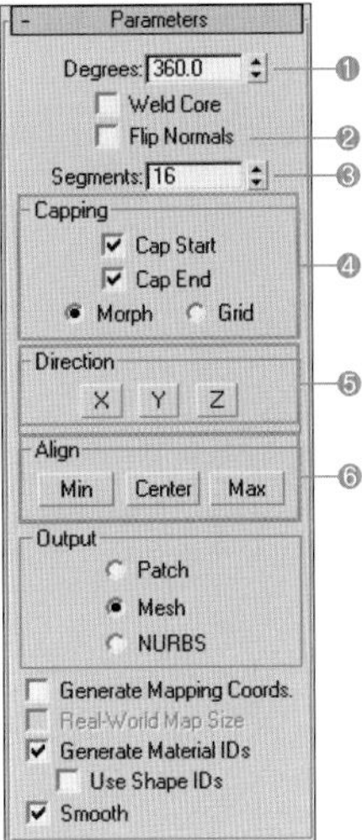

1. **Degrees:** Defines a line-rotating degree
2. **Flip Nomal:** Reverses the segment generated through rotation, if it is turned over
3. **Segment:** Defines the number of segments to be generated through line rotation
4. **Capping:** Determines whether to close the top/bottom or front/rear of a revolving object
5. **Direction:** Defines the central axis for rotation
6. **Align:** Defines the minimum, central, and maximum positions for the internal axis of an object

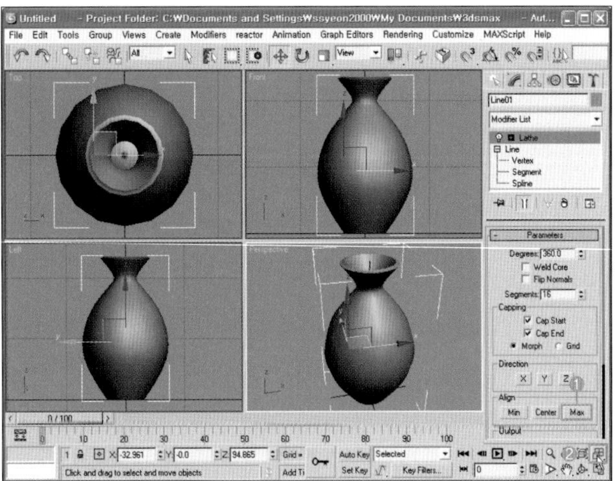

09 Return to the normal shape by clicking [Lathe]–[Parameters]–Max and revolving it based on the Y–axis positioned at the left end of the line. Click [Zoom Extents All] in the Viewport Control to extend the vase to fit fully in each Viewport.

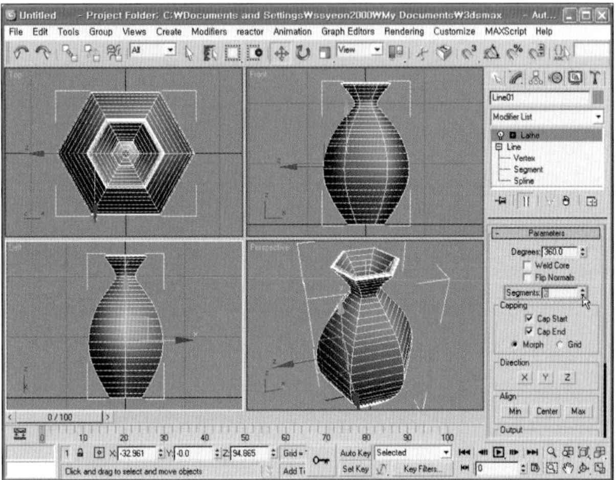

10 Convert the object to an angular shape by entering [6] for [Parameters]–[Segments].

Adding Sharpness using Chamfer

The MeshSmooth Modifier is used for polishing the overall face, but its shortcoming is to make jagged points look blurred. In order to complement this, when the MeshSmooth Modifier is used, Chamfer can be applied for dividing an angle in two, thereby reviving the sharpness.

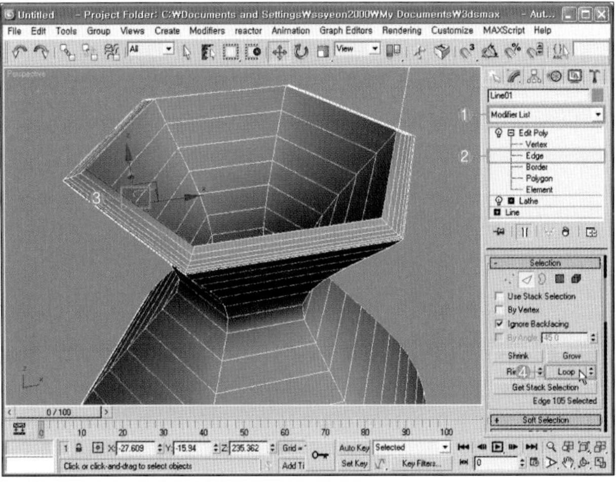

01 Click the [Modifier List] combo box and select [Edit Poly]. Select sub–object [Edge], and then select one of the upper angles of the vase. Subsequently, click [Selection]– Loop to auto–select angles that are connected to the right or left.

Edit Poly Modifier

Note >>>

The Edit Poly Modifier is a tool to help edit an object at will and is composed of sub–objects, such as Vertices, Edges, Borders, Polygons and Elements.

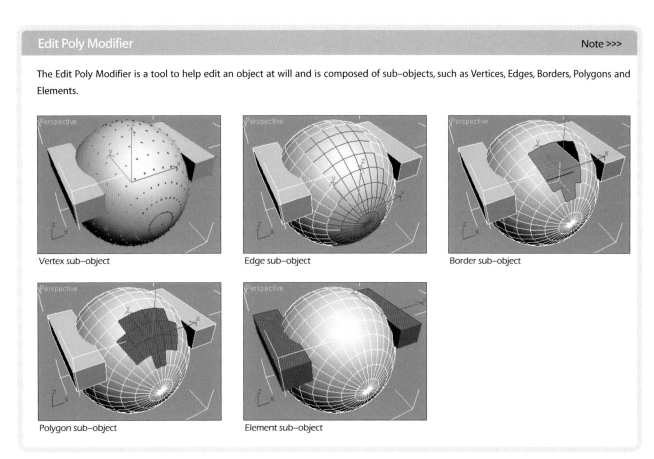

Vertex sub–object

Edge sub–object

Border sub–object

Polygon sub–object

Element sub–object

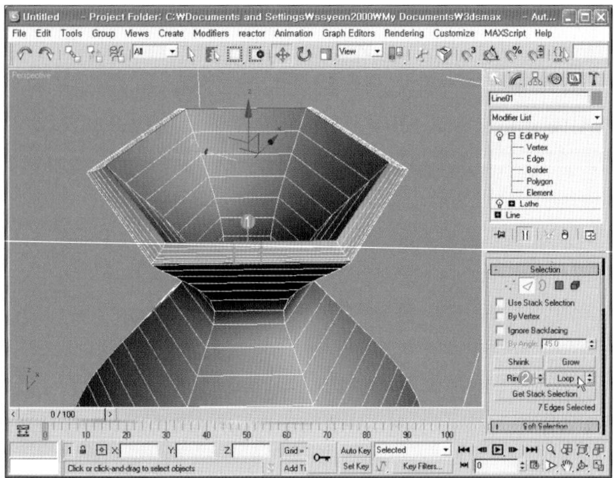

02 While holding the <Ctrl> key, select one of the interior angles, then click Loop again.

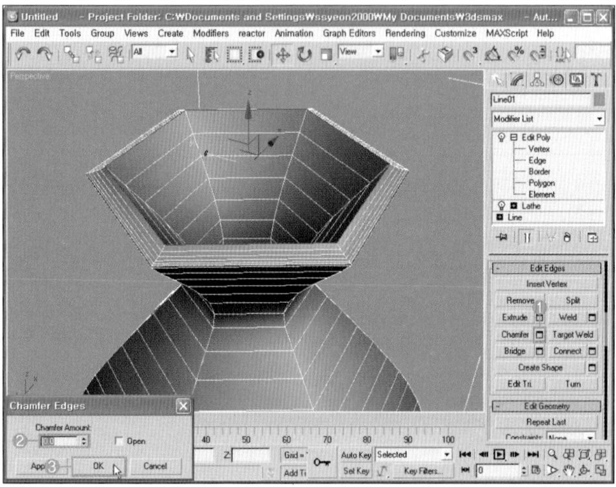

03 If you click [Edit Edges]–[Chamfer Settings], the [Chamfer Edges] dialog box will appear. Enter [0.0] for [Chamfer Amount], and click [OK].

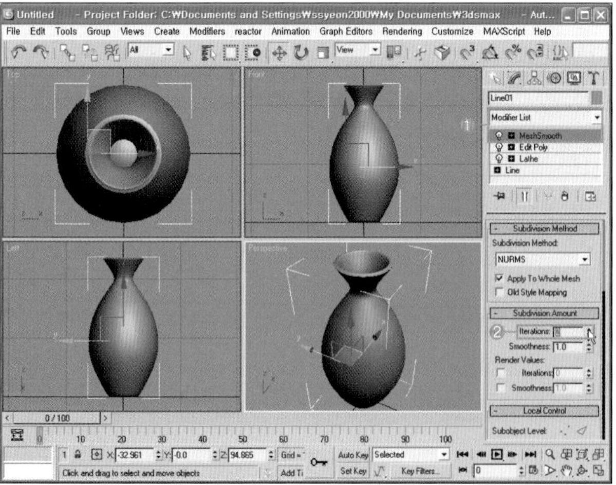

04 Click the [Modifier List] combo box and select [MeshSmooth]. By entering [2] for [Parameters]–[Iterations], the shape can be made smoother.

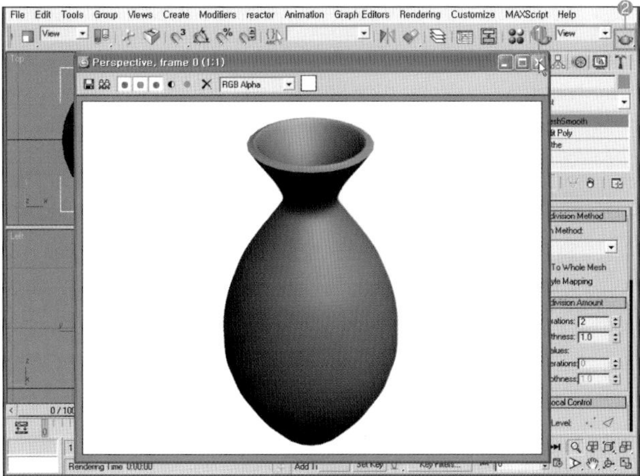

05 Select the Perspective Viewport, then click on [Quick Render] in the main toolbar. A rendered image will be displayed. You can close the rendered image window by clicking on the window.

Drilling Holes Using the Pro Cutter

Let's learn how to create a section using the NGon feature, rotate and copy with Array, and complete the object by drilling a hole in the pottery using the Pro Cutter.

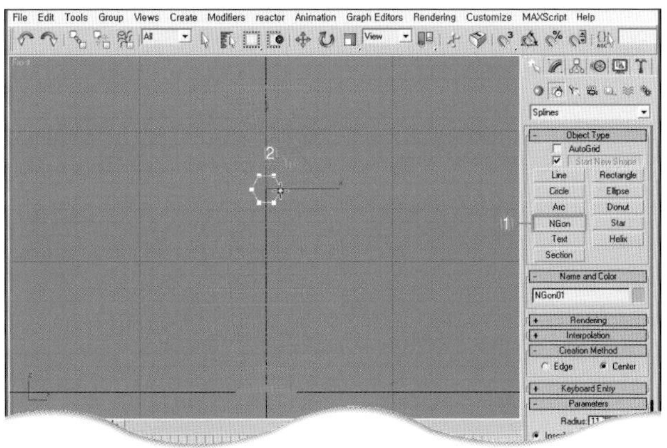

01 Click [Shapes]–[Splines]–[NGon] on the Create panel. Click–and–drag on the location shown in the picture in the Front Viewport to create a small NGon.

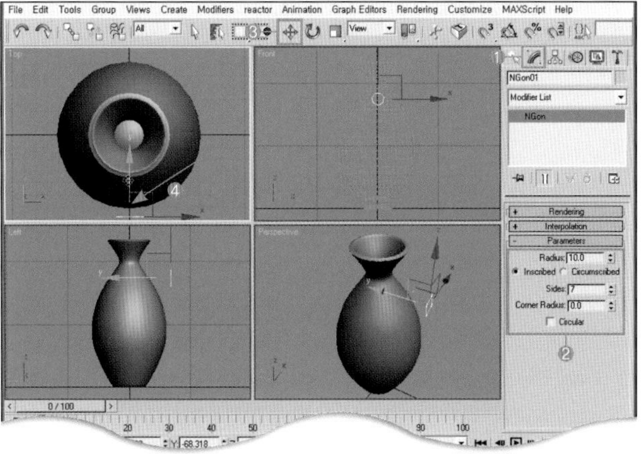

02 With the "NGon01" object selected, move to the Modify panel, and under [Parameters] enter [10] for [Radius] and [7] for [Sides]. Click [Select and Move] to move the "NGon01" object in front of the ceramic in the Top Viewport.

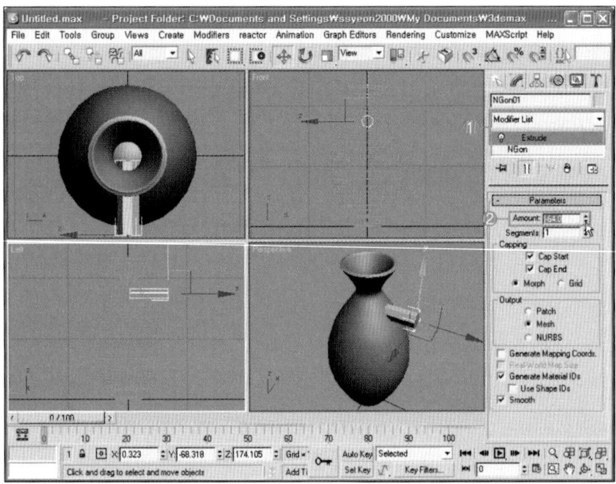

03 Click the [Modifier List] combo box, and select [Extrude]. Enter [–64] for [Parameters]–[Amount] to modify the NGon into a shape that penetrates the object.

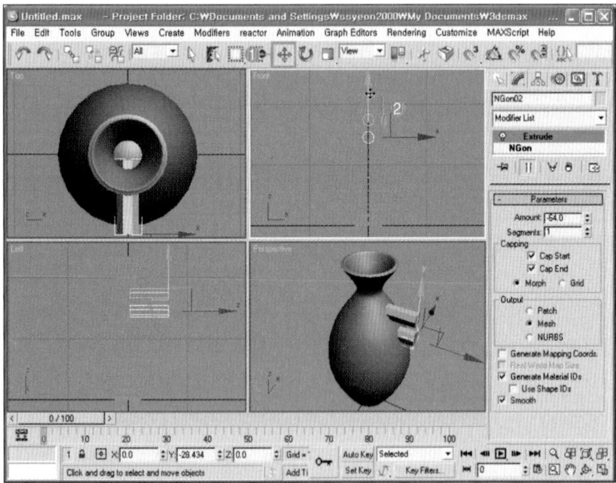

04 Click [Select and Move] on the main toolbar. While holding <Shift>, click–and–drag the NGon downwards in the Front Viewport.

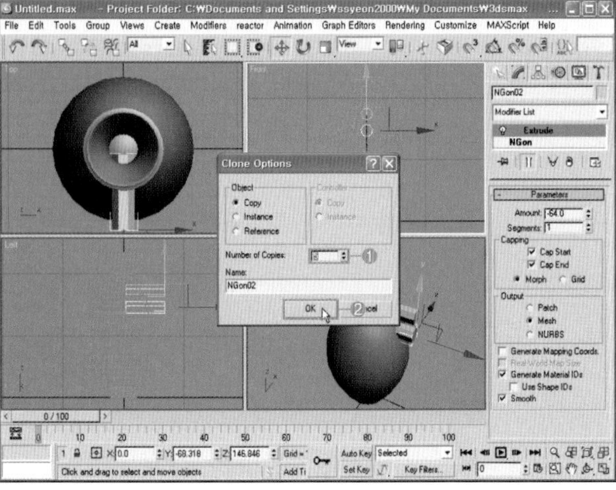

05 When the [Clone Options] dialog box appears, enter [5] in [Number of Copies] and click [OK].

tip >>

Clone Options Dialog Box

By click–and–dragging the object in the Viewport while pressing <Shift>, the user can copy a new object with the distance as much as the dragged length. The user can create a number of copies equal to the value of [Number of Copies].

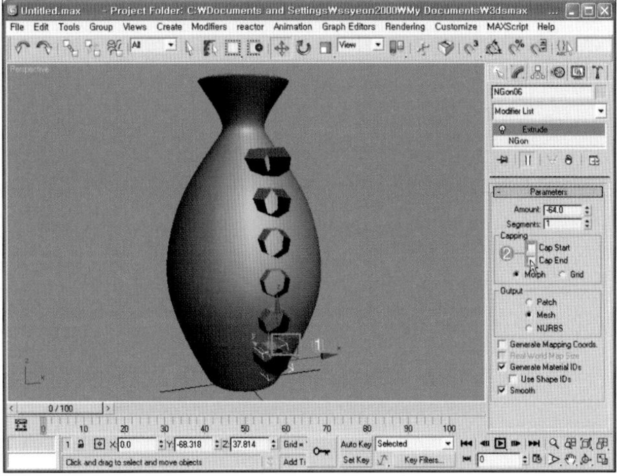

06 Confirm that five NGon objects have been copied vertically at equal intervals. Select each NGon one at a time, and uncheck [Cap Start] and [Cap End] under [Parameters] to depict a hole in the front and back of the NGon objects.

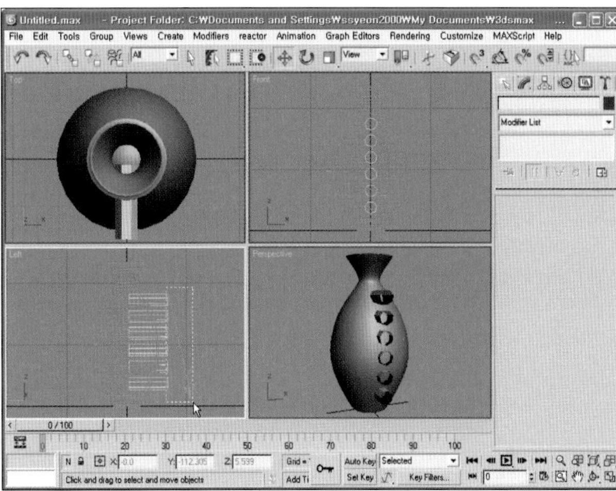

07 In the Left Viewport, select the NGon objects that have been copied.

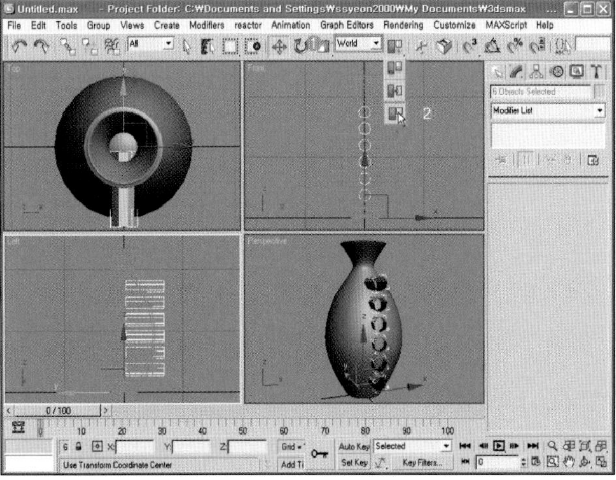

08 With the NGon objects selected, in the main toolbar select [World] and [Use Transform Coordinate Center] to move the central axis to the absolute axis.

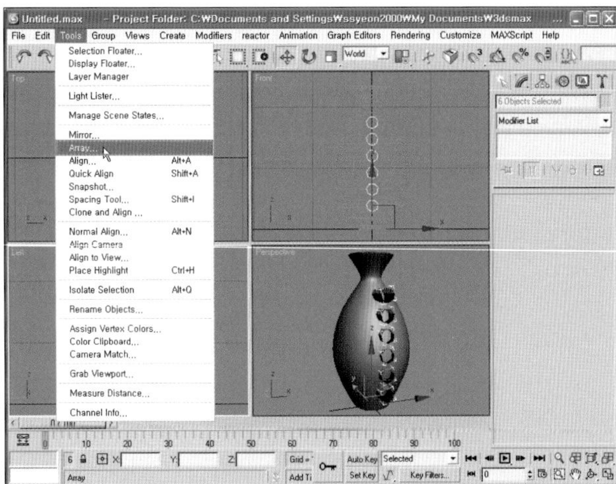

09 To rotate and copy the NGon objects, click [Tools]–[Array] on the menu bar.

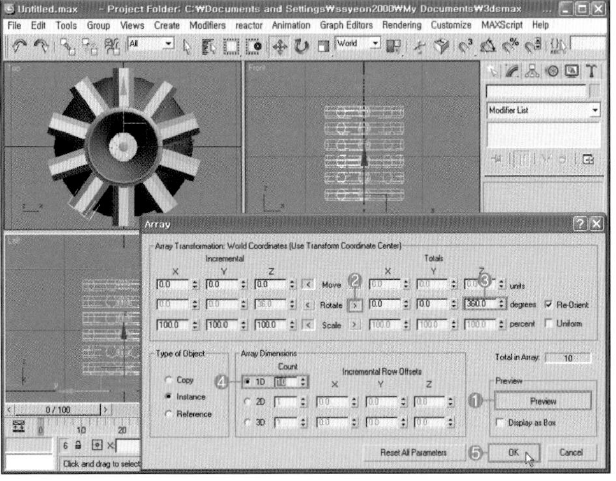

10 When the [Array] dialog box appears, follow these steps:

① Click [Preview] to monitor the changes in real-time.

② Click [Rotate right [>]] and enter [360] for [Array Transformation]–[Totals]–[Z] inline with [Rotate].

③ Click [Array Dimensions]–[1D] and enter [10]; ten rotated and aligned objects are completed.

④ Click [OK] to finish.

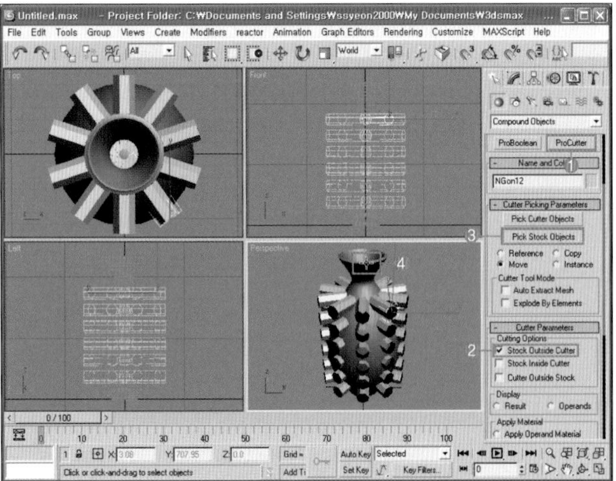

11 After selecting one NGon, go to the Create panel and click [Geometry]–[Compound Objects]–[ProCutter]. Click [Pick Stock Objects], and check [Cutter Parameters]–[Stock Outside Cutter], then select the "Line01" object.

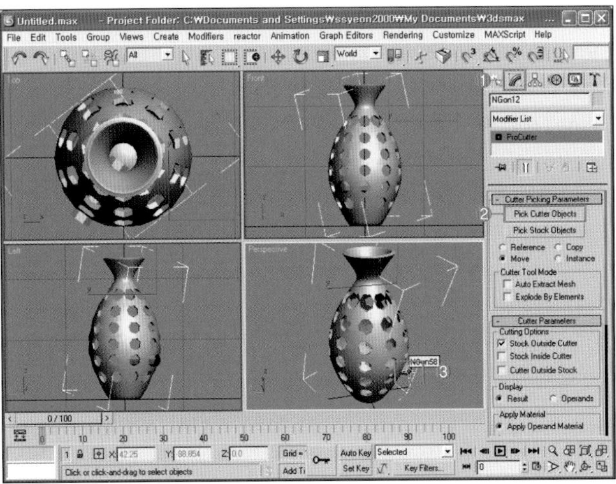

12 With the united object selected, move to the Modify panel. Click [Pick Cutter Objects], and select the rest of the NGon objects in the order they are in to drill holes.

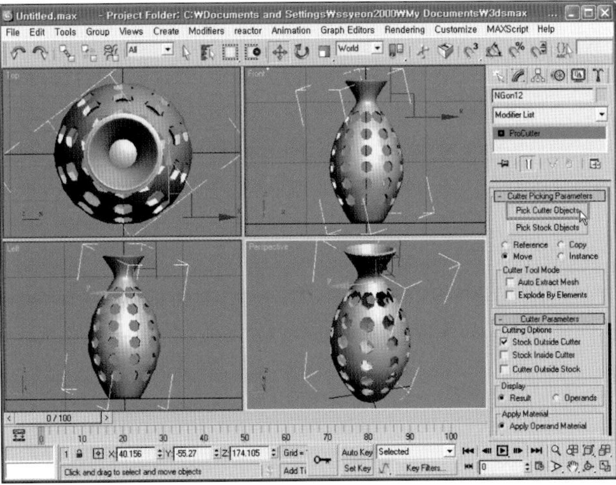

13 When the work is finished, click [Pick Cutter Objects] to exit the mode.

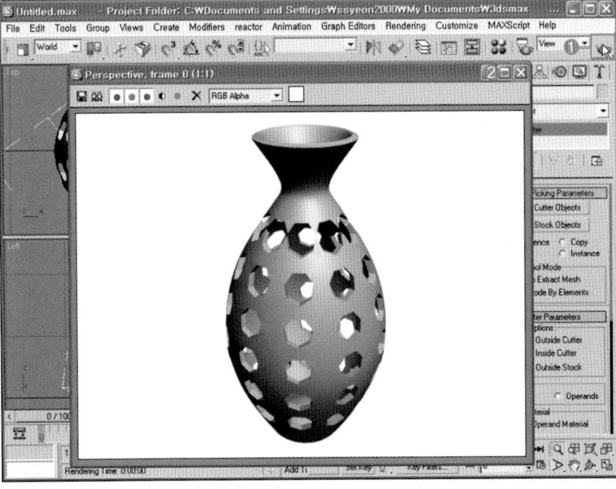

14 Select the Perspective Viewport, and click [Quick Render] on the main toolbar to confirm the rendered shape. Click the ☒ of the rendered image window to close the image window.

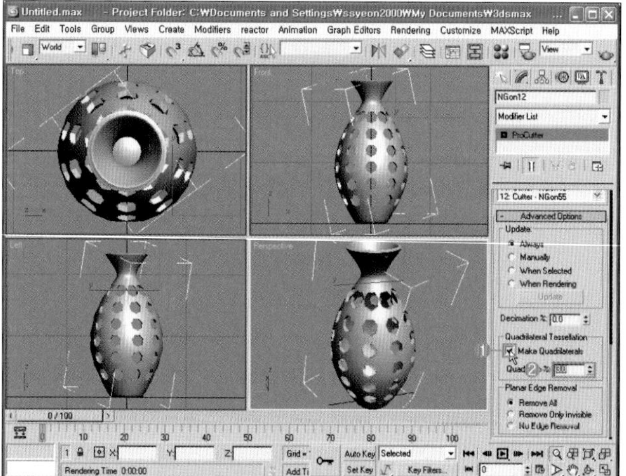

15 The polygons surrounding the hole may look a little fragmented; to solve this issue, check [Make Quadrilaterals] of [Quadrilateral Tessellation] to divide the polygons into small bits.

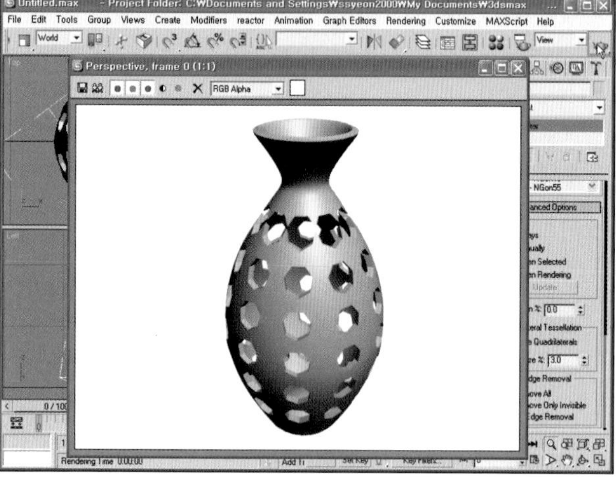

16 Select the Perspective Viewport, and click [Quick Render] on the main toolbar to view the rendered shape.

Supplementary CD\Sample\Chapter 3\Exercise 1\Pottery-final.max

Let's Go Pro!

Creating the Object Interior Using Pro Cutter

Pro Cutter is a tool that drills a hole using an object's perimeter. This tool enables the user to easily style the middle parts of objects that are difficult to modify through general modeling.

① Create a simple box, and create a new object made of text using [Shapes]–[Splines]–[Text]. Add the Extrude Modifier to the "Text01" object, and set the Parameters.

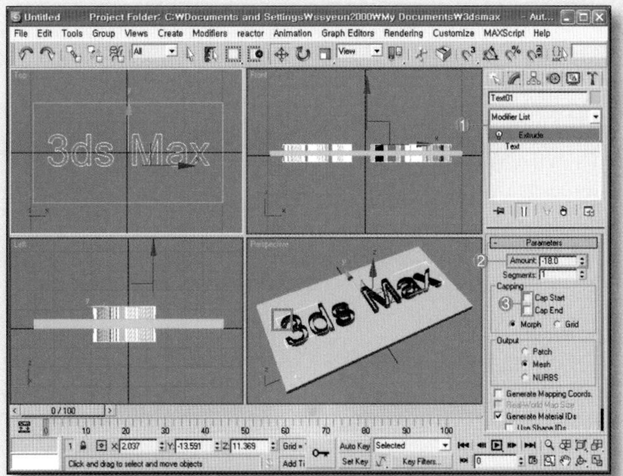

② With the "Text01" object selected, click [Geometry]–[Compound Objects]–[ProCutter]. Under [Cutting Options], check [Stock Outside Cutter] and [Stock Inside Cutter], click [Pick Stock Objects], and select the Box object.

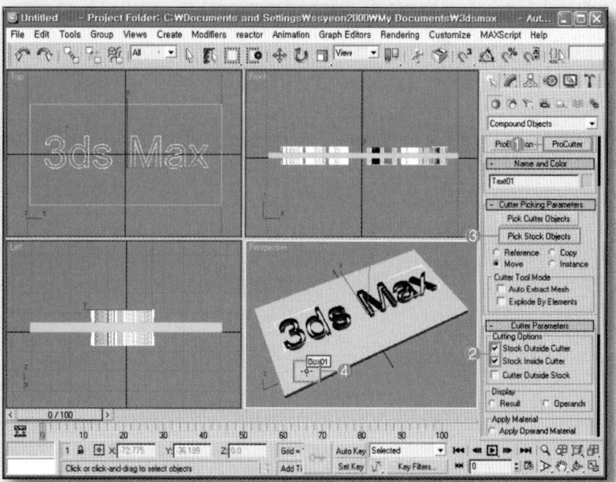

③ With the "Text01" object selected, move to the Modify panel. Confirm whether the form of the "Text01" object was changed into [ProCutter] in the Modify stack, and add an Edit Poly Modifier on the top. Select the [Element] sub-object, and select all of the text left inside the box. Then, move outwards using [Select and Move] to obtain the desired result.

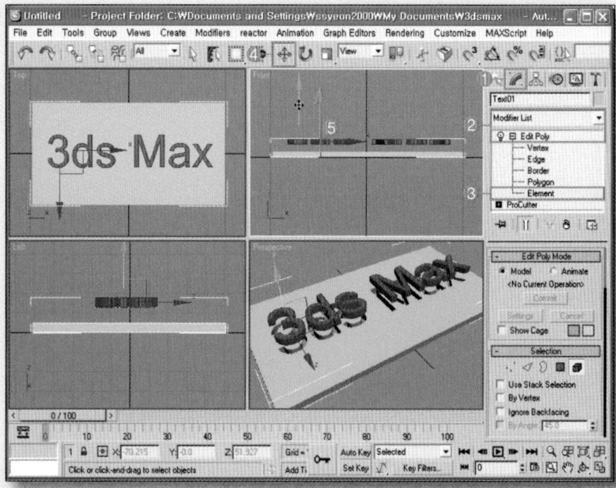

Exercise 02

Creating a Beer Mug

Final Image

Among the modeling methods using polygons, the Cylinder is the most widely used figure other than the Box. A beer mug requires much work on the handle, the inside, and the projections on the surface, although its overall shape is simple. Therefore, this section will use techniques such as Extrude Polygons Along Spline, Inset, and Bevel, to handle these aspects. The section will also cover how to divide edges in two and make sharp polygons appear smooth with the MeshSmooth Modifier.

Final File
\Sample\Chapter 3\Exercise 2\Beermug-final.max

Shaping the Mug

After placing the cylinder, the Edit Poly Modifier will be added to form the shape of the beer mug.

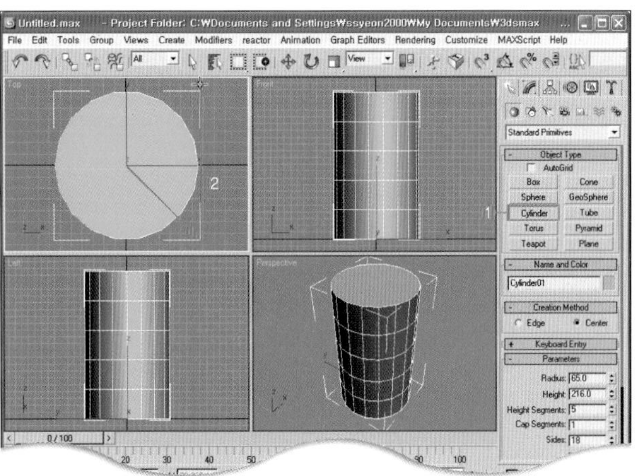

01 On the Create panel, click [Geometry]–[Standard Primitives]–. Click–and–drag in the Top Viewport as shown to create a new cylinder.

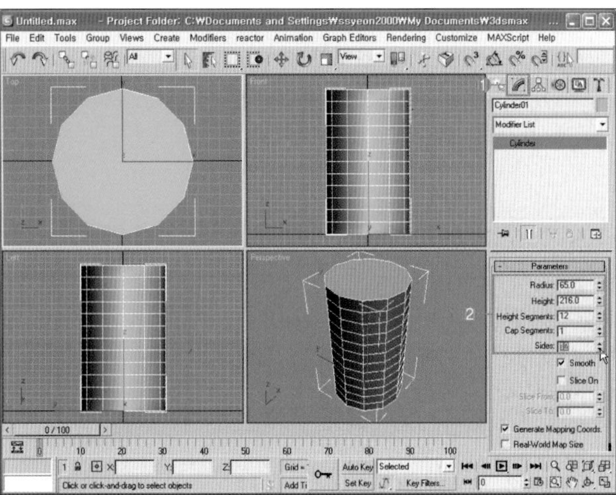

02 With the "Cylinder01" object selected, click [Modify] to move to the Modify panel, and set the Parameters. Enter [65, 216, 5, 1, 18] respectively for [Radius], [Height], [Height Segments], [Cap Segments], and [Sides].

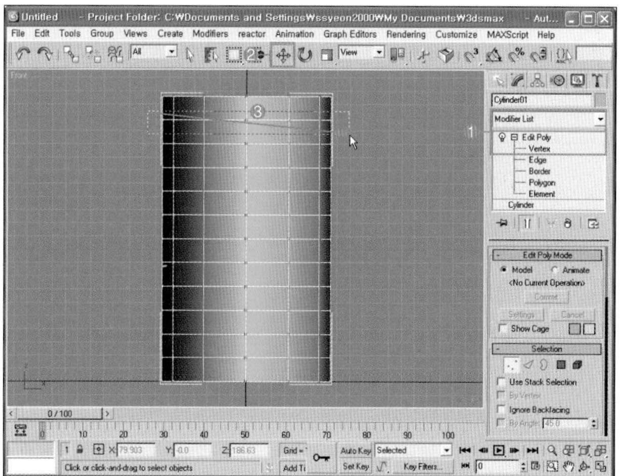

03 Click the [Modifier List] combo box, and select [Edit Poly]. Select the [Vertex] sub–object, and click [Select and Move] on the main toolbar. Click–and–drag as show in the picture to select the vertices of the horizontal line in the Front Viewport.

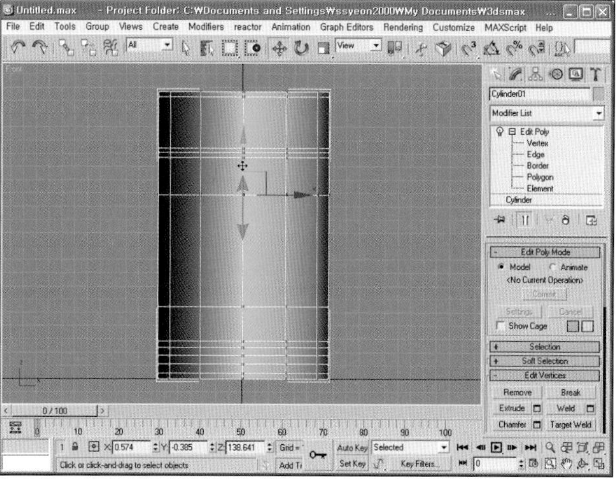

04 Move the selected vertices of the horizontal line to the location shown in the picture.

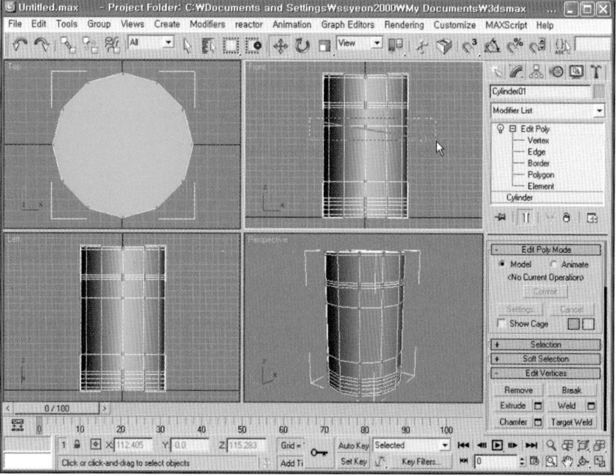

05 To give a sense of volume, select the sixth horizontal set of vertices in the Front Viewport.

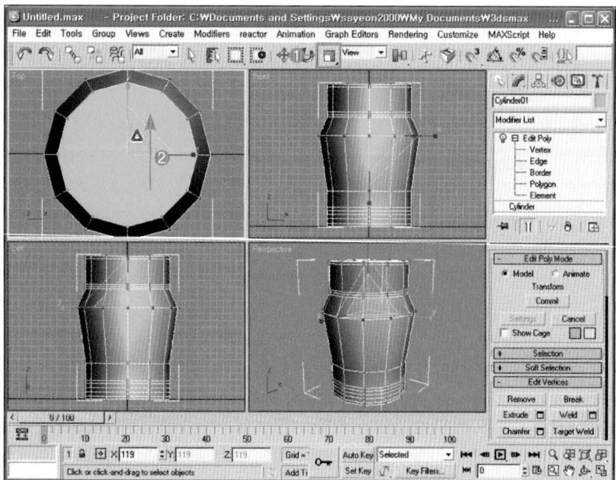

06 Click [Select and Scale] on the main toolbar, and click–and–drag in the Top Viewport to create the upper shape of the beer mug.

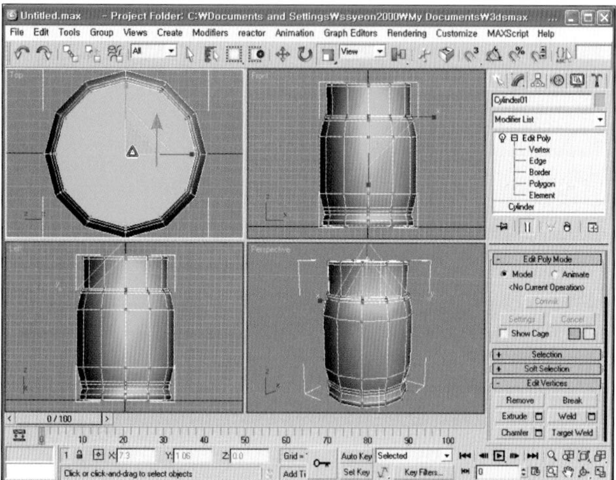

07 To complete the shape of the beer mug, modify the sizes of each of the horizontal sets of vertices.

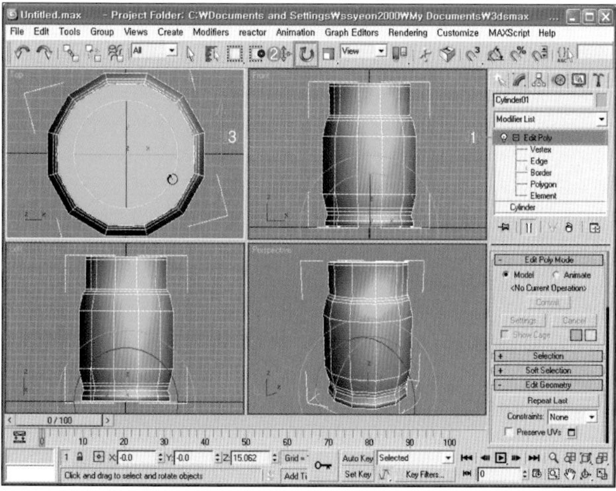

08 Click the text part of the [Edit Poly] modifier to exit the sub–object mode, and click [Select and Rotate] on the main toolbar. Rotate the "Cylinder01" object in the Top Viewport to change the left and right shape to be the same on the Y–axis.

Adding the Handle

Now, create the handle by extracting one polygon of the beer mug with the Extrude Polygons Along Spline function.

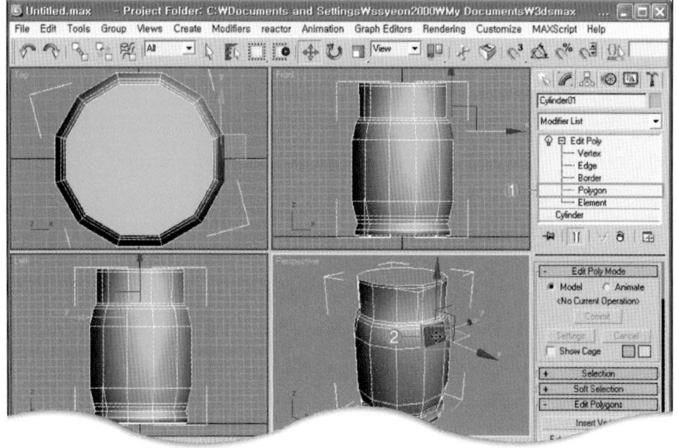

01 Select the [Polygon] sub–object of the [Edit Poly] modifier, and select one of the upper polygons in the Perspective Viewport to become the handle.

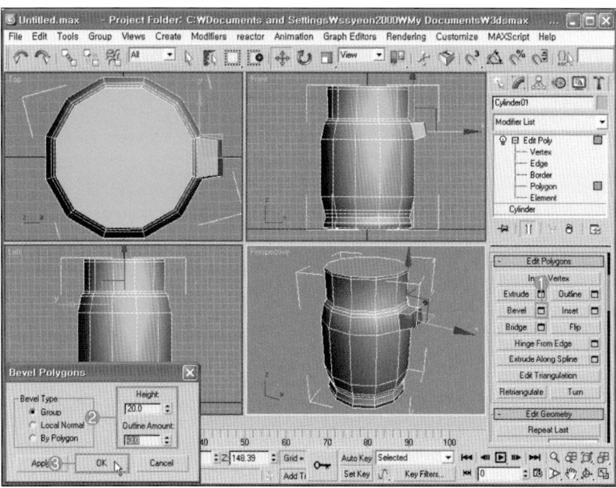

02 Under [Edit Polygons], click [Bevel Settings ▣] to activate the [Bevel Polygons] dialog box. Enter [20] for Height and [–3] for [Outline Amount], and click [OK].

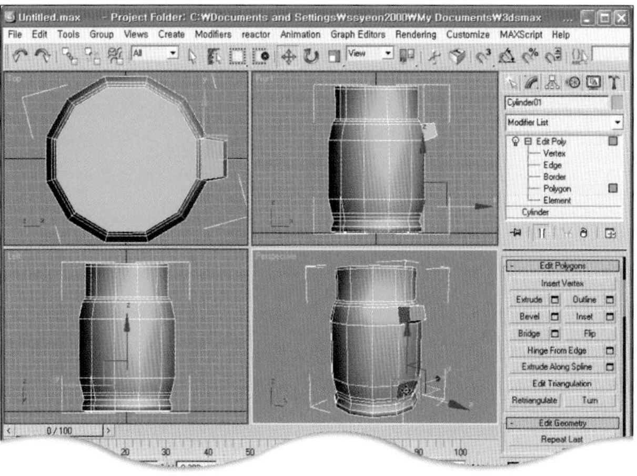

03 Select the appropriate polygon to make the protrusion that will connect the lower end of the handle. Reference the images to help determine the correct polygon for this step.

04 As with the upper polygon for the top part of the handle, under [Edit Polygons], click [Bevel Settings ▣] to activate the [Bevel Polygons] dialog box. Enter [20] for Height and [–3] for [Outline Amount], and click [OK]. Click the text part of the [Edit Poly] modifier to exit the sub–object mode.

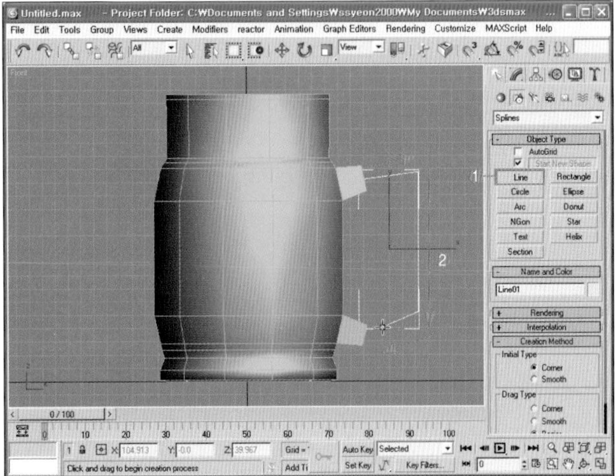

05 On the Create panel, click [Shapes]–[Splines]–[Line]. In the Front Viewport, create a line to connect the two protruding polygons.

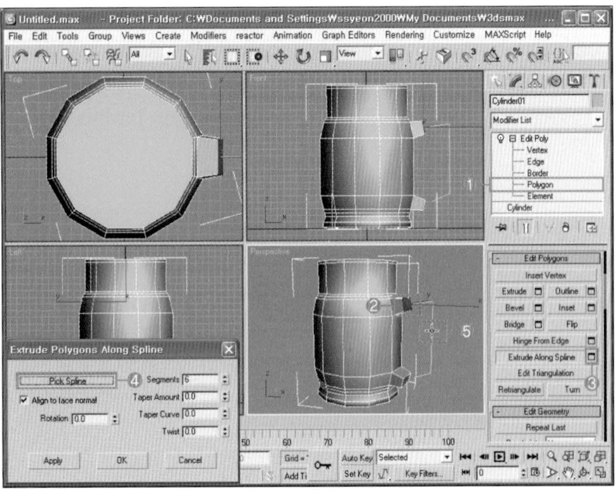

06 Again, select the "Cylinder01" object, select the [Polygon] sub–object of the [Edit Poly] modifier, and select the upper polygon. Click [Edit Polygons]–[Extrude Along Spline Settings ▣] to activate the [Extrude Polygons Along Spline] dialog box, click [Pick Spline], and select the "Line01" object in the Viewport.

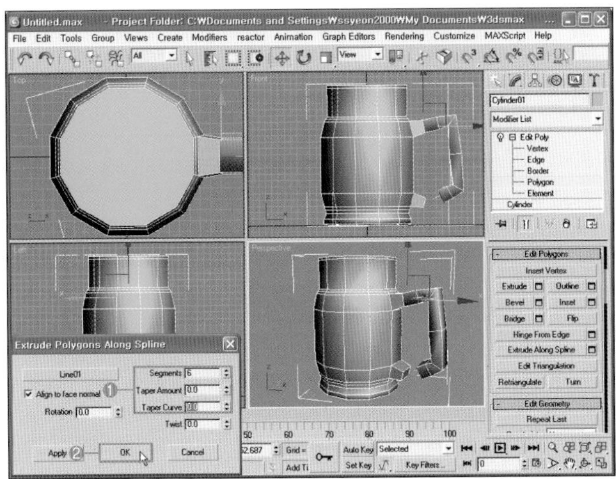

07 In the [Extrude Polygons Along Spline] dialog box, enter [6] for [Segments], [0] for [Taper Amount], and [0] for [Taper Curve]. Click [OK] to show the handle part.

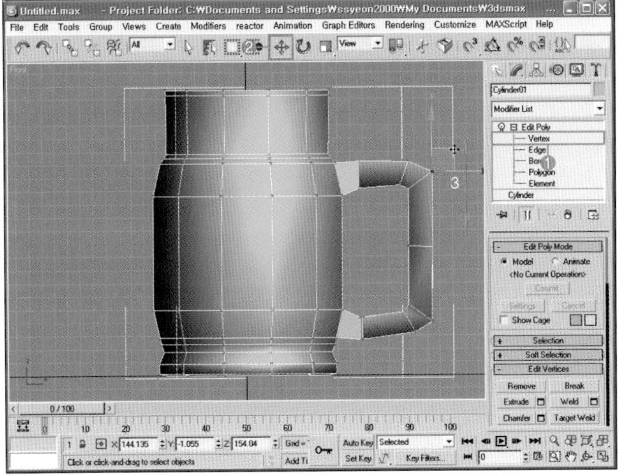

08 Select the [Vertex] sub-object of the [Edit Poly] modifier, and mold the handle shape using [Select and Move].

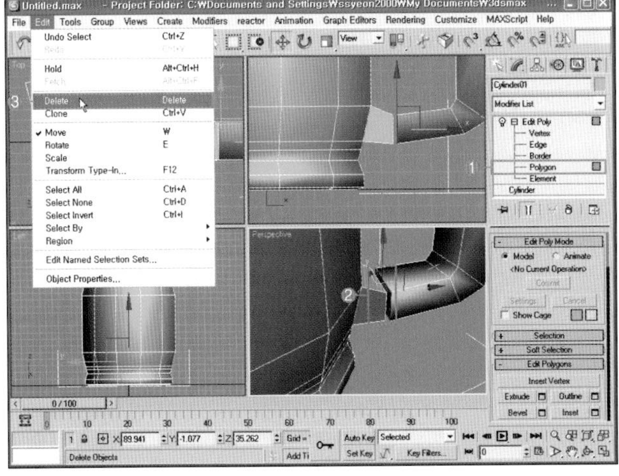

09 Select the [Polygon] sub-object of the [Edit Poly] modifier, and on the lower end of the handle, select the polygon facing the mug's lower protrusion in the Perspective Viewport. Click [Edit]–[Delete] on the menu bar to delete.

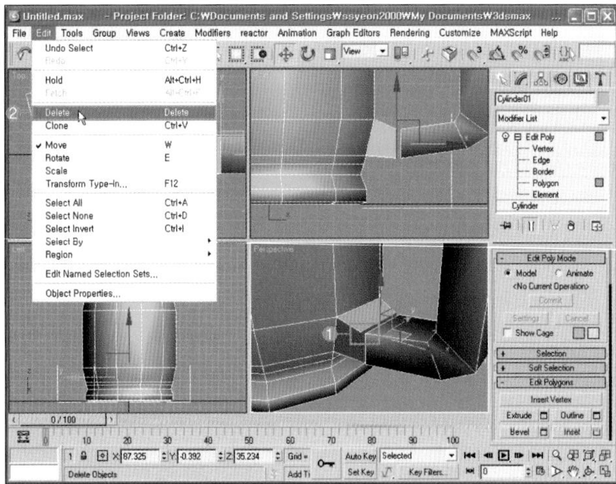

10 On the mug's lower protrusion, select the polygon facing the handle, and delete by clicking [Edit]–[Delete] on the menu bar.

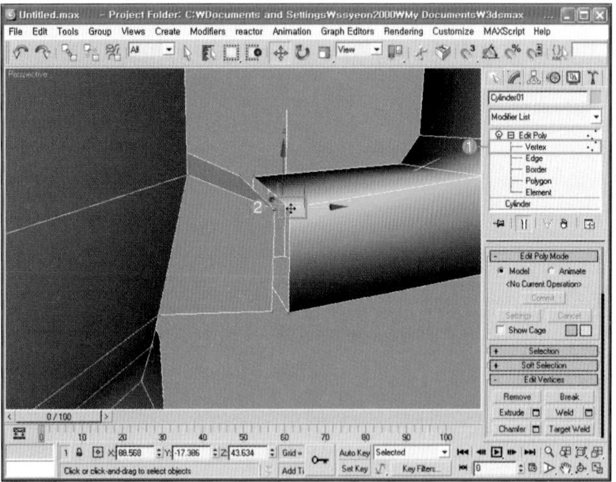

11 To merge the separate vertices, select the [Vertex] sub–object of the [Edit Poly] modifier first, then select the matching vertices while pressing <Ctrl>.

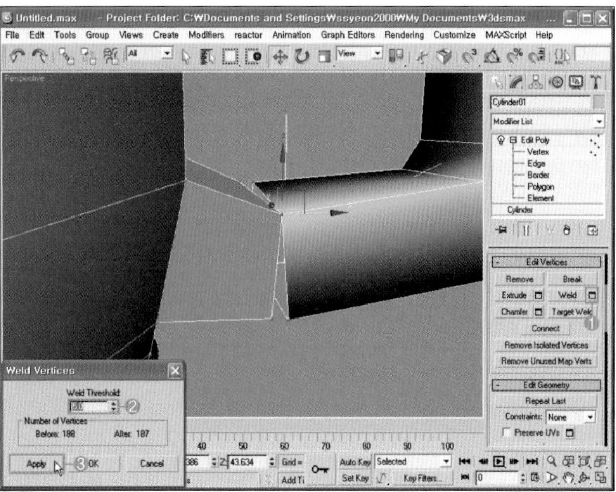

12 Click [Edit Vertices]–[Weld Settings ▣] to activate the [Weld Vertices] dialog box. Enter [5] for [Weld Threshold], and click [Apply]. Among those selected, the vertices within the set distance from each other are merged.

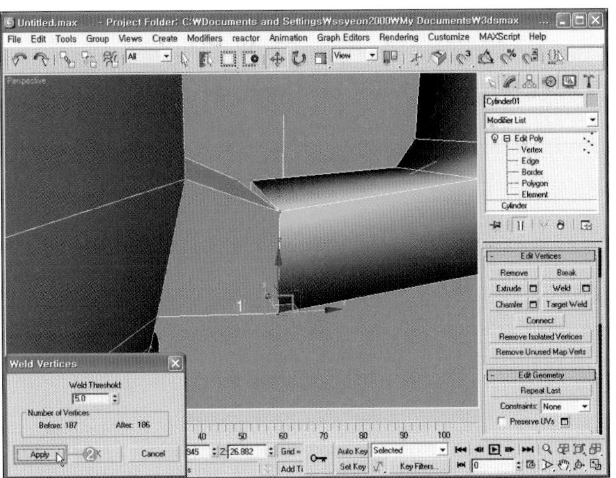

13 Select the lower set of vertices with the same method, and merge them by clicking [Apply].

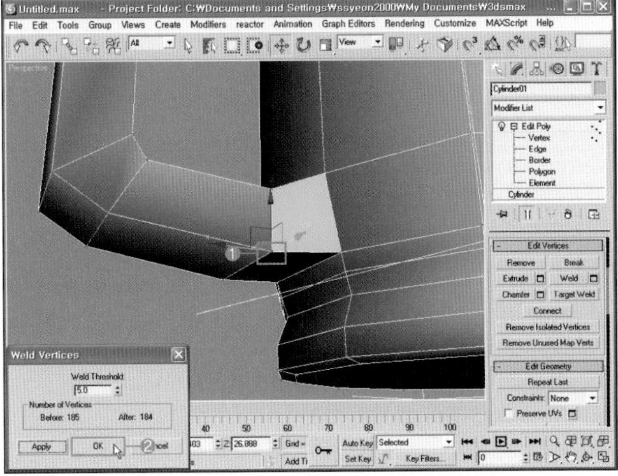

14 Merge the vertices on the opposite side in the same fashion. When done, click [OK].

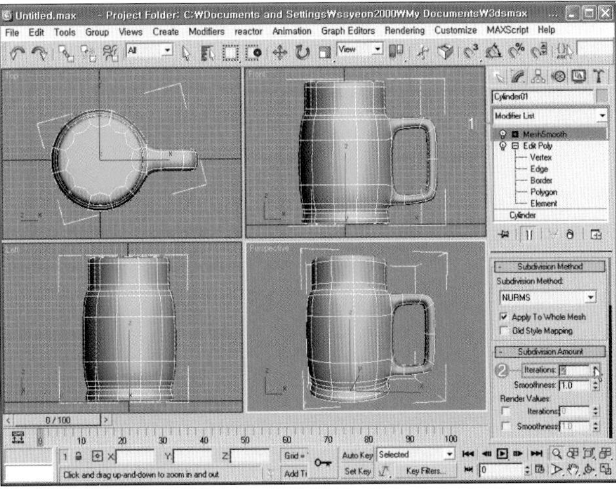

15 Click the [Modifier List] combo box, and select [MeshSmooth]. Enter [2] for [Subdivision Amount]–[Iterations] to round the contours of the overall polygon.

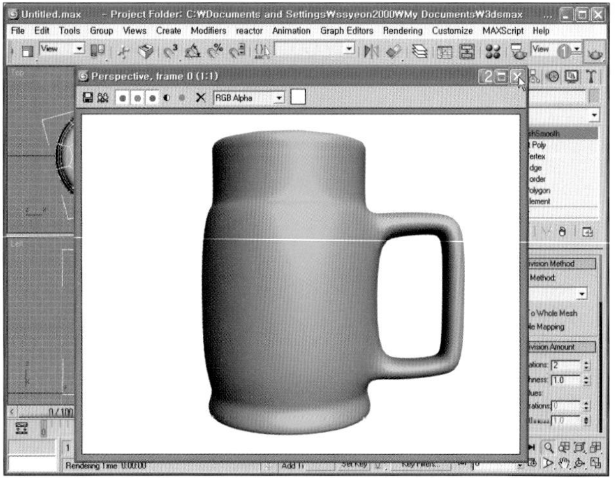

16 Select the Perspective Viewport and click [Quick Render] on the main toolbar to view the rendered shape. Click ☒ on the rendered image window to close it.

Adding Surface Texture

The Chamfer Edge feature sharpens only the necessary parts when the polygons are mashed by the MeshSmooth Modifier. Also, the Slice Plane function moves the separated vertices to obtain the desired shapes by separating the selected polygons entirely.

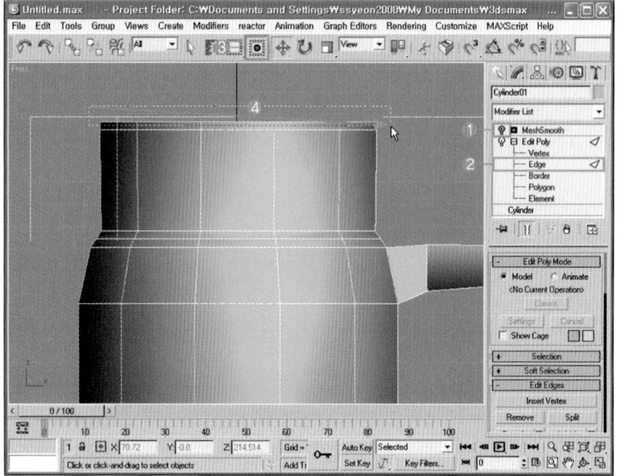

01 Click of the [MeshSmooth] modifier to deactivate the function. Select the [Edge] sub–object of the [Edit Poly] modifier, and select the topmost vertices in the Front Viewport.

tip >>

Selecting Desired Vertical Edges

To avoid selecting the unnecessary vertical edges, click [Window] on the main toolbar.

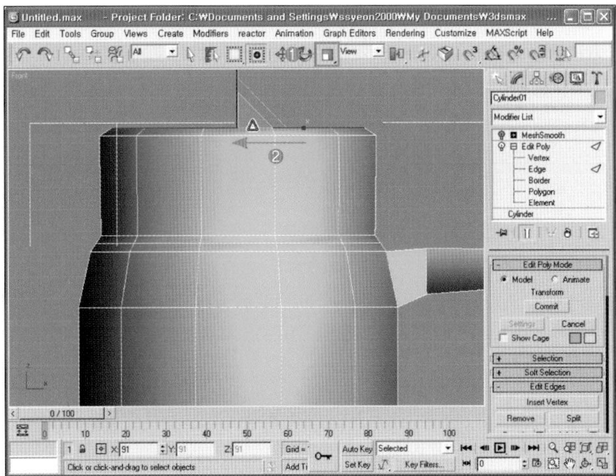

02 Click [Select and Scale] on the main toolbar, and reduce the size towards the X–axis.

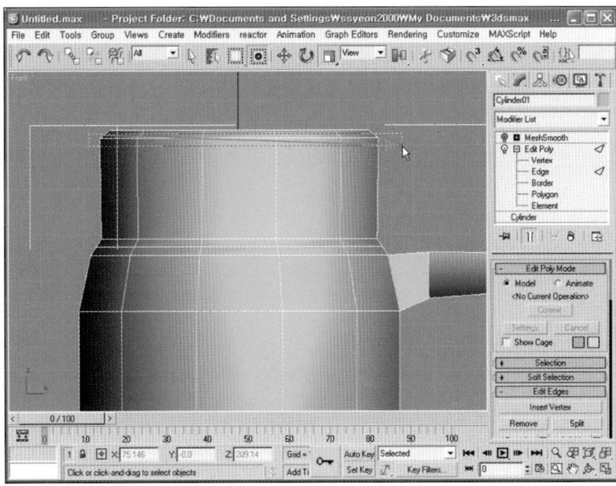

03 Select the second horizontal edge in the same way.

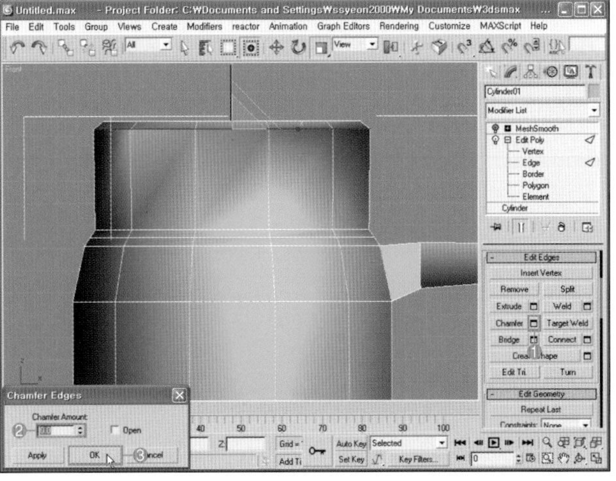

04 Click [Edit Polygons]–[Chamfer Settings] to activate the [Chamfer Edges] dialog box. The selected edges are divided into two at the same location. Enter [0] for [Chamfer Amount] and click [OK].

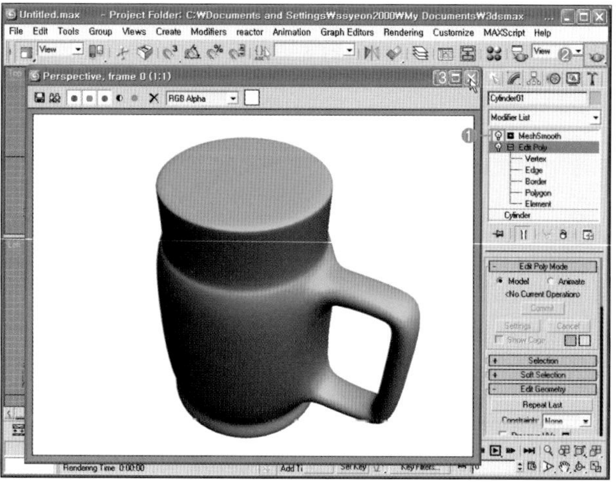

05 Click [icon] of the [MeshSmooth] modifier to activate the function, select the Perspective Viewport, and click [Quick Render [icon]] on the main toolbar to confirm the rendered shape. Click [icon] on the rendered image window to close it.

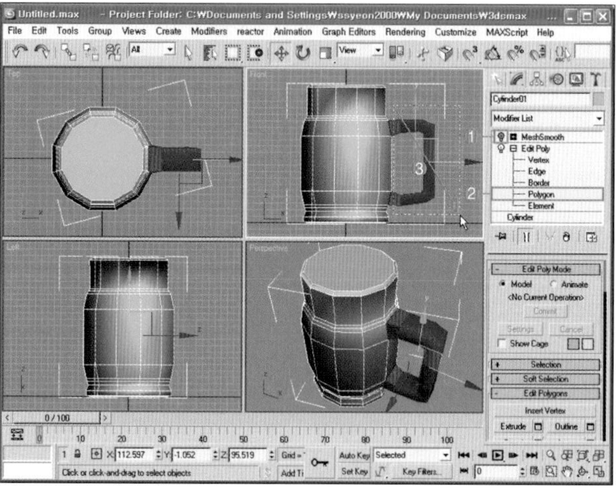

06 Click [icon] of the [MeshSmooth] modifier to deactivate the function. Select the [Polygon] sub–object of the [Edit Poly] modifier, and select the beer mug handle in the Front Viewport.

tip >>

Using the Crossing Feature

Click [Crossing [icon]] on the main toolbar to select the handle even when it is simply crossed by the selection region.

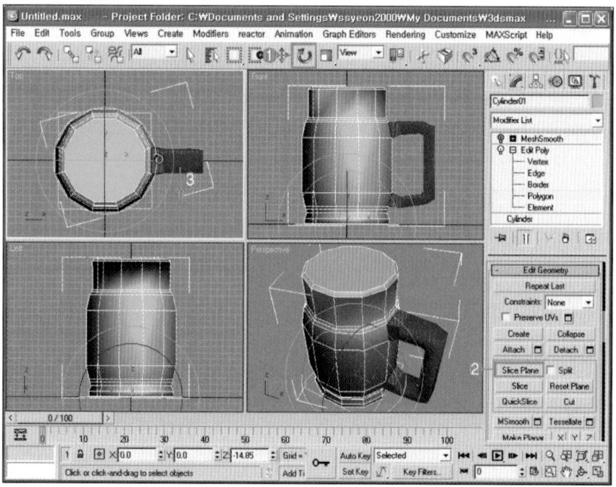

07 Click [Edit Polygons]–[Slice Plane] and click [Select and Rotate [icon]] on the main toolbar. Rotate the Slice Plane in the Top Viewport as shown in the picture.

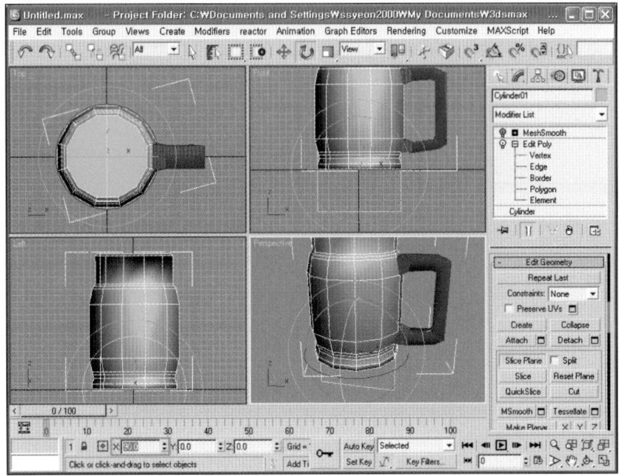

08 Enter [90] for the X–axis of the coordinate input line to place the Slice Plane vertically on the selected handle polygon.

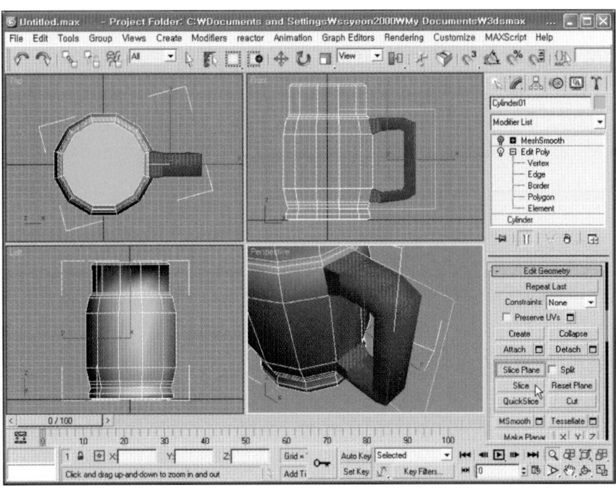

09 To set the final position, use the modification tool to move to the location of the selected handle. When the Slice Plane is located to vertically slice the selected polygon, click [Slice] to divide the polygon.

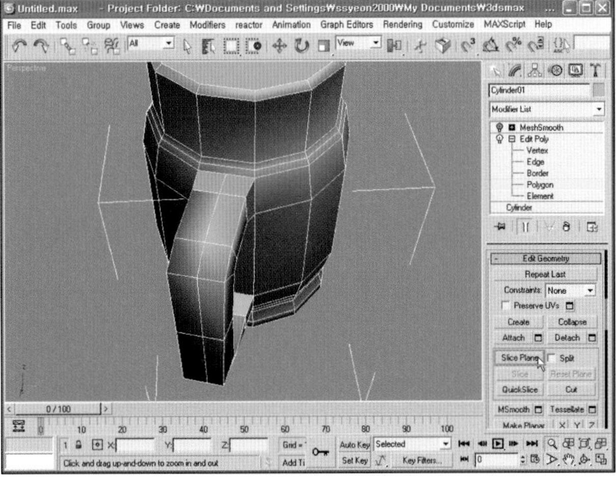

10 To finish the Slice Plane work, click [Slice Plane].

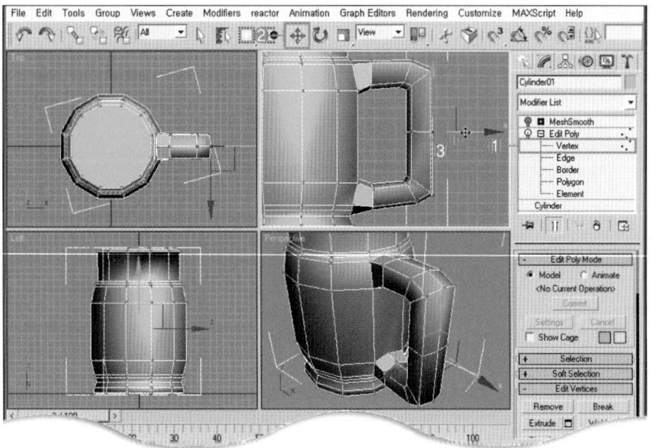

11 Select the [Vertex] sub–object of the [Edit Poly] modifier. Using [Select and Move], enlarge the sizes of the vertices at the divided location.

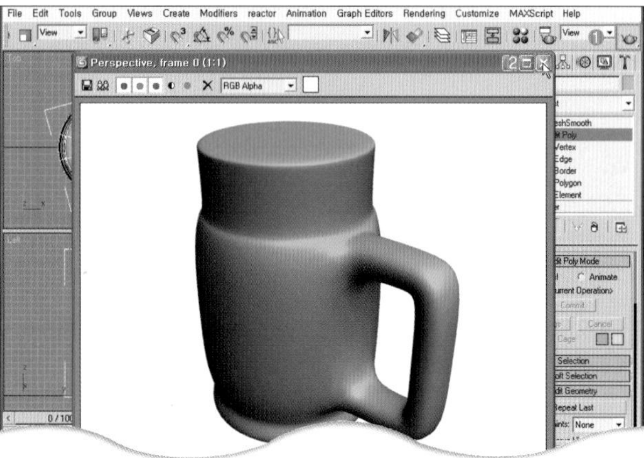

12 Click of the [MeshSmooth] modifier to activate the function, select the Perspective Viewport, and click [Quick Render] on the main toolbar to confirm the rendered shape. Click of the rendered image window to close it.

Beveling the Inside of the Mug

To create an opening in an object, use the Bevel feature to carve the top polygon inward.

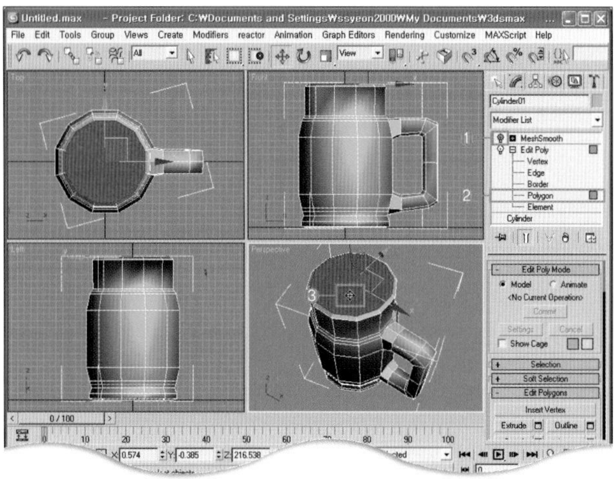

01 Click of the [MeshSmooth] modifier to deactivate the function. Select the [Polygon] sub–object of the [Edit Poly] modifier, and select the top of the beer mug.

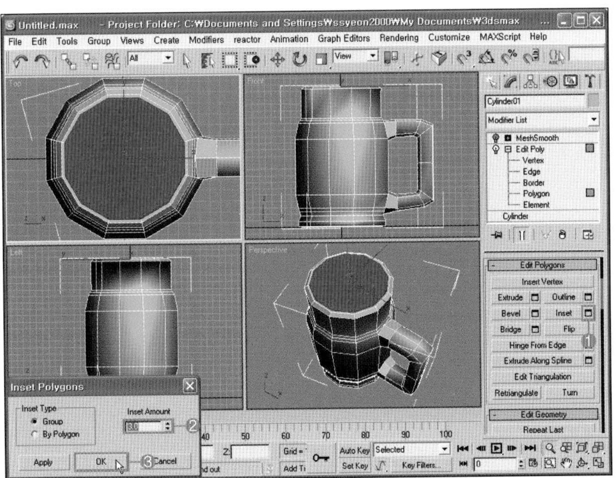

02 Click [Edit Polygons]–[Inset Settings ▣] to activate the [Inset Polygons] dialog box. To divide the polygon into smaller polygons, enter [3] for [Inset Amount], and click [OK].

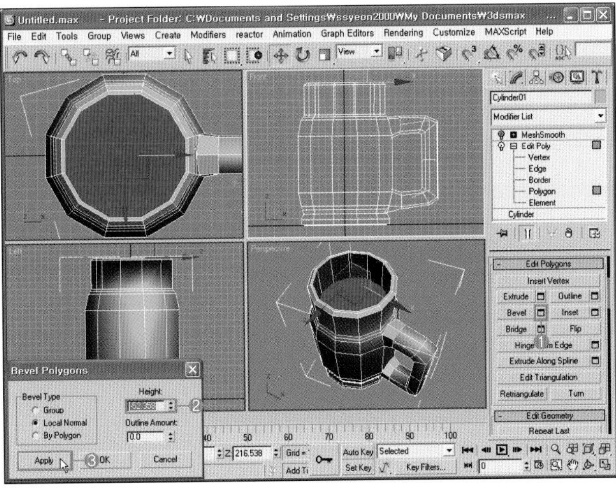

03 Click [Edit Polygons]–[Bevel Settings ▣] to open the [Bevel Polygons] dialog box. Enter [–52.358] for [Height], and click [Apply].

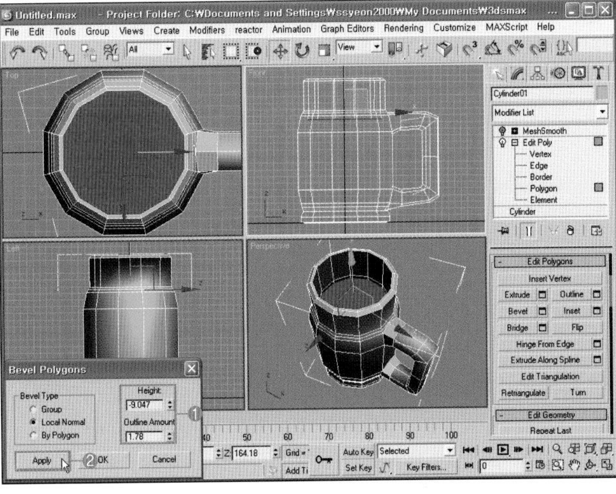

04 With the [Bevel Polygons] dialog box still open, enter [–9.047] for [Height] and [1.79] for [Outline Amount], and click [Apply].

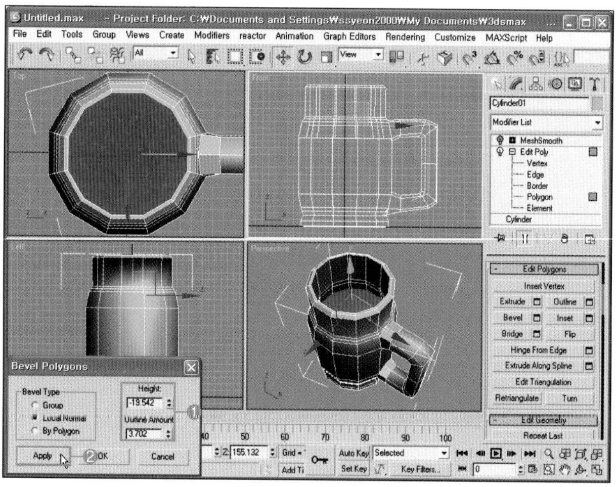

05 Enter [–19.542] for [Height] and [3.702] for [Outline Amount], and click [Apply].

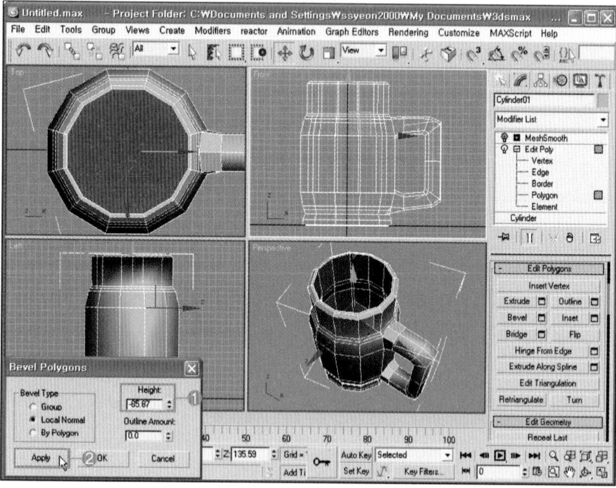

06 Enter [–85.87] for [Height], and click [Apply].

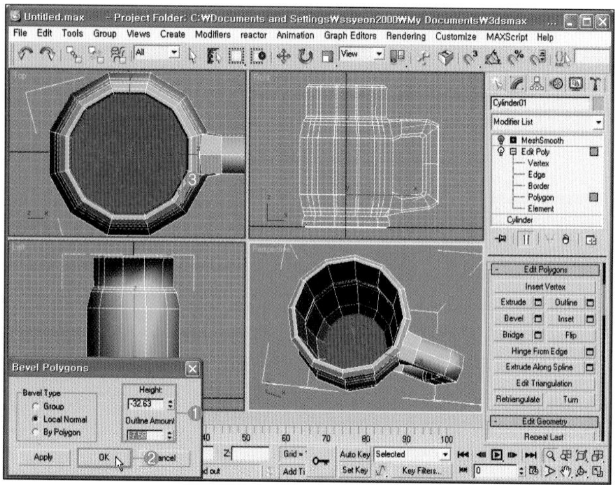

07 Enter [–32.63] for [Height] and [–7.58] for [Outline Amount], and click [OK].

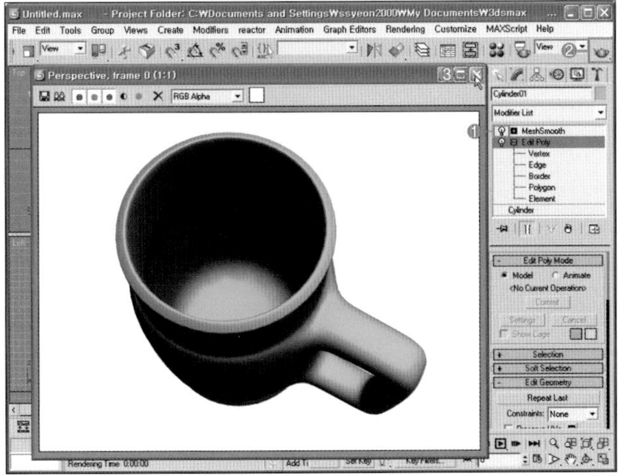

08 Click of the [MeshSmooth] modifier to activate the function, select the Perspective Viewport, and click [Quick Render] on the main toolbar to see the rendered shape. Click of the rendered image window to close it.

Smoothing the Mug Interior 

The inside bottom corners of the beer mug need a round shape. To express this, use the Soft Selection feature.

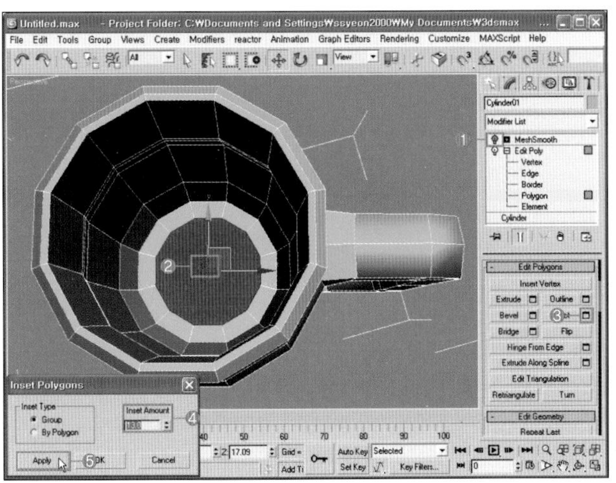

01 Click of the [MeshSmooth] modifier to deactivate the function. Select the [Polygon] sub–object of the [Edit Poly] modifier and select the inner bottom polygon of the beer mug. Click [Edit Polygons]–[Inset Settings] to activate the [Inset Polygons] dialog box. Enter [13] for [Insert Amount], and click [Apply].

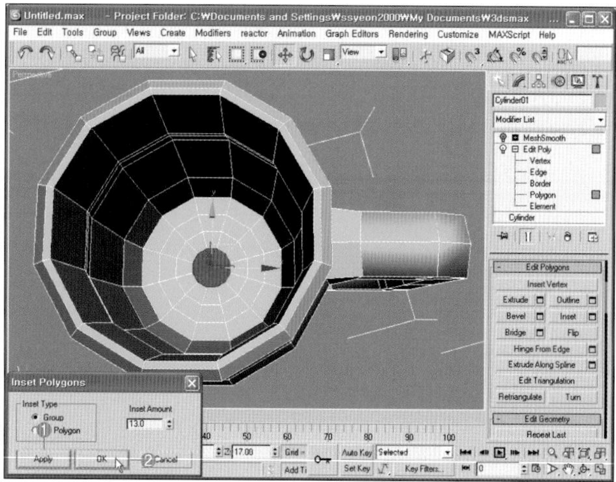

02 Click [Apply] again and then [OK] to finish the shaping of the inside polygon.

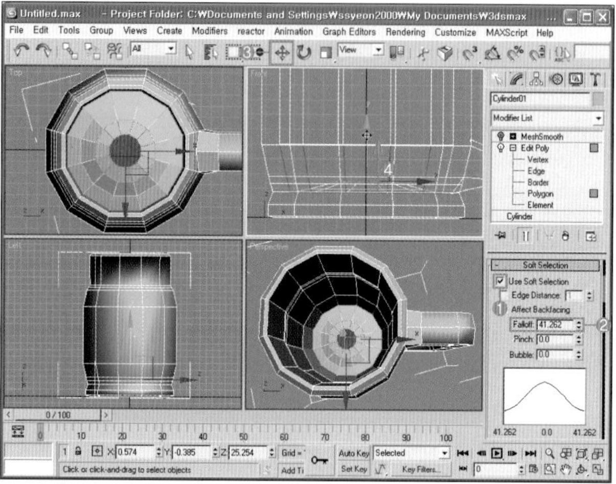

03 Select the innermost of the inside bottom polygons. Click [Select and Move] on the main toolbar, and click–and–drag a little upwards in the Front Viewport. Check [Use Soft Selection], and enter [41.262] for [Falloff].

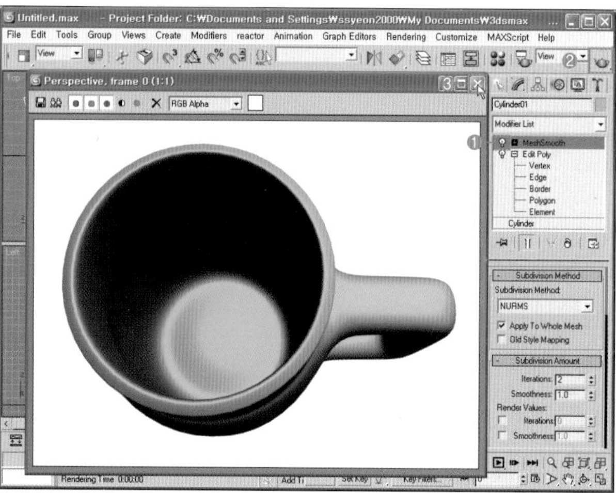

04 Click of the [MeshSmooth] modifier to activate the function, select the Perspective Viewport, and click [Quick Render] on the main toolbar to see the rendered image. Click in the rendered image window to close it.

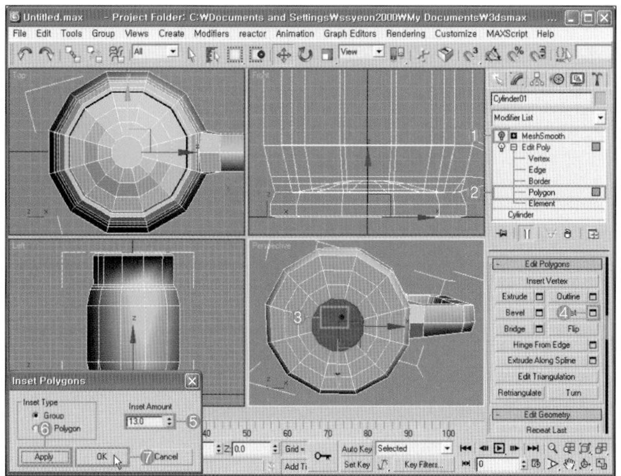

05 Click of the [MeshSmooth] modifier to deactivate the function. Select the [Polygon] sub–object of the [Edit Poly] modifier, select the polygon on the bottom of the beer mug, click [Edit Polygons]–[Inset Settings] to open the [Inset Polygons] dialog box, enter [13] for [Insert Amount], click [Apply] twice, and click [OK].

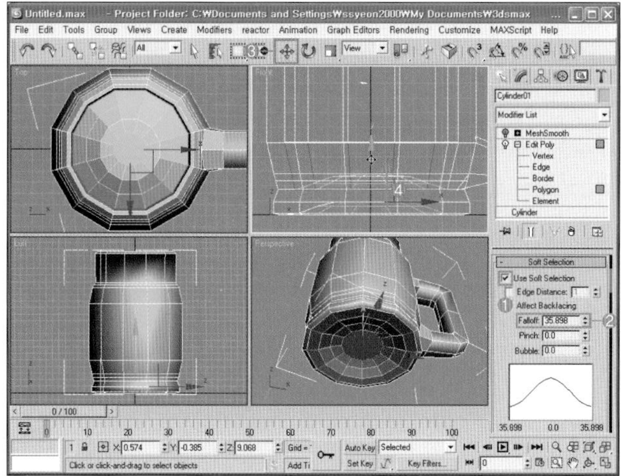

06 Select the innermost polygon on the bottom selected. Click [Select and Move] on the main toolbar, and click–and–drag a little upwards in the Front Viewport. Check [Use Soft Selection] in the polygon selection state, and enter [35.898] for [Falloff].

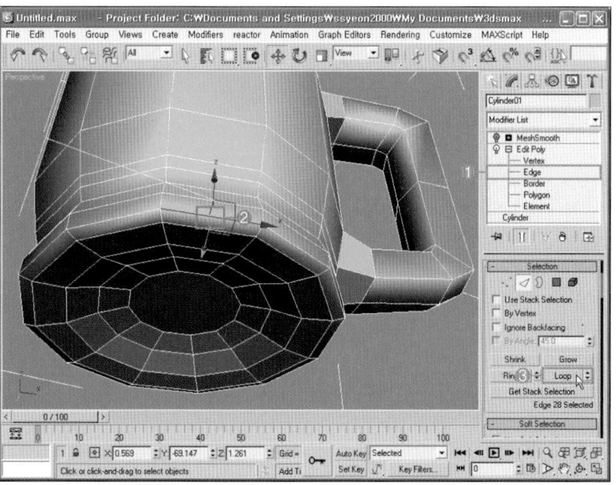

07 Select the [Edge] sub–object of the [Edit Poly] modifier, and select the bottom edge in the Perspective Viewport. To select the adjacent edges, click [Loop] while pressing <Ctrl>.

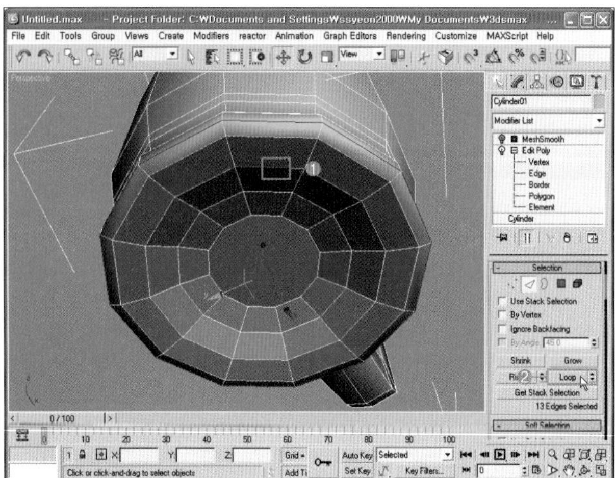

08 While pressing <Ctrl>, select the edge on the location shown in the picture, and click Loop again.

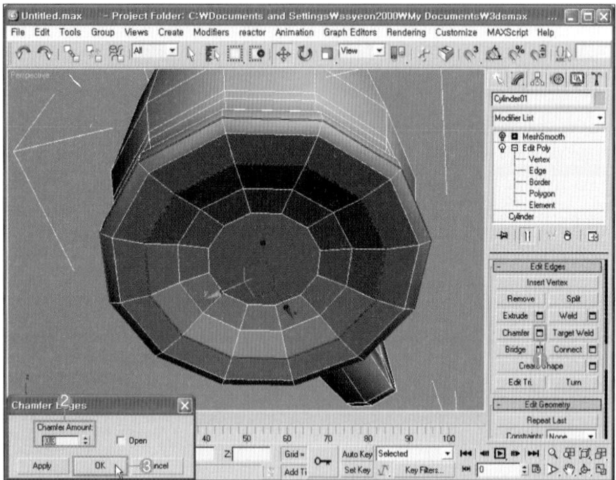

09 Click [Edit Edges]–[Chamfer Settings] to activate the [Chamfer Edges] dialog box. Enter [0.3] for [Chamfer Amount], and click [OK]. The selected edges are divided in two.

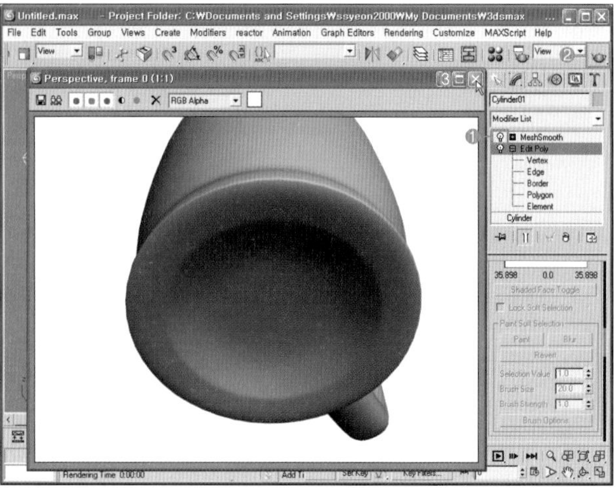

10 Click of the [MeshSmooth] modifier to activate the function, select the Perspective Viewport, and click [Quick Render] on the main toolbar to see the rendered shape. Click in the rendered image window to close it.

Extrude the Surface

Add projections to the surface of the beer mug using Inset and Extrude. This example shows how to create the projections on each of the individual polygons among those selected and on the overall polygon group.

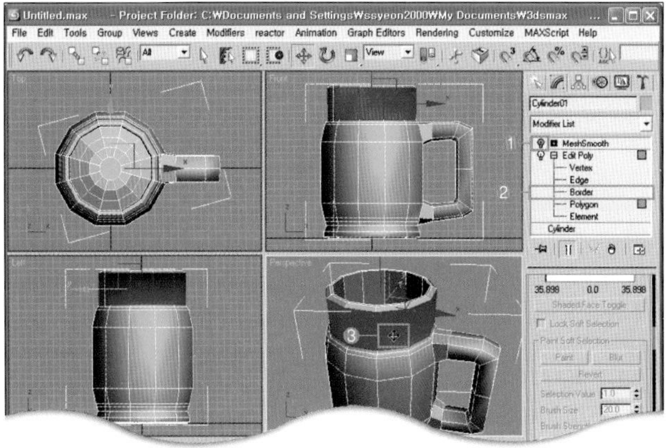

01 Click of the [MeshSmooth] modifier to deactivate the function. Select the [Polygon] sub–object of the [Edit Poly] modifier, and select the upper polygons in the Perspective Viewport while pressing <Ctrl>.

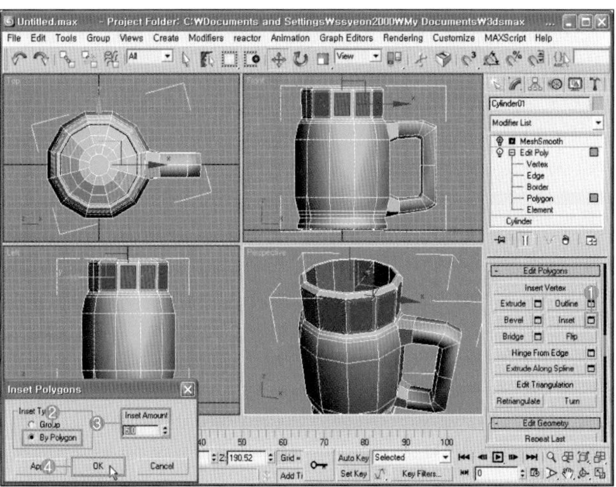

02 Click [Edit Polygons]–[Inset Settings] to open the [Inset Polygons] dialog box. Select [By Polygons], enter [3] for [Insert Amount], and click [OK]. The selected polygons are divided inwards into smaller polygons.

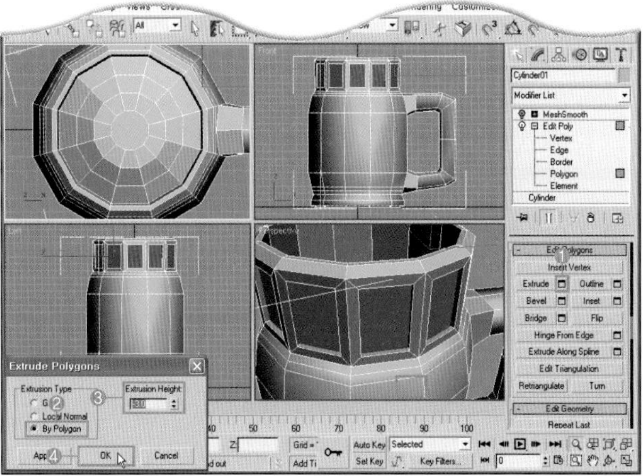

03 With each polygon selected, click [Edit Polygons]–[Extrude Settings] to activate the [Extrude Polygons] dialog box, enter [3] for [Extrusion Height], and click [OK]. The selected polygons move inwards.

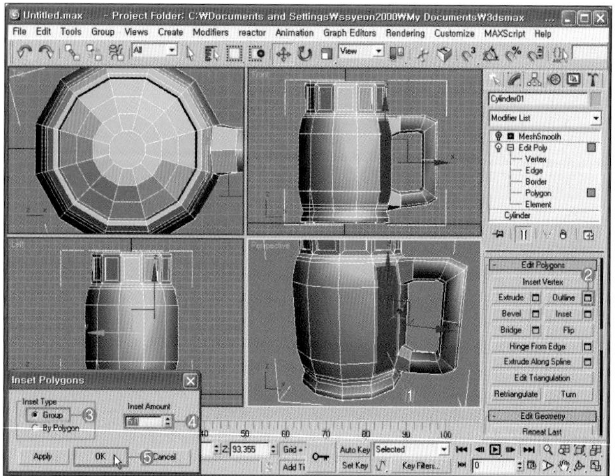

04 In the Perspective Viewport, press <Ctrl> while selecting the side polygons as shown in the picture. Click [Edit Polygons]–[Inset Settings] to activate the [Inset Polygons] dialog box. Select [Group], enter [5] for [Inset Amount], and click [OK]. The selected polygons are divided into smaller polygons.

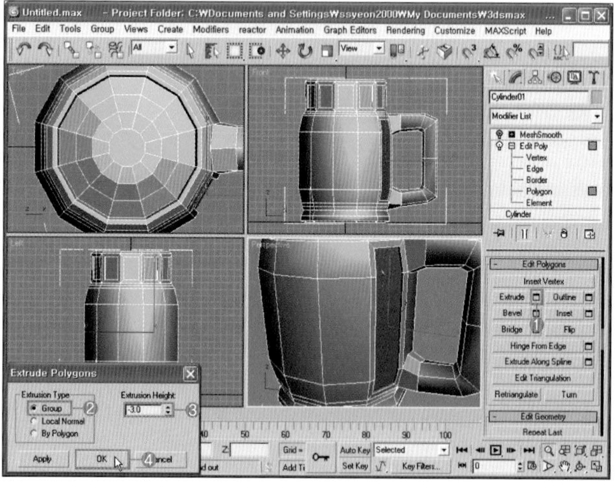

05 Click [Edit Polygons]–[Extrude Settings] to activate the [Extrude Polygons] dialog box. Select [Group], enter [–3] for [Extrusion Height], and click [OK]. The selected polygons move inwards according to the [Extrusion Height] value.

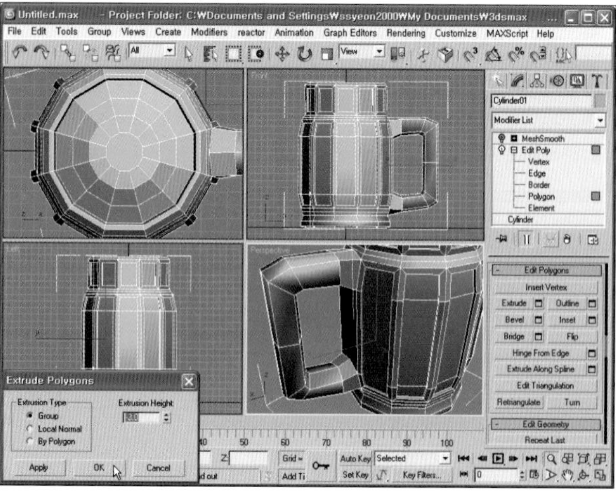

06 Repeat this process for each of the similar polygons around the mug.

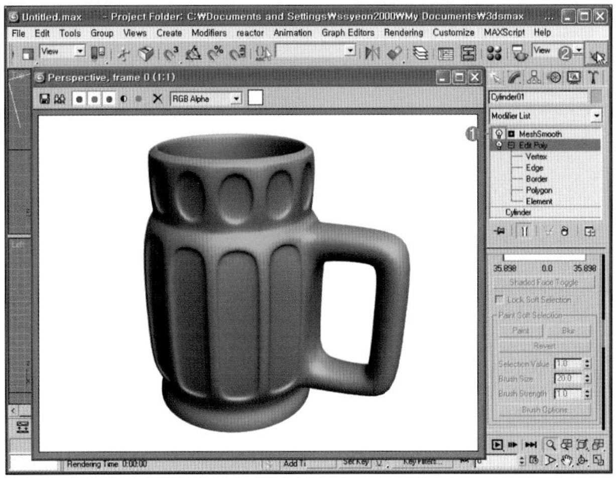

07 Click of the [MeshSmooth] modifier to activate the function, select the Perspective Viewport, and click [Quick Render] on the main toolbar to see the rendered shape.

Supplementary CD\Sample\Chapter 3\Exercise 2\Beermug–final.max

Exercise 03

Designing a Cello

Final Image

Using the MeshSmooth Modifier to finish a design would seem like a natural choice for an object with several curves, such as a cello. However, in this scenario it is best not to use the MeshSmooth Modifier because of all the edges that need to be finalized. This lesson will show a modeling method for creating a realistic cello without the use of the MeshSmooth Modifier.

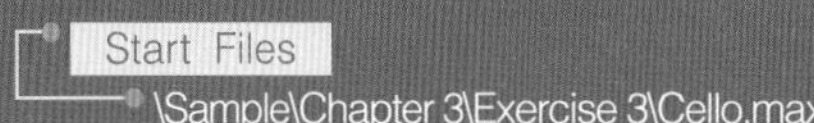

Start Files
\Sample\Chapter 3\Exercise 3\Cello.max

Final File
\Sample\Chapter 3\Exercise 3\Cello-mapping-final.max

Outlining the Cello Body

The cello is a symmetric object, so you can create half of the object with the Line tool, and then apply the Mirror function.

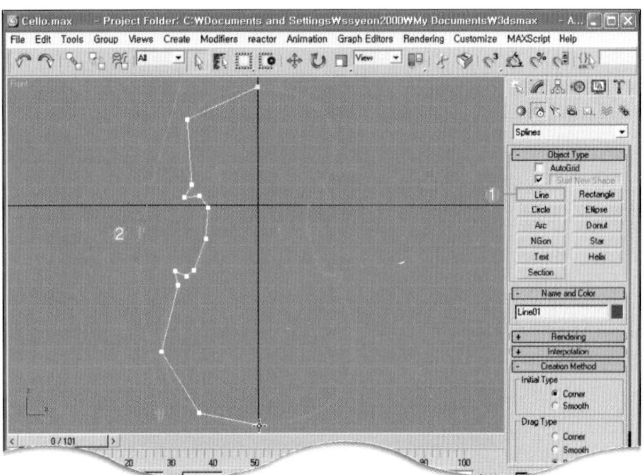

01 Open the "cello.max" file from the supplementary CD and enlarge the Front Viewport. On the Create panel, under [Shapes]–[Splines], click on  and trace the shape of the object on the left side of the Y–axis.

Supplementary CD\Sample\Chapter 3\Exercise 3\Cello.max

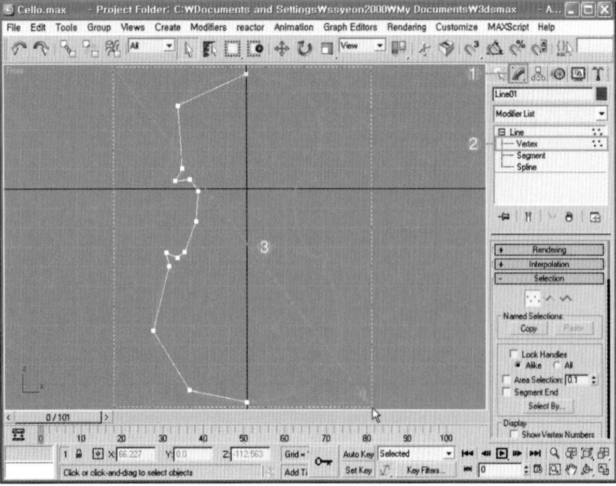

02 Move to the Modify panel with the "Line01" object selected. Select the [Vertex] sub–object of [Line], and drag to select all vertices.

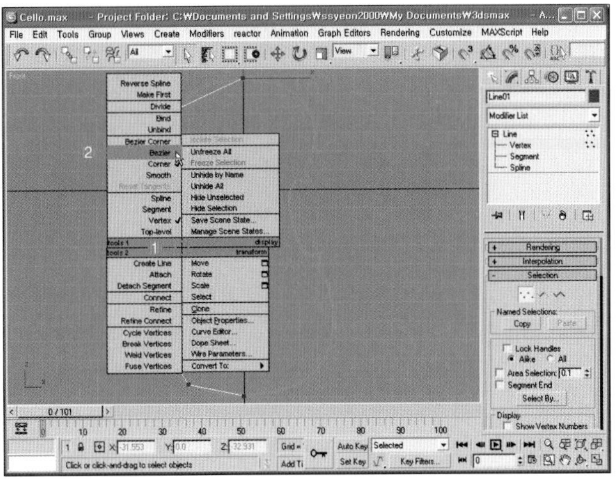

03 Right–click on the selected vertices to show the quad menu, then select [Bezier] to transform straight lines into curves.

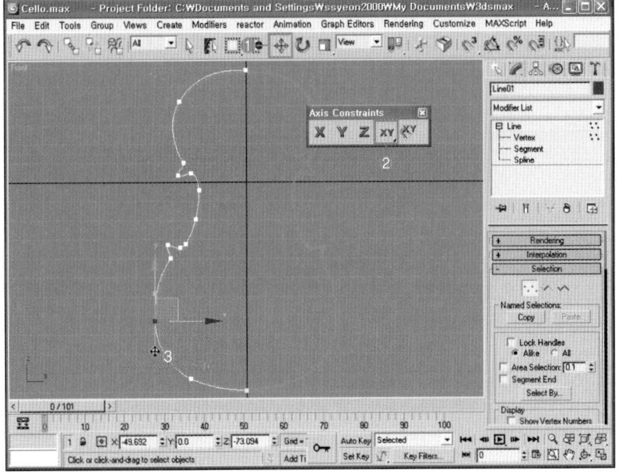

04 Soften the handlebar of each vertex with [Select and Move].

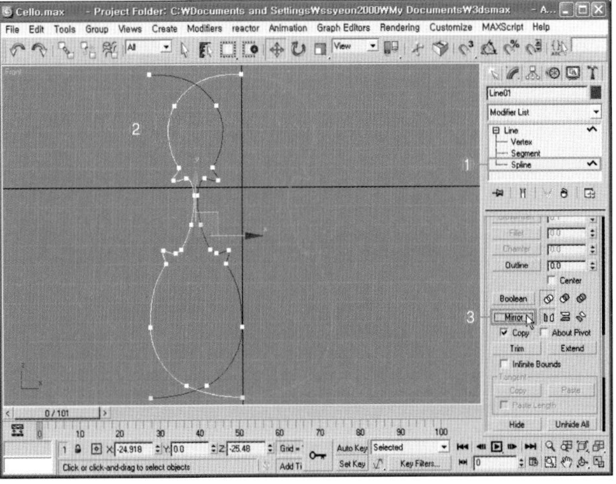

05 Select the [Spline] sub–object of [Line] and then the cello curve. By clicking [Mirror] under [Parameter], the object will be copied symmetrically.

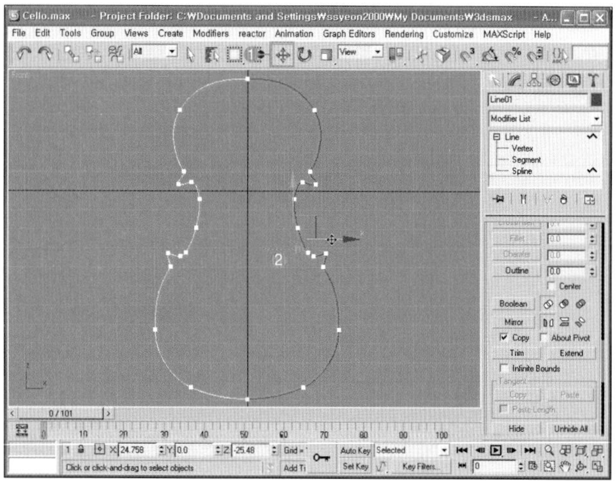

06 Click on [Select and Move] in the main toolbar to drag and align the copied "Line01" object to the right.

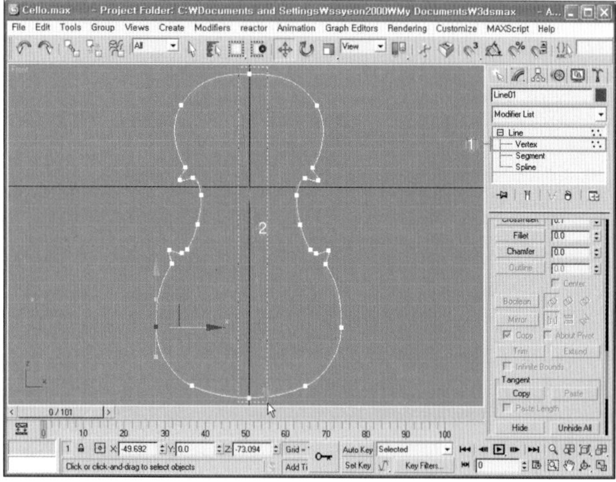

07 Select the [Vertex] sub–object of [Line], and drag to select the intersecting vertices of the two lines.

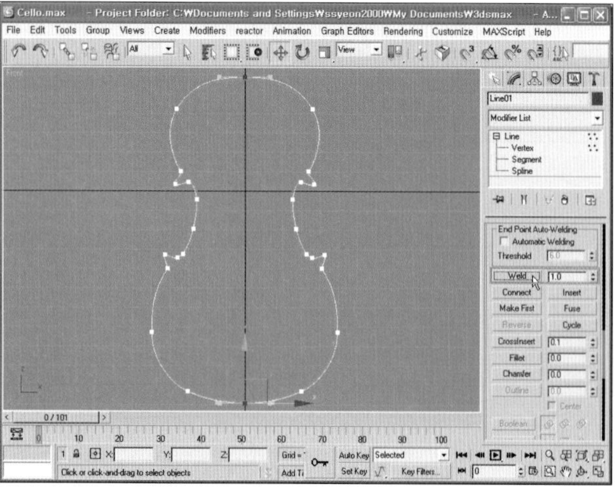

08 Enter [1] for [Geometry]–[Weld], then click Weld to combine the two halves.

tip >>

Welding

Intersecting vertices of two lines copied with the use of Mirror may be in the same position, but they are not joined. This can become a problem when working in three dimensions. To avoid this, use Weld to join all intersecting vertices or overlapping end points.

Modeling the Cello Body 

To make the cello appear three–dimensional, protrude a surface using the Extrude Modifier, and smooth the edges with Chamfer.

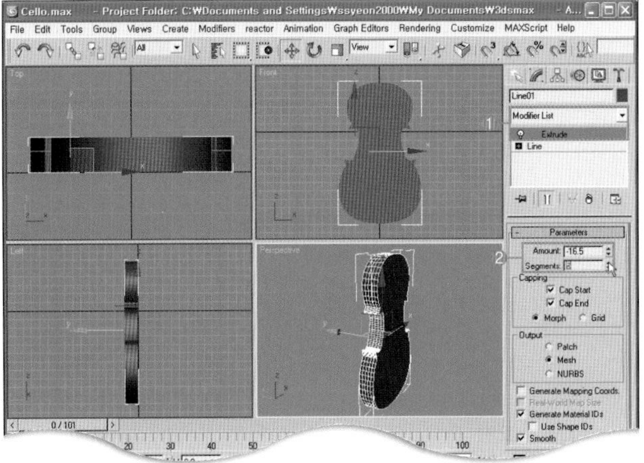

01 Click on the [Modifier List] combo box and select [Extrude] to transform the "Line01" object, which will be the cello body, into a three–dimensional object. Under [Parameters], enter [–16.5] for [Amount] and [5] for [Segment].

tip >>

The Extrude Modifier

The Extrude Modifier tool adds depth to an object made of lines to create a three–dimensional object.

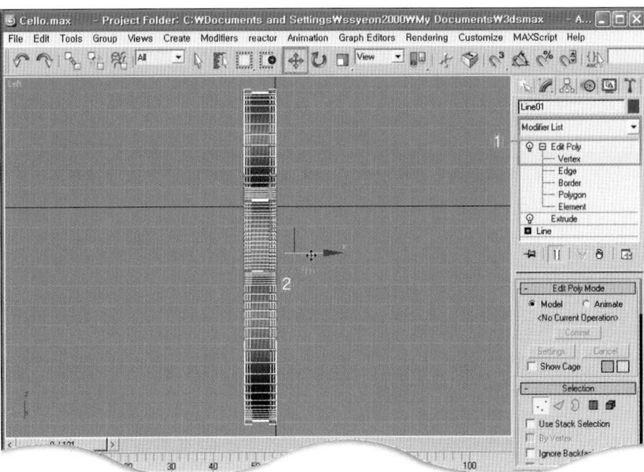

02 Click on the [Modifier List] combo box and select [Edit Poly]. After selecting the [Vertex] sub–object, move the vertices in the center of the Left Viewport to both sides.

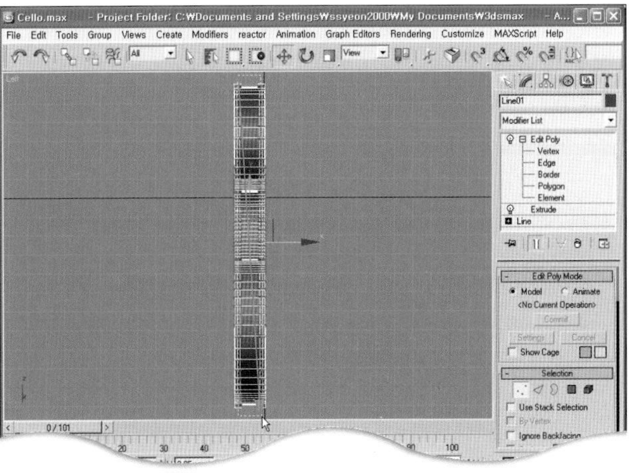

03 Drag to select all of the inner–most vertices.

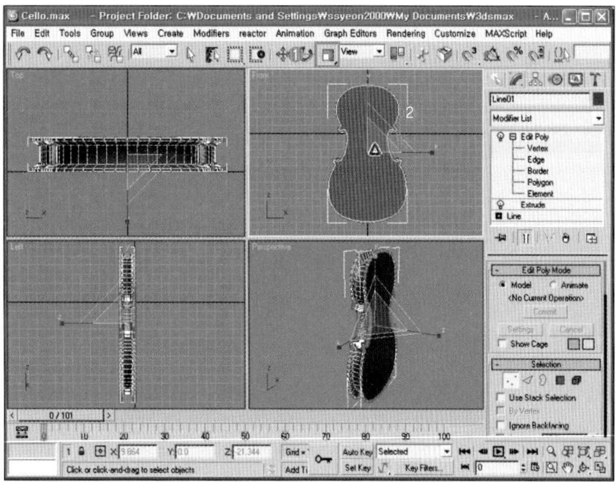

04 Click on [Select and Scale] on the main toolbar, then decrease the size slightly in the Front Viewport.

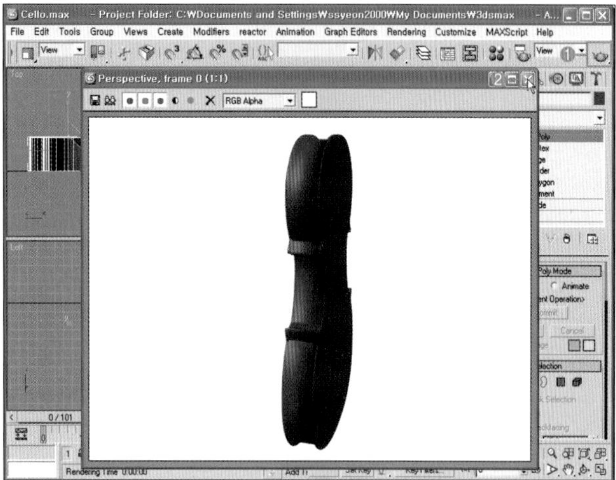

05 Select the Perspective Viewport, then click on [Quick Render] in the main toolbar to see the rendering. Click on the rendered image window to close it.

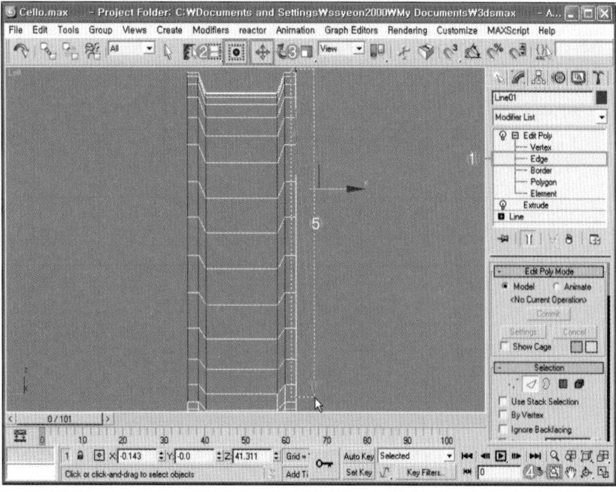

06 Select the [Edge] sub–object of [Edit Poly], activate [Window] on the main toolbar, and [Select and Move] as well. Enlarge the Left Viewport with [Zoom Region] and click–and–drag while pressing <Ctrl> to select all vertical edges.

tip >>

Window and Crossing Tools

Crossing [] is a tool used in complicated configurations when selecting objects or sub–objects in the Viewport, and it also selects objects that are partially in the mouse–drag region. Window [] only selects objects that lie completely within the boundaries of the mouse–drag region.

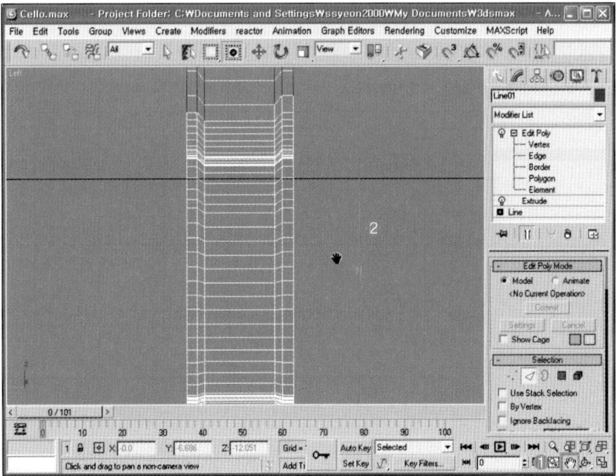

07 Click on [Pan View] in the Viewport control and move the view by click–and–dragging the Viewport up.

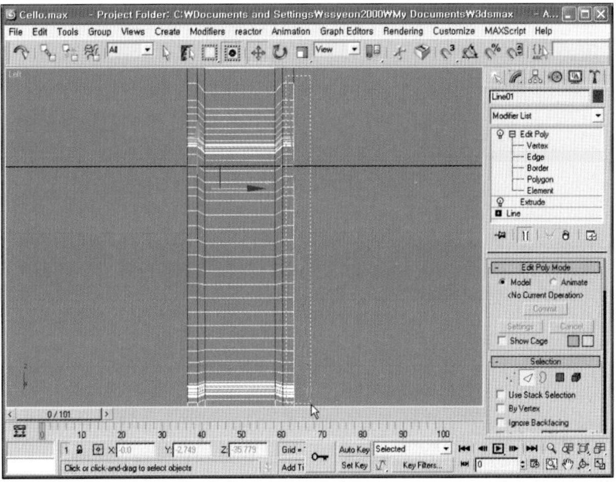

08 While pressing <Ctrl>, select the vertical edges.

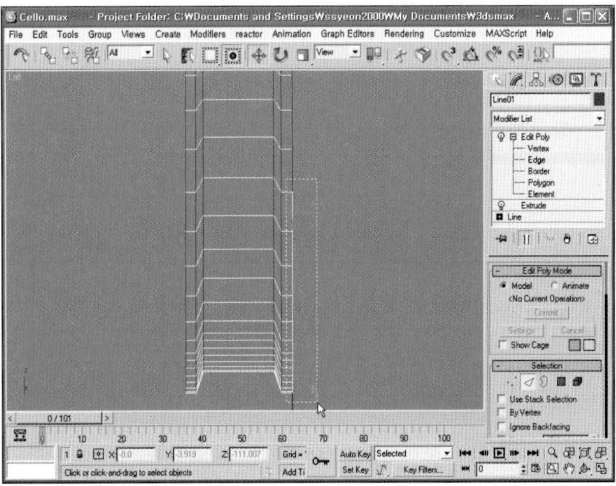

09 Select all of the other edges by pressing <Ctrl> and click–and–dragging downward.

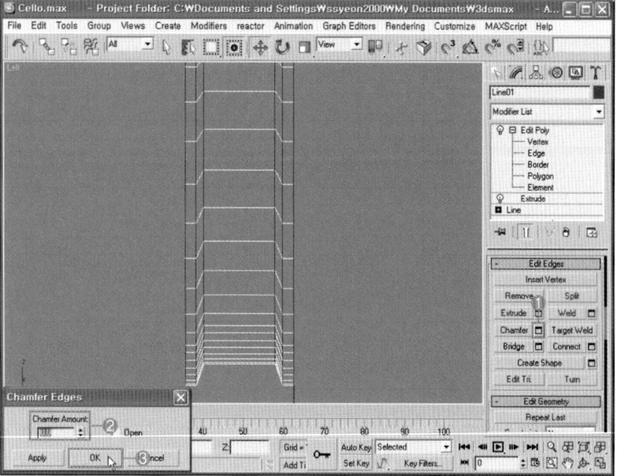

10 Under [Edit Poly], select the [Edit Edge] sub–object and click [Chamfer Settings]. The Chamfer Settings dialog box will appear. Enter [0] for [Chamfer Amount] and click [OK].

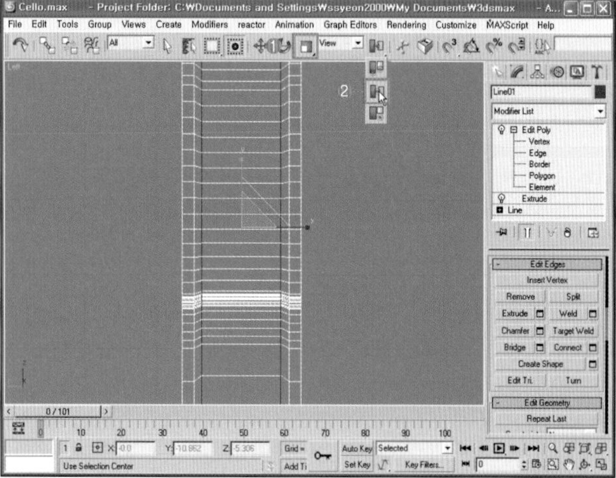

11 After selecting all of the edges inside, click on [Select and Scale] on the main toolbar and then click [Use Selection Center].

tip >>

Use Selection Center [ ]

When you need to transform an object while many components are selected, this feature allows you to make the changes with the center of all the selected components as the base. For example, the Use Selection Center feature can shrink spheres arranged in a circle.

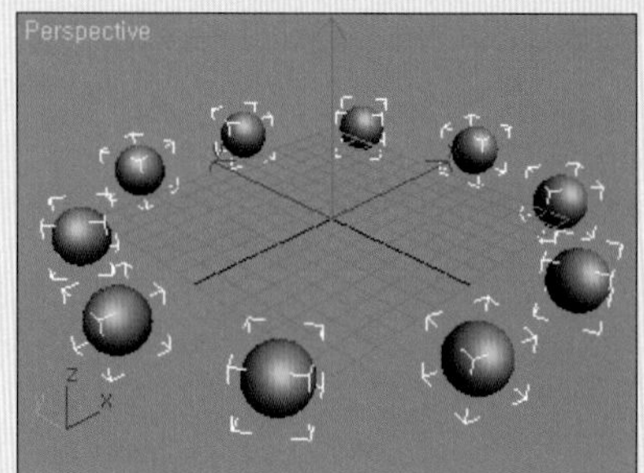

Select a circular array of objects.

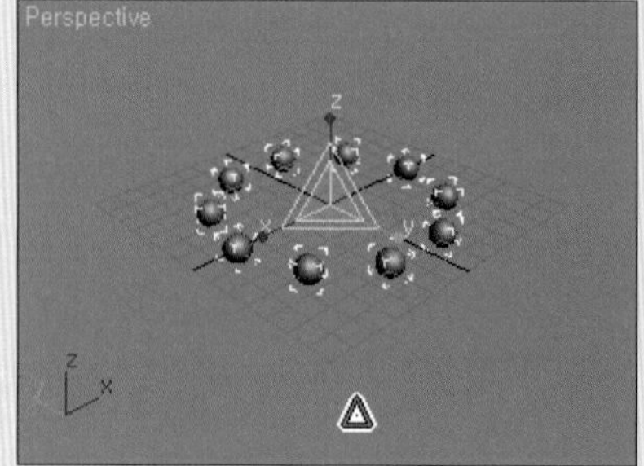

Shrink objects around the center point with [Select and Scale].

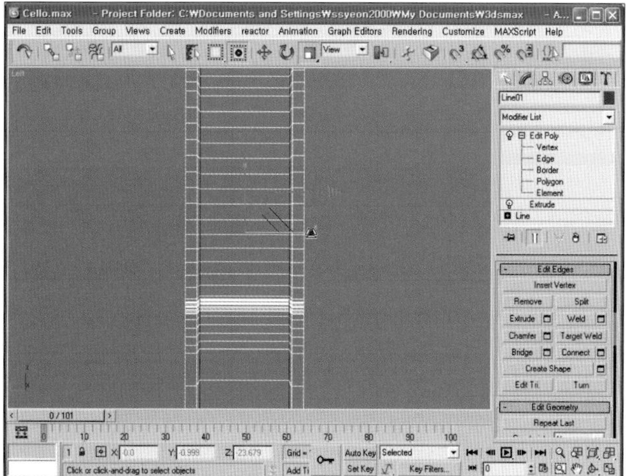

12 Drag selected edges along the X–axis to move them to both verges.

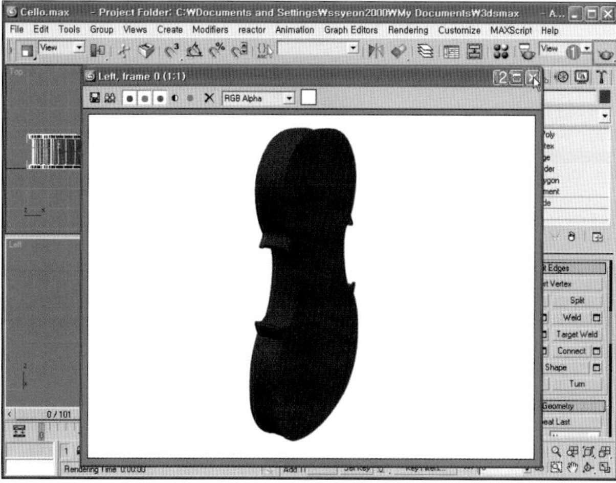

13 Select the Perspective Viewport, then click [Quick Render] on the main toolbar to see the rendering. Click on the rendered image window to close it.

Enhancing the Object Depth

The next step is to enhance the volumetric sense on the surface of the flat body using the Inset and Extrude functions.

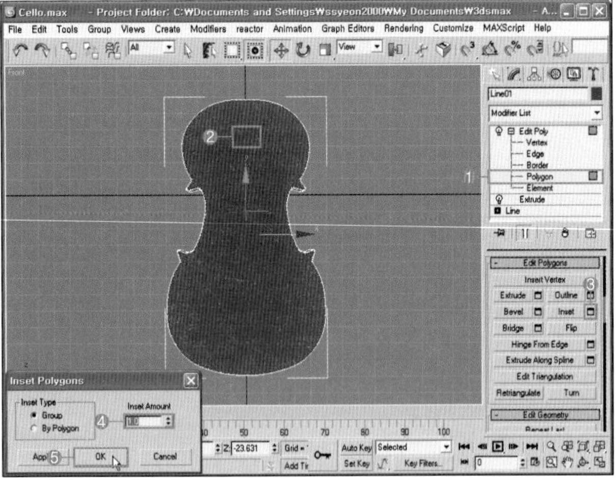

01 Select the [Polygon] sub-object of [Edit Poly], and select the polygon in the Front Viewport. Select [Inset Settings ▣] under [Edit Polygons] and click [OK]. When the [Inset Polygons] dialog box appears, enter [1] for [Inset Amount]. Click [OK]. The selected polygons are divided into smaller polygons inwards.

tip >>

Inset

In previous versions of 3ds Max, creating small polygons of the same shape required the polygons to be individually divided. However, with the addition of the Inset function, the system easily divides new polygons while preserving their precise shape; this is a very useful tool for modeling.

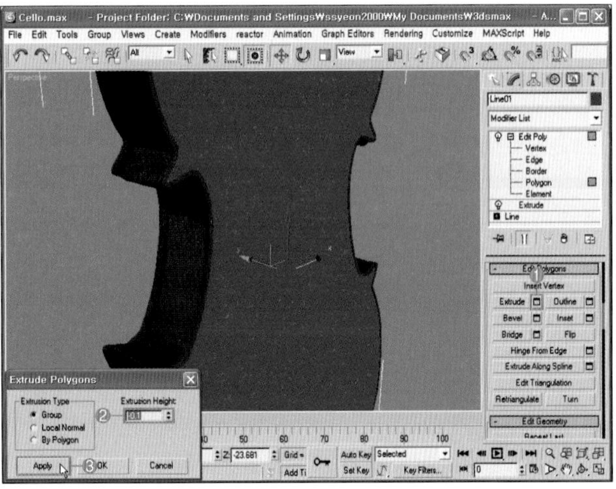

02 Click [Extrude Settings ▣] of [Edit Polygons]. When the Extrude Polygons dialog box appears, enter [–0.1] for [Height], and click [Apply]. The selected polygon retracts this distance inward.

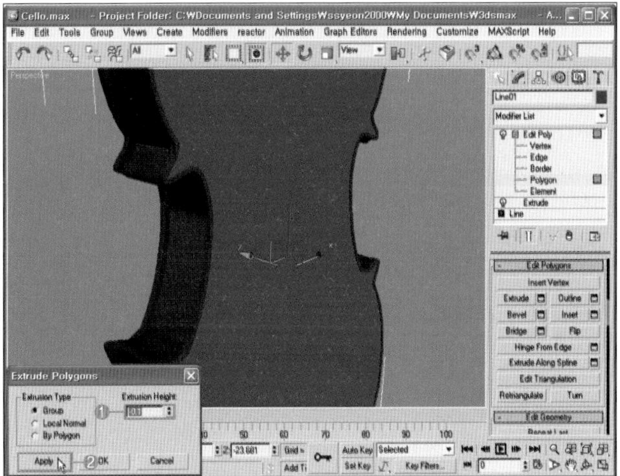

03 Enter [–0.1] for [Height] of the Extrude Polygons dialog box, and click [Apply] once again.

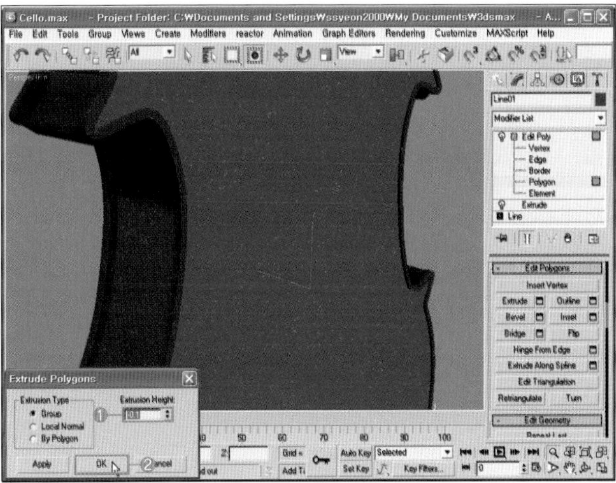

04 Enter [–0.1] for [Height] of the Extrude Polygons dialog box and click [OK] to show the sharpened shapes overall.

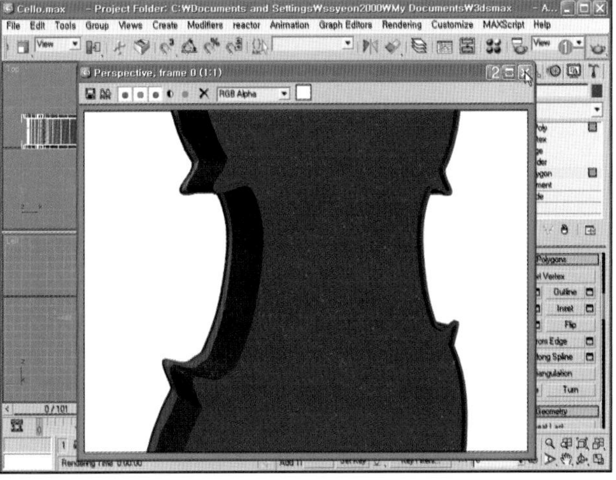

05 Select the Perspective Viewport, then click [Quick Render] on the main toolbar to see the rendered shape. Click on the rendered image window to close it.

Adding F Holes

The f–shaped holes in a cello allow sound to escape from the instrument. To depict them, you will create a line and circle, and proceed with the Boolean operation to unite them at the Spline.

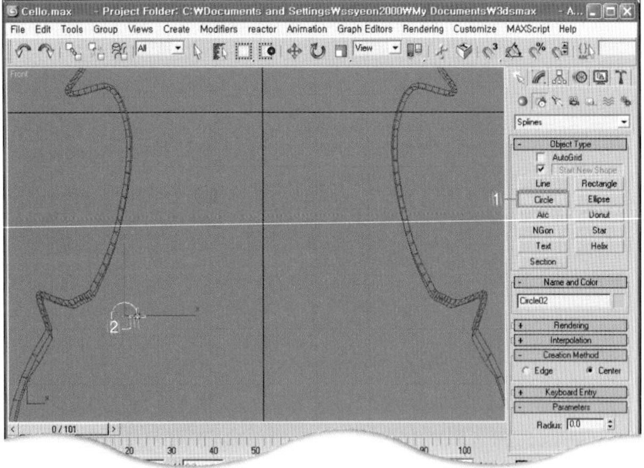

01 On the Create panel, under [Shapes]–[Splines], click Circle. Create two small circles at the center–left of the cello on the Front Viewport, as shown in the image.

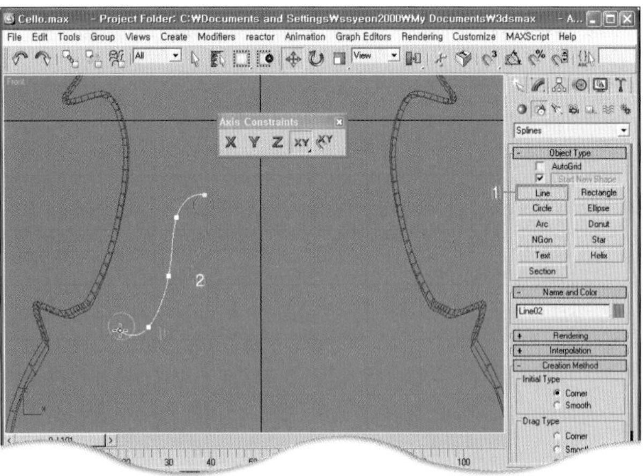

02 On the Create panel, under [Shapes]–[Splines], click Line, and create an S–shaped line that connects the two circles.

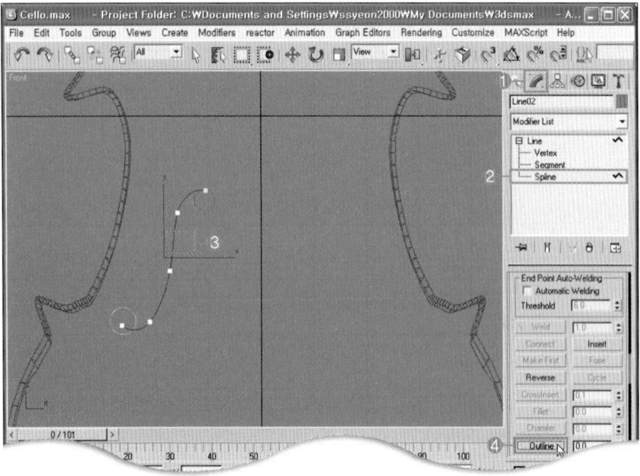

03 Select the S–shaped line and move to the Modify panel. Select the [Spline] sub–object of [Line], click the S–shaped line, and click [Geometry]–Outline.

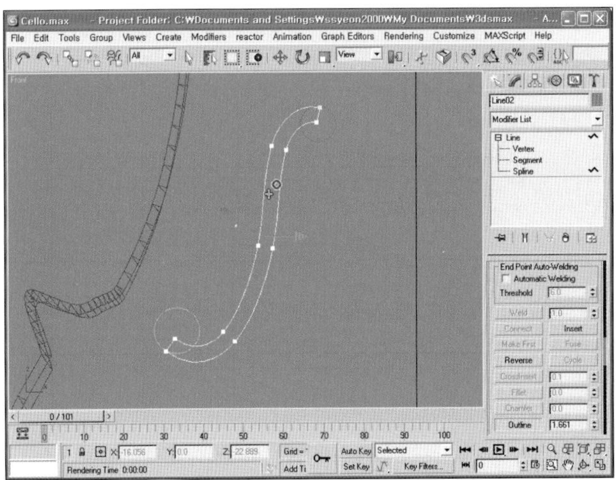

04 Create an outline by click–and–dragging the S–shaped curve towards the right. Both lines should still align with the small circles.

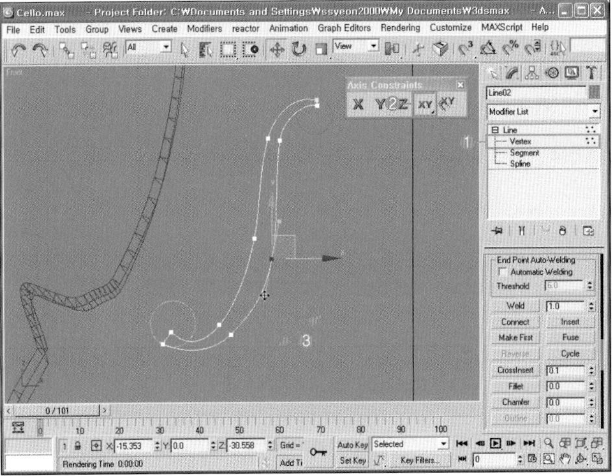

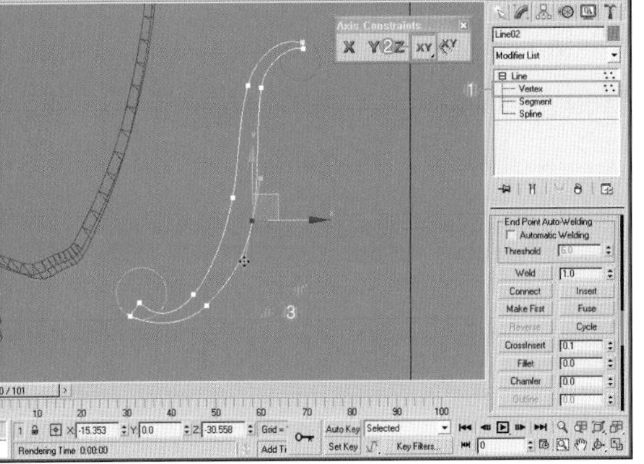

05 Select the [Vertex] sub–object of [Line] and modify the shape to make the center of the S–curve thicker, as shown.

tip >>

[Axis Constraints] dialog box

In order to open the [Axis Constraints] dialog box, right–click on the empty space on the main tool bar then select [Axis Constraints] from the menu.

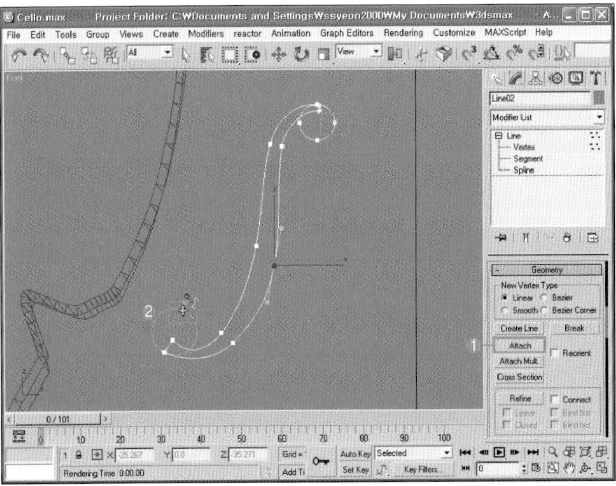

06 Click [Geometry]–[Attach], and select and unite both of the small circles.

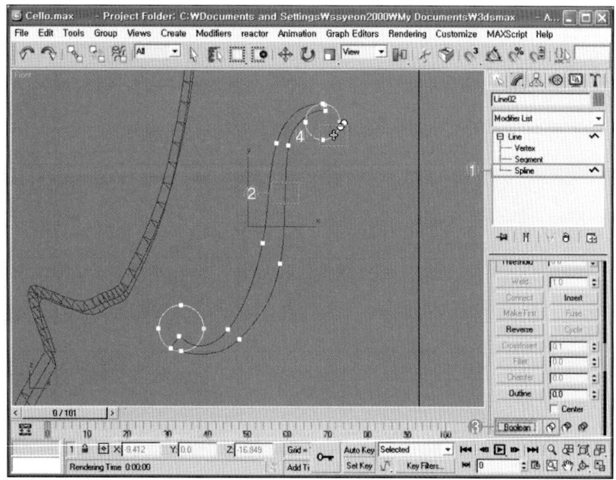

07 Click on the [Spline] sub–object of [Line], and select the right–hand line of the S–curve. Then select [Geometry]–Boolean, and select and unite the upper small circle.

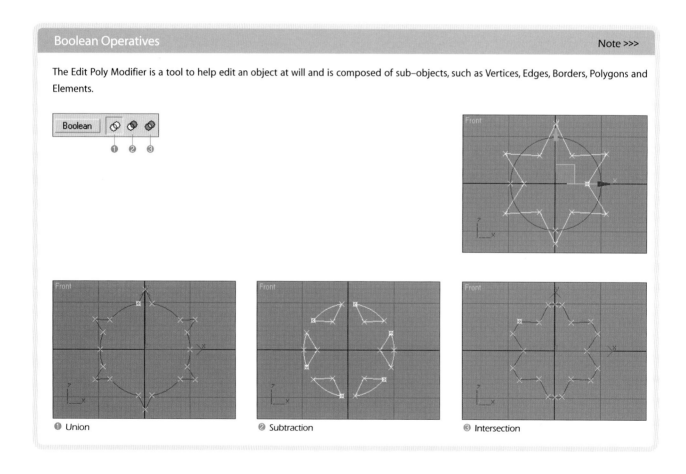

Boolean Operatives

Note >>>

The Edit Poly Modifier is a tool to help edit an object at will and is composed of sub–objects, such as Vertices, Edges, Borders, Polygons and Elements.

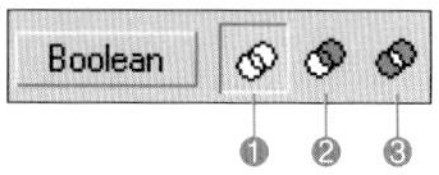

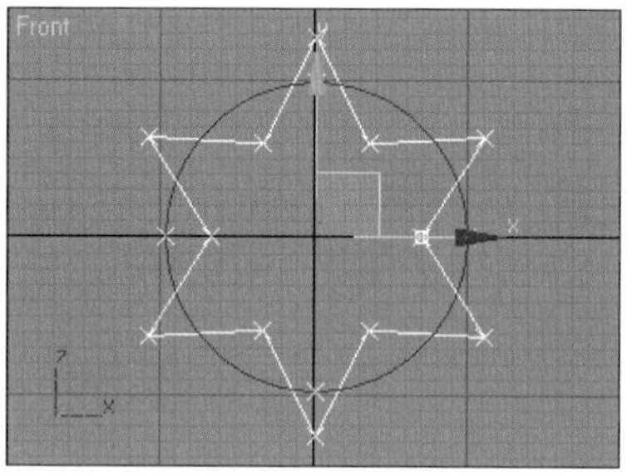

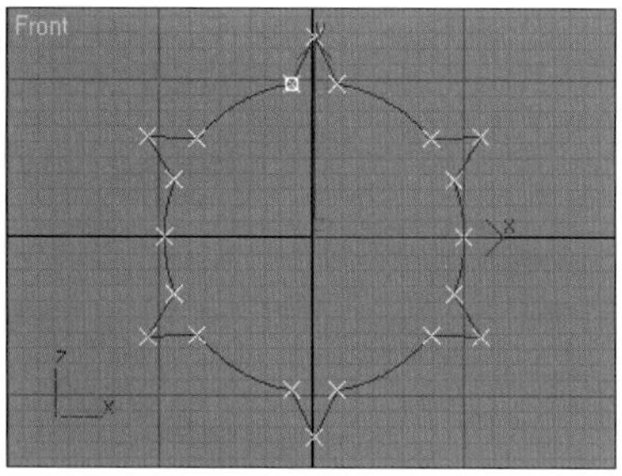

❶ Union

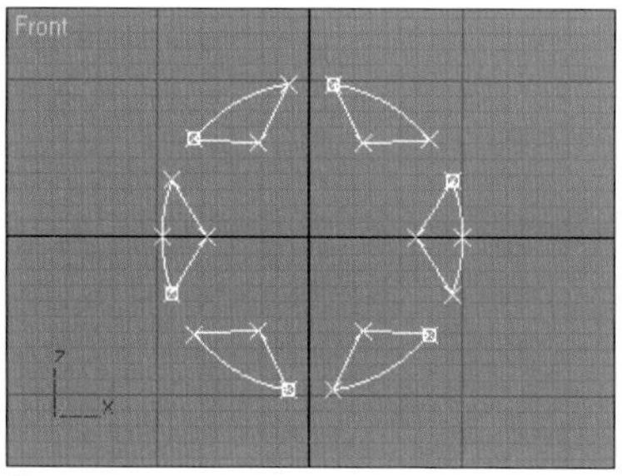

❷ Subtraction

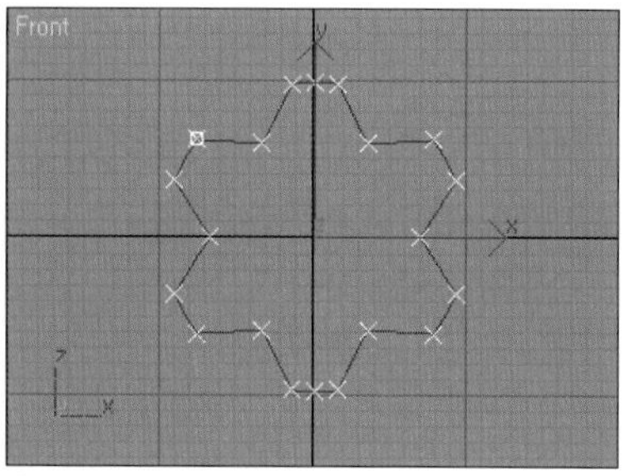

❸ Intersection

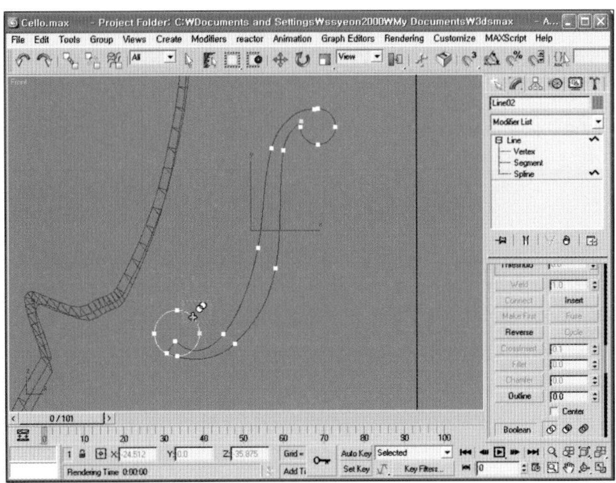

08 Select and unite the lower circle in the same way.

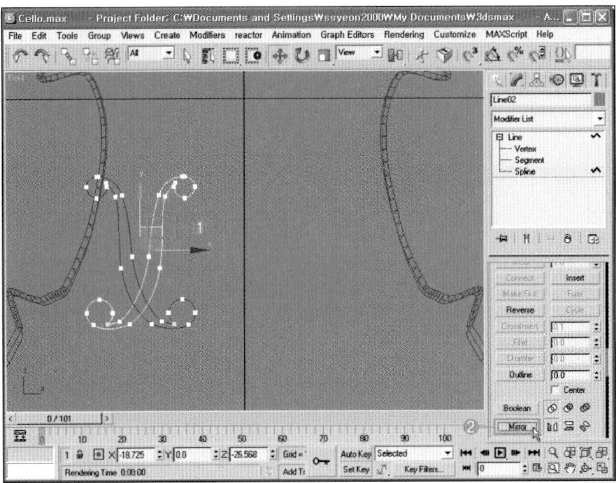

09 Select the completed S–curve, and click [Geometry]–Mirror to symmetrically copy the object.

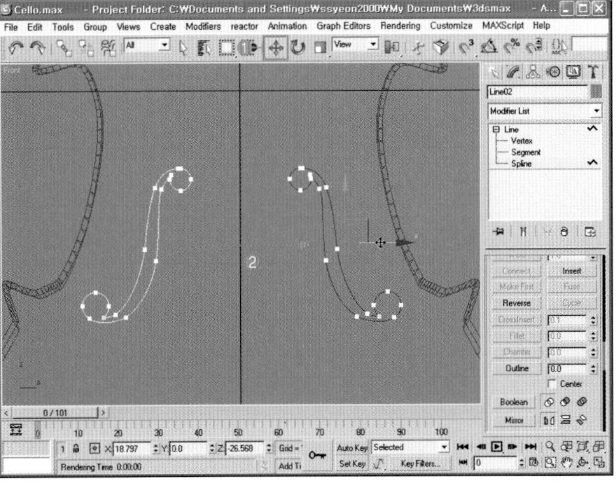

10 Click [Select and Move] on the main toolbar, and move the copied line to the opposite side of the cello.

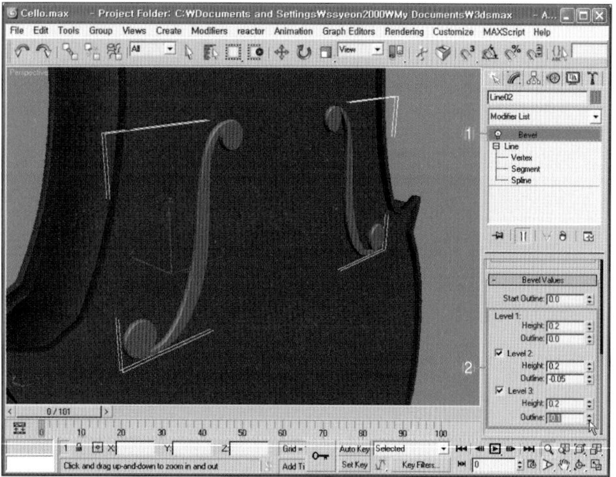

11 To make the S–curve into a 3D object, click the [Modifier List] combo box, and select [Bevel]. Set the [Bevel Values]. For [Level 1], enter [0.2] for [Height]. For [Level 2], enter [0.2] for [Height] and [–0.05] for [Outline]. For [Level 3], enter [0.2] for [Height] and [–0.1] for [Outline].

Bevel Modifier

Note >>>

The Bevel Modifier has the same function as the Bevel function of the Edit Poly Modifier, but it is more convenient for creating curved polygons of up to three layers from individual lines.

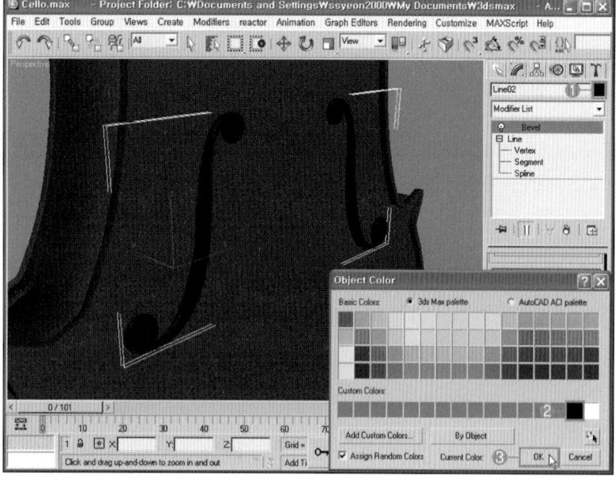

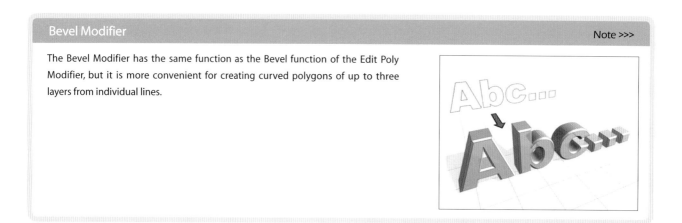

12 Click the color button for the line and change the color to black.

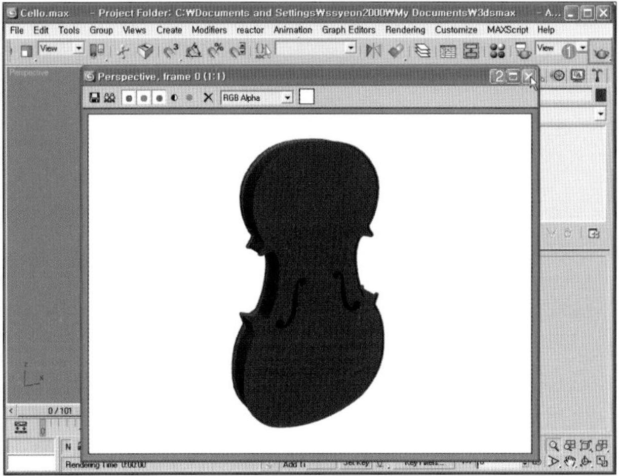

13 Select the Perspective Viewport, and click [Quick Render] on the main toolbar to see the rendered shape. Click on the rendered image window to close it.

Creating the Fingerboard and Scroll

The detailed structures of a cello are shaped differently from right to left, so attention to detail is important here. It is recommended that you create the section with the Line, sufficiently add the vertices, and adjust the shape with the FFD Modifier.

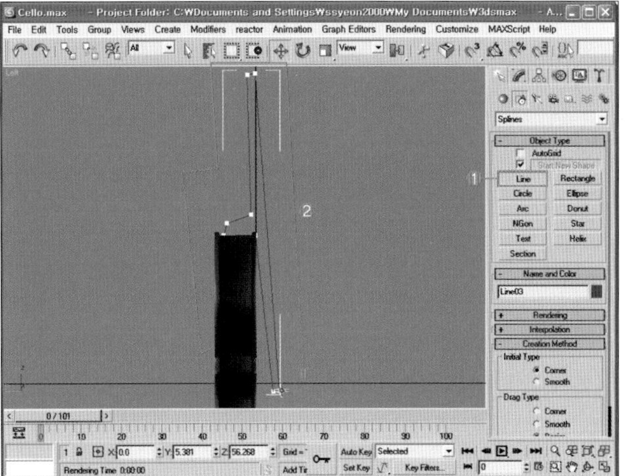

01 On the Create panel, under [Shapes]–[Splines], click Line and create a closed line in the Left Viewport, as shown.

tip >>

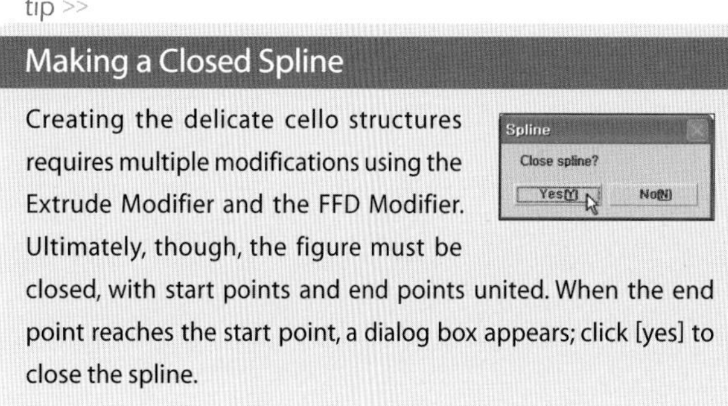

Making a Closed Spline

Creating the delicate cello structures requires multiple modifications using the Extrude Modifier and the FFD Modifier. Ultimately, though, the figure must be closed, with start points and end points united. When the end point reaches the start point, a dialog box appears; click [yes] to close the spline.

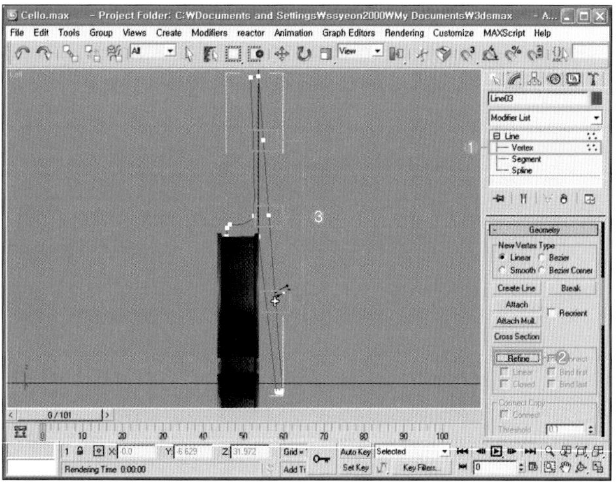

02 Select the [Vertex] sub–object of [Line], click [Geometry]–[Refine], and click the straight line at the right hand three times to add a new vertex.

tip >>

Adding a New Vertex Using Refine

The FFD Modifier modifies the figure in proportion to the number of divided vertices. Therefore, normal object editing can only be done if the vertices occur on the structure at regular intervals.

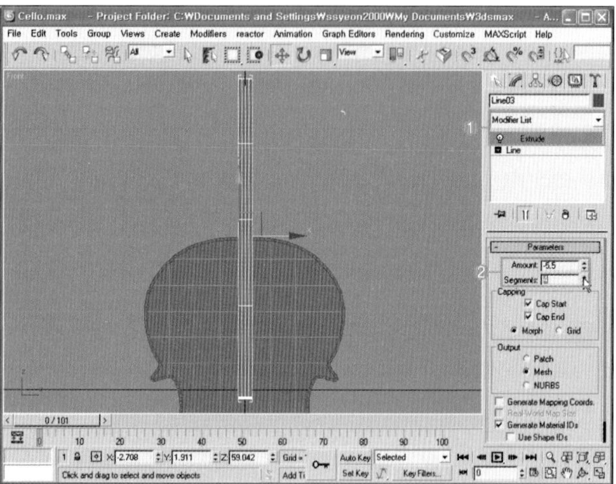

03 Click the [Modifier List] combo box, select the [Extrude], and, under [Parameters], enter [–5.5] for [Amount] and [4] for [Segment].

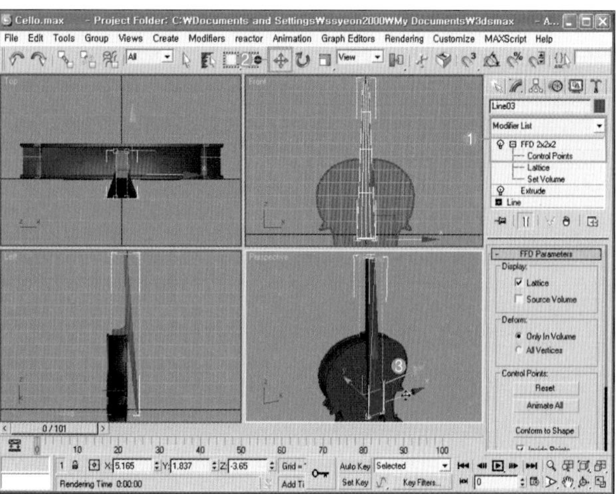

04 Click the [Modifier List] combo box, and select the [FFD 2x2x2] Modifier. Select the [Control Point] sub–object, and move the lower adjustment vertex right and left with [Select and Move] to model the fingerboard, as shown.

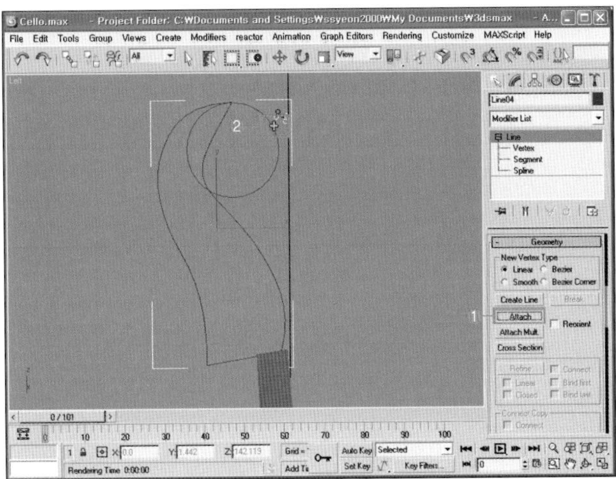

05 To model the scroll at the end of the fingerboard, create a line and circle, and unite the circle with the line, as shown.

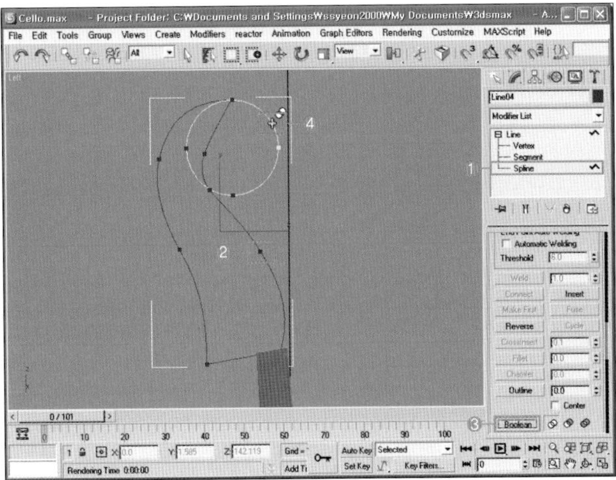

06 Select the [Spline] sub–object of [Line], select the curve, click [Geometry]–Boolean, and unite by selecting the circle.

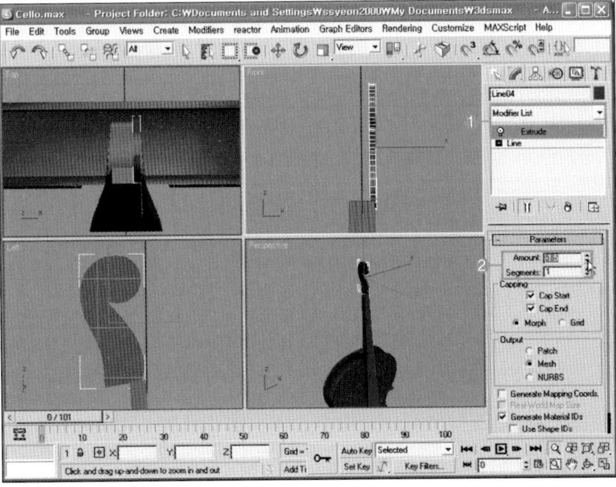

07 Click the [Modifier List] combo box, select [Extrude], and, under [Parameters], enter [–1.5] for [Amount] and [1] for [Segment].

08 On the Create panel, under [Geometry]–[Extended Primitives], click [Chamfer Cylinder ChamferCyl]. Create a Chamfer Cylinder in the Left Viewport in the size shown.

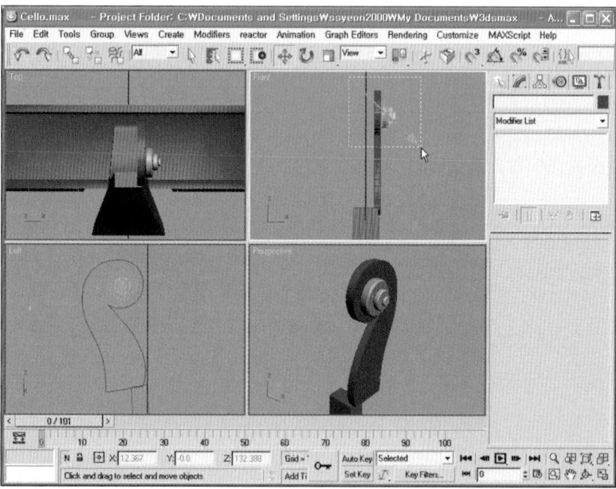

09 Use [Chamfer Cylinder ChamferCyl] to add another small Chamfer Cylinder, and select the objects in the Front Viewport.

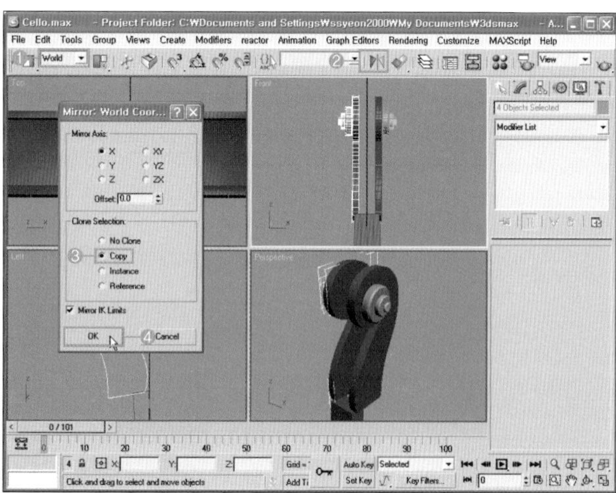

10 On the main toolbar, select World and [Use Transform Coordinate Input], and move the central axis to the absolute axis. Select [Mirror] on the main toolbar, and when the Mirror dialog box appears, select the X–axis direction and [Copy], and click [OK]. The selected objects are copied symmetrically to the opposite side.

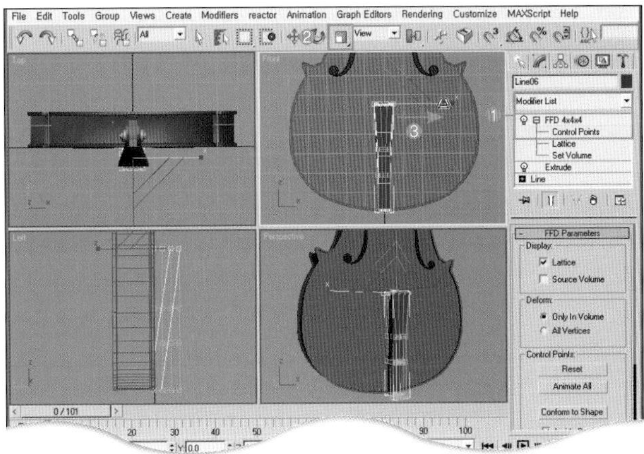

11 Model the cello's tailpiece by creating a basic line in the Left Viewport. Complete the shape with the [Extrude] and [FFD 4x4x4] modifiers.

Creating Pegs and Strings

The cello's pegs and strings can easily be designed with lines, but the drawback is that they do not appear when rendering. Therefore, you must forcefully render the lines.

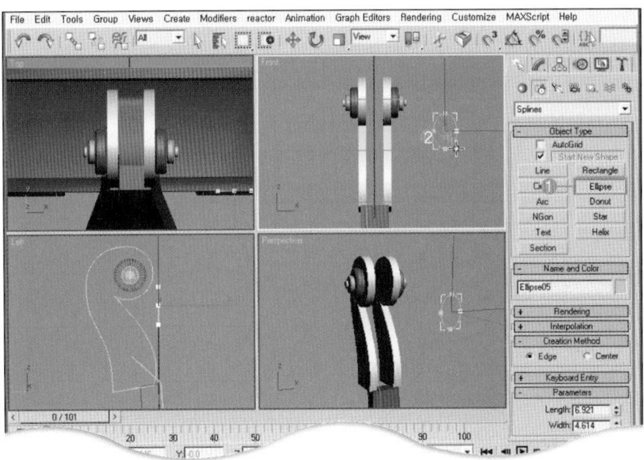

01 On the Create panel, under [Shapes]–[Splines], click [Ellipse], and create a small ellipse by click–and–dragging in the Front Viewport.

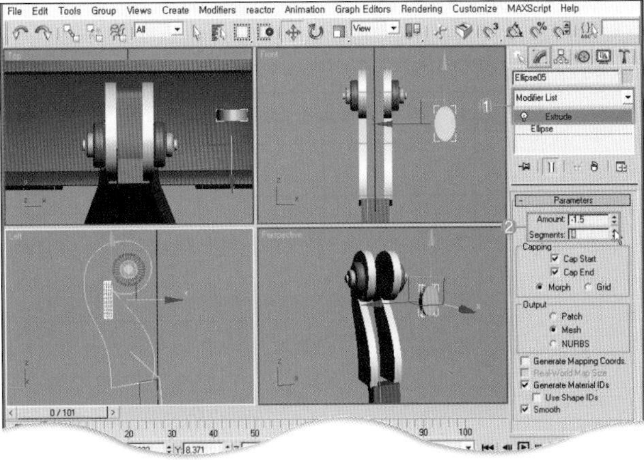

02 Move to the Modify panel, and click the [Modifier List] combo box. Select [Extrude], and set the [Parameters]. Enter [–1.5] for [Amount] and [4] for [Segment].

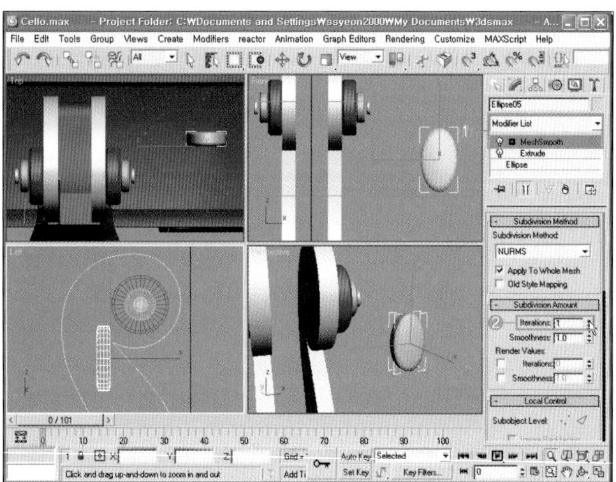

03 Again, click the [Modifier List] combo box, and select [MeshSmooth] to smooth the object.

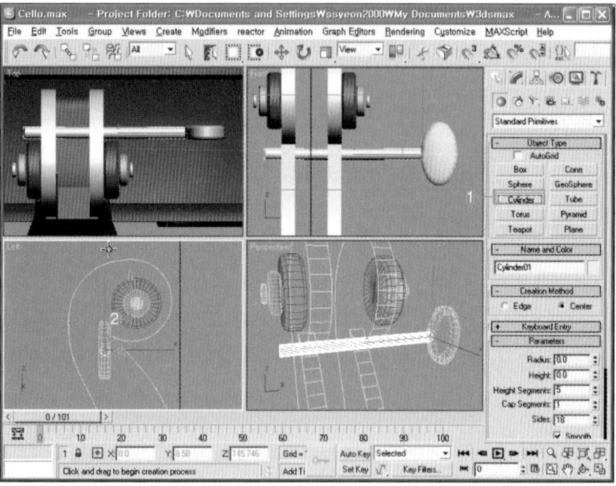

04 On the Create panel, under [Geometry]–[Standard Primitives], click Cylinder. Click–and–drag in the Left Viewport to create a long, rod–shaped cylinder.

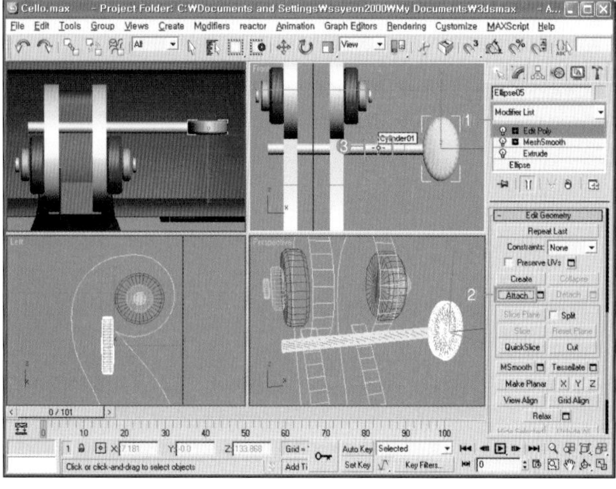

05 Select the "Ellipse01" object just created, click the [Modifier List] combo box, and select [Edit Poly]. Click [Edit Geometry]–Attach, and select the "Cylinder01" object in the Viewport.

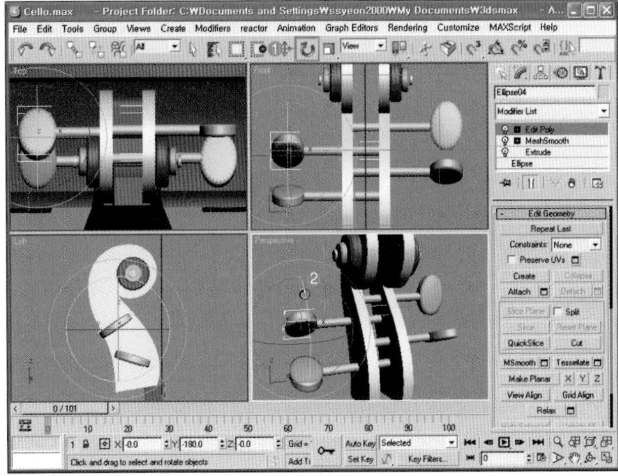

06 Create three more ellipses in the same way, then click [Select and Rotate] on the main toolbar, and rotate in irregular directions.

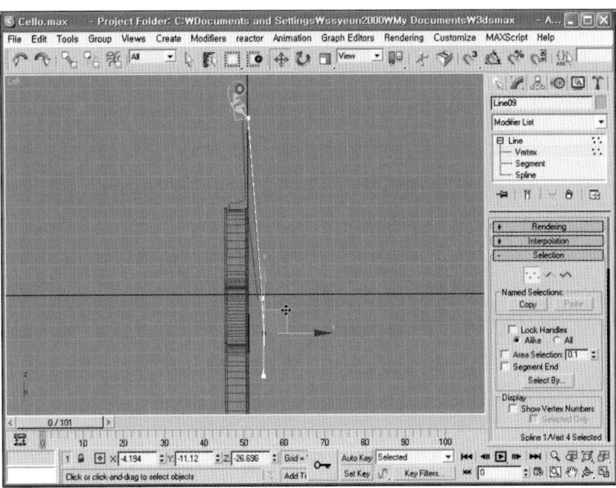

07 To create the cello strings, create a curve in the Left Viewport with a line, as shown, and adjust the shape with the [Vertex] sub–object.

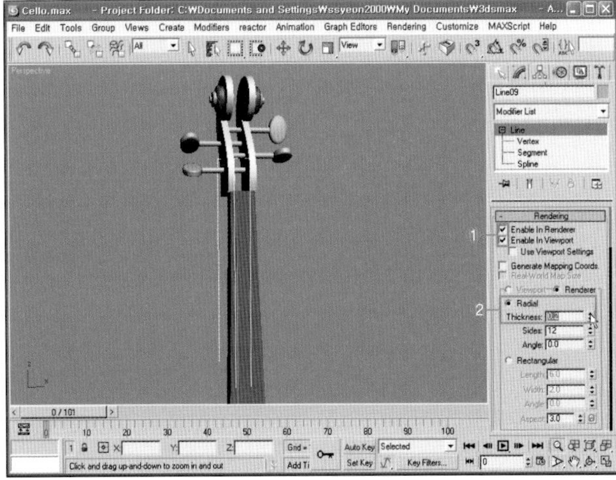

08 Go to the Modify panel, and, under [Rendering], check [Enable in Renderer] and [Enable in Viewport]. Check [Radial], and enter [0.2] for [Thickness] to complete the cello strings.

Enable in Renderer and Enable in Viewport

Note >>>

Line type objects do not show when rendering, and therefore they must be set to enable forced rendering. The user can make the lines appear only in the Viewport (Enable in Viewport), or only during rendering (Enable in Renderer), or select Radial or Rectangular shapes for the line's vertical polygon figure.

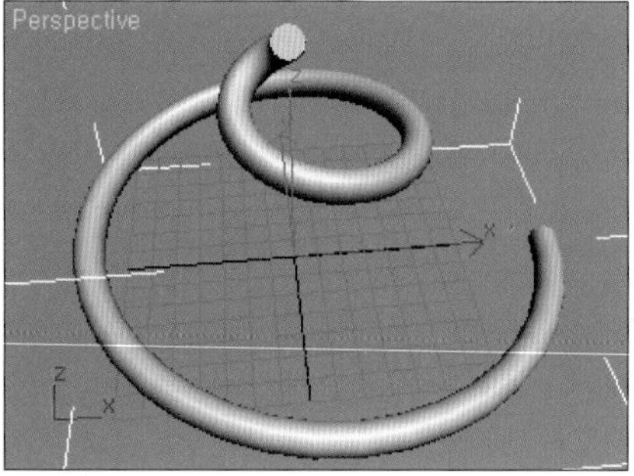

Radial

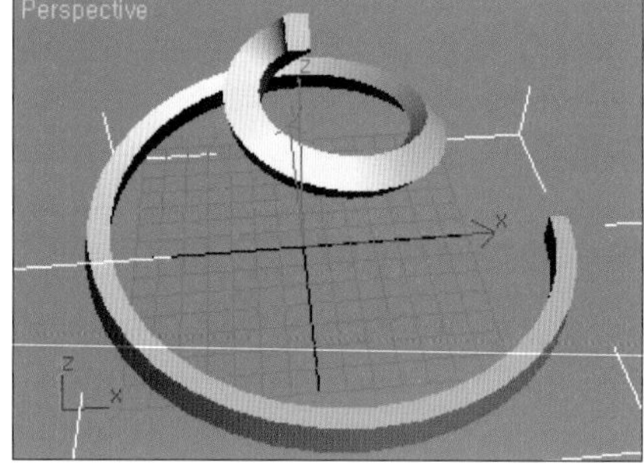

Rectangular

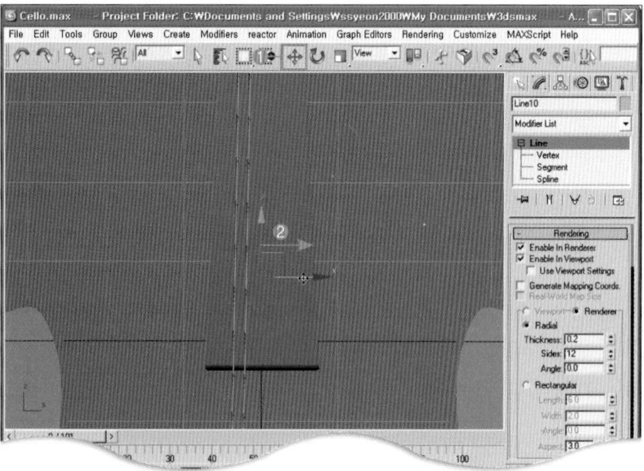

09 To create the rest of the lines, click [Select and Move] on the main toolbar, and, while holding <Shift>, click–and–drag the basic line towards the right.

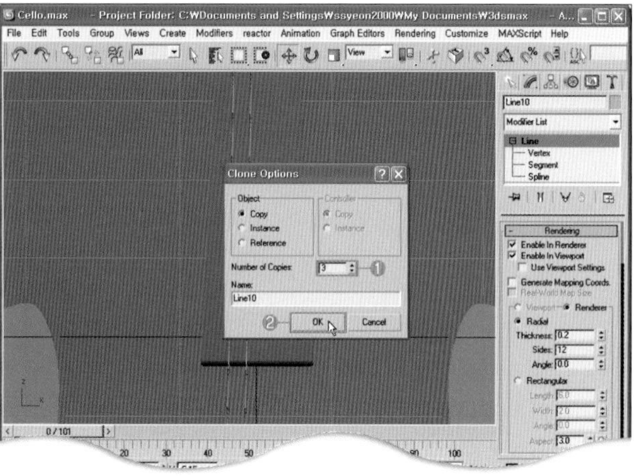

10 When the [Clone Options] dialog box appears, enter [3] for [Number of Copies], and click [OK] to finish the strings.

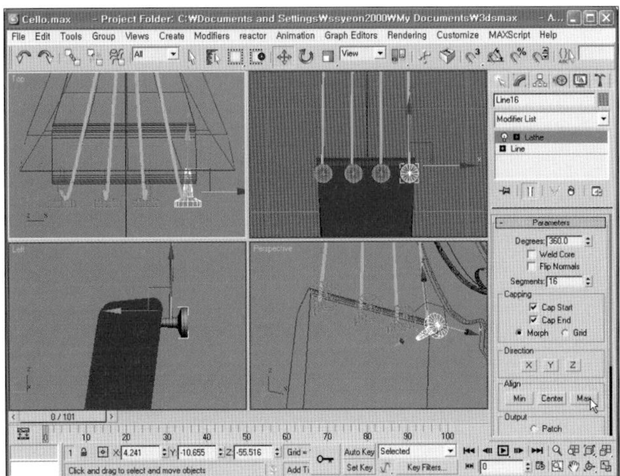

11 Add the fine tuners that hold the lower end of the cello strings using [Line] and the Lathe Modifier.

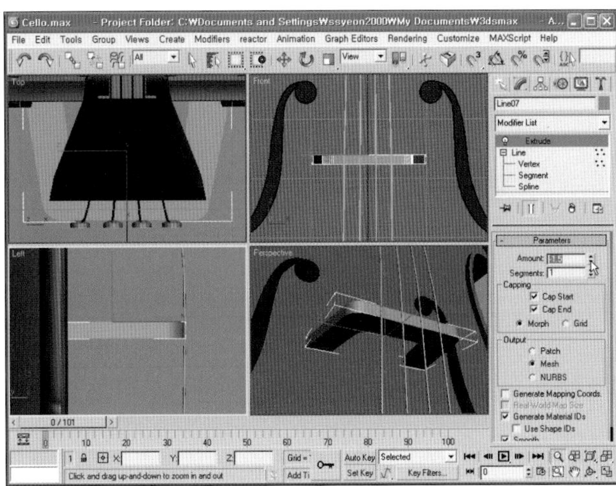

12 Add the cello bridge, which supports the strings in the middle of the cello, using [Line] and the Extrude Modifier.

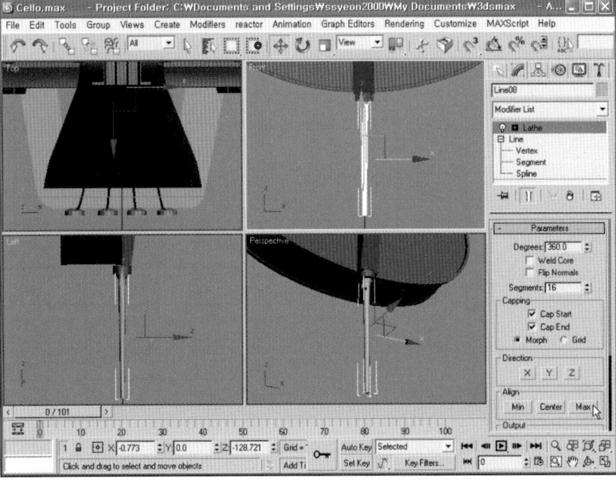

13 To create the endpin, the lower support for the cello, use [Line] and the Lathe Modifier, as shown.

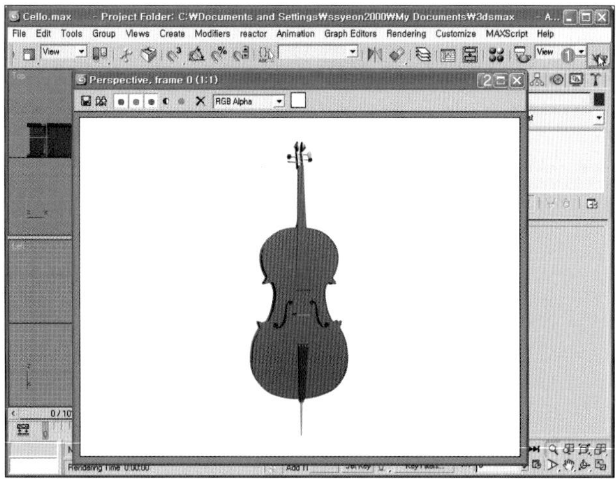

14 Select the Perspective Viewport, and select [Quick Render] on the main toolbar to see the rendered shape. Click on the rendered image window to close it.

Supplementary CD\Sample\Chapter 3\Exercise 3\Cello–final.max

Mapping a Wood Pattern

For modeling that requires careful attention to detail, making mapping sources using the Unwrap UVW Modifier is recommended. In this example, the side body of the cello is to be perpendicular to the front part, and without using the Unwrap UVW Modifier, the object may appear unnatural.

① Select the body of the cello, click the [Modifier List] combo box, and select [UVW Map]. Select the [Face] sub-object of the [Unwrap UVW] Modifier, and select the front part of the cello body.

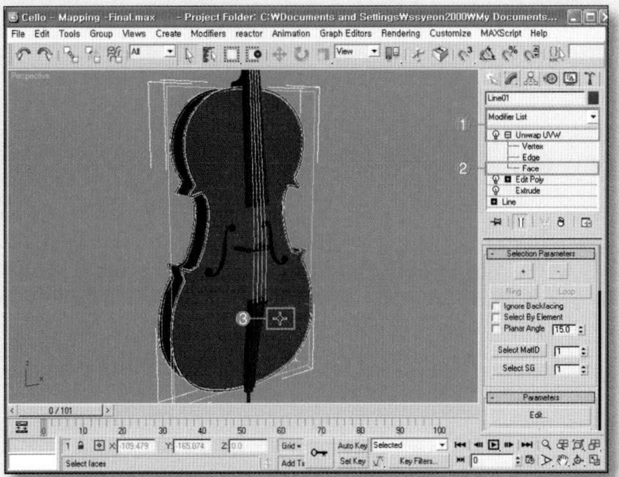

② Under [Unwrap UVW]–[Map Parameters], click [Planar] to spread the selected front polygon.

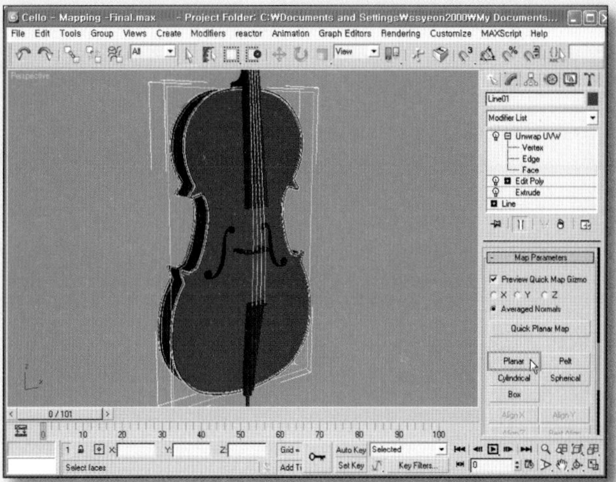

③ When the [Edit UVWs] window appears, place the front polygon at an appropriate location, as shown, then select the back and side polygons of the cello and place them for creating the mapping source.

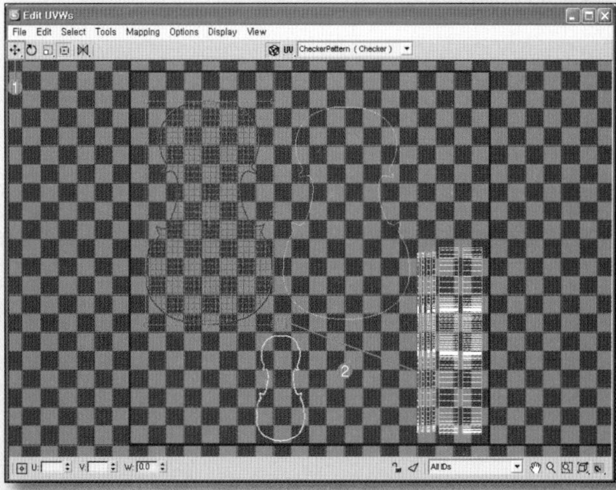

④ Complete the mapping source image according to the fields in the [Edit UVWs] window, and align the images in the [Edit UVWs] window.

Supplementary CD\Sample\Chapter 3\Exercise 3\Cello body.psd

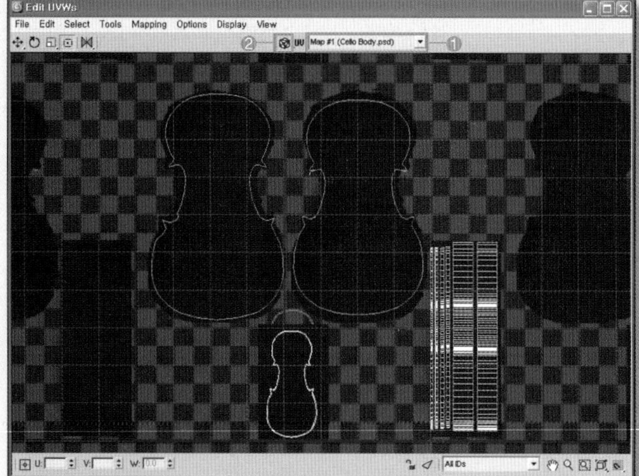

⑤ To make the mapping source image appear in the Viewport, click [Material Editor] on the main toolbar to show the Material Editor options. Select the first sample slot and click None for [Diffuse Color] to open the material/map browser. Select [Bitmap] at the material/map browser, and click [OK]. Apply the "Cello body.psd" file created with PhotoShop, and click [Show Map in Viewport] and [Assign Material to Selection] to apply the surface texture to the selected object.

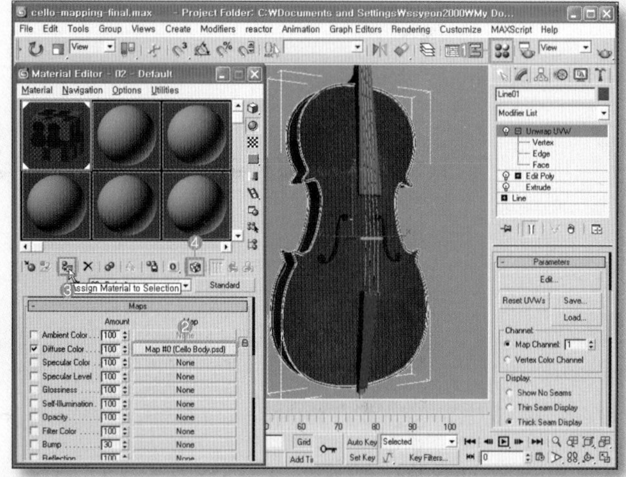

⑥ Complete the mapping by using the Unwrap UVW Modifier for the rest of the cello parts.

Supplementary CD\Sample\Chapter 3\Exercise 3\Cello-mapping-final.max

Exercise 04

Modeling an F–15 Fighter Jet Cylinder

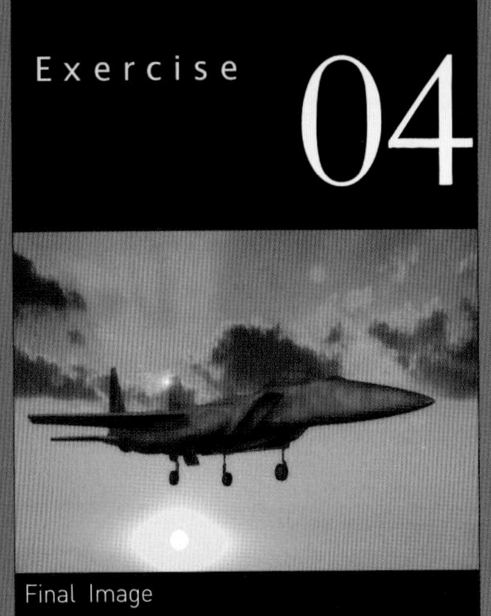
Final Image

Modeling an F–15 fighter jet may seem difficult, but it can be created in several simple steps. The most important part of an F–15 is the body, which has an elegant aerodynamic shape. Therefore, it is best to start with using a cylinder.

Final File
\Sample\Chapter 3\Exercise 4\F15–mapping–final.max

Using Cylinder to Form the Basic Structure

First, create a cylinder and manipulate the necessary vertices to form the nose. This will begin the basic structure of the fighter jet.

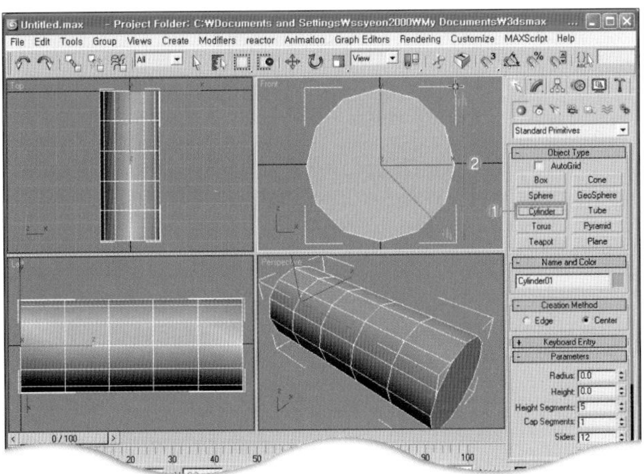

01 Open a new file and go to the Create panel. Click [Geometry]–[Standard Primitives]–. Click–and–drag in the Front Viewport along the absolute axis to create a new cylinder.

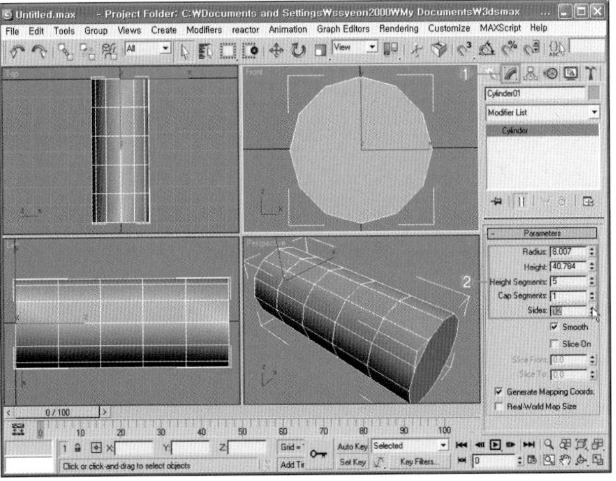

02 With "Cylinder01" selected, move to the Modify panel, and set the [Parameters]. Enter [8] for [Radius], [40] for [Height], [5] for Height Segment], [1] for [Cap Segment], and [12] for [Sides].

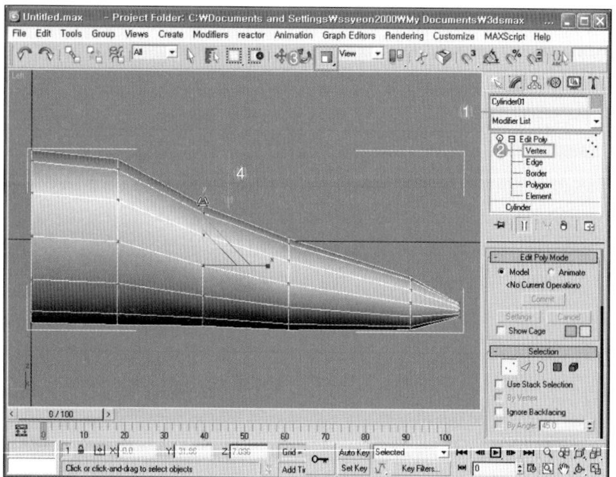

03 Click the [Modifier List] combo box, and select the [Edit Poly] Modifier. Select the [Vertex] sub–object of the [Edit Poly] Modifier, and click [Select and Scale] on the main toolbar. Then, change the vertical positions of the vertices in the Left Viewport as shown in the picture.

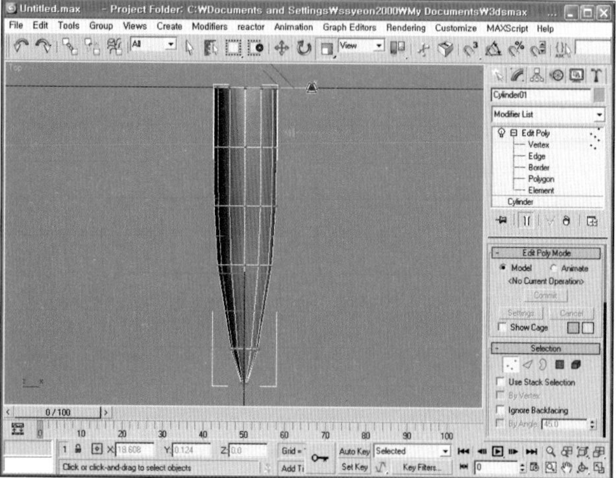

04 In the same way, change the positions of the vertices in the Top Viewport as shown.

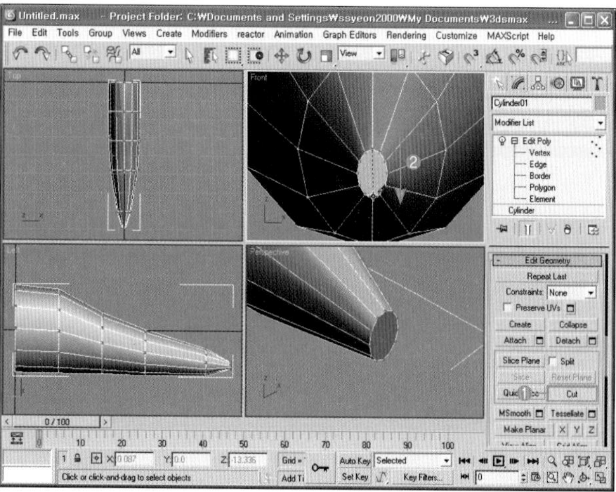

05 In the Front Viewport, zoom in on the front part of the "Cylinder01" object, click [Edit Geometry]–[Cut], and divide the polygon along the Y–axis.

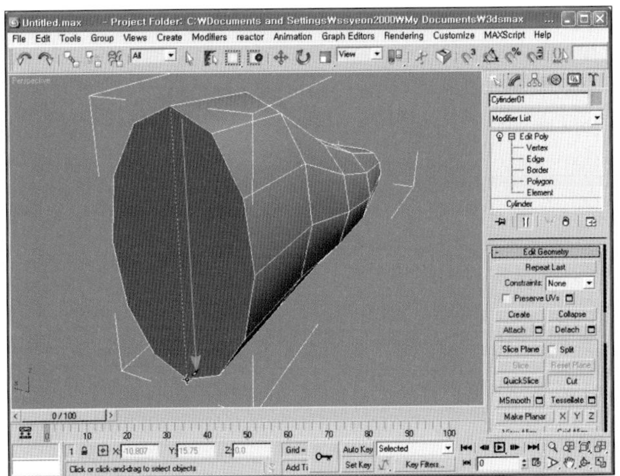

06 Follow the same steps to divide the back polygon of the "Cylinder01" object along the Y–axis.

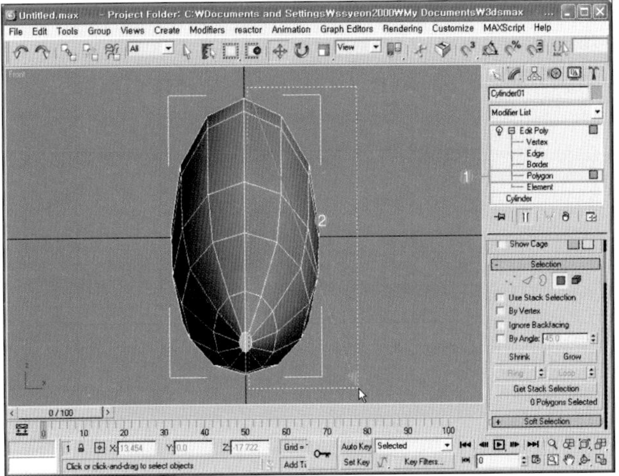

07 Select the [Polygon] sub–object of the [Edit Poly] modifier, and select the polygons by click–and–dragging the right half in the Front Viewport as shown.

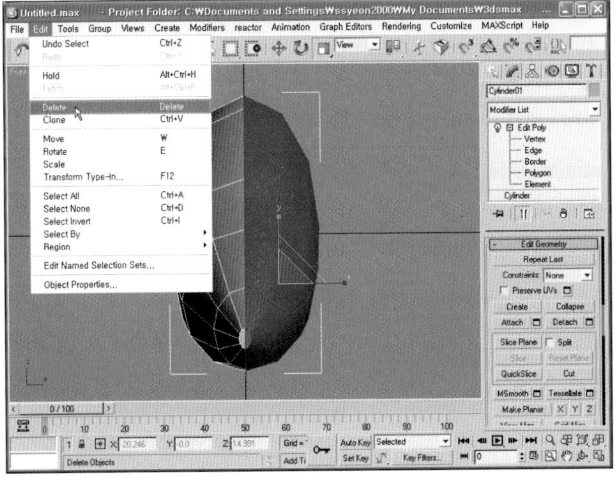

08 To delete the selected polygons, click [Edit]–[Delete] on the menu bar.

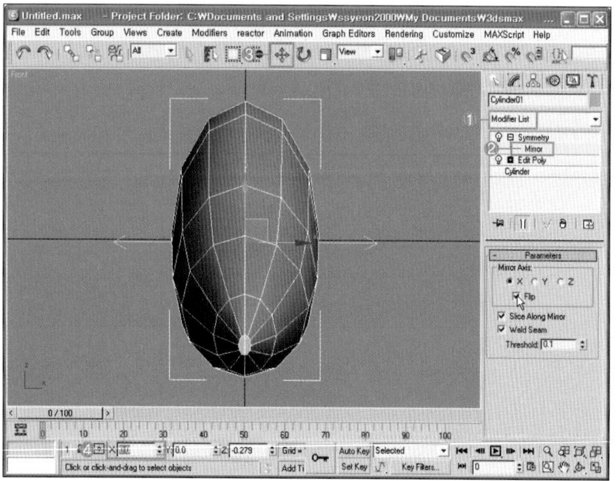

09 To create the opposite side of the cut shape, click the [Modifier List] combo box, and select [Symmetry]. Select the [Symmetry] Modifier's [Mirror] sub–object, click [Select and Move], and enter [0] for the X–axis in the coordinate input line.

10 From the [Modifier List] combo box, select the [MeshSmooth] Modifier, and click to deactivate the function. Select the [Vertex] sub–object of [Edit Poly] Modifier, and move the left vertex in the Top Viewport. The user will see the other vertices on the right moving together.

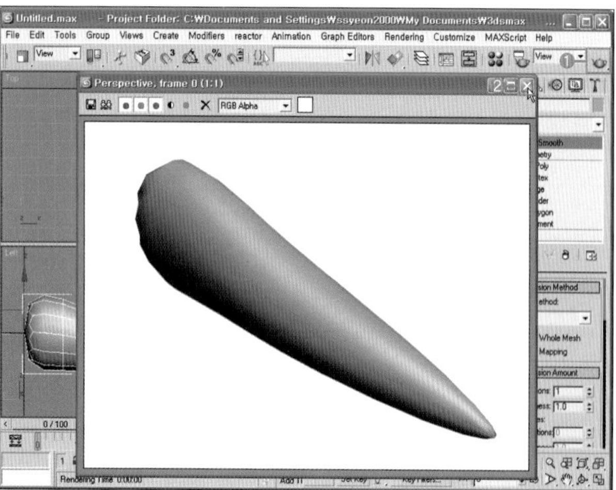

11 Activate the of the [MeshSmooth] Modifier, select the Perspective Viewport, and click [Quick Render] on the main toolbar to see the rendered shape. Click on the rendered image window to close it.

Completing the Body Using Extrude

Let's use [Extrude] to create the pilot seat, air inlet, and the jet orifice of the fighter jet. The process of editing the soft curves of the F–15 fighter jet requires much careful attention.

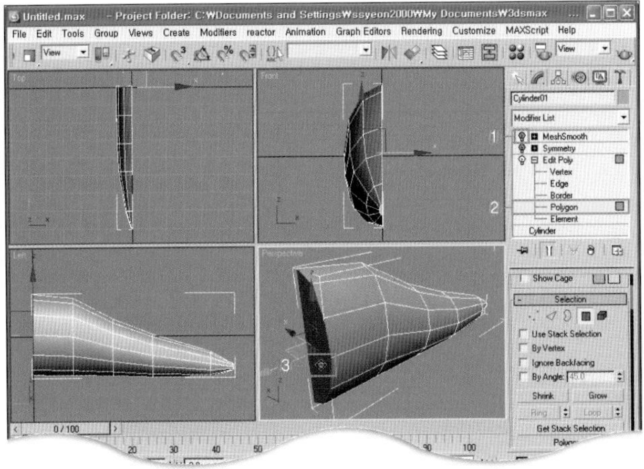

01 Click of both the [MeshSmooth] and [Symmetry] Modifiers to deactivate them. Select the [Polygon] sub–object of the [Edit Poly] Modifier, and select the rear part of the "Cylinder01" object.

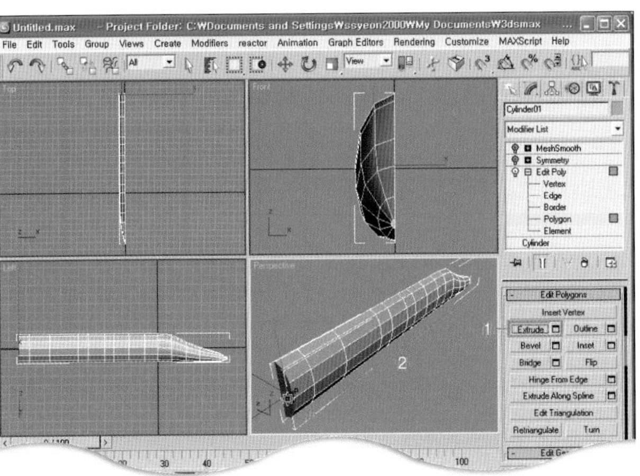

02 Click [Edit Polygons]–Extrude, and extrude the polygon by dragging nine times in the Perspective Viewport as shown in the picture.

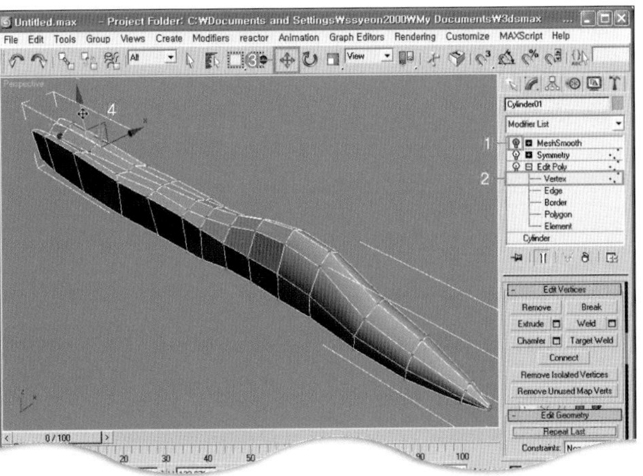

03 Click of the [Symmetry] Modifier, and select the [Vertex] sub–object of the [Edit Poly] Modifier. Click [Select and Move] on the main toolbar, and create the central part of the F–15 fighter jet.

tip >>

Polishing the Details

The details of the F–15 model will differ depending on the effort invested in completing the model. The remaining parts cannot be expressed smoothly unless the curve connecting the pilot seat and the jet orifice at the back is elegant and smooth.

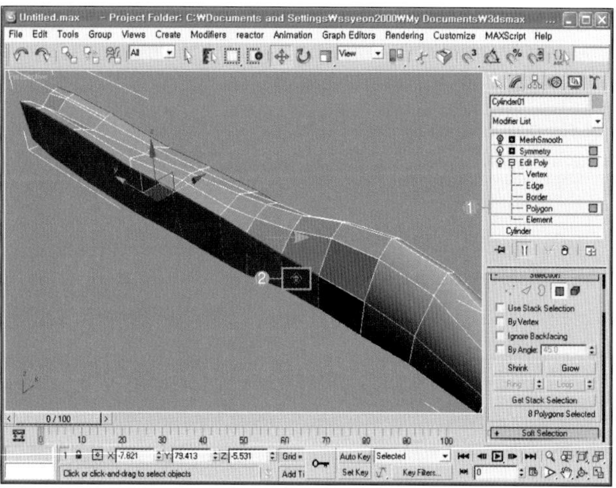

04 Select the [Polygon] sub–object of the [Edit Poly] Modifier, and, while pressing <Ctrl>, select the polygons to become the body of the F–15 fighter jet.

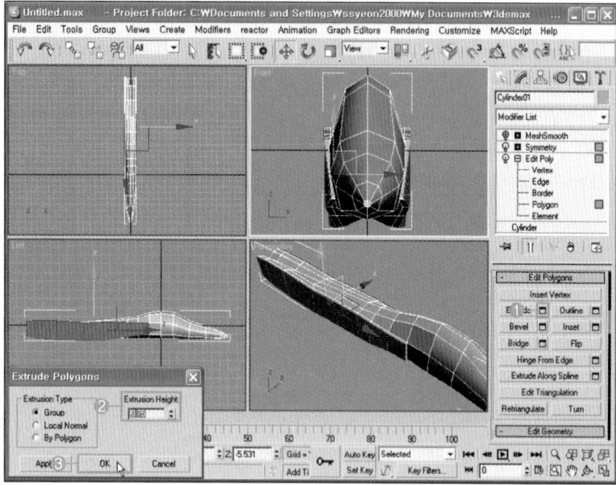

05 Click [Edit Polygons]–[Extrude Settings ▣]. In the [Extrude Polygons] dialog box, enter [0.75] for [Extrusion Height], and click [OK]. The selected polygon extrudes a little sideward according to the value entered.

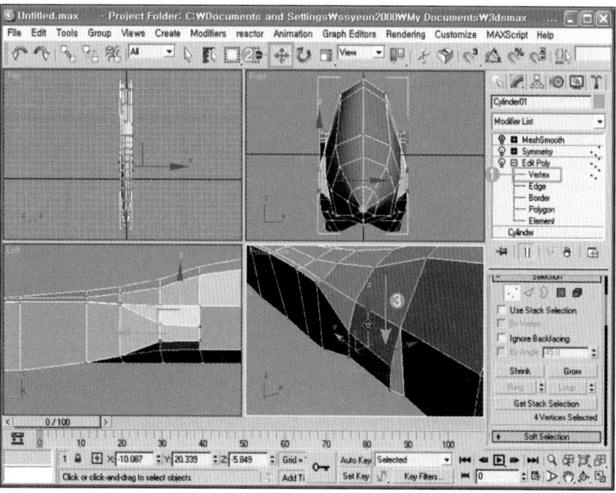

06 Select the [Vertex] sub–object of the [Edit Poly] Modifier, and move the vertex at the pilot seat slightly.

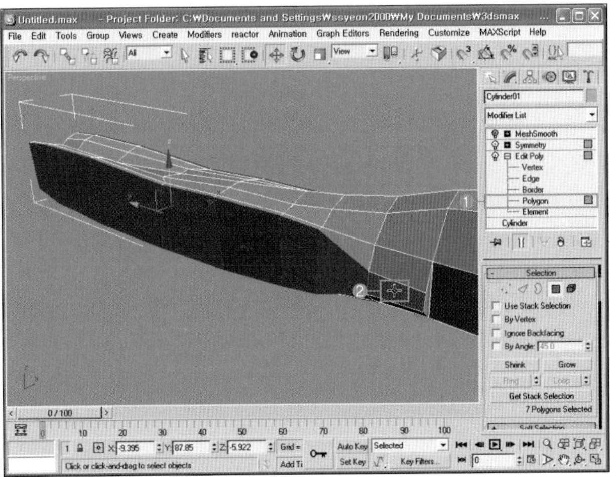

07 Select the [Polygon] sub–object of the [Edit Poly] Modifier, and select the body part polygons while pressing <Ctrl>.

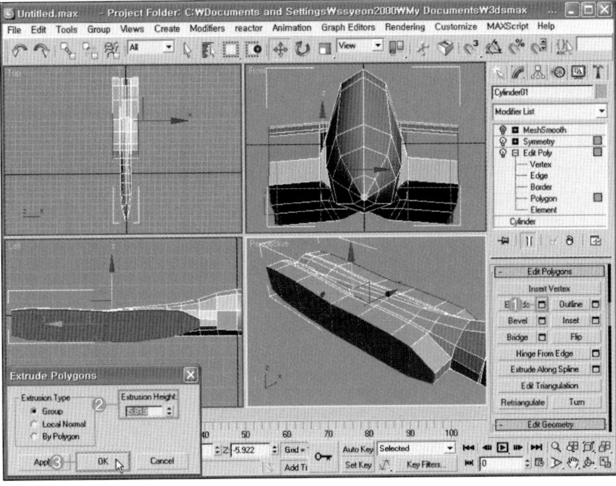

08 Activate the [Extrude Polygons] dialog box by clicking on [Edit Polygons]–[Extrude Settings ▣]. Enter [5.819] for [Extrusion Height], and click [OK]. The selected polygon extrudes a little sideward according to the entered value.

09 Select the [Vertex] sub–object of the [Edit Poly] Modifier, and modify the extruding polygons into square shapes.

Creating a Right-Angled Air Inlet 

It can be very difficult to create an air inlet from the square shape of the F–15. Let's examine the best way to do this.

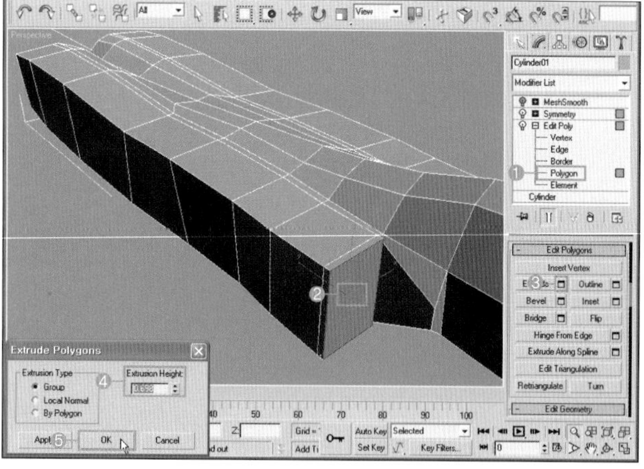

01 Select the [Polygon] sub–object of the [Edit Poly] Modifier, and select the polygon on the air inlet side of the F–15 fighter jet. Then, activate the [Extrude Polygons] dialog box by clicking on [Edit Polygons]–[Extrude Settings]. Enter [0.69] for [Extrusion Height], and click [OK]. The selected polygon extrudes forward according to the entered value.

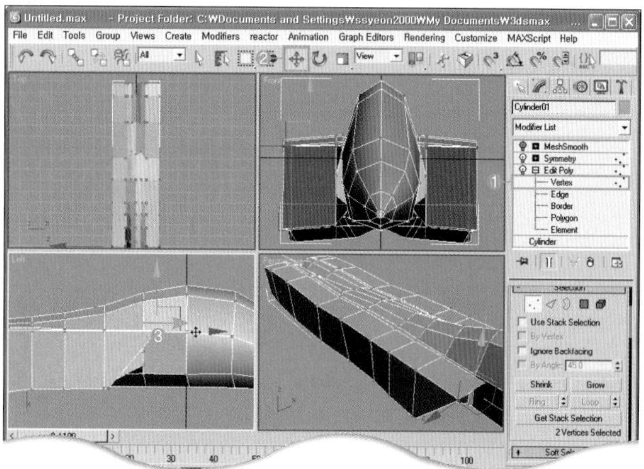

02 Select the [Vertex] sub–object of the [Edit Poly] Modifier, and, in the Left Viewport, sharpen the shape of the air inlet using [Select and Move].

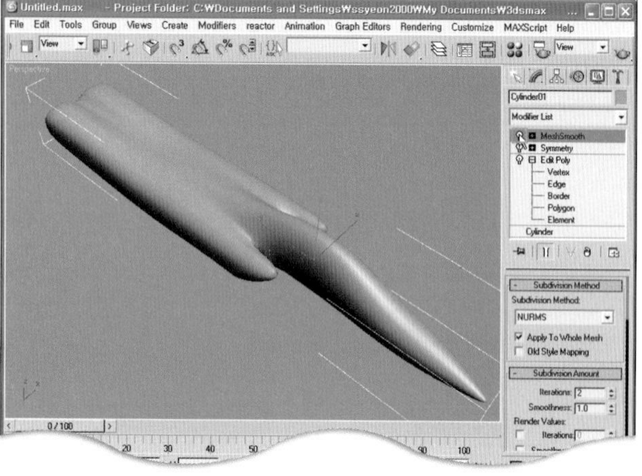

03 Click of the [MeshSmooth] Modifier to activate it, and look at the shape.

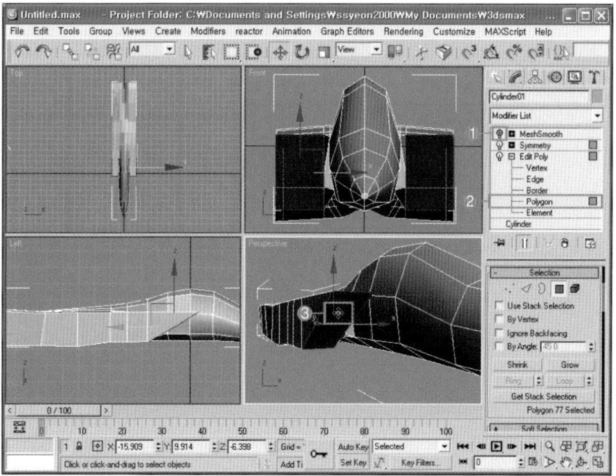

04 Click of the [MeshSmooth] Modifier to deactivate the function. Select the [Polygon] sub–object of the [Edit Poly] modifier, and click the inside of the air inlet to select it.

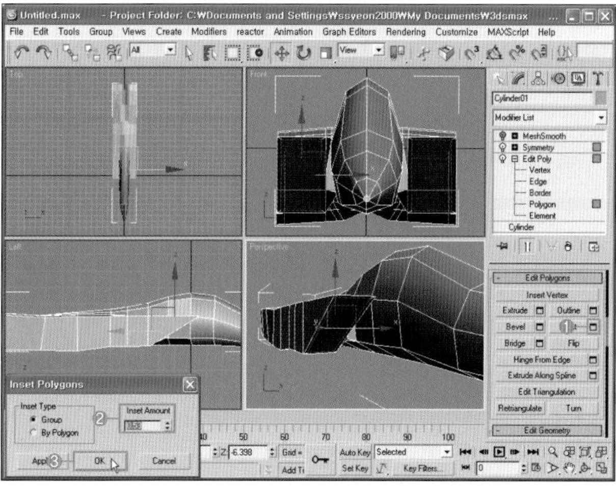

05 Activate the [Inset Polygons] dialog box by clicking [Edit Polygons]–[Inset Settings]. Enter [0.53] for [Inset Amount], and click [OK]. The selected polygon is divided into smaller polygons inward.

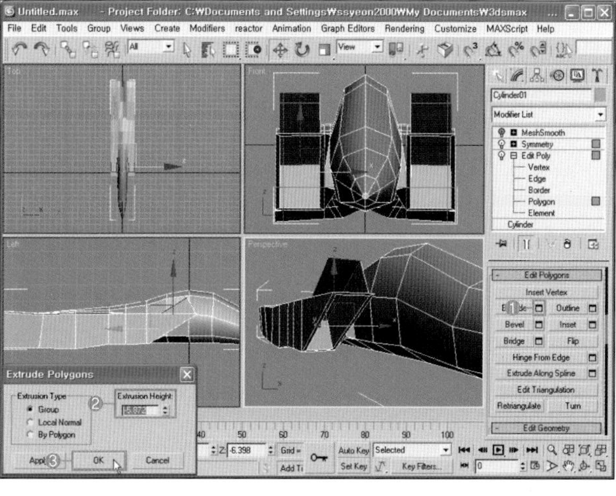

06 Activate the [Extrude Polygons] dialog box by clicking the [Edit Polygons]–[Extrude Settings]. Enter [–5.872] for [Extrusion Height], and click OK. The selected polygon folds inward according to the entered value.

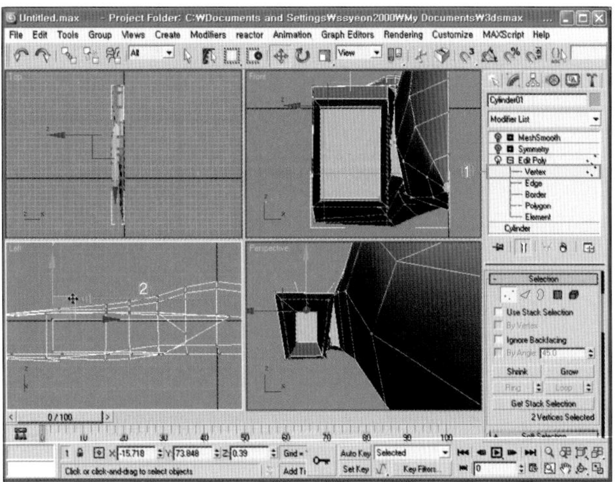

07 Select the [Vertex] sub-object of the [Edit Poly] Modifier, and move the vertices of the inward-folded polygon further into the air inlet.

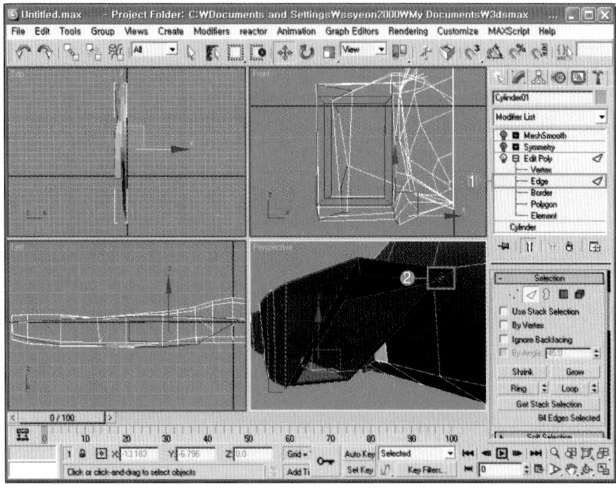

08 Select the [Edge] sub-object of the [Edit Poly] Modifier, and, while pressing <Ctrl>, select the edge on the air inlet as shown.

Selecting Edges for the Air Inlet

Note >>>

Only the crosswise and lengthwise edges are to be divided with the [Chamfer] function, and it is difficult to obtain a square as a result. To achieve this, the user must select the diagonal edges to create the desired result.

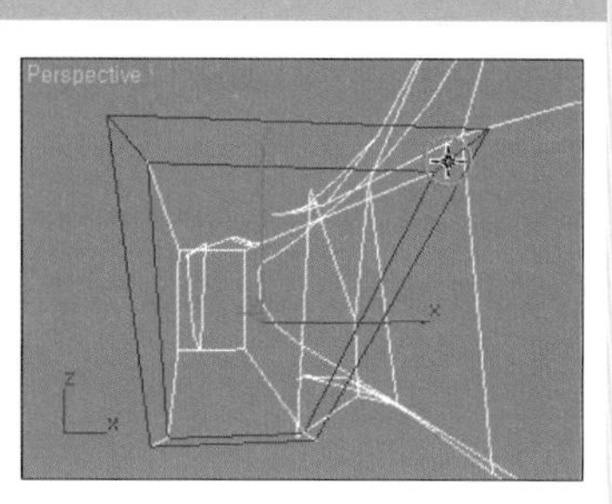

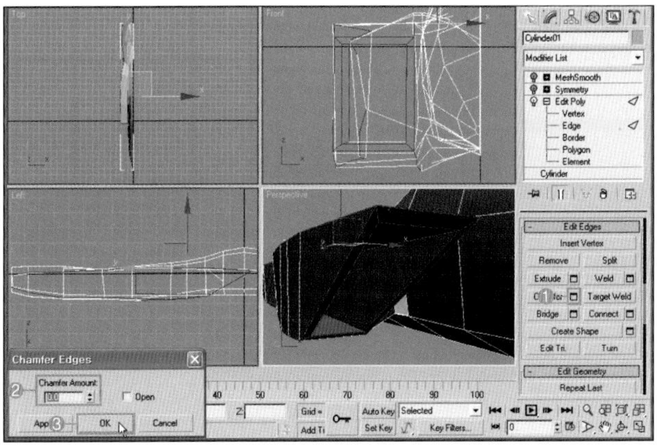

09 Activate the [Chamfer Edges] dialog box by clicking [Edit Edges]–[Chamfer Settings]. Enter [0] for [Chamfer Amount], and click [OK].

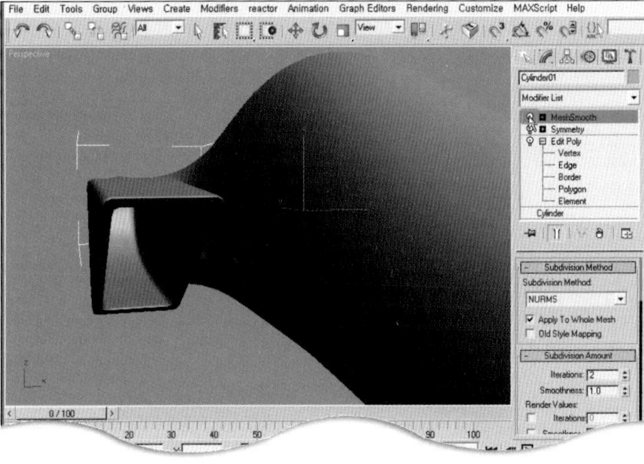

10 Click of the [MeshSmooth] Modifier to activate it, and look at the shape. You can see the exact square figure of the air inlet.

Expressing the F–15 Fighter Jet Orifice

Jet orifices can be easily created using the general [Extrude] feature.

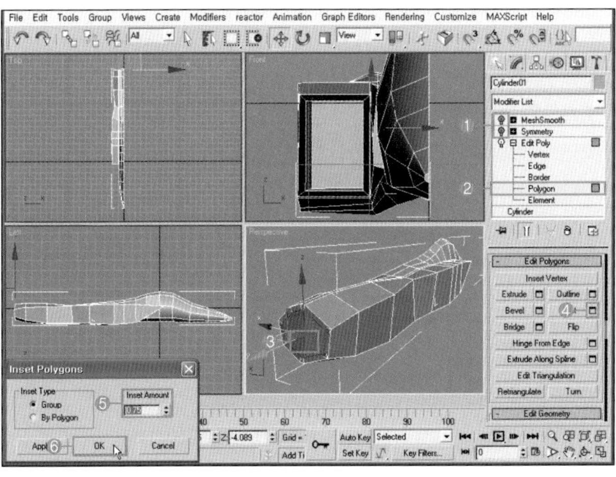

01 Click of both the [MeshSmooth] and [Symmetry] Modifiers to deactivate the functions. Select the [Polygon] sub–object of the [Edit Poly] Modifier, and select the polygon on the side of the F–15's jet orifice. Activate the [Inset Polygons] dialog box by clicking [Edit Polygons]–[Inset Settings]. Enter [0.75] for [Inset Amount], and click [OK]. The selected polygon is divided into smaller polygons inward.

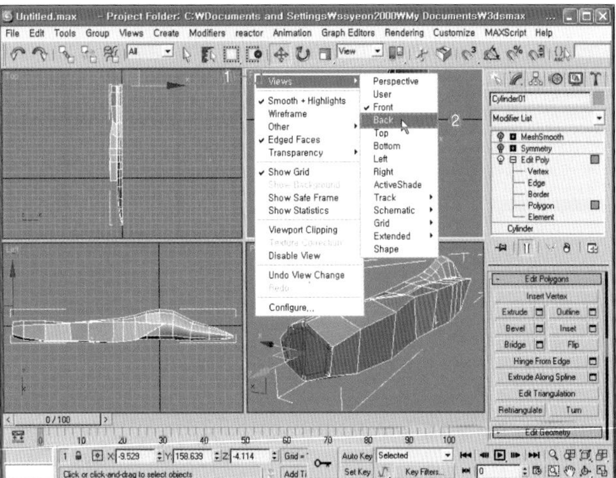

02 To see the back of the jet, click [Views]–[Back] in the Front Viewport.

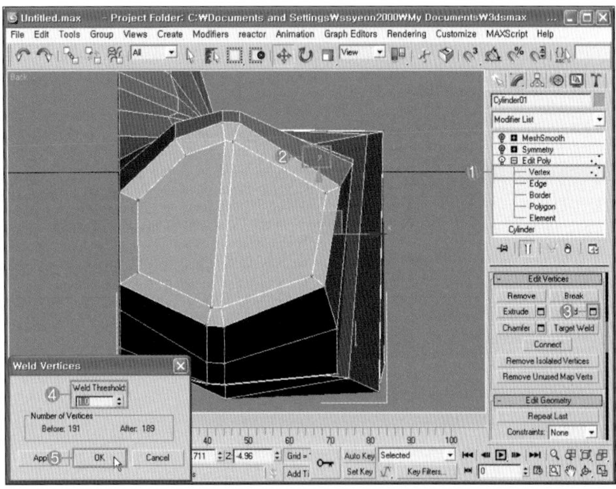

03 Select the [Vertex] sub–object of the [Edit Poly] Modifier, and select all of the vertices that are crossed in the Back Viewport. Activate the [Weld Vertices] dialog box by clicking [Edit Vertices]–[Weld Settings ▣]. Enter [1] for [Weld Vertices], and click [OK]. The vertices within the set distance are merged.

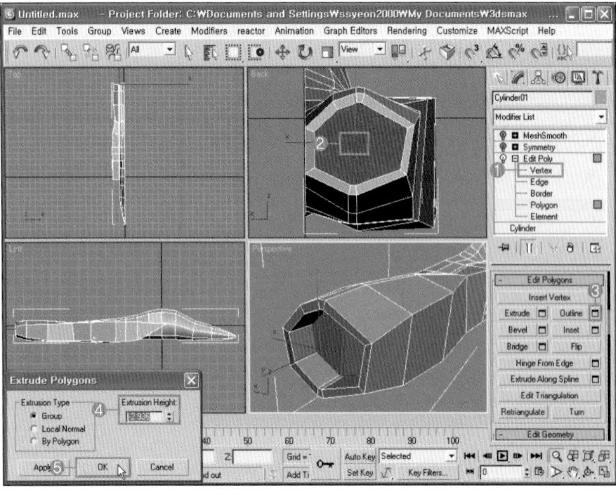

04 Select the [Polygon] sub–object of the [Edit Poly] modifier, and select the polygon on the jet orifice side. Activate the [Extrude Polygons] dialog box by clicking [Edit Polygons]–[Extrude Settings ▣]. Enter [–2.936] for [Extrusion Height], and click [OK]. The selected polygon folds inward according to the value entered.

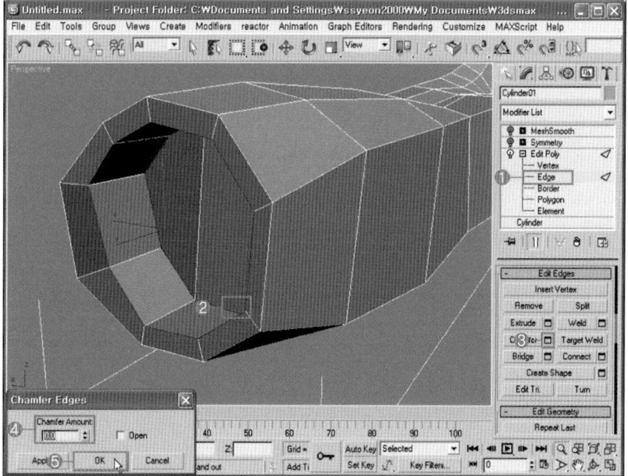

05 Select the [Edge] sub–object of the [Edit Poly] Modifier, and select the edges on the jet orifice's side. Activate the [Chamfer Edges] dialog box by clicking [Edit Edges]–[Chamfer Settings]. Enter [0] for [Chamfer Amount], and click [OK].

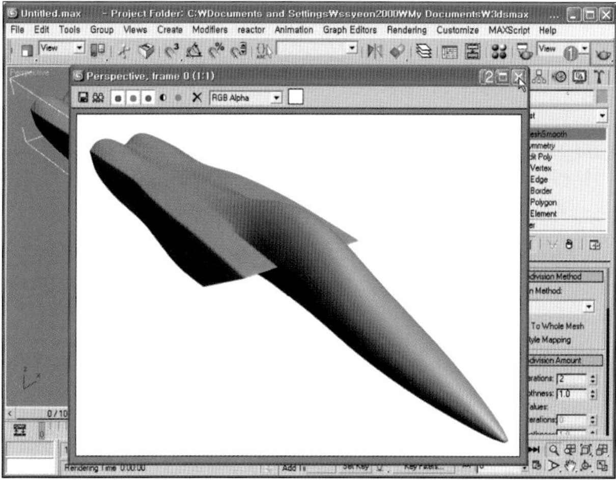

06 Click to activate of both the [MeshSmooth] and [Symmetry] Modifiers. Select the Perspective Viewport, and click [Quick Render] on the main toolbar to see the rendered shape. Click on the rendered image window to close it.

Creating the Cockpit 

Since the MeshSmooth Modifier is used, it can be very difficult to create the pilot seat. The Detach and ShapeMerge functions are good solutions. Their use is rather complicated, but worth learning.

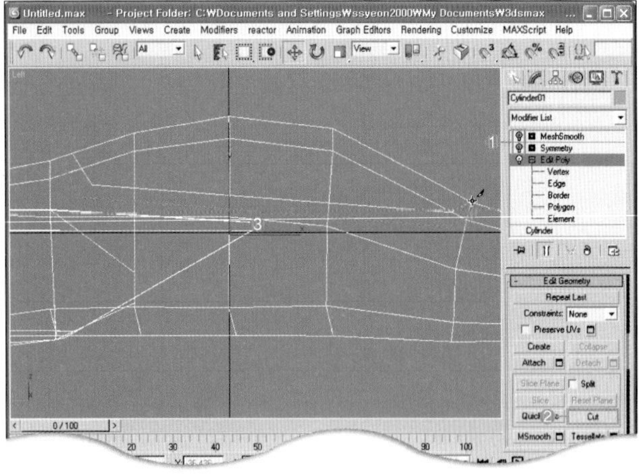

01 Click [light bulb icon] of both the [MeshSmooth] and [Symmetry] Modifiers to deactivate them. Zoom in the Left Viewport, and, using [Cut], divide the polygon at the pilot seat as shown in the picture.

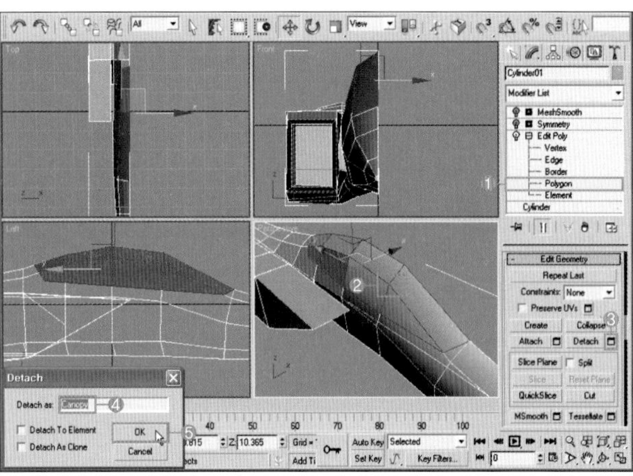

02 Select the [Polygon] sub–object of the [Edit Poly] Modifier, and the polygons at the pilot seat area. Activate the [Detach] dialog box by clicking [Edit Geometry]–[Detach]. Enter the name as "canopy", and click [OK].

03 Select the "canopy" object, and click the [Modifier List] combo box twice; once to select [Symmetry] and once to select [MeshSmooth]. Set the [MeshSmooth] Modifier's [Iterations] as [2] to maintain the vertex of the jet body.

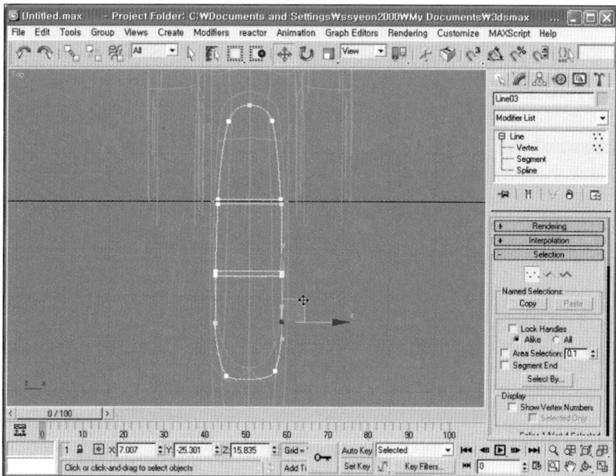

04 Zoom in the Top Viewport, go to the Create panel, and click [Shapes]–[Splines]–[Line]. Create lines in the shapes shown in the picture, and unite them with [Attach].

05 Move the set of lines above the "canopy" object. Select the "canopy" object, and click [Geometry]–[Compound Objects]–[ShapeMerge]. Then, click [Pick Shape], and select the newly created line.

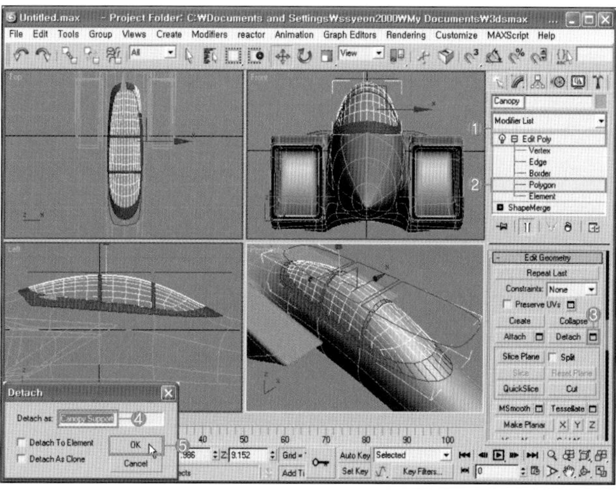

06 With the "canopy" object selected, click the [Modifier List] combo box and select [Edit Poly]. Select the [Polygon] sub–object of the [Edit Poly] Modifier, and select the canopy frame polygons. Activate the [Detach] dialog box by clicking [Edit Geometry]–[Detach]. Enter the name as "canopy support", and click [OK].

tip >>

One Inconvenience of 3ds Max 9

Up to the last version of 3ds Max, the slice of polygons was automatically selected by adding the [Edit Poly] Modifier after using [Shape Merge]; however, in 3ds Max 9, the automatic selection function has been removed. Therefore, it is necessary to select the desired polygons one by one. This is one inconvenience of the current version.

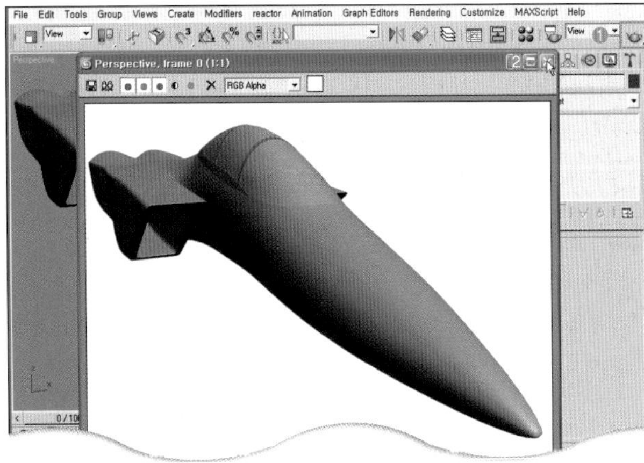

07 Select the Perspective Viewport, and click [Quick Render] on the main toolbar to see the rendered shape. Click on the rendered image window to close it.

Creating the Fuel Drum and Wings

There are fuel drums on either side of the F–15 fighter jet, and the wings protrude from them. To make these, let's learn how to edit with a box as the basic format.

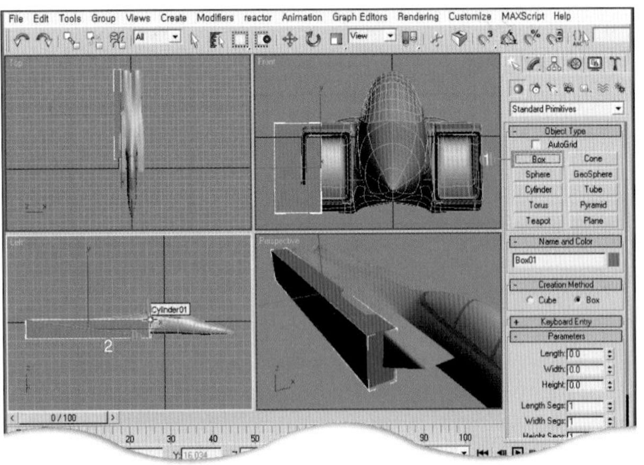

01 On the Create panel, click [Geometry]–[Standard Primitives]–Box. Click–and–drag in the Left Viewport as shown in the picture to create a box for the fuel drum.

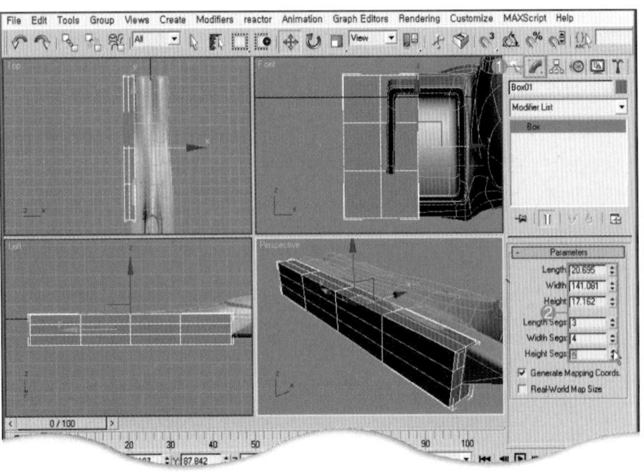

02 With the previously created "Box01" object selected, move to the Modify panel, and set the [Parameters]. Enter [20] for [Length], [141] for [Width], [17] for [Height], [3] for [Length Segs], [4] for [Width Segs], and [2] for [Height Segs].

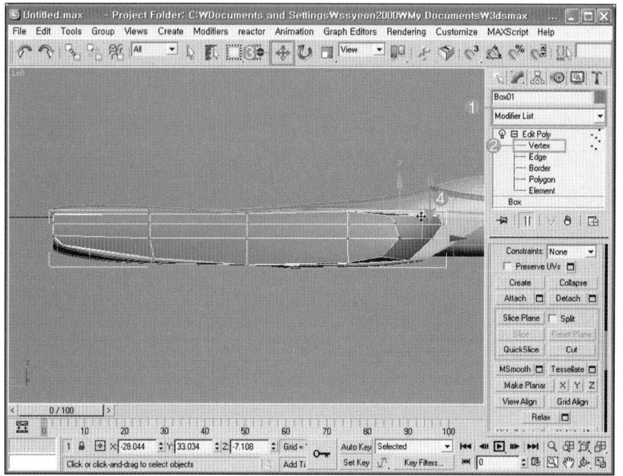

03 Click the [Modifier List] combo box, and select [Edit Poly]. Select the [Vertex] sub–object of the [Edit Poly] Modifier, and modify the shape in the Left Viewport with [Select and Move] as shown in the picture.

04 While checking each of the Viewports, modify the air inlet shape into the desired shape.

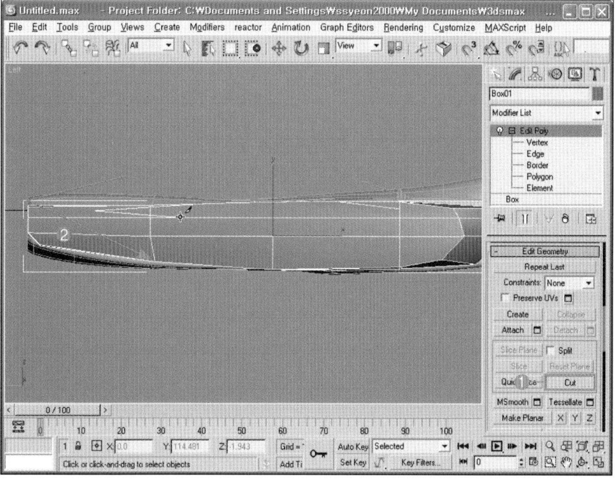

05 To create the polygon from which the wings will protrude, click Cut and divide the polygon in the Left Viewport as shown.

06 Select the [Polygon] sub–object of the [Edit Poly] Modifier, and, while pressing <Ctrl>, select the polygons from which the wings protrude. Activate the [Extrude Polygons] dialog box by clicking [Edit Polygons]–[Extrude Settings]. Enter [41.777] for [Extrusion Height], and click [OK]. The selected polygons extrude sideward according to the value entered.

07 Click [Select and Scale] on the main toolbar, and reduce the extruding polygon's size in the Top Viewport as shown.

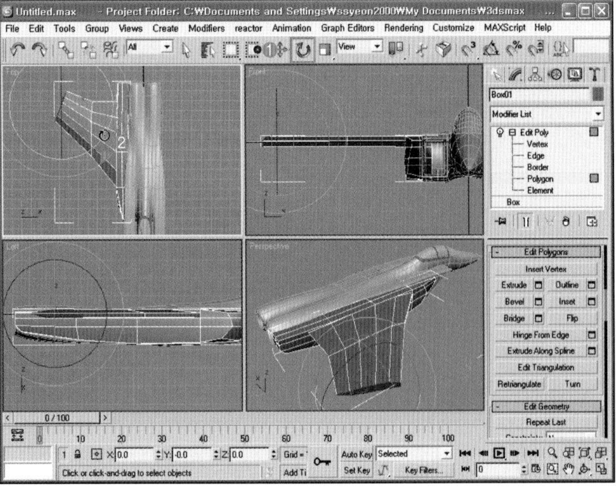

08 Extrude the wing once again with [Extrude], click [Select and Rotate] on the main toolbar, and rotate it slightly in the Top Viewport.

09 In the same way, create the tail wing. Select the [Vertex] sub–object of the [Edit Poly] modifier, and modify its shape.

10 To create the other wing, click the [Modifier List] combo box, and select [Symmetry].

11 Click the [Modifier List] combo box, and select [MeshSmooth]. Then, select the [Edge] sub–object of the [Edit Poly] Modifier, select the edges that should look sharp, and complete the shape by dividing the edge in two with [Chamfer].

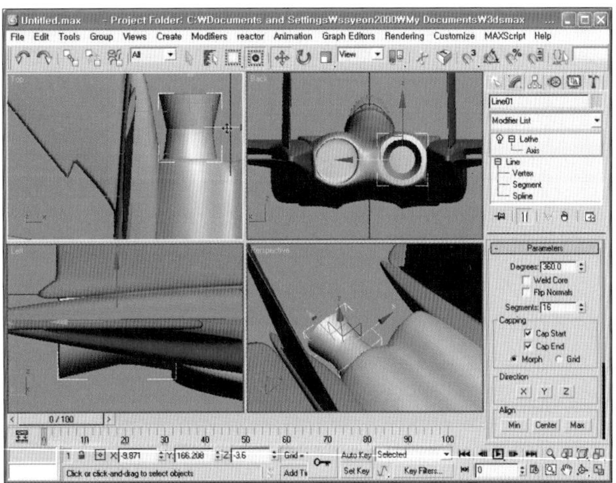

12 Create a section for the jet orifice in the Top Viewport, and complete by rotating with the [Lathe] Modifier.

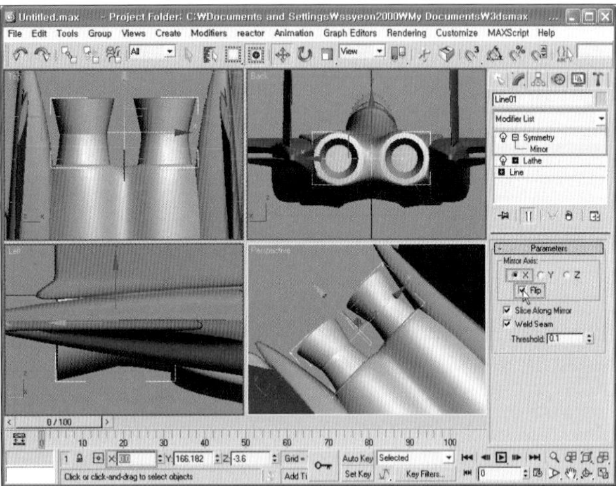

13 Click the [Modifier List] combo box, select the [Symmetry] Modifier, and then the [Mirror] sub–object, and enter [0] for the X–axis to create the other jet orifice.

14 To create a support for the front wheels of the jet, model the landing gear using previously learned methods, and unite them all with [Attach].

Supplementary CD\Sample\Chapter 3\Exercise 4\Wheels support.max

15 In the same way, create the support for the rear wheels, and complete the other support with the [Symmetry] Modifier.

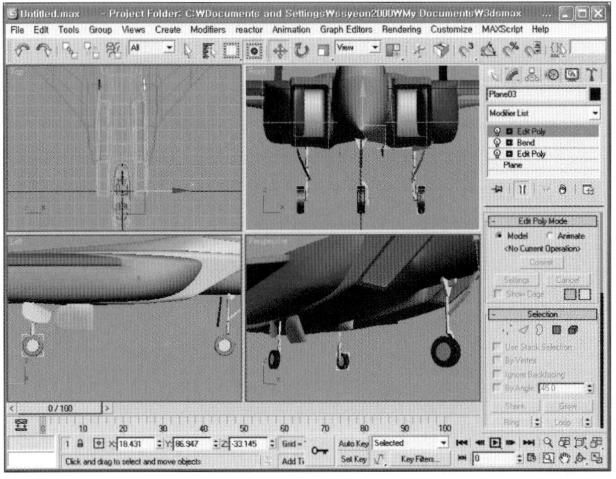

16 Create each of the jet wheels with [Cylinder], or create one and copy it to the other locations.

17 Select the canopy object, right–click on it to open the quad menu, and hide the canopy with [Hide Selection].

18 Use [Cylinder] and [Box] to create the pilot seat.

19 Use [Box] and the [Edit Poly] modifier to create the seat for the cockpit, add it, and re–show the canopy that was hidden on the quad menu.

Supplementary CD\Sample\Chapter 3\Exercise 4\Cockpit.max

20 Add the auxiliary device of the wing to complete the shape of the jet.

Supplementary CD\Sample\Chapter 3\Exercise 4\Auxiliary device.max

21 Select the canopy object, open its quad menu, and select Properties. When the [Object Properties] dialog box appears, enter [0.3] for [Visibility] to make it semi–transparent.

22 Confirm the final version.

Supplementary CD\Sample\Chapter 3\Exercise 4\F15–final.max

Let's Go Pro!

Mapping the F–15 with the Unwrap UVW Modifier

Mapping an F–15 is difficult using the standard method because of its complicated surface. In order to make the surface look more authentic, flatten the surfaces using the Unwrap UVW Modifier, design the texture in Photoshop, then place that texture on the surfaces. The detailed usage of Unwrap UVW will be addressed in Chapter 5, so only the general process will be covered here.

① First, select the wing object. Then, click the 💡 of both the [Symmetry] and [MeshSmooth] Modifiers to deactivate them.

② To hide objects other than the wing, right–click to open the quad menu, and then select [Isolate Selection].

③ To simplify the handling of the different surfaces of a wing, assign unique material IDs to each of them. First, select the [Polygon] sub–object of the [Edit Poly] Modifier, select all of the surfaces of the body as shown in the picture, then enter [1] for [Polygon Properties]–[Set ID]. Assign the material "ID 2" to the main wing, and "ID 3" and "ID 4" respectively to the tail wings in the same way.

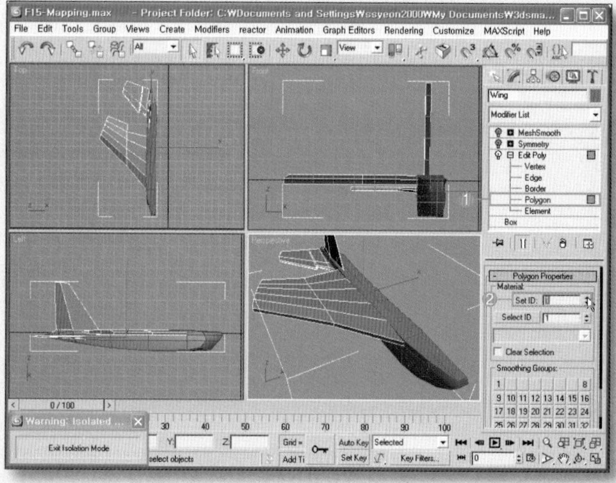

④ With the [Edit Poly] Modifier selected, click on the [Modifier List] combo box and select [Unwrap UVW]. Select the [Face] sub-object and enter [1] for [Selection Parameters]–[Select MatID], then click to select the corresponding surfaces.

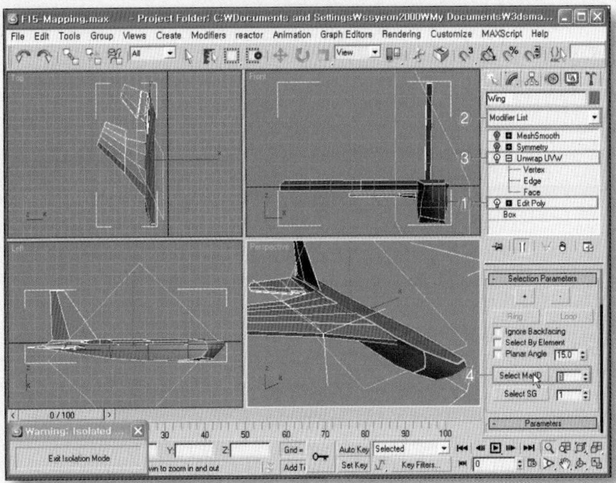

⑤ To gather the selected surfaces into one image, position the vertices using the [Edit UVWs] window. After assigning material IDs to the other surfaces, capture the blue region, and design the surface in Photoshop according to the picture.

Supplementary CD\Sample\Chapter 3\Exercise 4\Wing.psd, Body.psd

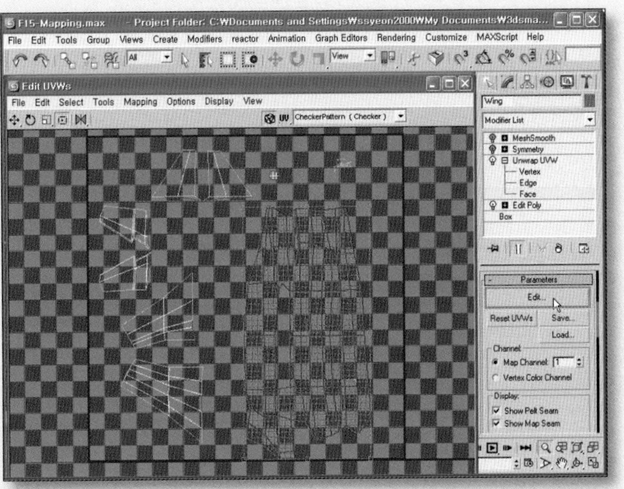

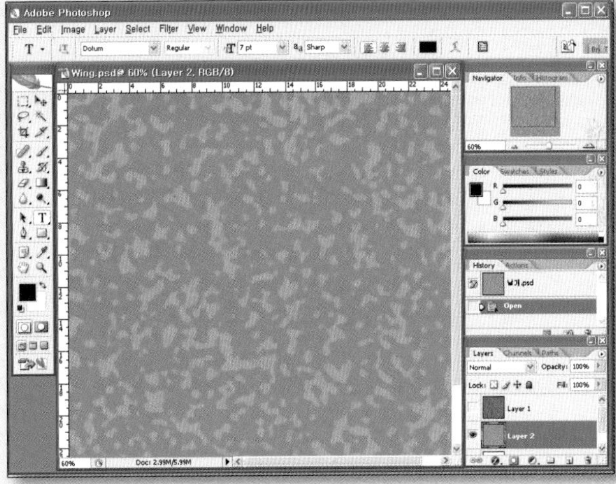

tip >>

Editing with Unwrap UVW

Editing the surface using [Unwrap UVW] is complex. This process will be dealt with in more detail in Chapter 4.

⑥ Open the image created with Photoshop from the [Edit UVWs] window of the [Unwrap UVW] Modifier, and adjust the images to the corresponding surfaces.

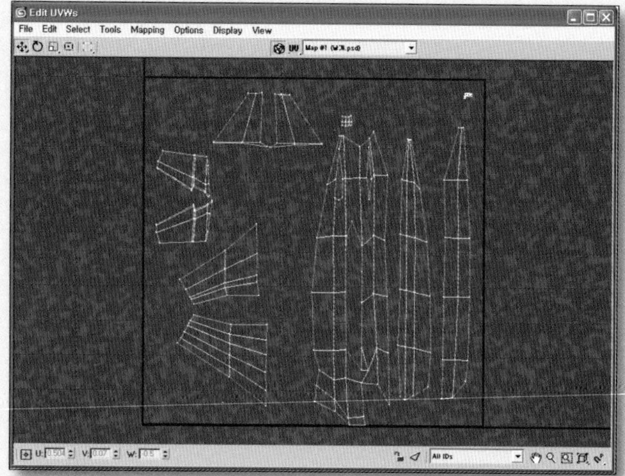

⑦ In order to view the adjustment results made to the [Unwrap UVW] Modifier in the Viewport in real time, map the image onto the wing in [Material Editor] mode. If the mapped image is not visible, repeat the adjustment process of positioning the vertices and surfaces with the [Edit UVWs] dialog box.

⑧ Map the body of the F-15 with this same method.

⑨ The following image is a rendering of a fighter jet.

Supplementary CD\Sample\Chapter 3\Exercise 4\F15-mapping-final.max

Chapter 4

Lights, Cameras, and Realistic Mapping

Even in objects that have been precisely and delicately modeled, it is difficult to convey a sense of reality without accurate light and shadow effects. For this, 3ds Max 9 provides various Lights and Cameras. The Light feature provides various effects for manipulating brightness, color, and range, as well as for creating shadows. The Cameras feature has several camera options as well. This chapter will demonstrate how to use Light to special effects methods, and how to handle a Camera to create dynamic scenes.
Mapping allows the user to add realism to an object by applying characteristic colors and materials. This section will discuss the key mapping techniques of 3ds Max 9, such as the Paint Mapping technique, which expresses real life textures, the Real–World Map Size technique, which maps with tools that are identical to the actual measuring tools, and the Unwrap technique, which enables the user to use all of the techniques of PhotoShop.

SECTION 01

Lights, Cameras, and the Basics of Mapping

The Light feature of 3ds Max 9 includes not only Standard Light, but also Photometric Light, which is used for building simulations and provides almost every function that can be expressed with light. The Camera feature provides all of the general functions of a real camera. Furthermore, this section will discuss mapping that will make an object look more realistic.

Standard Light

The value of Standard Light has decreased somewhat due to the advent of the more realistic Photometric Light feature, but it is still widely used for animations or the rendering of still objects. On the other hand, the mental ray renderer, highly esteemed for its fast speed and precise resolution, defaults to Standard Light.

Light Options

The Light feature on the Create panel offers Spot, Direct, and Omni, as well as Skylight, which gives a natural lighting effect, and two lights for mental ray rendering: mr Area Omni and mr Area Spot.

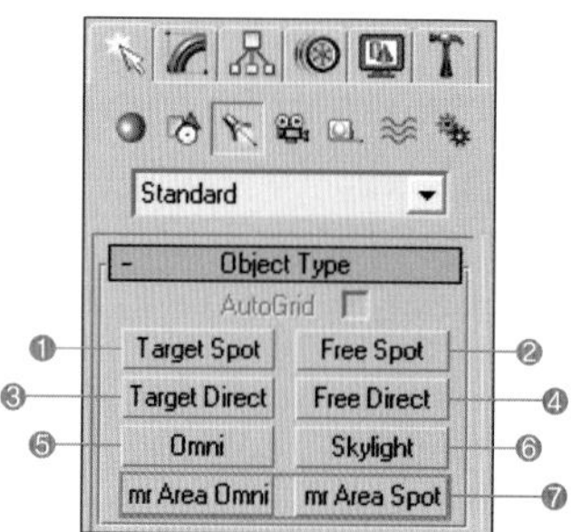

❶ **Target Spot**—Lights up the object on the screen from multiple directions.
❷ **Free Spot**—Directs a narrow beam at a fixed location.
❸ **Target Direct**—Simulates the multi–directional lighting of the sun.
❹ **Free Direct**—Simulates the sun, but as a narrow beam.
❺ **Omni**—Creates light sources such as incandescent electric lamps, light bulbs, or the sun.
❻ **Skylight**—Creates diffused light, like the sun on a cloudy day.
❼ **mr Area Omni/mr Area Spot**—Only useable when the mental ray renderer is active.

Light Source and Target

A Light is defined by the basic Light and Light Target. Light indicates the source of the light, and the Light Target means the area illuminated by the Light. The Light and Light Target can move together or separately. The Falloff area shows the range in which the Light becomes gradually weaker. This can be controlled by the parameters.

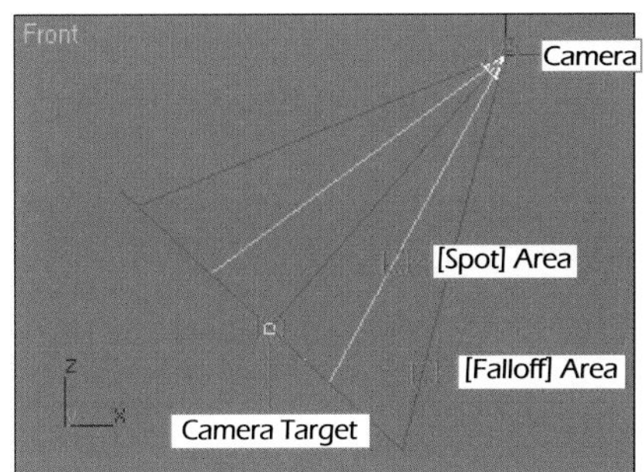

Light Parameters

After installing the Light in the Viewport, the user can create different effects by changing some or all of the elements in the Modify panel's parameters, such as the color and shadow settings. You can add effects, such as Fog, to the area illuminated by the light.

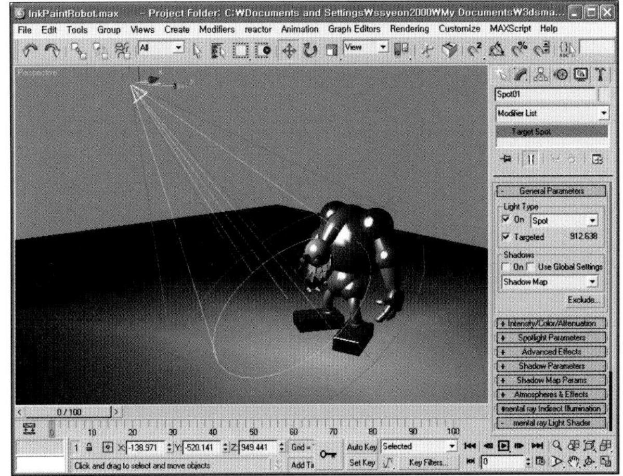

General Parameters

The Light can be turned on or off and the type of Light can also be changed. Moreover, the Target Light can be turned on or off, and the Free Light may be changed to a Target Light. In addition, the shadows can be selected, and the shadow effect can be turned on or off.

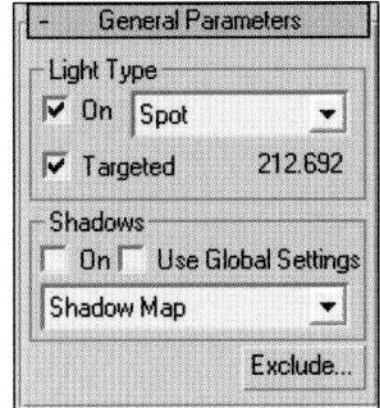

Intensity/Color/Attenuation

The Multiplier—the strength of the Light—and the color can be manipulated as well. The program offers the Decay function, which controls the diminution effect of the Light. The user can also control the Near and Far Attenuation point of the Light in detail.

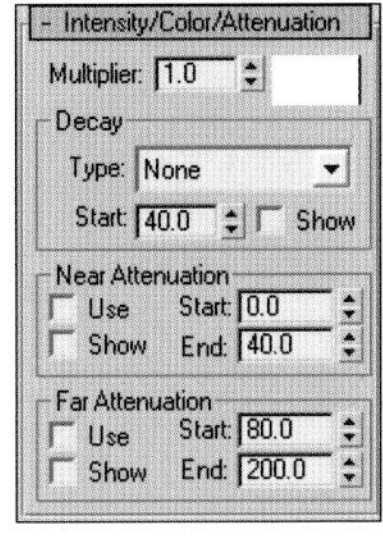

Spotlight Parameters

This is the part that appears differently depending on the type of Light. The user can change the shape and size of the Spot Light. Also, the user can adjust the area according to the proportion of the image's size using Bitmap Fit.

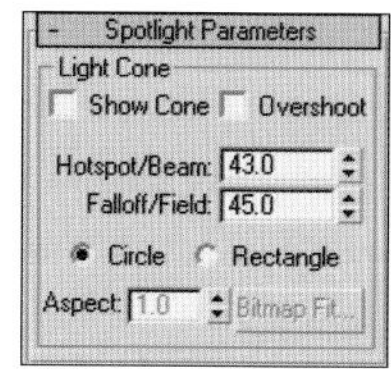

Advanced Effects

The user can selectively use Advanced Effects to control the segments that are brightly lit, the contrast, and the spreading form of light when projected on the object. Also, the program offers the Projector Map feature for inserting different effects in the middle of the lighting process.

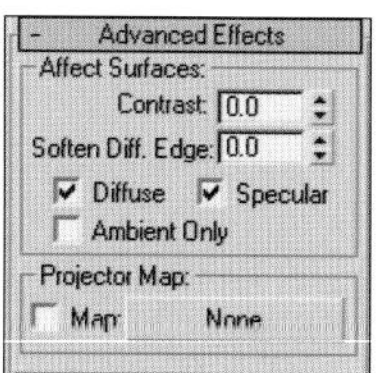

Shadow Parameters

Shadow Parameters involves detailed settings for strength and special effects applied to the shadow. Also, Atmosphere Shadows offers shadow effects for particles in the air.

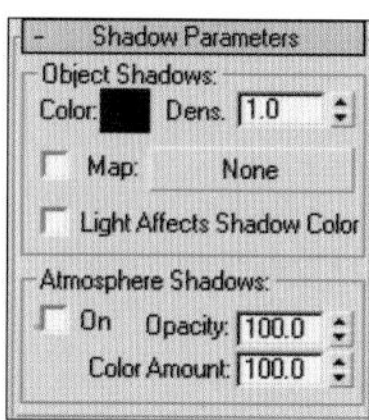

Shadow Map Params

Shadow Map Parameters allow detailed control over the diffusion and range of the shadow.

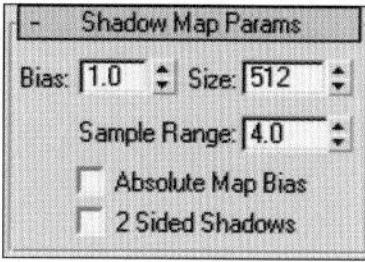

Atmosphere & Effects

The Atmosphere & Effects feature enables the user to add special effects to the lighted area. The user can use Volume Lights for fog effects and brightly illuminating Lens Effects. To add an effect, select it and click Add.

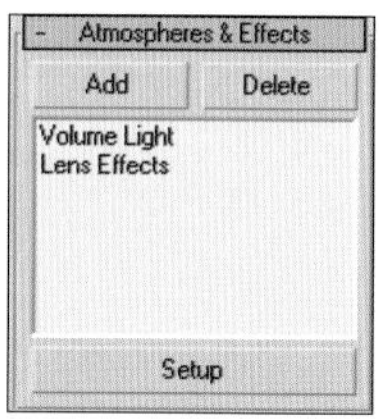

Mental Ray Parameters

This function, in the mental ray renderer, is where the user sets the energy value of the Light by calculating the Global Illumination.

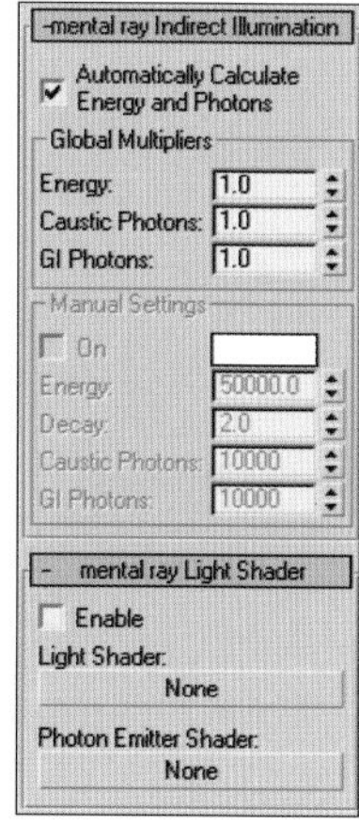

Using the Light Viewport

The Viewport can be changed over to the Light view. When the Light Viewport appears, the Viewport controls change accordingly.

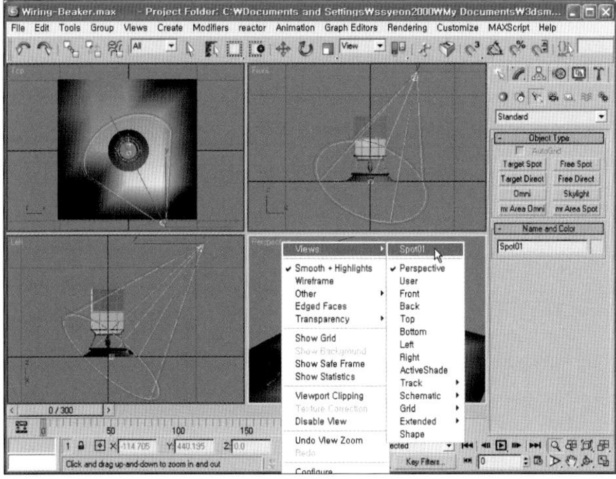

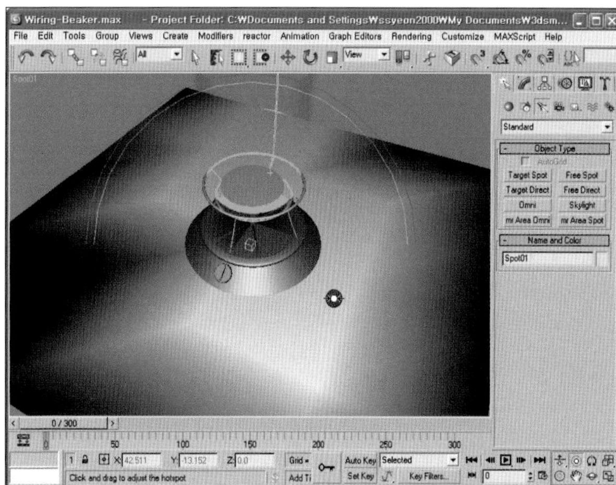

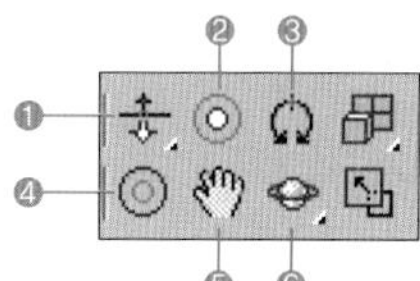

❶ **Dolly Light**—Moves the entire Light up and down.
❷ **Light Hotspot**—Changes the Hotspot area of the Light.
❸ **Roll Light**—Rotates the Light.
❹ **Light Falloff**—Changes the Falloff area of the Light.
❺ **Truck Light**—Moves the entire Light horizontally.
❻ **Orbit Light**—Moves the Light only, leaving the Light target the same.

Creating Realistic Lighting Effects with Photometric Light

For scenes that require realistic lighting effects, the user can use Photometric Light. This is primarily used to render buildings. The directions for use are similar to that of the Standard Light, but for precise lighting effects, click [Rendering]–[Advanced Lighting]–[Radiosity] on the menu bar for the Radiosity Solution calculation process.

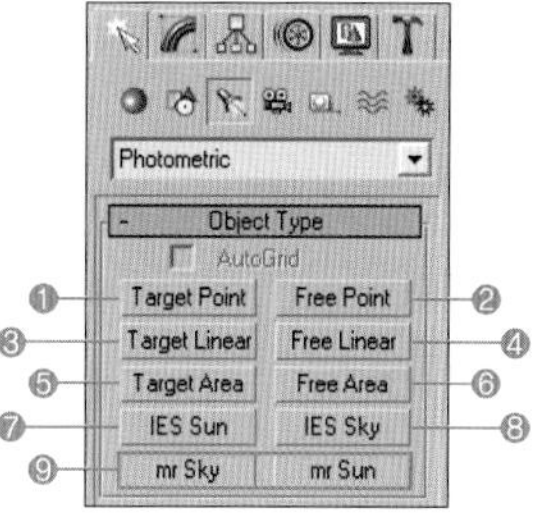

❶ **Target Point**—Light is projected in many directions. This can control light that is more elaborate than an Omni Light. It is capable of following a moving object.
❷ **Free Point**—Light is projected in many directions, but at fixed locations.

❸ **Target Linear**—Light is emitted straight in many directions, and is often used to express fluorescent light. It is capable of following a moving object.

❹ **Free Linear**—Light illuminates one location at a fixed position.

❺ **Target Area**—Light illuminates a certain area in various directions. The target can move around following the object. The data from professional lighting companies can be imported and used.

❻ **Free Area**—Light can illuminate a certain area at a fixed location.

❼ **IES Sun**—Light imitates the luminosity of the sun.

❽ **IES Sky**—Light imitates the diffusion of sunlight.

❾ **mr Sky/mr sun**—The setting of Render must be switched to the mental ray Renderer in order to get the best results.

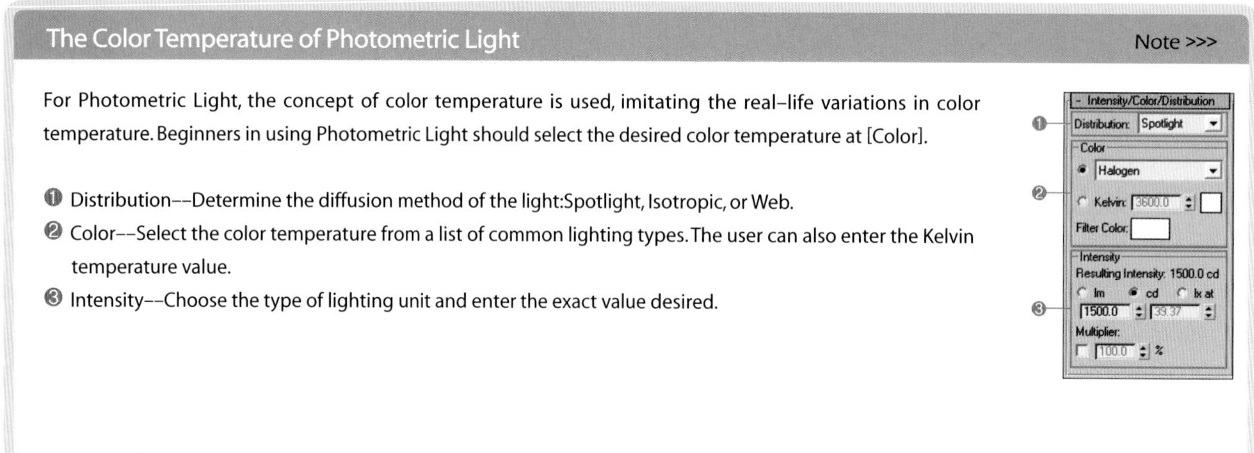

The Color Temperature of Photometric Light

Note >>>

For Photometric Light, the concept of color temperature is used, imitating the real-life variations in color temperature. Beginners in using Photometric Light should select the desired color temperature at [Color].

❶ Distribution--Determine the diffusion method of the light:Spotlight, Isotropic, or Web.

❷ Color--Select the color temperature from a list of common lighting types. The user can also enter the Kelvin temperature value.

❸ Intensity--Choose the type of lighting unit and enter the exact value desired.

Camera Handling for a Dynamic Screen

Let's examine the camera options available in the program.

Types and Installation of Cameras

The cameras provided by 3ds Max 9 include the Target Camera, which will follow if its target point moves, and the Free Camera, which has a fixed target point.

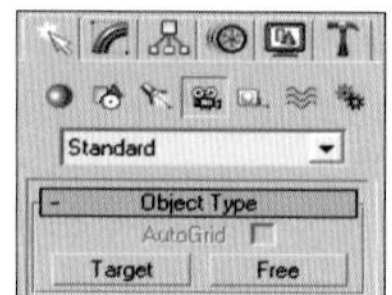

Target Camera photographs the object from various directions.

Free Camera can photograph in only one direction.

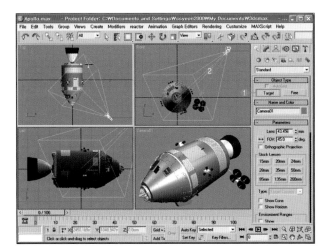

Camera parameters

After installing the camera, the user can control the camera's parameters on the Modify panel.

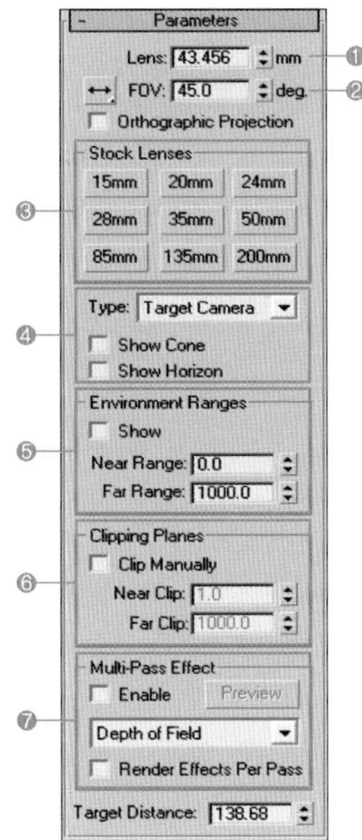

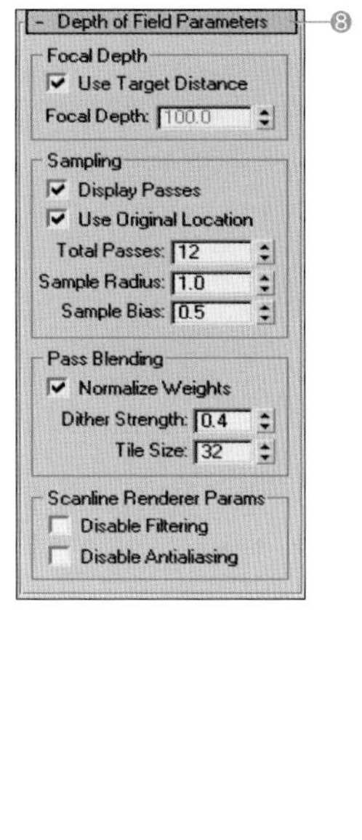

❶ **Lens**—Sets the size of the camera's lens.

❷ **FOV**—Controls the lens size by angle.

❸ **Stock Lenses**—The designated lens can be used just by clicking. The smaller the size of the lens, the more it becomes a wide–angle lens that distorts the screen. The bigger the size, the more it becomes a telephoto lens.

❹ **Type**—The user can change the type of camera, hide or show the viewing field icon (Show Cone), and hide or show the Horizon (Show Horizon).

❺ **Environment Ranges**—Determines the area photographed by the camera. Setting the Environment Ranges of the 3D space using virtual spaces is very important.

❻ **Clipping Planes**—Sets the Clipping area, cutting out objects that are outside of the range created by the entered values.

❼ **Multi–Pass Effect**—Emphasizes an object at a certain distance with Depth of Field, and blurs according to the speed of an object in motion with Motion Blur.

❽ **Depth of Field Parameters**—By selecting Depth of Field or Motion Blur, the user can confirm the respective parameters and control the effects.

Using the Camera's Viewport Control

By right–clicking on the Viewport's text label, the user can change over to the Viewport of an installed camera and control its movements and angles.

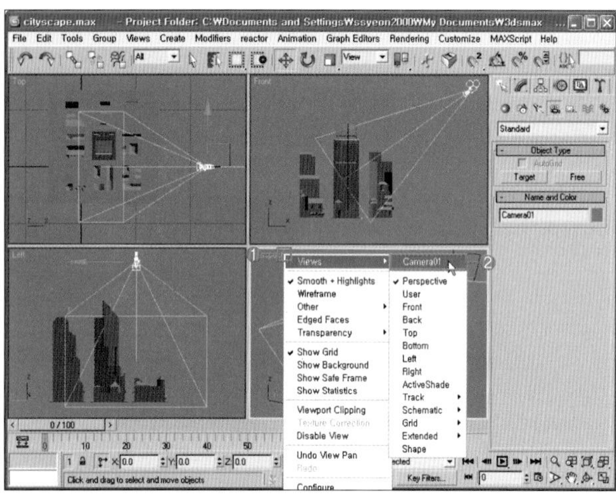

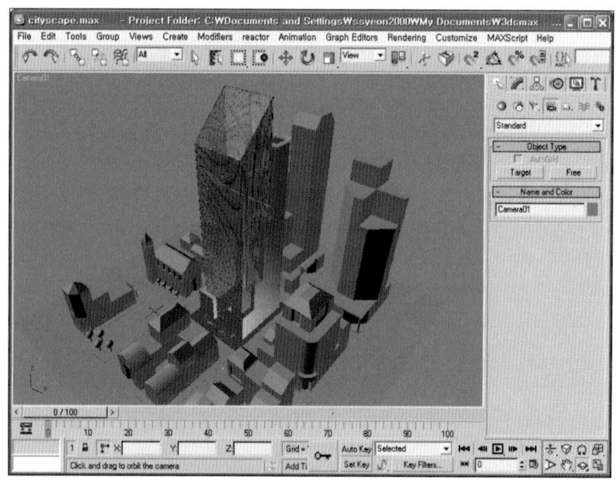

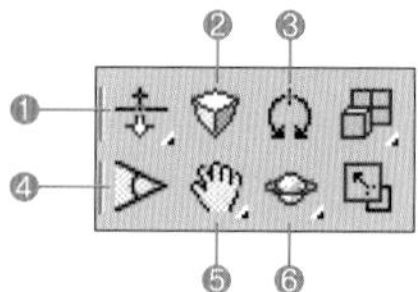

❶ **Dolly Camera**—Controls the height of the camera, up and down.

❷ **Perspective**—Controls the perspective of the camera.

❸ **Roll Camera**—Rotates the camera.

❹ **Field of View**—Same as the Zoom function.

❺ **Truck Camera**—Moves the camera horizontally.

❻ **Orbit Camera**—Rotates the camera only, leaving the camera target still.

User Interface of Basic Mapping Tools

Before mapping, the user must first be familiar with the Materials options. Materials define the color, transparency, light reflection, and the surface condition of the objects that compose the scene. The Materials that are applied to an object can be classified as Material Type, Shader, and Map. Before studying each of the elements that compose a Material, let's look at the tools for editing the Materials.

Material Editor

The Material Editor is where the Material to be applied to the object is tested; it includes the basic Material Type, which determines the properties of the Material, as well as Shader and Map, which indicate the object properties. The Material Editor can be opened by clicking [Rendering]–[Material Editor] on the menu bar, or by clicking [Material Editor] on the main tool bar.

The Material Editor is composed of the menu bar, Sample Slot, and the Material tools, and the user can set various Shader parameters in the lower section.

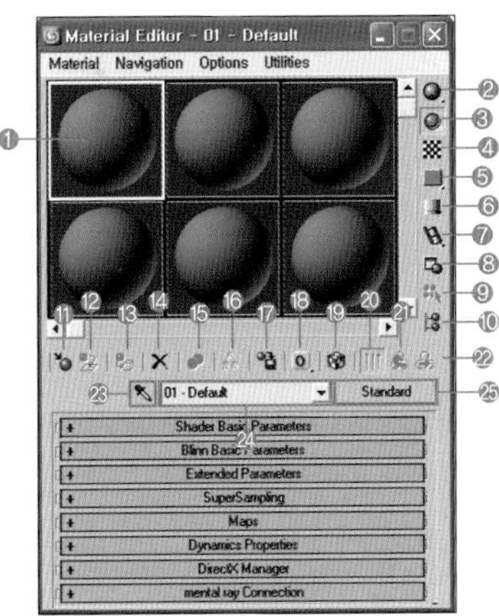

❶ **Sample Slot** —The Sample Slot is where the materials can be edited. The user can preview the color, transparency, and light reflection of the Material. There default is six sample slots, but the user can adjust the number of Sample Slots by right-clicking on it and choosing one of the "Sample Windows" options from the menu.

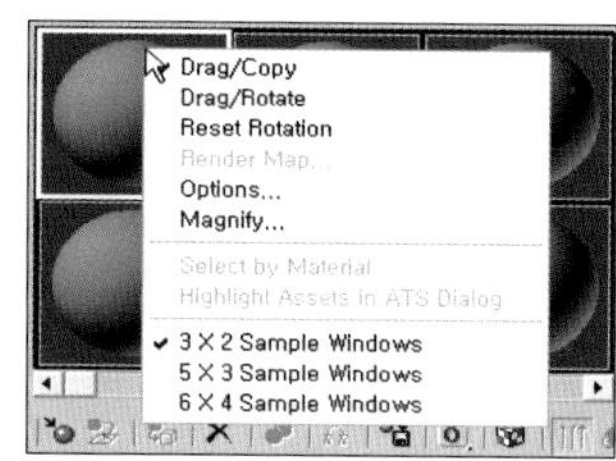

❷ **Sample Type**—The user can change the shape in the Sample Slot to spheres, cylinders or hexagon for, previewing the results of mapped objects.

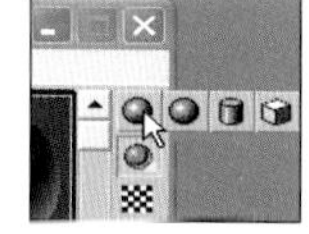

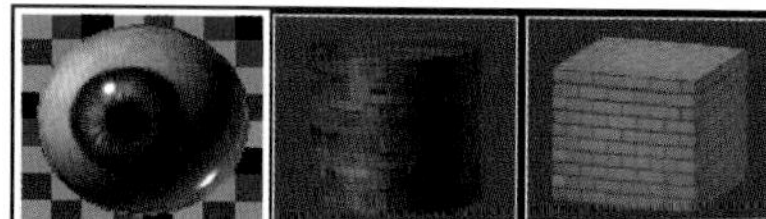

❸ **Backlight** ( ) —Preview the background lighting effects in the Sample Slot.

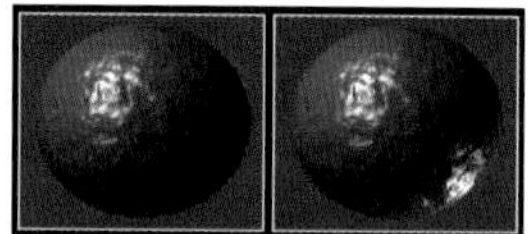

❹ **Background** ( ) —Preview the background image in the Sample Slot to see the transparency of the Material.

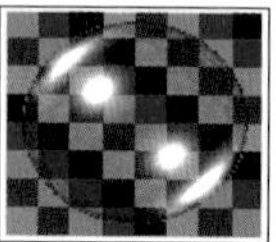

❺ **Sample UV Tiling**( ) —Preview the Map and Material tiled.

❻ **Video Color Check**( ) —Preview how the colors will differ if the Material is recorded on film.

❼ **Make Preview**( ) —View an animated preview rendering.

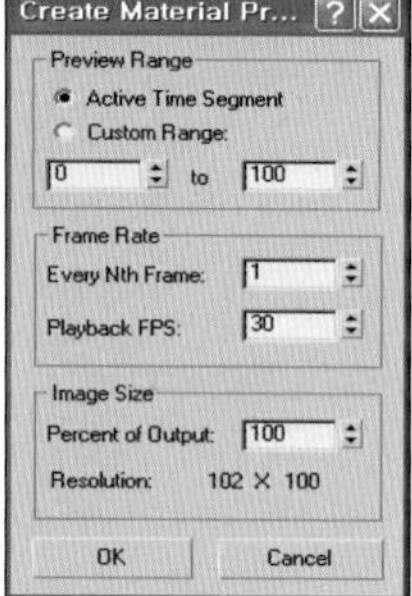

❽ **Options**( ) —Modify all of the settings required for the Material Editor.

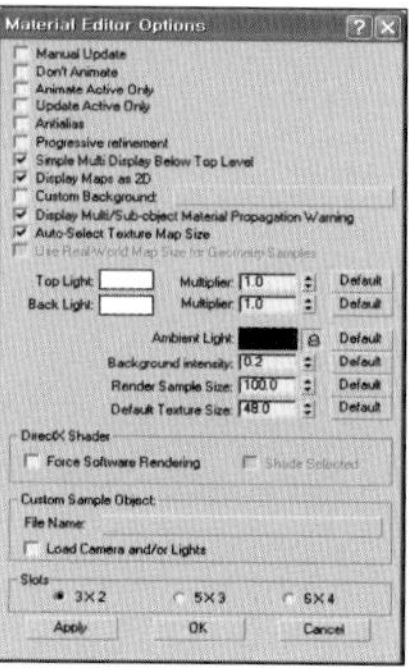

⑨ **Select by Material( )** —Select all of the objects by Material in the Select Objects dialog box.

⑩ **Material/Map Navigator( )** —Observe the currently selected Sample Slot's Material structure in the Material/Map Navigator dialog box.

⑪ **Get Material( )** —Opens the Material/Map Browser dialog box which features pre-made Materials and Maps.

⑫ **Put Material to Scene( )** —Refreshes the currently modified Material on the selected object in the Viewport.

⑬ **Assign Material to Selection ( )** —Apply the Material in the selected Sample Slot to the object selected in the Viewport.

⑭ **Reset Map/Material to Default Setting ( )** —Deletes the Material in the Sample Slot or remove the Material applied to the object.

⑮ **Make Material Copy ( )** —Displays the Material applied to the object as a non-applied Material.

⑯ **Make Unique( )** —Makes the interrelated sub-Material into an individual Material.

⑰ **Put to Library ( )** —Registers the currently selected Material in the Material library along with its name.

⑱ **Material Effect Channel ( )** —Registers the currently selected Material as the Material of the rendering effect existing in the G-Buffer.

⑲ **Show Map in Viewport ( )** —Shows the Material applied to the object in the Viewport as well.

⑳ **Show End Result ( )** —Iimmediately shows the changed Material in the Sample Slot. It is activated by default.

㉑ **Go to Parent ( )** —Moves the Material from the lower stage to the upper stage.

㉒ **Go Forward to Sibling ( )** —Moves the Material of the same level in their order.

㉓ **Pick Material from Object ( )** —Click an object in the Viewport to copy its Material to a Sample Slot.

㉔ **Material Name Field (01 - Default)** —Displays the name of the currently selected Material or rename it.

㉕ **Material Type (Standard)** —Change the form of the Material currently selected in the Sample Slot to a different form.

Material/Map Browser

The Material/Map Browser dialog box enables the user to easily select a Material from the pre–made Material Library or to select a new type of Material. Also, the user can preview the Materials in the Material Editor and identify the Materials of only the objects selected in the Viewport.

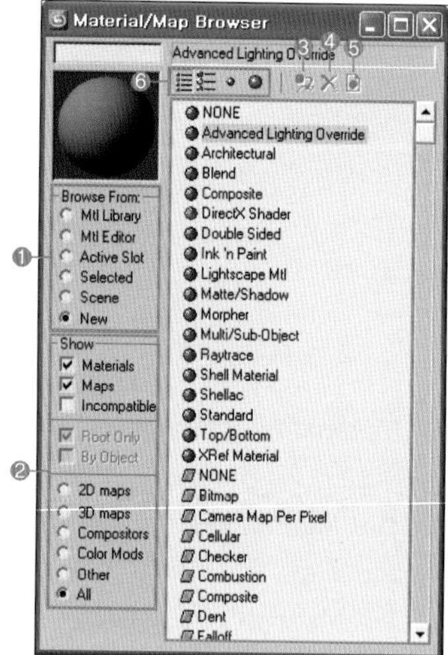

❶ Browse From

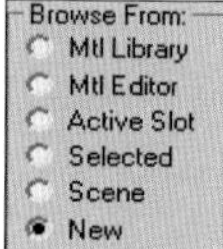

The user can selectively invoke the Material Library that stores the pre–made materials, Materials in the Material Editor, the Materials in the Active Slot, the Material of the object Selected in the Viewport, or the Materials of all the objects in the Viewport Scene.

❷ Show

The user can selectively observe the Material, Map, and Incompatible Materials in the Sample List, or display only the representative name (Root Only) on the top among the names shown as the list view, or vary the selection of display methods for each object (By Object). Also, the user can selectively classify and observe the 2D maps, 3D maps, or other composite maps.

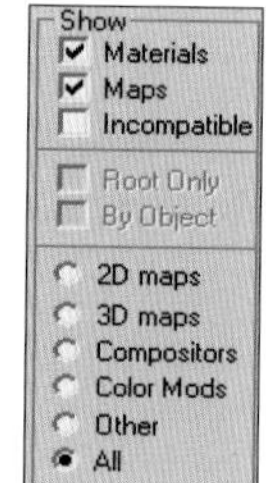

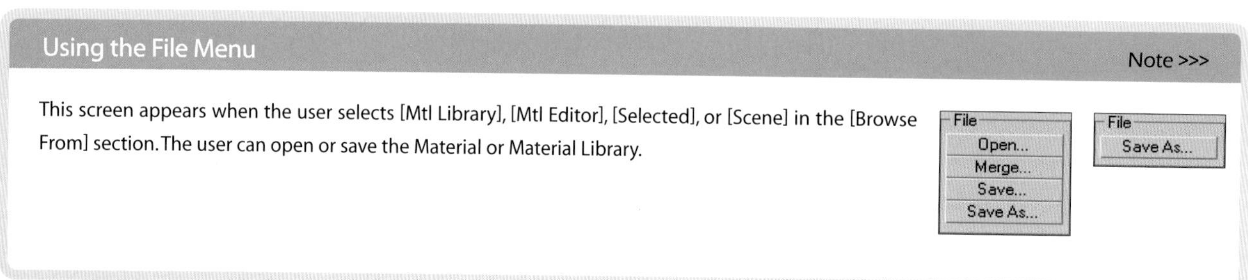

Using the File Menu — Note >>>

This screen appears when the user selects [Mtl Library], [Mtl Editor], [Selected], or [Scene] in the [Browse From] section. The user can open or save the Material or Material Library.

❸ **Update Scene Materials from Library** (icon) : Renew the Material with the same name in the Viewport.
❹ **Delete from Library** (X) : Delete the Material selected in the Viewport.
❺ **Clear Material Library** (icon) : Delete everything in the Material library.

⑥ View

See the Sample List as text or icons.

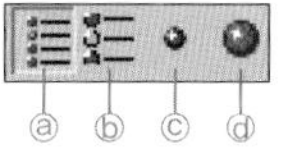

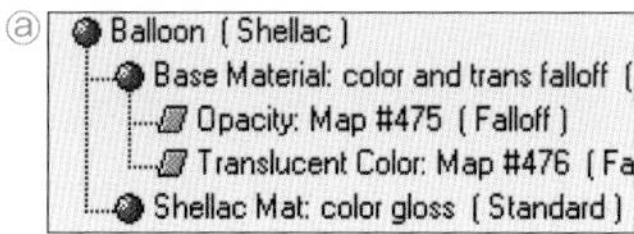

The Basic Mapping Procedure

When editing Materials with the Material Editor, first determine whether to use an individual Material or a mix of various Materials. The mixed format of the Materials is called the Material Type, and the user can click [Standard] to open the Material/Map Browser for selection. After determining the Material Type, the user must decide on the Shader, which is a basic property of Materials. The Shader affects the nature of the Material; for example, it may resemble cloth, metal, or glass. Once the Shader is determined, the user can change or apply the basic color or various maps in the Shader parameter.

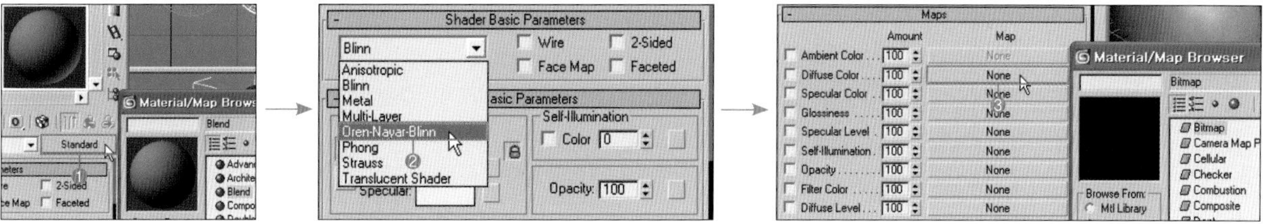

The Mapping Hierarchy

Note >>>

3ds Max 9 mapping is complex because the program has a multi-layer structure that involves many levels shown systematically in a small screen. First, the user selects the Material Type, and then the Shader, and uses many Maps as the lower stage; this workflow is depicted in the diagram below. Since the menu structure flows downward and then back up, the user needs to fully understand the format. To move to the previous menu level, click [Go to Parent].

Standard (Material Type)
- Blinn(Shader)
  - Diffuse Map – Mask – Map – Bitmap
    - Mask – Bitmap

Controlling the Overall Material Type, Shader, and Map

As explained previously, the first stage of creating Materials begins with deciding on the Material Type. Let's learn about the Material Type options and discuss Shader and Map.

Material Type

When working with a Material Type in the Material/Map Browser dialog box, click .to work with two or more materials.

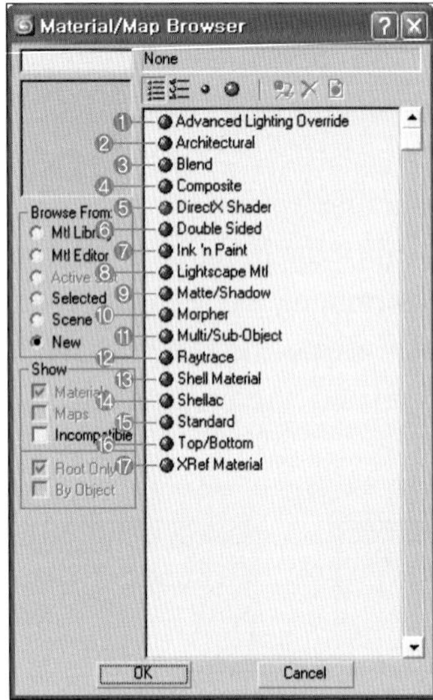

1. **Advanced Lighting Override**—Selected when Materials are required to process very bright light, such as fluorescent light. The user must use Radiosity Solution to obtain a normal result.
2. **Architectural**—A special Material for interiors, which was used in 3D Studio VIZ. It can express very realistic paper, plastic, stone, water, and trees.
3. **Blend**—Used to subtly mix two types of Materials.
4. **Composite**—Mix up to ten types of selected Materials to create a soft Material.
5. **DirectX Shader**—Used to create Materials for DirectX games.
6. **Double Sided**—Used when a polygon needs different Materials for its opposing surfaces.
7. **Ink 'n Paint**—Used to express a 3D object in a 2D cartoon format.
8. **Lightscape Mtl**—A special Material for Radio City, used for objects manufactured by Lightcape.
9. **Matte/Shadow**—Used for composite work combining 3D objects with 2D backgrounds.
10. **Morpher**—Used on objects using the Morpher Modifier. It is often used for lip–syncing.
11. **Multi/Sub–Object**—Used when applying different Materials to the inside of an object.
12. **Raytrace**—Used to express realistic light reflection.
13. **Shell Material**—Enables the user to map the rendered image with Render to Texture.
14. **Shellac**—Mixes two types of Materials to create a blazing effect.
15. **Standard**—The standard Material used in 3ds Max 9.
16. **Top/Bottom**—Can apply Materials to objects that have different upper and lower polygons.
17. **XRef Material**—Used when the object in the Viewport uses a Material in a different file.

Maps Applied to the Material Surface

Maps are various colors or mathematical structures that can be applied to the surface of objects. They are categorized into 2D types that are simple color images, 3D types created by mathematical calculations, and Composite types that are created by mixing the previous two types of Maps. Perhaps the most widely used is the Bitmap Map, which is applied directly to a surface. The Noise Map, which can depict an unclear surface, is also commonly used.

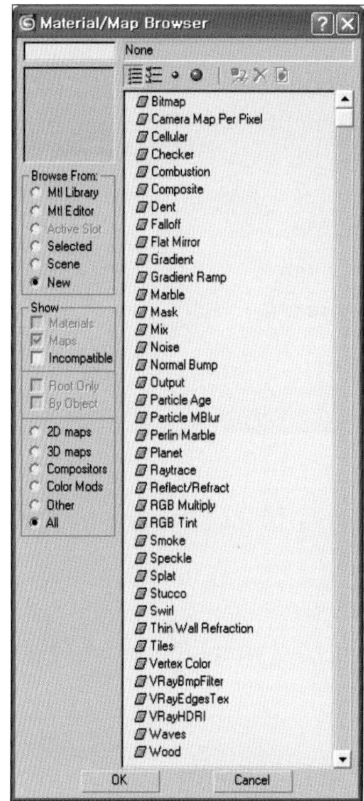

Type	Map
2D Map Type	Bitmap, Bricks, Checker, Gradient, Gradient Ramp, Paint, Swirl
3D Map Type	Cellular, Dent, Falloff, Marble, Noise, Particle Age, Particle Blur, Perlin Marble, Planet, Smoke, Speckle, Splat, Stucco, Water, Wood
Compositors	Composite, Mask, Mix, RGB Multiply, Normal Bump
Color Modifiers	Output, RGB Tint, Vertex Color
Miscellaneous	Camera Map Per Pixel, Combustion, Flat Mirror, Raytrace, Reflect/Refract, Thin Wall Refraction

Exercise 01

Creating a Still–Life Scene

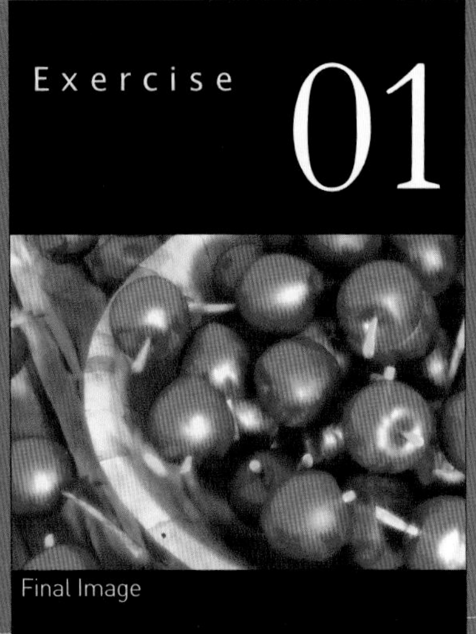

Final Image

Users may think much effort would be required to create detailed still–life scenes, but by using the Reactor simulation provided in 3ds Max 9, you can quickly create realistic scenes. This section will show you how to design a natural–looking basket full of cherries. Other features, such as Skylight and Project Map, can be used to develop natural lighting effects, enhancing the realism of the scene.

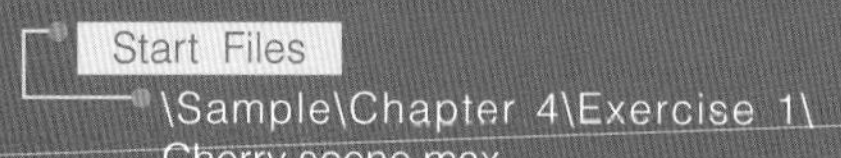

Start Files
\Sample\Chapter 4\Exercise 1\
Cherry scene.max

Final File
\Sample\Chapter 4\Exercise 1\
Cherry scene–final.max

Creating Uniquely–Shaped Cherries with Line

To better simulate reality, the cherries must be various shapes and sizes. Therefore, we can first create four types of cherries with Line and the Lathe Modifier.

01 Open the "Cherry Scene.max" file on the supplementary CD. Select the Front Viewport, and click [Maximize Viewport Toggle] on the Viewport control to zoom.

Supplementary CD\Sample\Chapter 4\Exercise 1\Cherry Scene.max

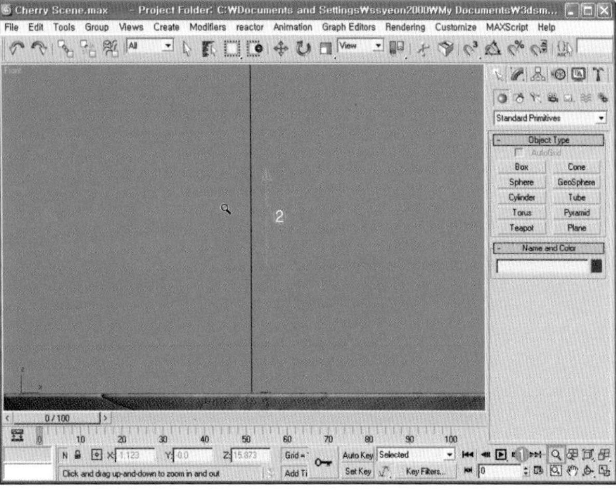

02 Click [Zoom] on the Viewport control, and drag the Top Viewport upward to magnify the objects in the Viewport.

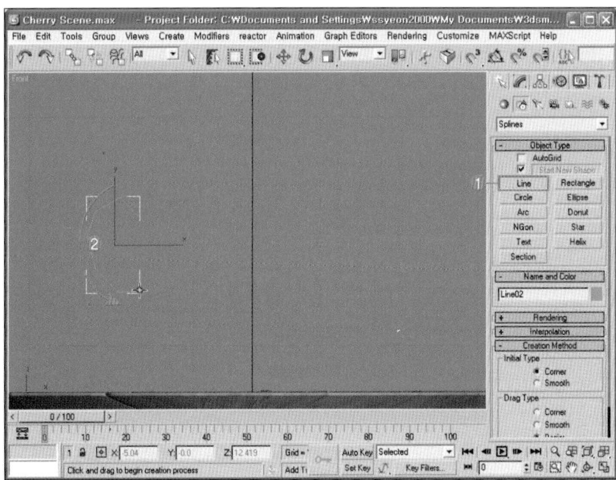

03 Click [Shapes]–[Splines]–Line on the Create panel. Draw half of the contour of the Cherry in the Front Viewport, as shown in the picture.

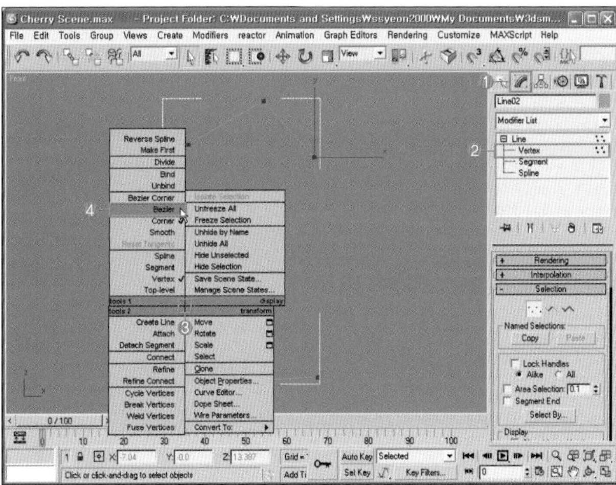

04 With the previously created "Line02" object selected, move to the Modify panel. Select the [Vertex] sub–object of [Line], and select all the vertices. Then right–click on one of the selected vertices to open the quad menu, and select [Bezier] to change the straight lines into curves.

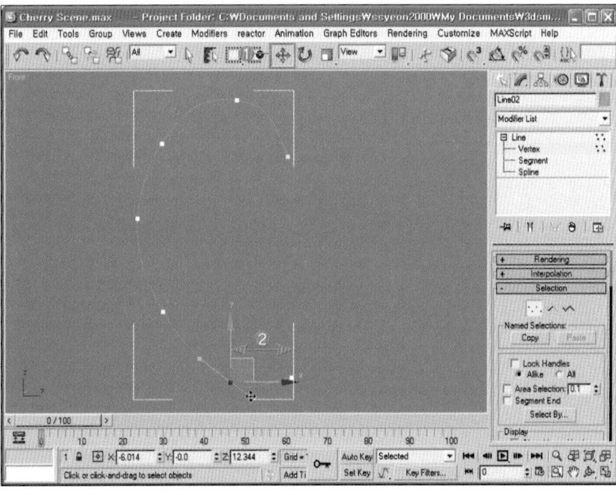

05 Move the Bezier handlebar of each vertex to form a heart–shaped curve, as shown in the picture.

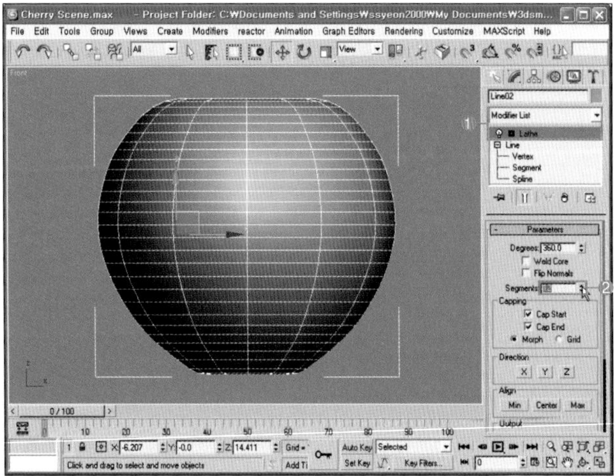

06 To transform the “Line02” object into a 3D object, click the [Modifier List] combo box, select the [Lathe] Modifier, and enter [12] for [Parameters]–[Segments].

07 Click the [Modifier List] combo box, select the [FFD 3x3x3] Modifier, and select the [Control Point] sub–object. Click [Select and Move] on the main toolbar, and modify each of the vertices to create an irregular figure.

08 Click [Select and Move] on the main toolbar, and press <Shift> while click–and–dragging to copy the “Line02” object in the Front Viewport.

09 When the [Clone Options] dialog box appears, check [Copy], enter [3] for [Number of Copies], and click [OK].

10 Move the adjustment vertices of the [FFD 3x3x3] modifier on each of the cherry objects to vary the shapes slightly.

11 To make the cherry objects look smooth, click the [Modifier List] combo box on each of the objects, select the [MeshSmooth] Modifier, and enter [2] for [Iterations].

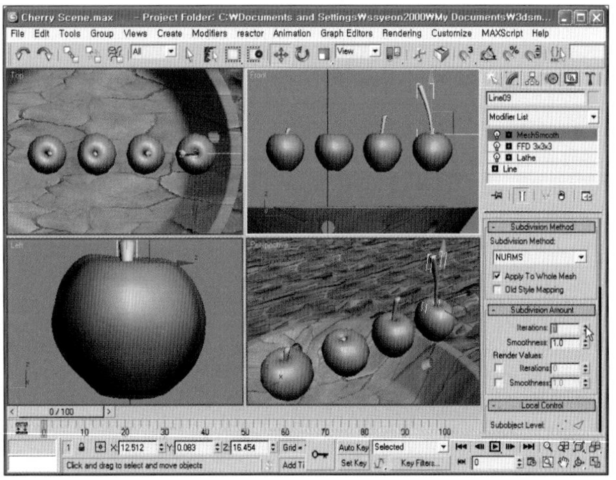

12 Use [Line] to create and place different shapes for each cherry.

tip >>

Creating Stems

Use [Line] to create unique stems for each cherry and place them.

Mapping a Semi–Transparent Cherry Surface

The surface of a cherry looks semi–transparent, as if the inside can be seen below the surface. To simulate this appearance, you can use Raytrace, which reflects the surrounding environment.

01 Click [Material Editor] on the main toolbar to open the Material Editor dialog box. Select the cherry objects to map first by click–and–dragging.

02 Select the third Sample Slot of the Material Editor, and select [Anisotropic] in [Shader Basic Parameters] to give it a glass–like appearance. Click the [Diffuse] color button and modify to red (RGB: 242, 0, 25) in the [Color Selector] dialog box. Click the [Close] button to close the dialog box.

tip >>

Shader

When selecting the Material, the first step is to determine the Shader settings. Shader refers to the basic properties of the object. Select from Anisotropic, Metal, and Oren–Nayar–Blinn.

03 Change the settings of [Specular Highlight], as shown, to generate soft reflections.

04 To add a bit of transparency to the outside of the cherry object, set the [Extended Parameters]. Select [Extended Parameters]–[Falloff]–[Out], enter [5] for [Amt] and select [Subtractive].

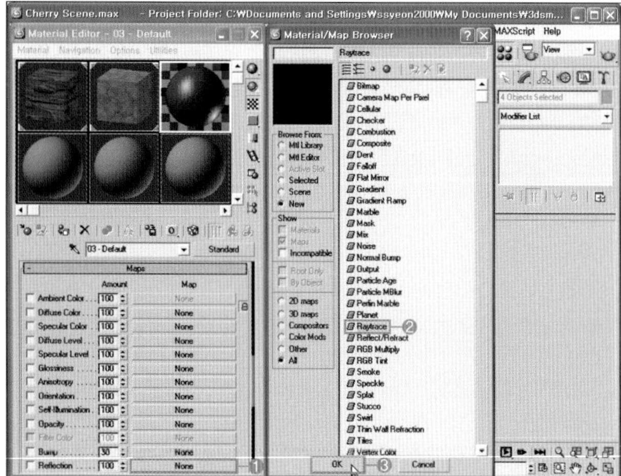

05 To create a reflection effect on the surface of the cherry, select [Maps]–[Reflection]–[None] to activate the [Material/Map Browser] dialog box, select [Raytrace], and click [OK].

tip >>

Map

Map is used after selecting the Shader settings in the Material Editor. Select a map from Diffuse, Reflection, and Opacity. Each of the characteristic maps can be selected from the Material/Map Browser.

06 Click [Go to Parent] to return to the previous level.

tip >>

Using "Parent" in the Material Editor

The 3ds Max Material Editor has a hierarchic management structure. When the user selects a new Sample Slot to work with, it begins with the Standard Material type. Then, the user determines the Shader and adds Maps as desired. When viewing options in the submenus, the user can click [Go to Parent] to return to the first level and proceed with the work.

Standard – Anisotropic Shader
- Diffuse Map – Bitmap Image File
- Reflection Map – Raytrace

07 Click [Show Map in Viewport] and [Assign Material to Selection] to apply the Material to the selected object.

08 Select the Perspective Viewport, and click [Quick Render] on the main toolbar to see the rendered scene. Click on the rendered image window to close it.

Mapping the Cherry Stalks with Uneven Textures

Cherry stalks have uneven surfaces. To simulate this, you may use [Diffuse] for the surface and [Bump] for the texture.

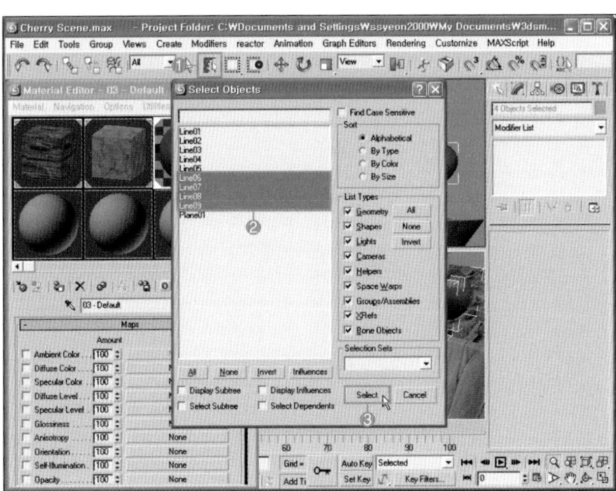

01 Click [Select by Name] on the main toolbar. While pressing <Ctrl>, select the objects specific to the cherry stalks in the [Select Objects] dialog box, and click the [Select] button.

02 Click the fourth Sample Slot in the Material Editor. Click [Maps]–[Diffuse Color]–[None] to activate the [Material/Map Browser] dialog box, click [Bitmap], and click [OK].

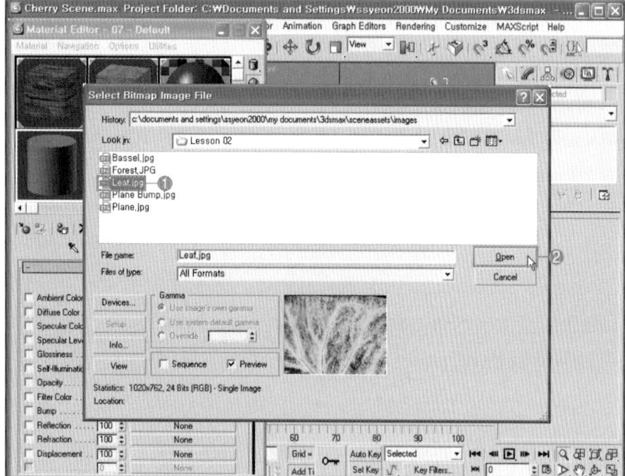

03 In the [Select Bitmap Image File] dialog box, select the "Leaf.jpg" file of the appendix CD, and click [Open].

Supplementary CD\Sample\Chapter 4\Exercise 1\Leaf.jpg

04 Click [Go to Parent] to return to the initial screen.

05 To express the curves on the surface of the branches, copy [Map #5 (Leaf.jpg)] of [Diffuse Color] by click–and–dragging with [Bump].

06 When the [Copy (Instance)] dialog box appears, select [Instance] so that the [Bump] image changes according to changes in the [Diffuse Color] image.

tip >>

The Instance Command

Instance is a function that updates an object's copies whenever changes are made to the original object.

07 Click [Show Map in Viewport] and [Assign Material to Selection] to apply the Material to the selected object.

08 To set mapping options for each stem, click the [Modifier List] combo box, and then the [UVW Map] modifier. Check [Cylinder] and [Cap] in [Parameters] to select how to map the Cylinder.

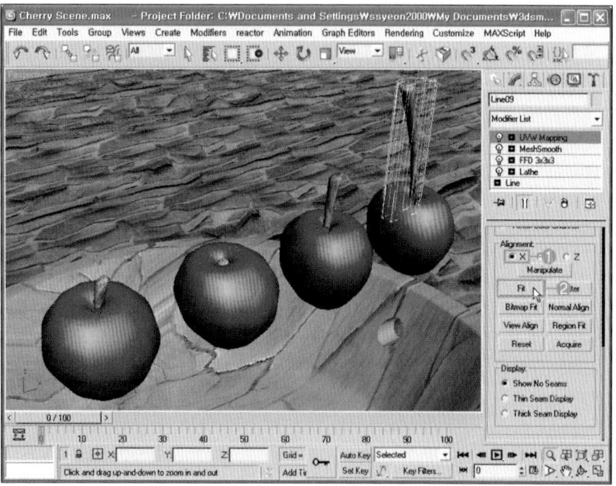

09 Select [Alignment]–[X], and click [Fit] so that the cylinder–shaped Gizmo surrounds a stem.

10 Apply the [UVW Map] modifier to the other stems using the same method.

11 Select the Perspective Viewport, and click [Quick Render] on the main toolbar to see the rendered scene. Click on the rendered image window to close it.

Combining the Cherries and Stalks 

The cherry and its stalk are separately created, which makes it difficult to handle them. Also, they are not fit to the [Reactor] simulation, which comes next. To correct this problem, let's learn how to combine the cherry with its stalk into one object.

01 Select one cherry stem object, and click the [Remove modifier from the stack] to remove the [MeshSmooth] Modifier from the Modifier stack.

02 Click the cherry object under it, and click to select [FFD 3x3x3]. Then click the [Modifier List] combo box and add the [Edit Poly] Modifier.

03 Click [Edit Poly]–[Edit Geometry]–[Attach], and click the cherry stem object above to combine them.

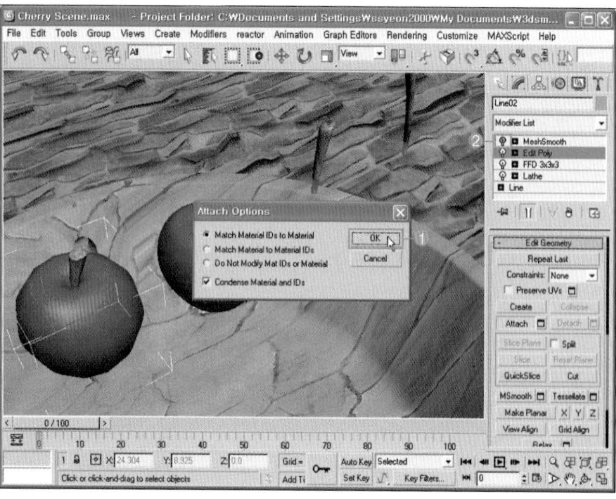

04 When the [Attach Options] dialog box appears, check [Match Material ID to Material] so that the material of the cherry stem object is maintained. Lastly, click [icon] of the cherry object's [MeshSmooth] Modifier to deactivate the function.

tip >>

Using [icon] on the MeshSmooth Modifier

When processing the Reactor simulation, [MeshSmooth] can modify a large number of polygons, sapping a lot of system resources and processing power. To prevent this, the user can deactivate the functions of each of the [MeshSmooth] Modifiers. The functions can be re–activated when the simulation is over.

05 With the same method, combine the cherry objects with each of the cherry stems.

Randomizing the Positions and Orientation of the Cherries

When numerous cherries are placed in a basket, they each have irregular positioning, poses, and forms. Before running the simulation, make numerous copies of the four cherry objects and vary their rotations and positions.

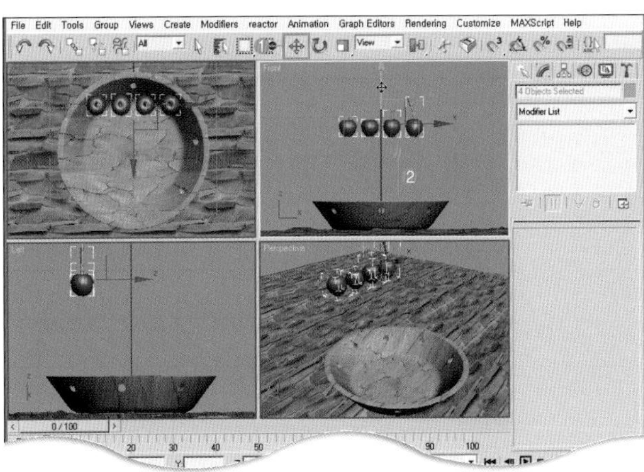

01 Click [Select and Move ] on the main toolbar, and click–and–drag in the Viewport to select all of the cherry objects. Then, in the Front Viewport, move the selection above the basket.

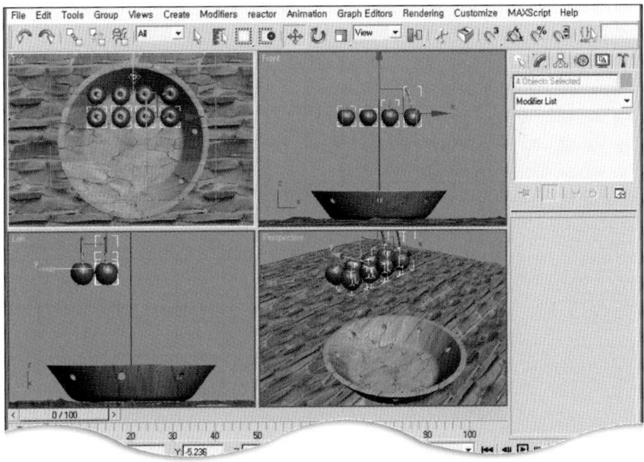

02 Go back to the Front Viewport, hold <Shift>, and click–and–drag the selection downward to copy them.

03 When the [Clone Options] dialog box appears, select [Copy] and enter [5] for [Number of Copies].

04 Select all of the cherry objects, and copy them with <Shift>+click–and–dragging in the Front Viewport upwards. When the [Clone Options] dialog box appears, check [Copy] and enter [5] for [Number of Copies].

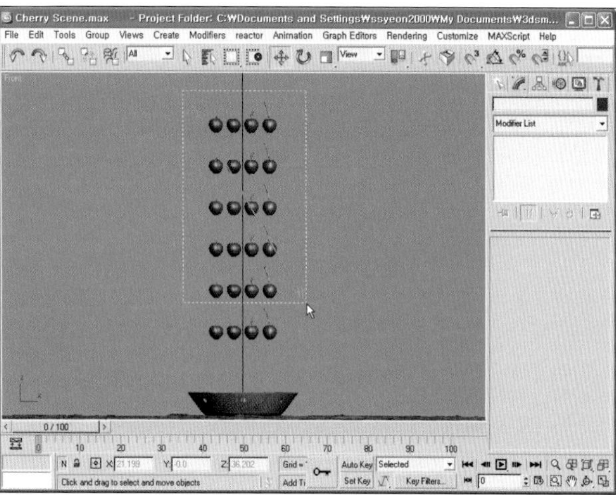

05 Zoom in on the Front Viewport and select the cherry objects from the top down to the fifth row.

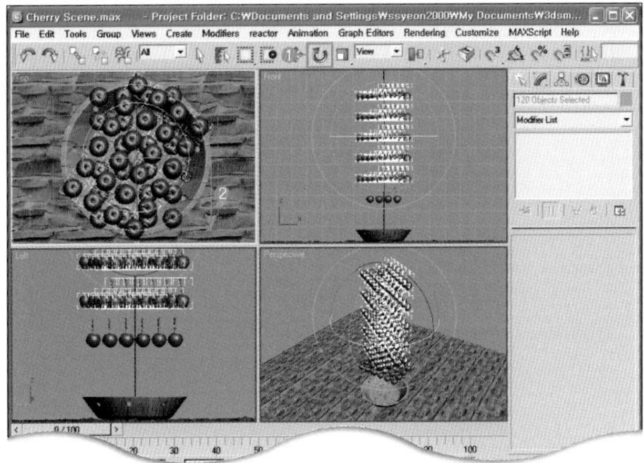

06 Click [Select and Rotate] on the main toolbar, and slightly rotate the selection in the Top Viewport.

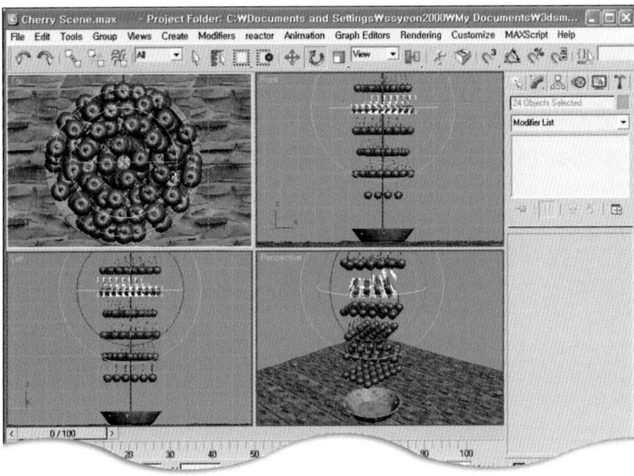

07 Now, select only the cherry objects from the top down to the fourth row, and rotate them slightly more in the Top Viewport. Repeat this method for the remaining rows.

Positioning the Cherries Using Reactor

The Reactor function can be used to calculate the effect of gravity on the cherries, the basket, and the floor polygon.

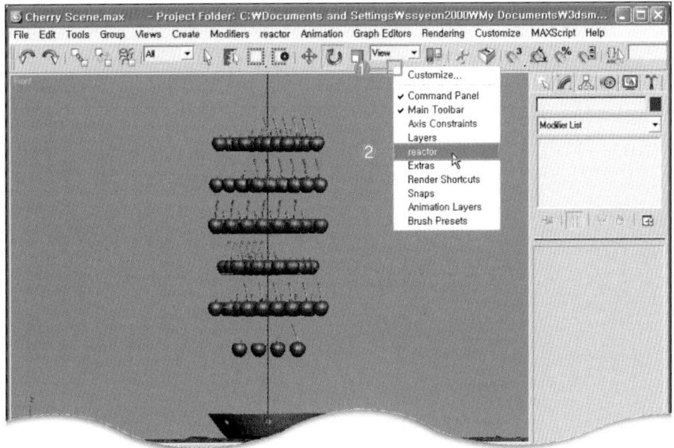

01 Right–click on the blank space on the main toolbar and select [Reactor] to open the [Reactor] toolbar.

tip >>

The Reactor Toolbar

In previous versions of 3ds Max, the Reactor toolbar displayed to the left of the Viewport. However, probably because the simulations are not a commonly used feature, the toolbar does not appear in 3ds Max 9.

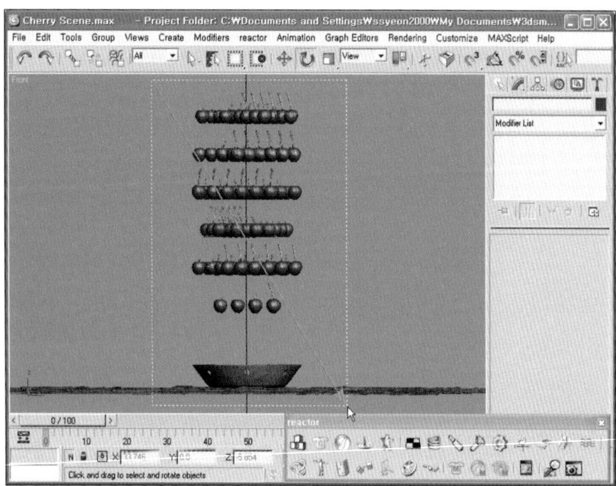

02 Click–and–drag in the Front Viewport to select the cherries and the bottom of the basket.

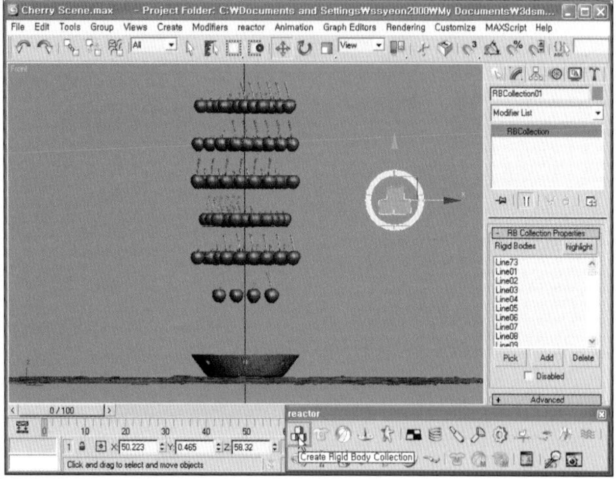

03 Click [Create Rigid Body Collection] on the [Reactor] toolbar to register the selected objects in a [Rigid Body Collection]. The new [Rigid Body Collection] object appears in the Viewport.

tip >>

Create Rigid Body Collection

The Rigid Body Collection is a Reactor simulation tool that calculates the interaction of the selected objects due to gravity. It is the foundation for other tools such as Cloth or Wind.

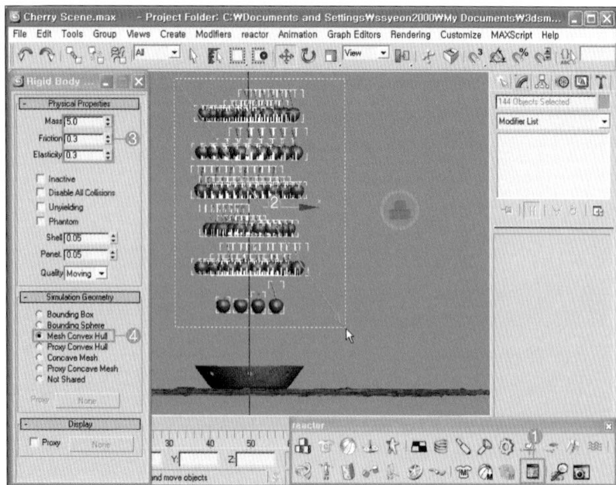

04 Click [Open Property Editor] on the [Reactor] toolbar. Select all the cherry objects in the Viewport, enter [5] for [Mass], [0.3] for Friction, and [0.3] for [Elasticity], and modify the object properties with [Mesh Convex Hull].

Object Properties in the Reactor Simulation

Note >>>

The objects selected for the [Reactor] simulation basically have Mass, Friction, and Elasticity. Gravity automatically applies in the simulation, and the objects collide according to their properties. The values of Mass, Friction, and Elasticity are relative, and if Mass is 0, the object is not influenced by gravity, staying put at its position.

Also, the Simulation Geometry determines the form of the object to calculate the amount of collision. Refer to the images below for the geometry options.

Bounding Box

Bounding Sphere

Mesh Convex Hull

Proxy Convex Hull

Concave Mesh

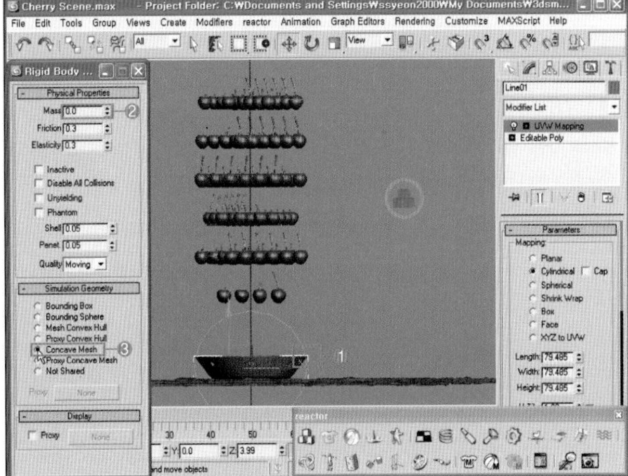

05 Select the basket object in the Viewport, and enter [0] for [Mass] to fix the object in place, and modify the object properties as [Concave Mesh].

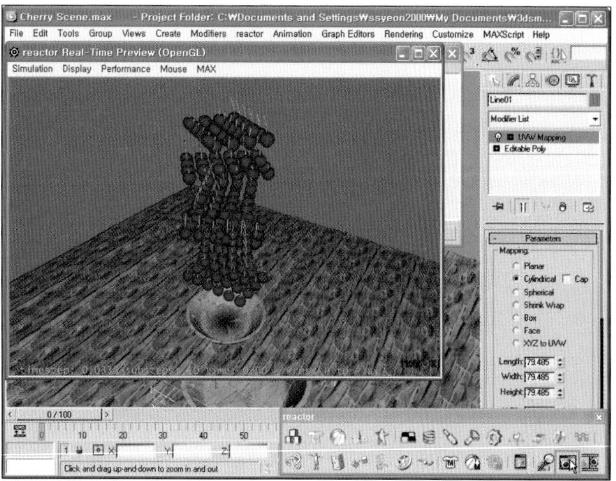

06 Click [Preview Animation] on the [Reactor] toolbar to open the [Reactor Real–Time Preview] window.

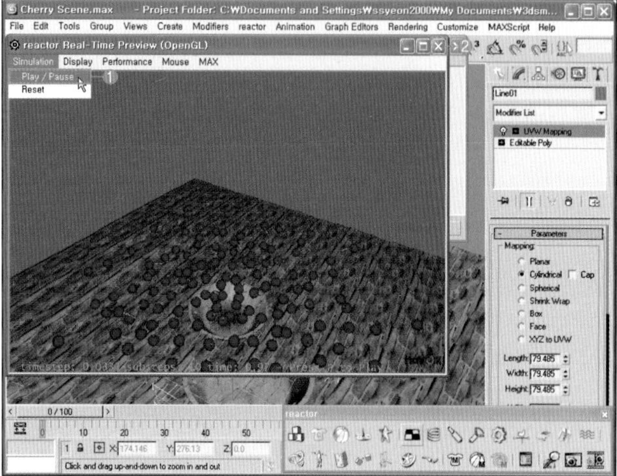

07 Click [Simulation]–[Play/Pause] on the menu bar of the [Reactor Real–Time Preview] window to view the simulation. You will see all the cherries drop to the "floor." Click on the image window to close it.

tip >>

Running Simulations in Reactor Real–Time Preview

To run the simulation on the [Reactor Real–Time Preview] window, it is faster to execute play and pause functions by pressing <P>, rather than using the menu.

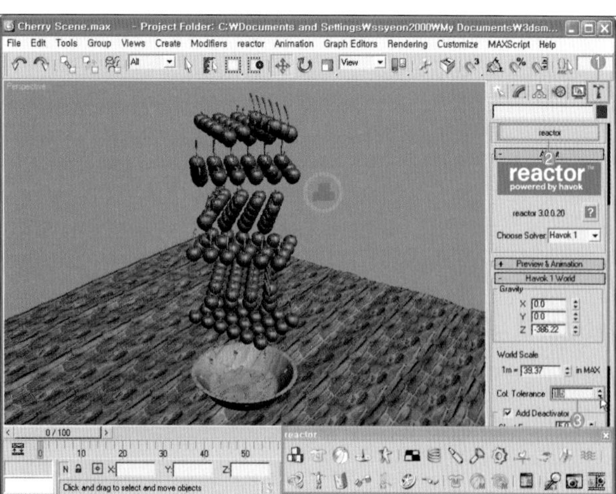

08 To obtain a natural simulation effect, click [Utilities] to view the Utility panel, and click [reactor]. Enter [1.5] for [Col. Tolerance], which will lower the collision value.

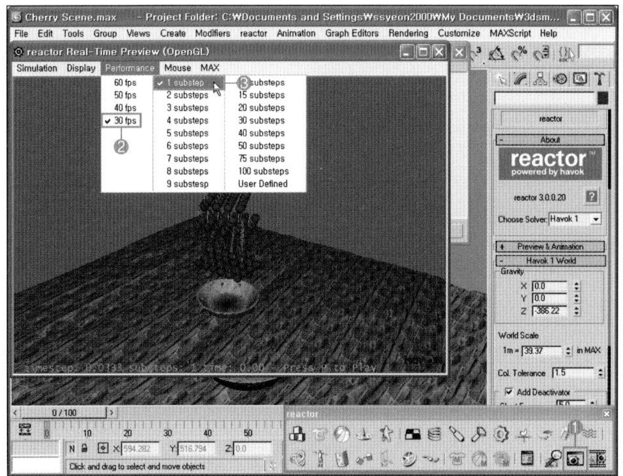

09 Click [Preview Animation] again on the [Reactor] toolbar. When the [Reactor Real-Time Preview] window appears, check [30 fps] and [1 Substep] in [Performance] to see detailed results of the simulation.

tip >>

Frames per Second (fps) and Substep

The command [fps] determines the frames per second, which is the speed at which the animation plays, and [Substep] determines the detailed stages that show the simulation. The higher the [fps], the more detailed the simulation, but higher [Substep] values lower the realism of the simulation.

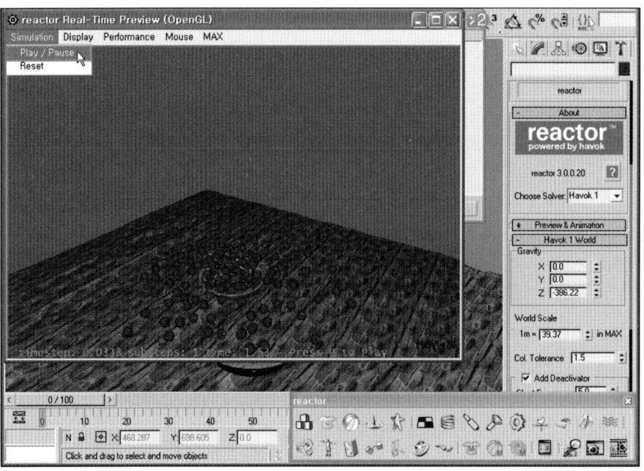

10 Click [Simulation]–[Play/Pause] on the menu bar of the [Reactor Real-Time Preview] window to see the desired results.

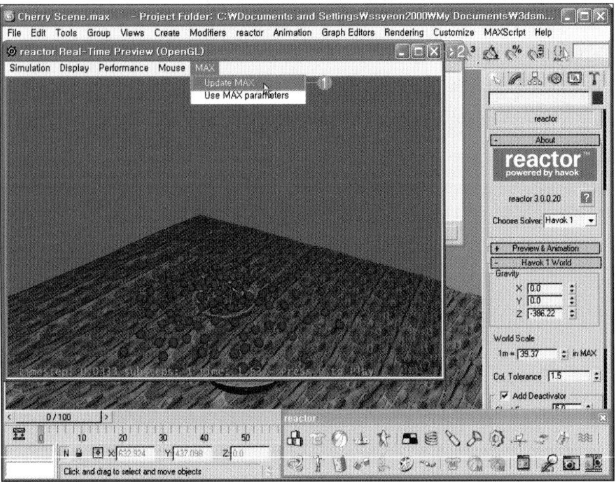

11 When the simulation of the cherries dropping is almost over, click [Max]–[Update Max] on the menu bar to renew the current screen as the scene for the 3ds Max screen. Click ☒ to close the [Reactor] toolbar.

tip >>

The Simulation Process and the Animation Key

It is possible to modify the simulation with the animation function. [Create Animation ▣] is listed at the end of the [Reactor] toolbar. By clicking this button, it is changed to a 3ds Max animation key. However, once this change is made, the aligned forms of the cherries in the initial stage cannot be retrieved. Therefore, it is best to use [Create Animation ▣] only when creating the final animation.

Adding Cameras and Lighting

This section will demonstrate how to install cameras and lighting to finalize the image.

01 Click [Cameras]–[Standard]–[Target] on the Create panel. Install the camera in the Front Viewport at the location shown in the picture, and change the Perspective Viewport to Camera01 Viewport.

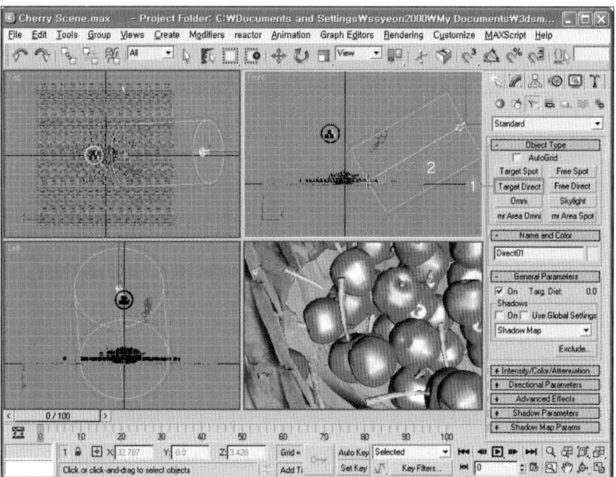

02 Click [Lights]–[Standard]–[Target Direct] on the Create panel. This will simulate sunlight shining from the right to the left in the Front Viewport.

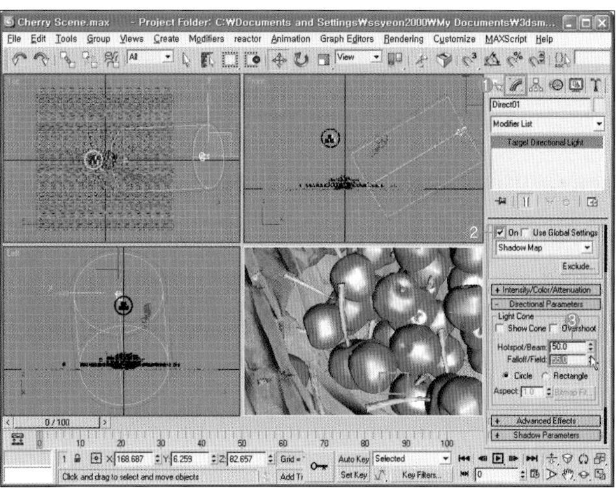

03 With the light selected, move to the Modify panel. Turn on shadows for the light, and enter [50] for [Hotspot/Beam] and [55] for [Falloff/Field].

04 Select the Camera01 Viewport and click [Quick Render] on the main toolbar to see the rendered shape. Click on the rendered image window to close it.

tip >>

Adjusting the Brightness

To adjust the brightness of the sunlight, change the [Multiplier] to [2] or more in [Intensity/Color/Attenuation] of the light. However, be careful that the Skylight (discussed later) does not create an unnatural illumination effect when using a high value.

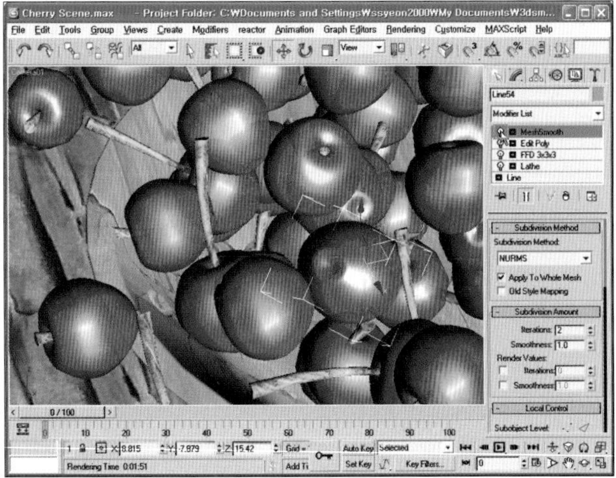

05 The cherry objects have their [MeshSmooth] Modifier functions deactivated, and thus they look as if they have some unnatural angles. Activate the [MeshSmooth] Modifier for each of the cherry objects shown on the screen to round out their shapes.

Using Project Map and Skylight 

It is difficult to create realistic images with basic light and cameras. But Project Map and Skylight can be used to add realism.

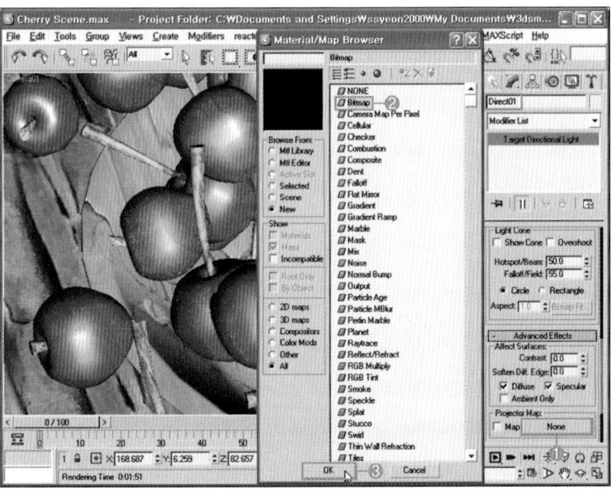

01 Select the "Direct01" object in the Viewport, and click [Project Map]–None. Select [Bitmap] in the [Material Editor], and click [OK].

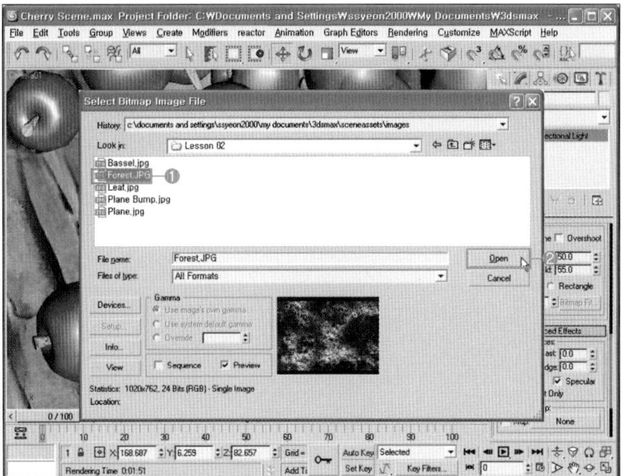

02 In the [Select Bitmap Image File] dialog box, select the "Forest.jpg" file on the supplementary CD, and click [Open].

Supplementary CD\Sample\Chapter 4\Exercise 1\Forest.jpg

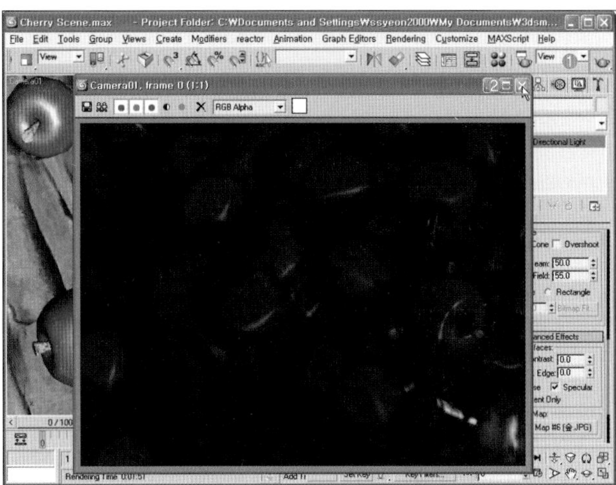

03 Select the Camera01 Viewport, and click [Quick Render] on the main toolbar to see the rendered shape. Click on the rendered image window to close it.

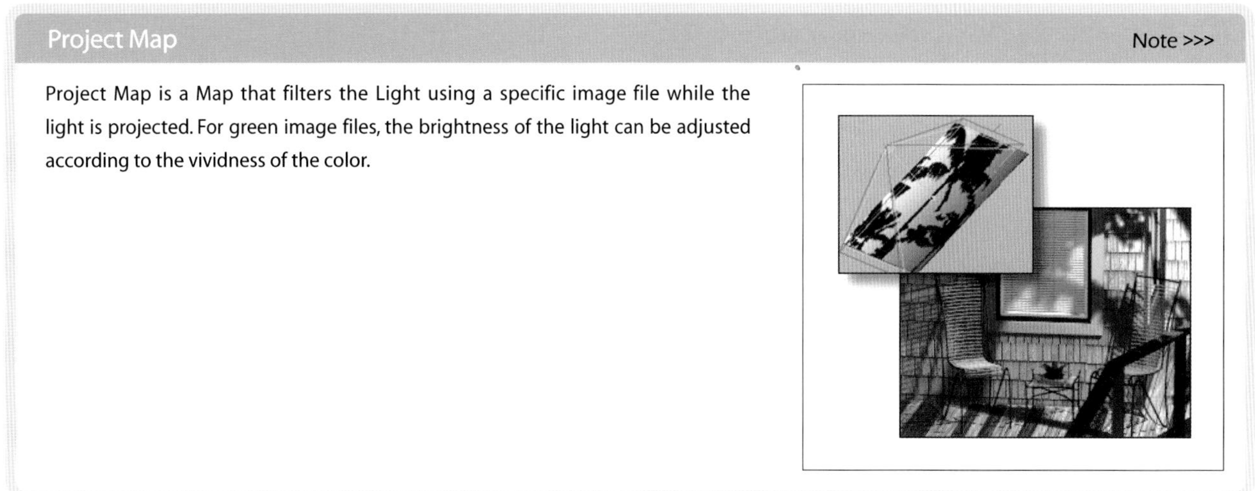

Project Map

Note >>>

Project Map is a Map that filters the Light using a specific image file while the light is projected. For green image files, the brightness of the light can be adjusted according to the vividness of the color.

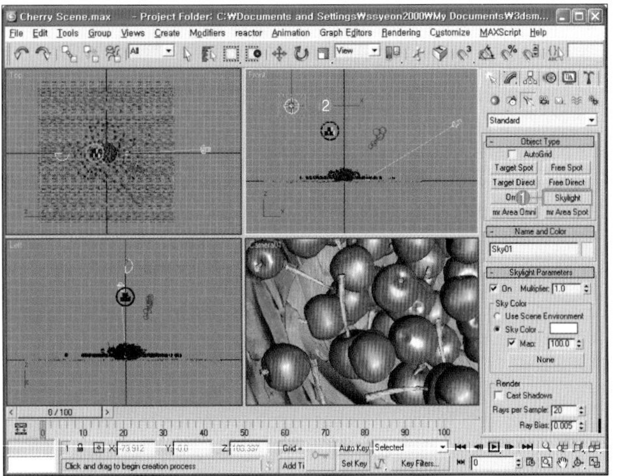

04 To enhance the overall brightness, click [Lights]–[Standard]–[Skylight] on the Create panel, and click the upper part in the Front Viewport.

Skylight

Note >>>

A Skylight is a light that assists the expression of diffused light, which cannot be expressed by a Standard Light. Since the function cannot be fully utilized with [Quick Render], the user must click [Rendering]–[Advanced Lighting]–[Light Tracer] on the menu bar to see the effects of the function.

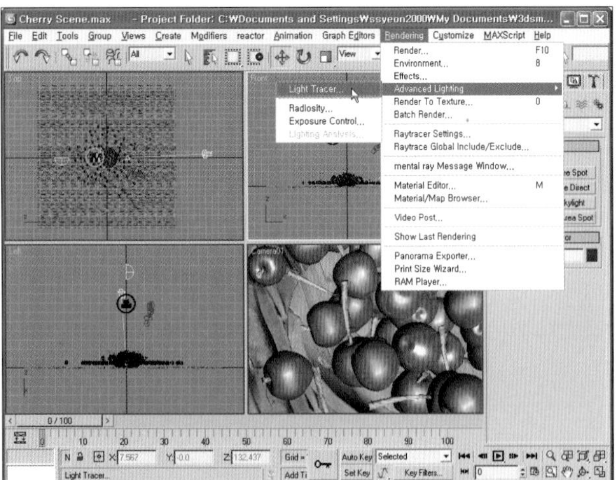

05 To see the effect of Skylight, click [Rendering]–[Advanced Lighting]–[Light Tracer] on the menu bar.

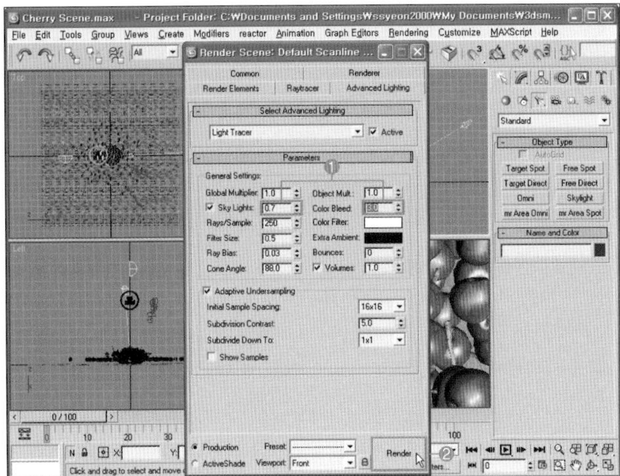

06 When the [Render Scene] dialog box appears, enter [0.7] for [Sky Lights], [3] for [Color Bleed], and click Render.

07 The screen, which was dark due to the [Project Map], becomes much more realistic with the Skylight effect. See how the rendered shape looks.

Supplementary CD\Sample\Chapter 4\Exercise 1\Cherry Scene-final.max

Color Bleed

Note >>>

The Color Bleed function makes blurred effects for the object colors based on the diffused light projected with Skylight.

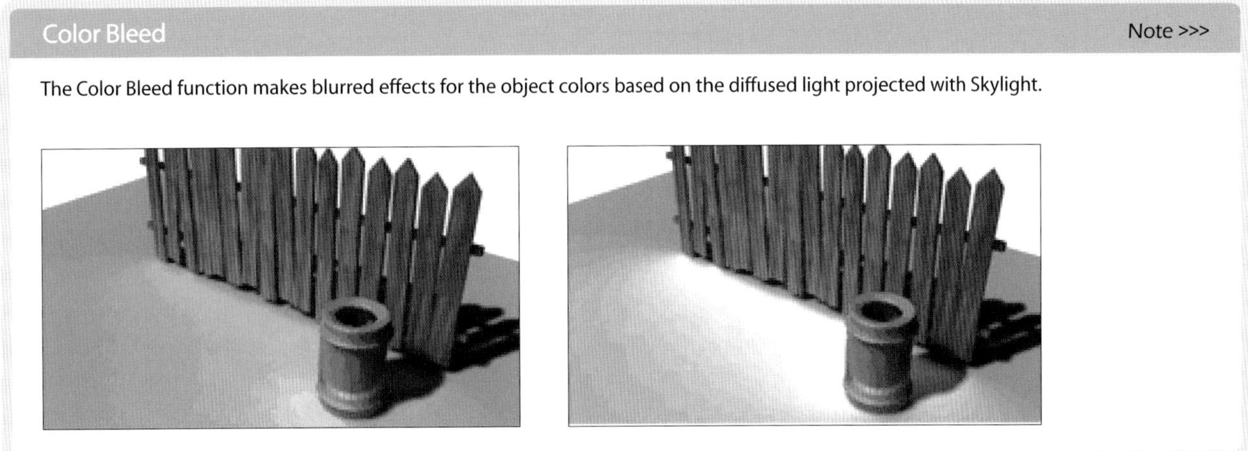

Exercise 02

Manipulating Light Effects

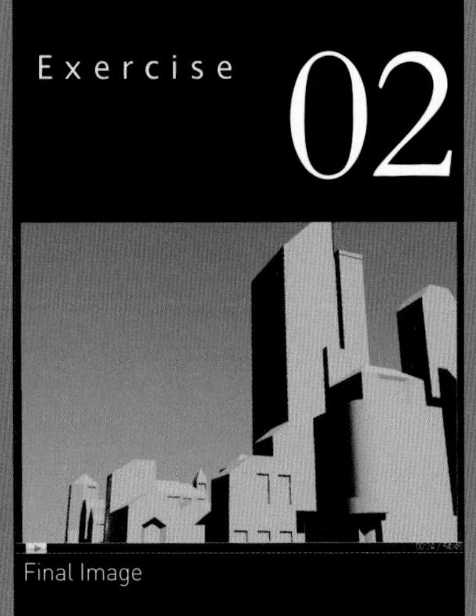
Final Image

The Daylight function expresses a variety of natural light conditions. This feature can produce the diffused light of sun seen through clouds, or mimic the movements of the sun to create realistic natural lighting. The mental ray renderer's mr Sun and mr Sky functions can also be used to create these effects.

Start Files
\Sample\Chapter 4\Exercise 2\
24 Hours.max

Final File
\Sample\Chapter 4\Exercise 2\
24 Hours–final.max

Using the mental ray Renderer's mr Physical Sky Shader

You can create a new camera on the Perspective Viewport and add a natural background with the mental ray renderer's mr Physical Sky shader.

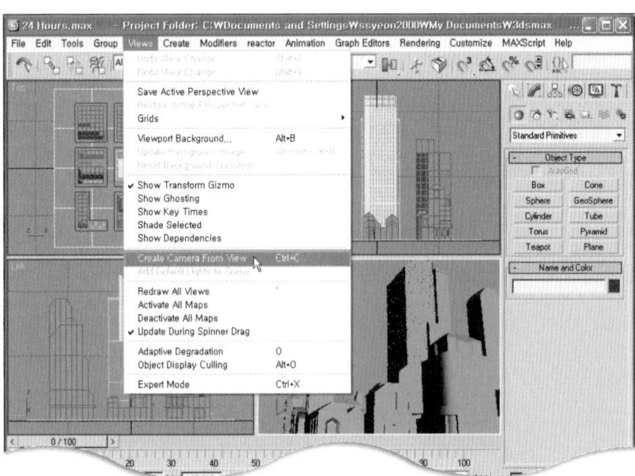

01 Open the "24 Hours.max" file of the supplementary CD and adjust the view of the Perspective Viewport as desired. To create a camera that shows the desired view of the Perspective Viewport, click [Views]–[Create Camera From View] on the menu bar.

Supplementary CD\Sample\Chapter 4\Exercise 2\24 Hours.max

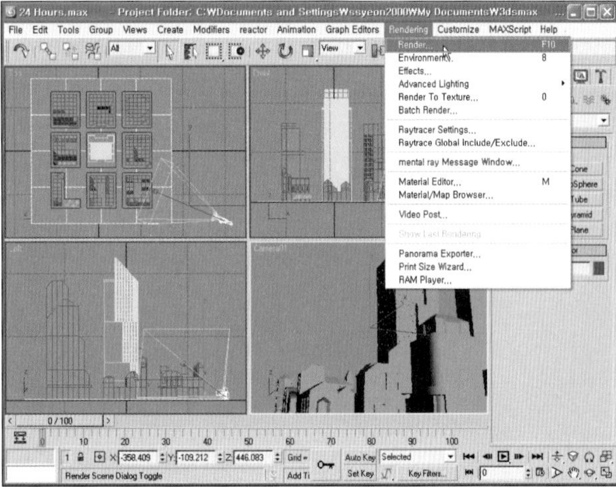

02 To change the basic Scanline renderer to the mental ray renderer, click [Rendering]–[Render] on the menu bar.

Scanline Renderer and mental ray Renderer

Note >>>

The Scanline renderer is the basic renderer used in 3ds Max 9. The user renders through an orderly calculation, from top to bottom. The Scanline renderer's strong point is that the rendering is done swiftly, but its drawback is that the 2D reflected light of the light source cannot be calculated. Therefore, it cannot be used when a precise and accurate image is required. To supplement this insufficiency, 3ds Max 9 also provides an advanced renderer called mental ray. The mental ray renderer is often used for the special effects in Hollywood movies. The Shader, used along with the mental ray renderer, provides various functions that enable the user to make realistic scenes.

The Day After Tomorrow

Matrix Revolution

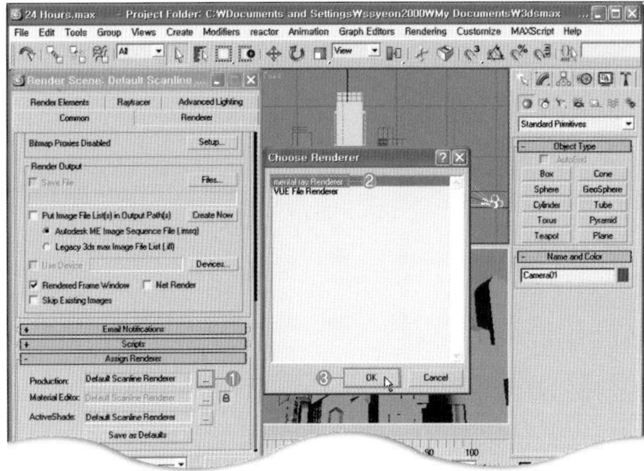

03 When the [Render Scene] dialog box appears, click [Assign Render]–[Production]–[...] to change the renderer, and select [mental ray Render] in [Choose Render].

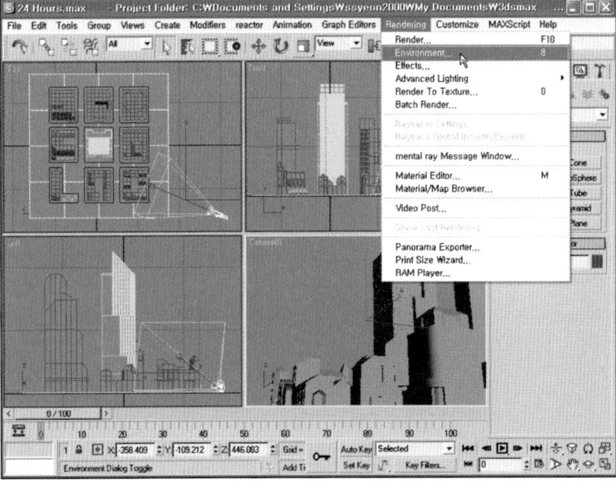

04 Click [Rendering]–[Environment] on the menu bar to set the background of the Scene.

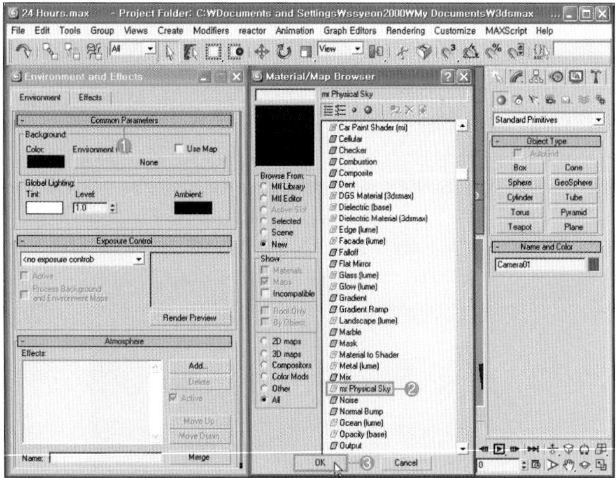

05 When the [Environment and Effects] dialog box appears, click [Background]–[None] to activate the [Material/Map Browser], select [mr Physical Sky], and click [OK].

tip >>

[Background]–[Environment and Effects] Window

When rendering by clicking [Quick Render] on the main toolbar, the background is black because the [Environment and Effects] window's [Background] is set to black. To change the background, modify [Background]–[Color] or click [None] and set the desired map.

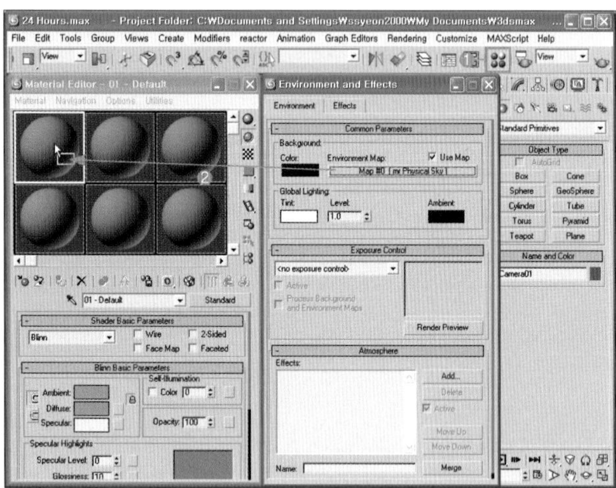

06 Click [Material Editor] on the main toolbar to open the [Material Editor]. Click–and–drag [Map #0 (mr Physical Sky)], which is applied to [Environment Map], and copy to the first Sample Slot of the [Material Editor].

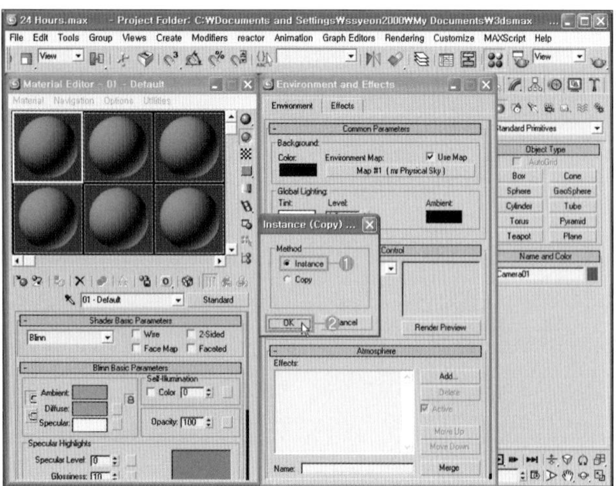

07 Select [Instance] in the [Instance (Copy)] dialog box.

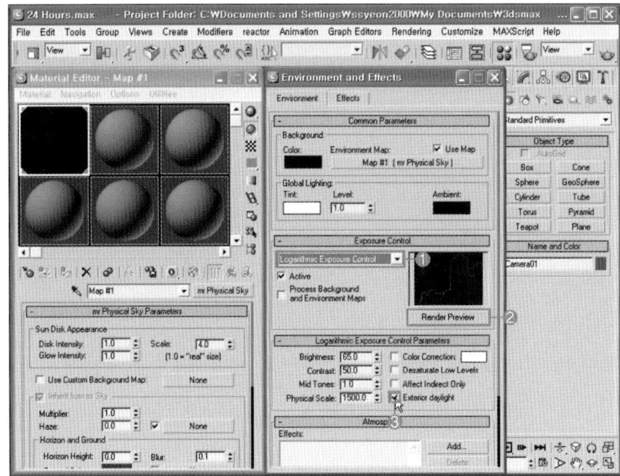

08 In the [Environment and Effects] dialog box, select [Logarithmic Exposure Control] in [Exposure Control], and click [Render Preview] to preview the rendering status of the Scene. Then, check the box for [Logarithmic Exposure Control Parameters]–[Exterior daylight] so that mr Physical Sky and Daylight are calculated when using Daylight.

Exposure Control

Note >>>

Exposure Control is one of the tools used to adjust the effect of the light on the scene's brightness. It is useful for interiors or construction designs. There are four degrees of exposure, including Automatic, which automatically adjusts the basic brightness, Linear, which removes the shadows as much as possible, Logarithmic, for expressing sunlight, and Pseudo, which adjusts based on specific colors.

Automatic Exposure Control

Linear Exposure Control

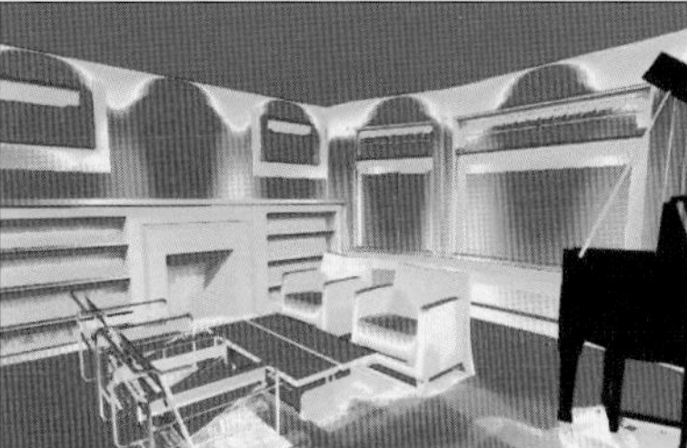

Pseudo Color Exposure Control

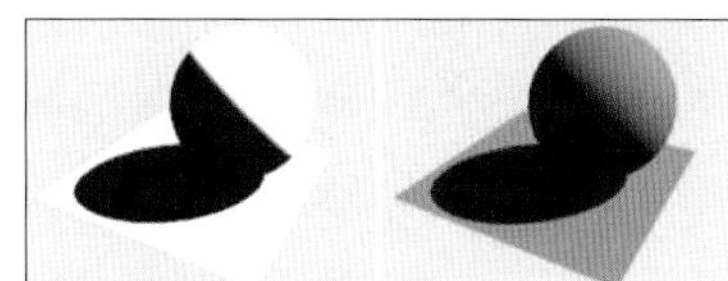

Logarithmic Exposure Control

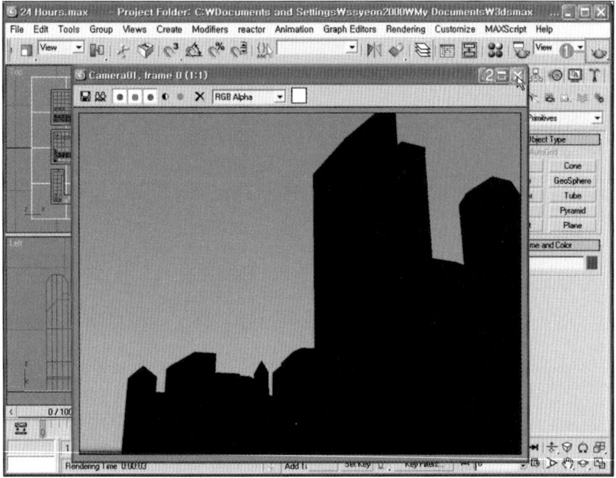

09 Select the Perspective Viewport, and click [Quick Render] on the main toolbar to see the rendered shape. Click on the rendered image window to close it.

Illustrating Time of Day

The Daylight option is a very effective tool that expresses light emitted by the sun in various positions in the sky. Combine it with the mental ray renderer's mr Sun and mr Sky features to achieve realistic sunlight effects.

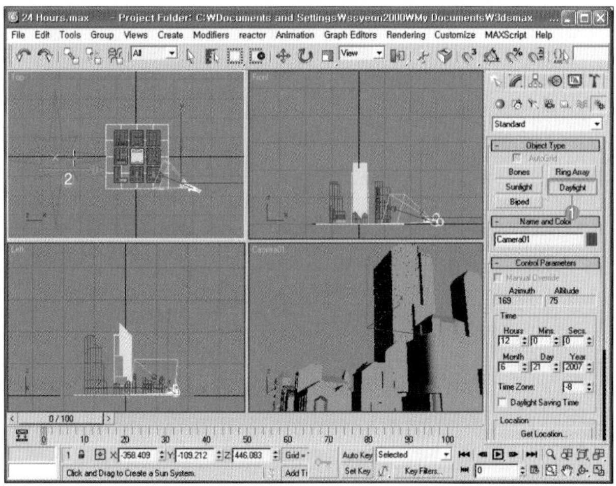

01 Click [Systems]–[Standard]– Daylight on the Create panel. In the Top Viewport, click–and–drag at the location shown in the picture to create the points to be illuminated.

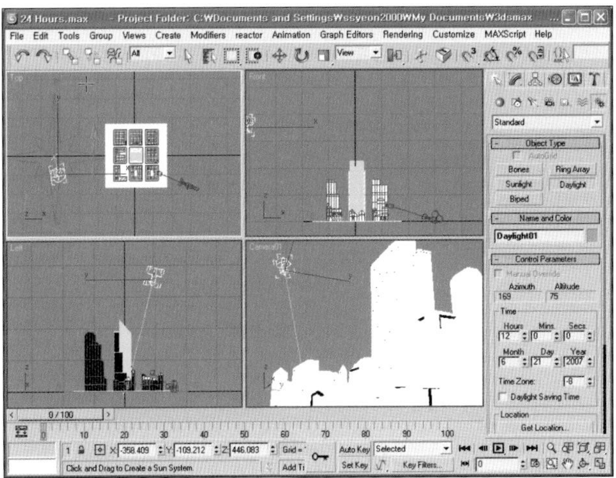

02 Then position the mouse to determine the location of the sun, and click in the Viewport.

tip >>

Setting the Direction of Light

After selecting the Daylight object, use [Select and Scale] to precisely set the object's direction.

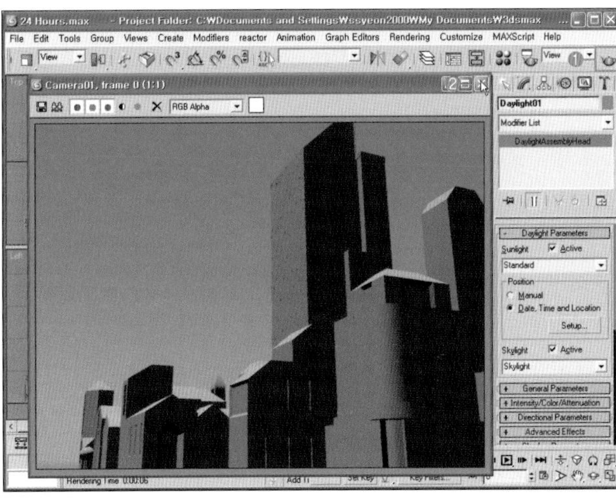

03 Select the Perspective Viewport and click [Quick Render] on the main toolbar to see the sunlight shining on the buildings. Click on the rendered image window to close it.

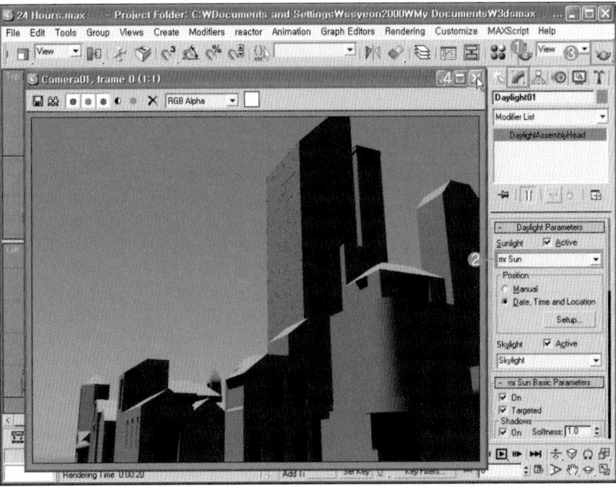

04 With the "Daylight01" light selected, move to the Modify panel. Select [mr Sun] for the Parameter's [Sunlight], and click [Quick Render] on the main toolbar for the Perspective Viewport to preview the scene. Click on the rendered image window to close it.

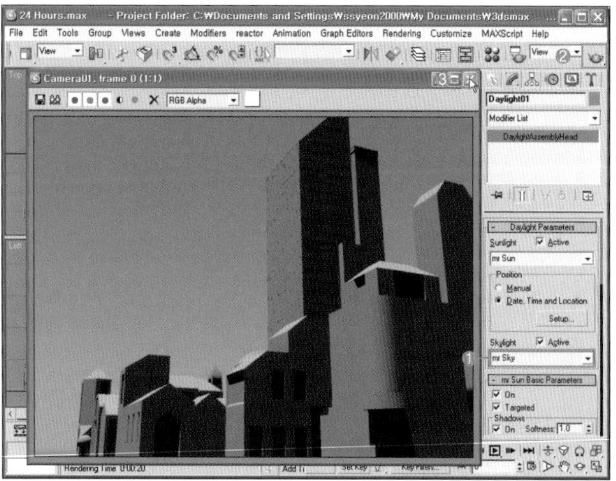

05 With the "Daylight01" object selected, select 'mr Sky' for [Daylight Parameters]–[Skylight]. Click [Quick Render] on the main toolbar for the Perspective Viewport to preview the change in the scene's lighting. Click on the rendered image window to close it.

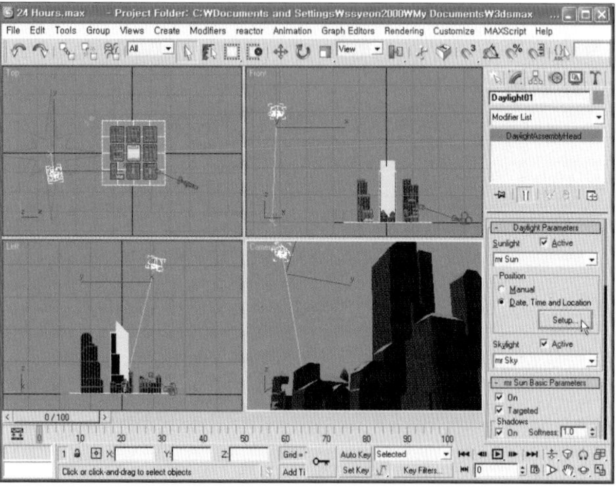

06 Under the [Daylight Parameters] menu for the "Daylight01" object, click [Position]–Setup.

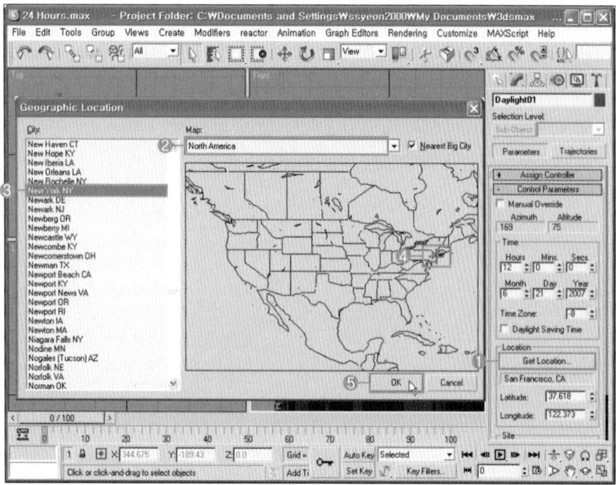

07 Click [Motion] to go to the Motion panel, then click [Location]–Get Location..., and set the desired region for the season in the [Geographic Location] dialog box.

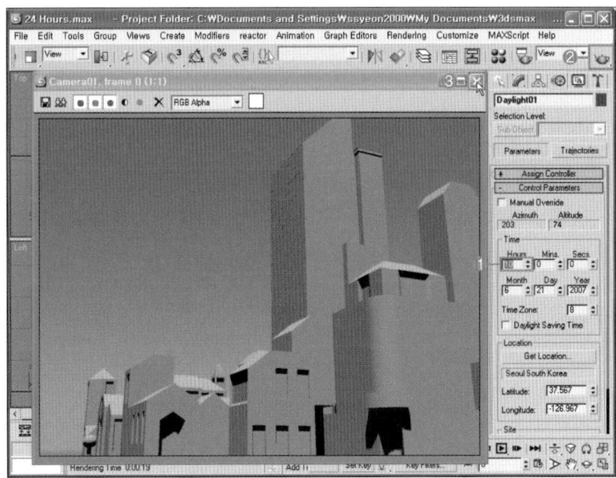

08 Enter [10] for [Control Parameters]–[Time], and click [Quick Render] on the main toolbar for the Perspective Viewport. Click on the rendered image window to close it.

09 Enter [16] for [Control Parameters]–[Time], and click [Quick Render] on the main toolbar of the Perspective Viewport to preview the change in the scene. Click on the rendered image window to close it.

10 Open the [Material Editor] by clicking [Material Editor] on the main toolbar. Manipulate the size of the sunlight and the range of the light source. Click to close the [Material Editor]. Select the [mr Physical Sky] Sample Slot in the [Material Editor], and under [Sun Disk Appearance], enter [6] for [Scale] and [2] for [Glow Intensity].

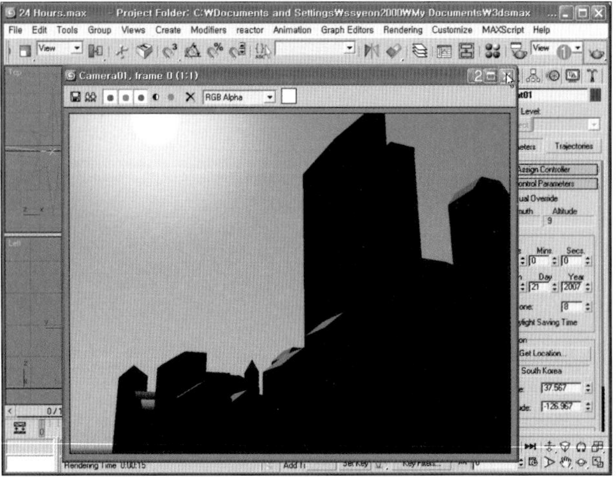

11 Select the Perspective Viewport, and click [Quick Render] on the main toolbar to preview the modified shape of the sun. Click on the rendered image window to close it.

Showing Progression of the Sun

It is possible to express the movement of the sun throughout a day using the Set Key animation method for Daylight.

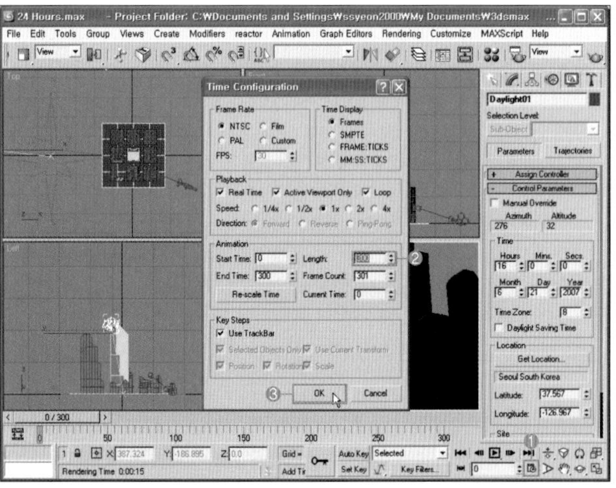

01 To change the animation's processing time, click [Time Configuration] on time control. When the [Time Configuration] dialog box appears, enter [300] for [Length], and click [OK].

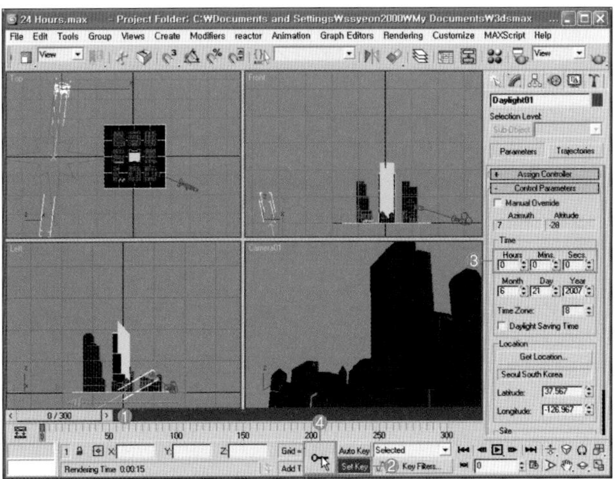

02 Move the time slider to Frame 0, and click [Set Key] to start the animation mode. For "Daylight01," under [Time], enter [0] for [Hours], and click [Key Click] to register a new key.

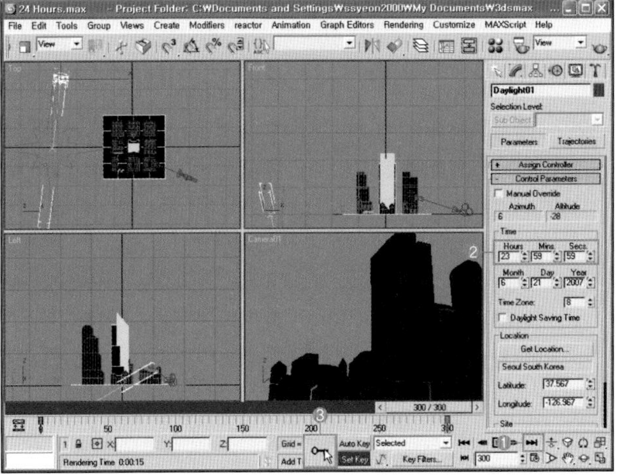

03 Click [Go to End] of the time control to move the time slider to the last frame, and under [Time], enter [23] for [Hours], [59] for [Mins], and [59] for [Secs]. Click [Key Click] to register a new key.

tip >>

Registering Keys for Animation Sections

Overall, two keys are registered. The sun's location in frame 0 is set to its midnight position (0 Hours), and its location in frame 300 is set to 23:59:59, or one second short of 24 hours later. 3ds Max 9 will fill in the frames between automatically.

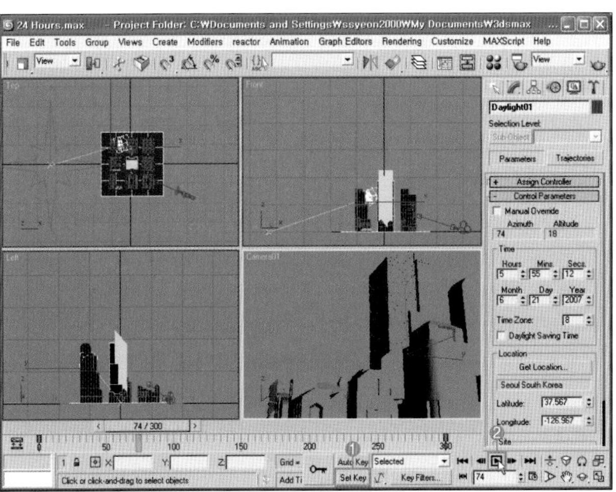

04 Click [Set Key] to exit the animation mode. Click [Play Animation] of time control to view the sun's movement over a simulated period of 24 hours.

Using Omni Light for Dawn and Dusk

The sunlight animation is not sufficient to reveal the objects during the darker hours, such as dawn and dusk. But the light can be turned on or off using Omni Light.

01 Click [Zoom Region] on the Viewport Control, and click–and–drag the front part of the camera in the Top Viewport to zoom the selected part.

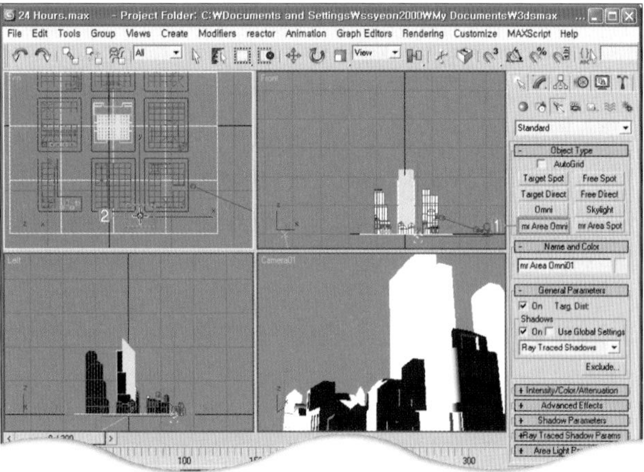

02 Click [Lights]–[Standard]–[mr Area Omni] on the Create panel. Click the front part of the camera in the Top Viewport to install a new mr Area Omni Light.

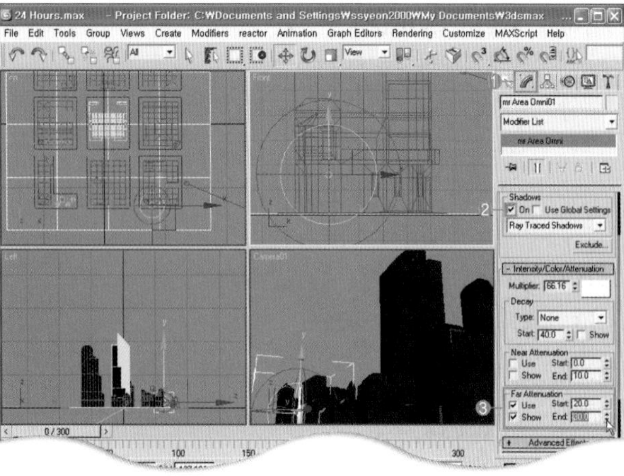

03 With the "mr Area Omni01" light selected, move to the Modify panel. Set the [Intensity/Color/Attenuation], to turn the shadows on and set the range of light, by checking [Use] and [Show] of [Far Attenuation]. Enter [20] for [Start] and [30] for [End].

tip >>

Using Far Attenuation

Essentially, a Light object emits light without being limited by distance. The user can set the desired distance using [Far Attenuation]. Also, [Far Attenuation] is used to create the fading effect of light with the increase of distance.

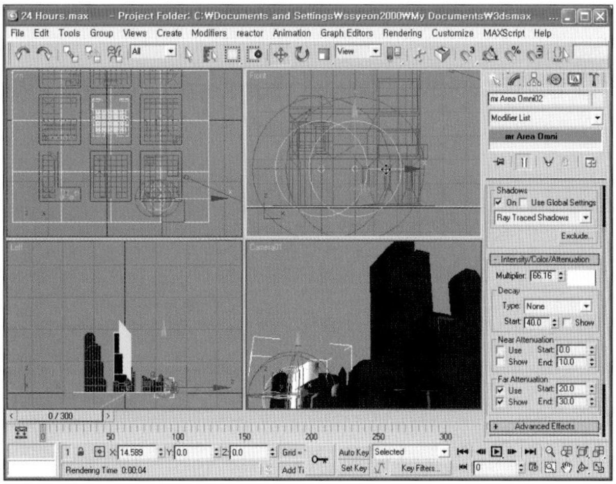

04 While pressing <Shift>, in the Front Viewport, click–and–drag the "mr Area Omni01" light towards the right to make a new light.

05 In the [Clone Options] dialog box that appears, enter [3] for [Number of Copies] and click [OK].

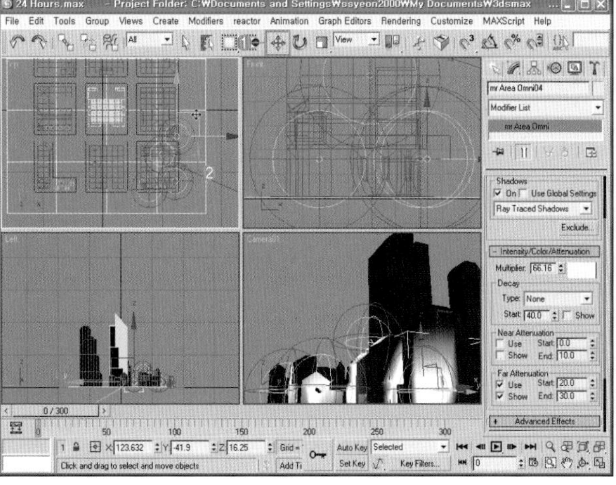

06 With the same method, create more light as desired, and make modifications in the Top Viewport using [Select and Move].

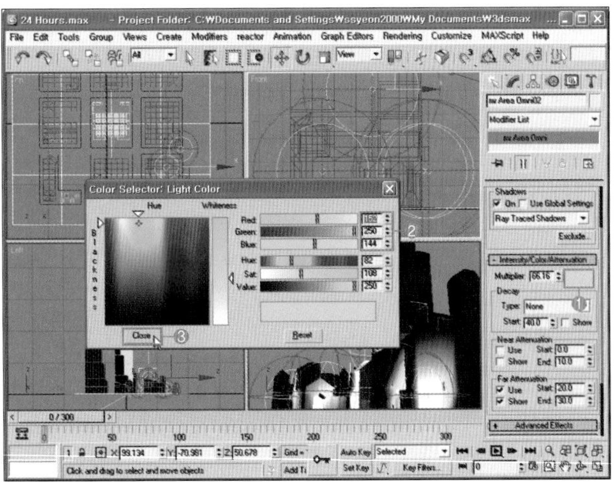

07 Click the color button of the copied "mr Area Omni02" light and modify to Green (RGB: 152, 250, 144) in the [Color Selector] dialog box.

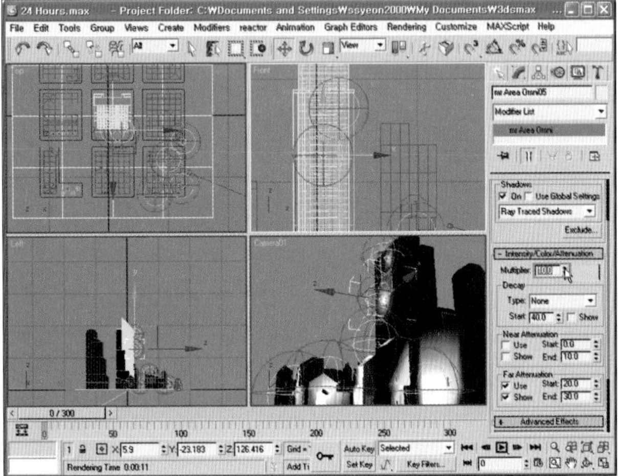

08 With the same method, change the colors of each light, as well as the value of [Multiplier] to adjust the brightness.

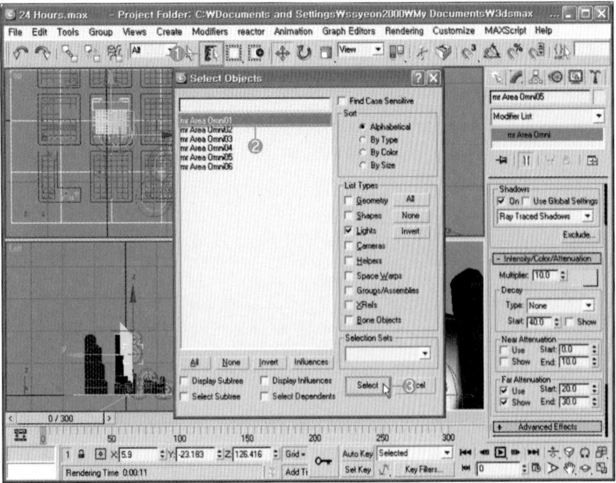

09 Click [Select by Name] on the main toolbar. Select "mr Area Omni01" in the [Select Objects] dialog box and click [Select].

10 With the time slider at frame 0, click [Auto Key] to enter the animation mode. Under [Intensity/Color/Attenuation] of "mr Area Omni01", enter [10] for [Multiplier], and click [Key Click [key]] to register a new key.

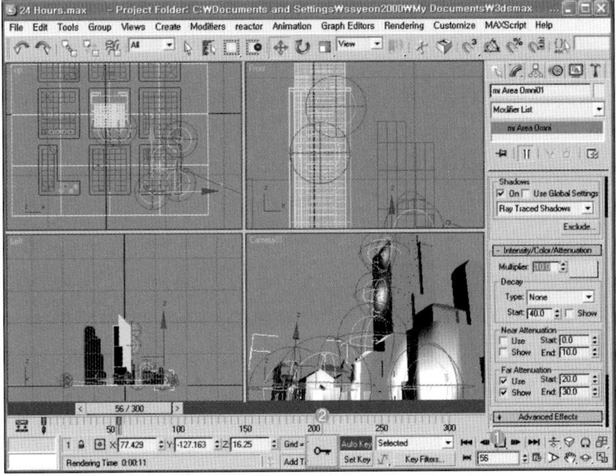

11 Enter [56] in time control to move the time slider, and click [Key Click [key]] again to register the key.

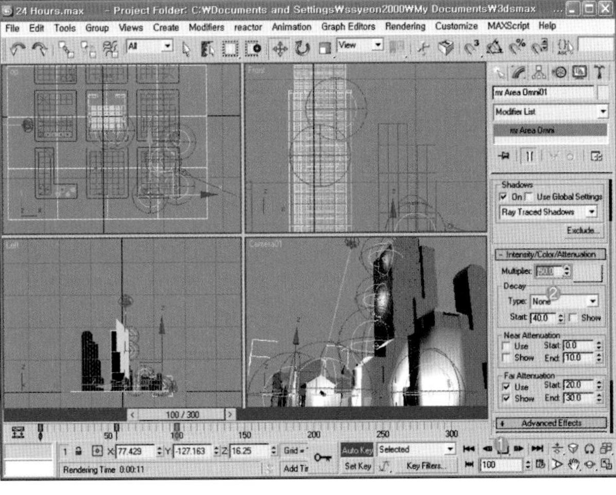

12 Enter [100] in the time control to move the time slider, and enter [50] for [Multiplier] to register a new key. As a result, the brightness of the light between frames 56 and 100 becomes gradually stronger.

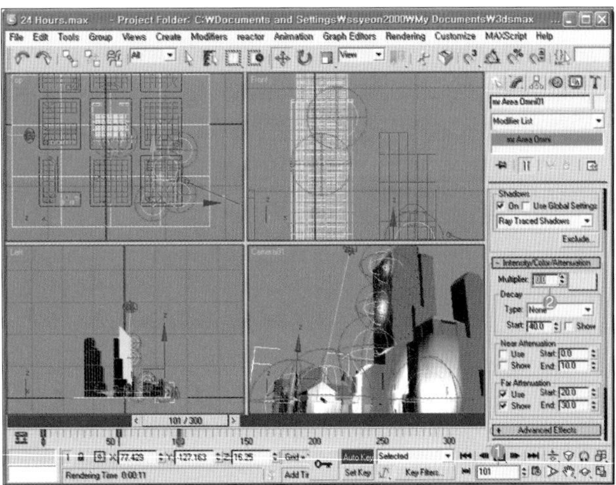

13 Enter [101] in the time control to move the time slider, and enter [0] for [Multiplier] to register a new key. The intensity of the light in frame 101 is minimized.

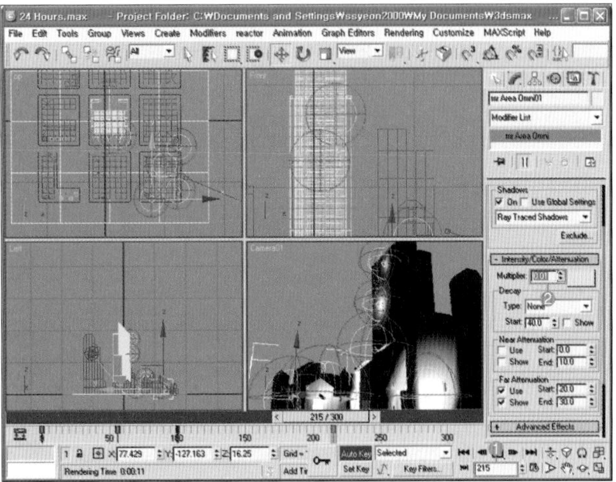

14 Enter [215] in the time control to move the time slider, and enter [0.01] for [Multiplier] to register a new key. The light between frame 101 and 215 is effectively disabled.

15 Enter [216] in the time control to move the time slider, and enter [50] for [Multiplier] to register a new key. The light suddenly appears.

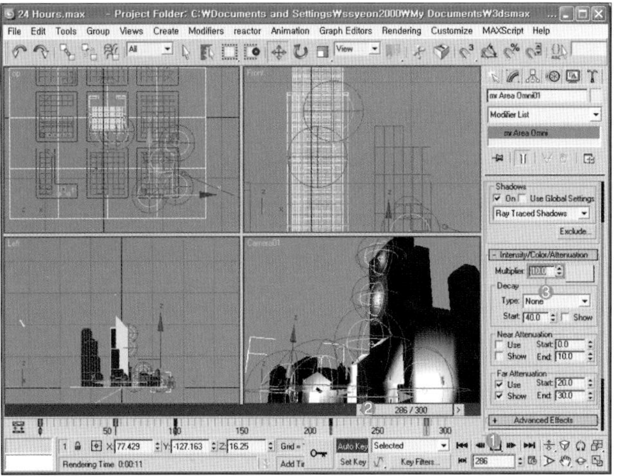

16 Enter [286] in the time control to move the time slider, and enter [10] for [Multiplier] to register a new key. The intensity of the light from frame 216 to 286 becomes gradually weaker.

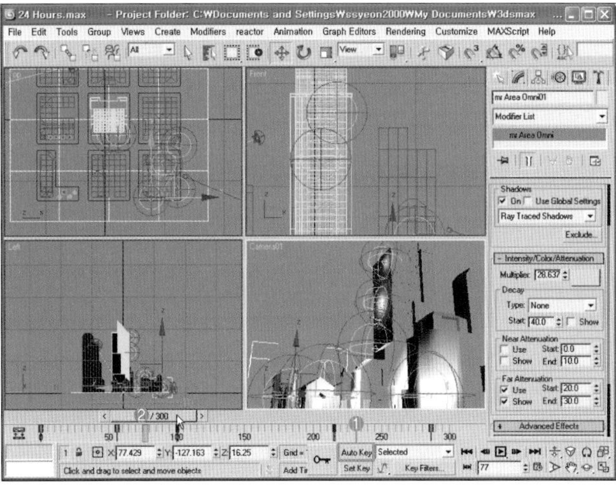

17 Click Auto Key to exit animation mode. Move the time slider to preview how the light changes.

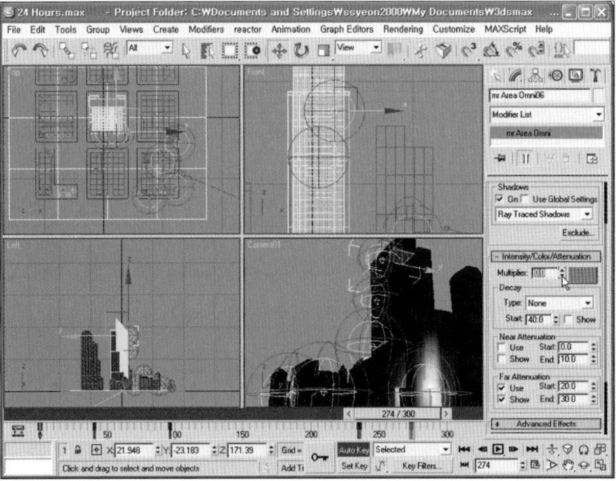

18 Just as with "mr Area Omni01", register some additional time keys that change the light at different times.

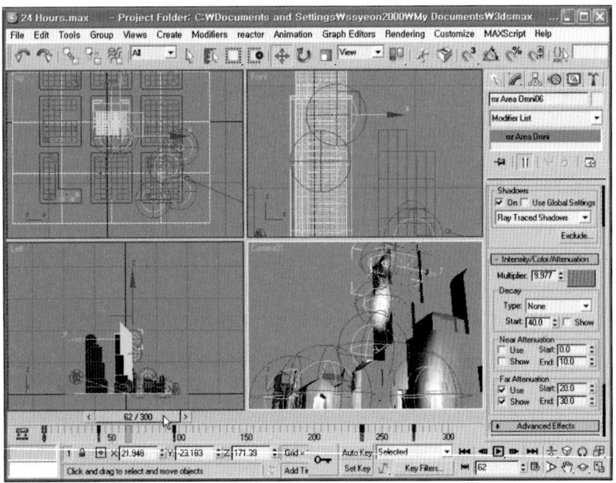

19 Exit the animation mode, and move the time slider to see how the brightness of the light changes.

Rendering for the Final Animation

When the animation for the 24–hour lighting effect is completed, you can proceed with the rendering to produce it as a separate movie.

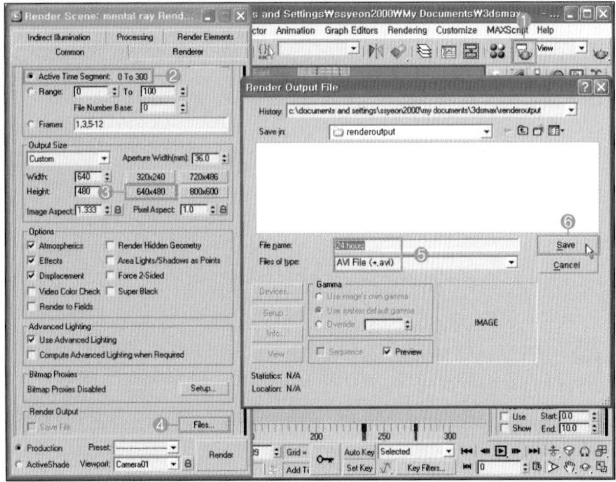

01 Click [Render Scene Dialog] on the main toolbar. When the [Render Scene] window appears, set it. To save the image to be rendered as a file, click Files... of [Render Output]. When the [Render Output File] dialog box appears, set it.

② When the [Render Scene] window appears, click [Active Time Segment: 0 to 300] on the [Common] tab, and at [Output Size], select 640x480.

⑤ When the [Render Output File] dialog box appears, enter "24 hours" in the name slot, and set the file format as "AVI File."

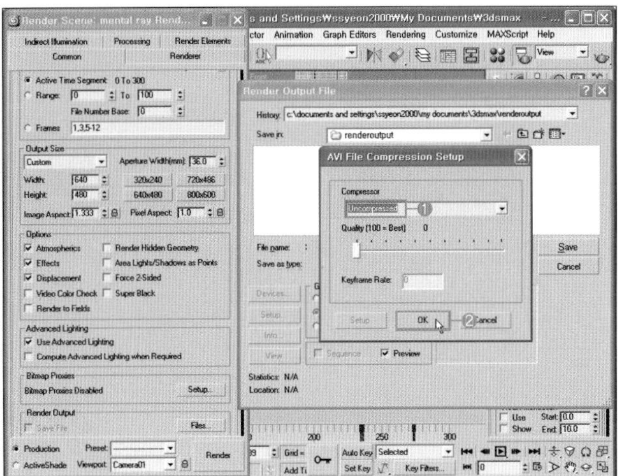

02 When the [AVI File Compression Setup] dialog box appears, select "Uncompressed" for the compression codec and click [OK].

03 Click Render on the [Render Scene] window to process the rendering of the entire animation.

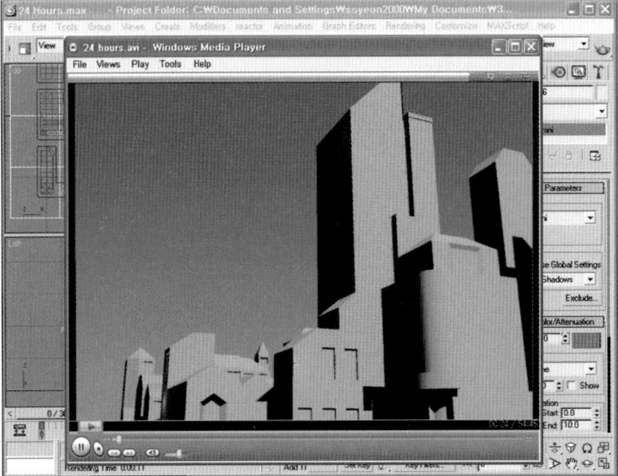

04 When the rendering is completed, play the saved "24 hours.avi" file.

Supplementary CD\Sample\Chapter 4\Exercise 2\24 Hours-final.max

Exercise 03

Producing Natural Textures

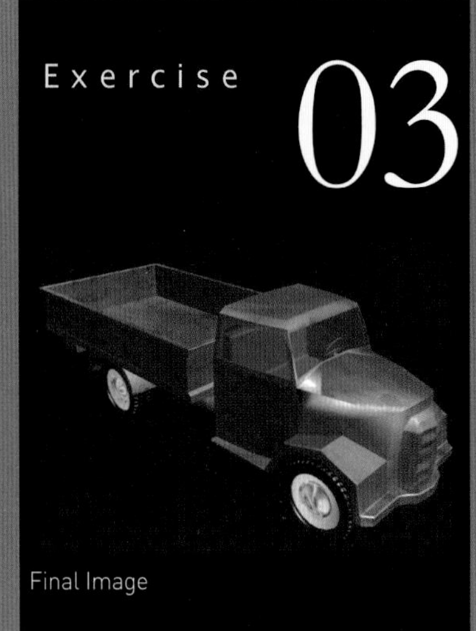

Final Image

Mapping can be described as applying image files to an object's surface using mathematical calculation. Before this can be done, the user must mix the Materials and determine the Material type. Mapping can be done by mixing various maps in a layered structure. This section will discuss how to mix two Materials by using the Vertex Paint Modifier.

\Sample\Chapter 4\Exercise 3\Truck.max

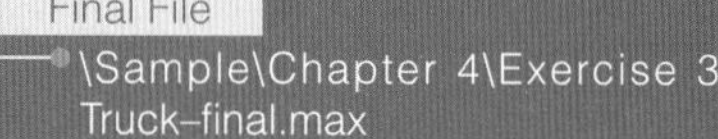

\Sample\Chapter 4\Exercise 3\Truck-final.max

Mapping with the Standard Materials and the Bump Map

The basics of 3ds Max 9 Mapping include using the Standard Material type. The Bump Map can be applied to simulate uneven polygons on the surface the objects.

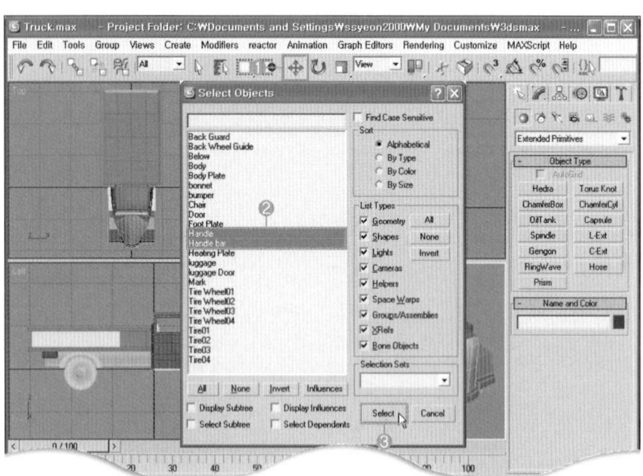

01 Open the "Truck.max" file from the supplementary CD and click [Select by Name] on the main toolbar. Select "Handle" and "Handle fixture" object in the [Select Objects] dialog box while pressing <Ctrl>, and click [Select].

Supplementary CD\Sample\Chapter 4\Exercise 3\Truck.max

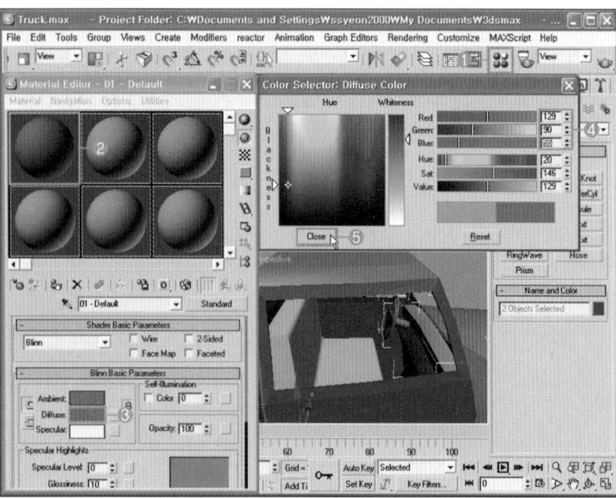

02 Click [Material Editor] on the main toolbar to open the [Material Editor] dialog box. Select the first Sample Slot in the [Material Editor], and click the [Diffuse] color button. Modify to light brown (RGB: 129, 90, 55) in the [Color Selector] dialog box.

03 Click [Show Map in Viewport] and [Assign Material to Selection] to apply the Material to the selected object.

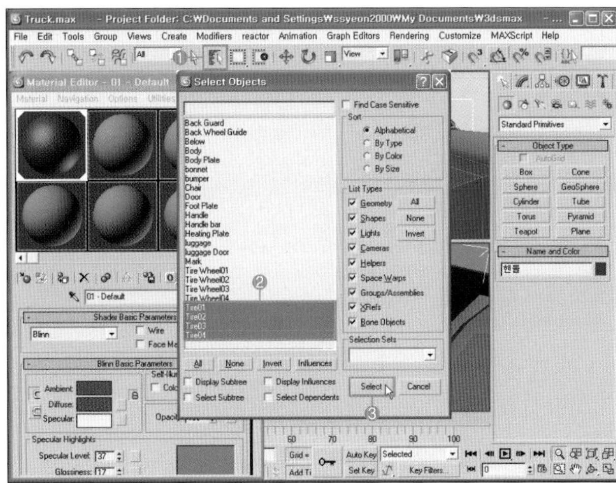

04 Click [Select by Name] on the main toolbar. Select the "tire" objects in the [Select Objects] dialog box while pressing <Ctrl>, and click [Select].

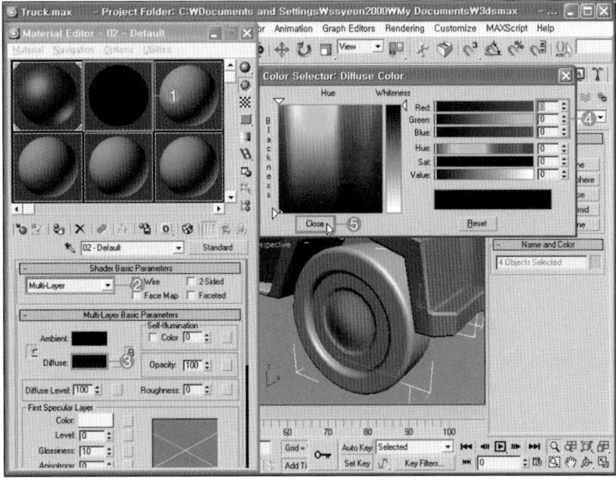

05 Click the second Sample Slot of the [Material Editor], and select "Multi–Layer" Shader to vary the light reflections. Then click the [Diffuse] color button, and modify to black (RGB: 0, 0, 0) in the [Color Selector] dialog box.

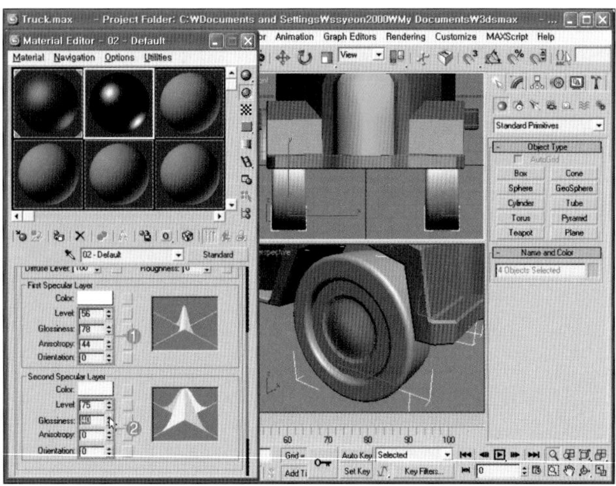

06 Set the [Level], [Glossiness], and [Anisotropy] for the [First Specular Layer] and the [Second Specular Layer] to set double reflections for the light.

1. Enter [56, 78, 44] in the [First Specular Layer] fields for [Level], [Glossiness] and [Anisotropy].
2. Enter [75, 40, 0] in the [Second Specular Layer] fields for [Level], [Glossiness] and [Anisotropy].

07 Select [Bitmap] map on the Material/Map Browser, which appears by clicking [Map]–[Map]–[None], and click [OK].

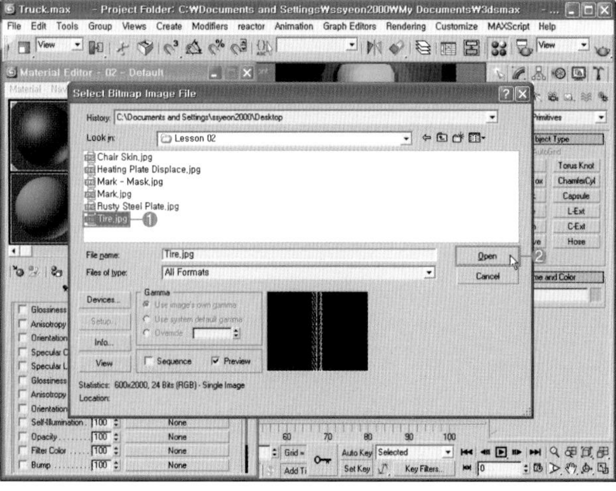

08 Select the "Tire.jpg" file from the supplementary CD in the [Select Bitmap Image File] dialog box and click [Open].

Supplementary CD\Sample\Chapter 4\Exercise 3\Tire.jpg

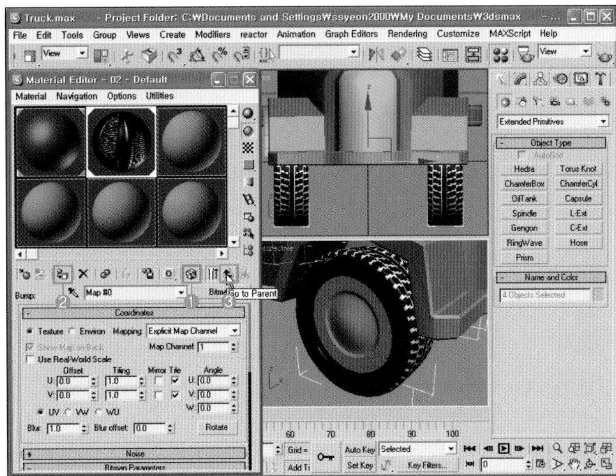

09 Click [Show Map in Viewport] and [Assign Material to Selection] to apply the Material to the selected object. Then, click [Go to Parent] to return to the initial screen.

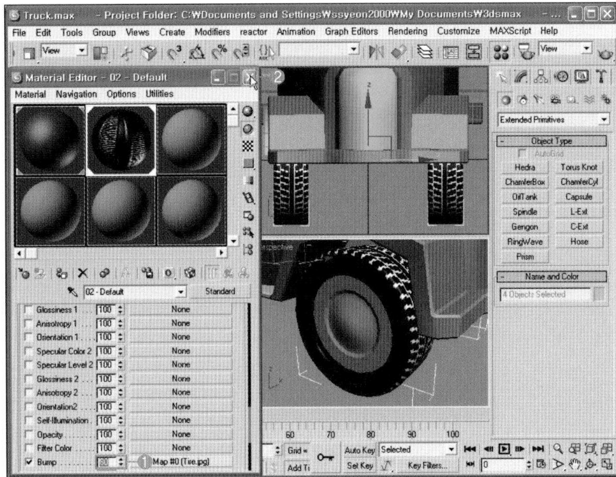

10 Enter [80] for [Bump] to adjust the weight of the [Bump] Map, and click to close the [Material Editor].

11 Check the mapping status of the tire.

tip >>

Do Not Apply UVW Map Modifier

If the UVW Map Modifier is applied, the tire mapping status cannot be adjusted. It is recommended not to use it.

12 Select the Perspective Viewport and click [Quick Render] on the main toolbar to see the rendered shape. Click ☒ on the rendered image screen to close it.

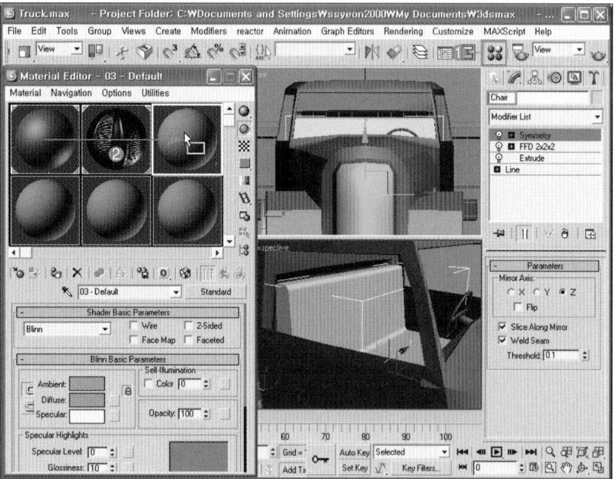

13 Click [Material Editor] on the main toolbar to open the [Material Editor] dialog box. Select the "Chair" object, and copy the first Sample Slot Material in the [Material Editor] to the third Slot by click–and–dragging.

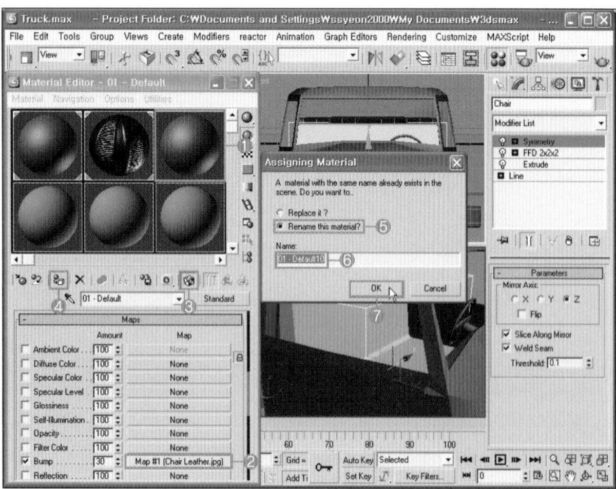

14 Select the copied third Sample Slot, and apply the "Chair Leather.jpg" file to [Bump], and apply the Material to the selected object. To avoid having Materials with the same name, check [Rename this material?] in the [Assigning Material] dialog box and rename it.

Supplementary CD\Sample\Chapter 4\Exercise 3\Chair Leather.jpg

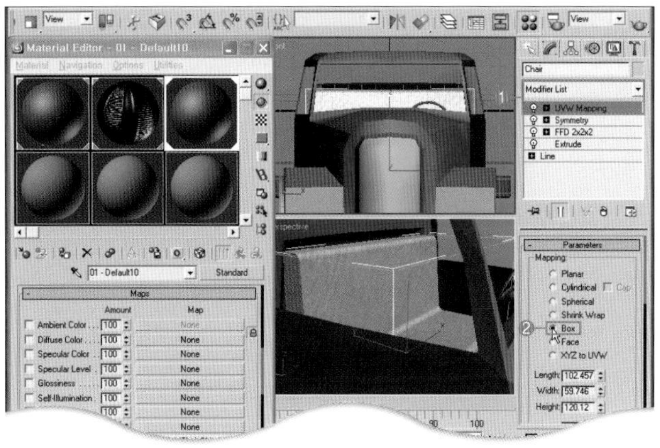

15 With the "Chair" object selected, click the [Modifier List] combo box and select the [UVW Map] modifier. Select [Box] in [Parameters] to change the applied mapping status into a box shape.

Observing the Bump Map Status in the Viewport

Note >>>

To see the status of the [Bump] map in the Viewport, click [Show Map in Viewport] on the [Bitmap] parameter screen, and click [Go to Parent].

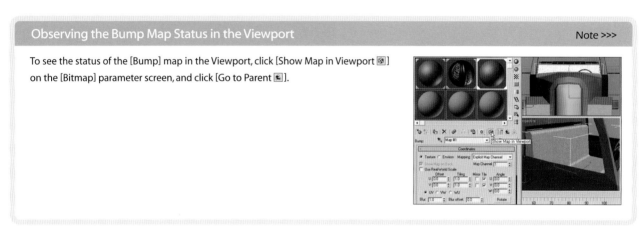

Mask Mapping Using Opacity

In some cases, the user will want to show some text or marks on the surface but make the rest of the object transparent. The Mask mapping technique is used to achieve this effect. To do mask mapping, the user will apply two image files to [Diffuse Color] and [Opacity]. This section will describe the principles and application techniques for this process.

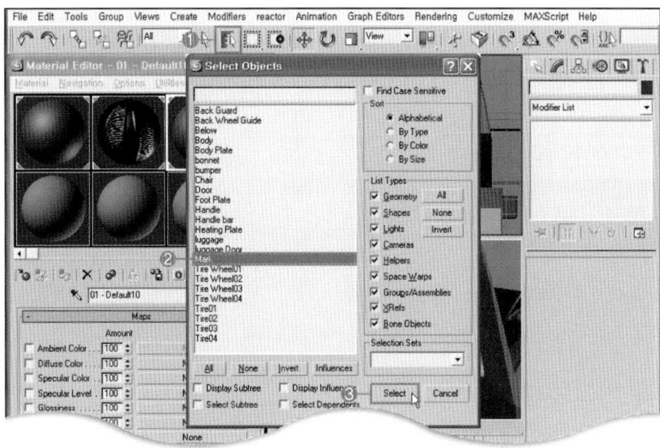

01 Click [Select by Name] on the main toolbar. Click the "Mark" object in the [Select Objects] dialog box, and click [Select].

02 Select the fourth Sample Slot of the [Material Editor], and apply "Mark.jpg'"and "Mark–Mask.jpg'" files to [Diffuse Color] and [Opacity], respectively. For the status of the applied Materials, click [Background ▩] to see the Sample Slot.

Supplementary CD\Sample\Chapter 4\Exercise 3\Mark.jpg, Mark–Mask.jpg

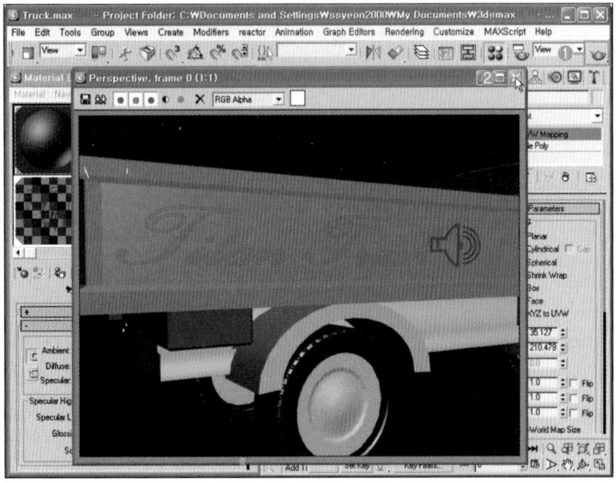

03 Select the Perspective Viewport and click [Quick Render] on the main toolbar to see the rendered shape. Click ☒ on the rendered image window to close it.

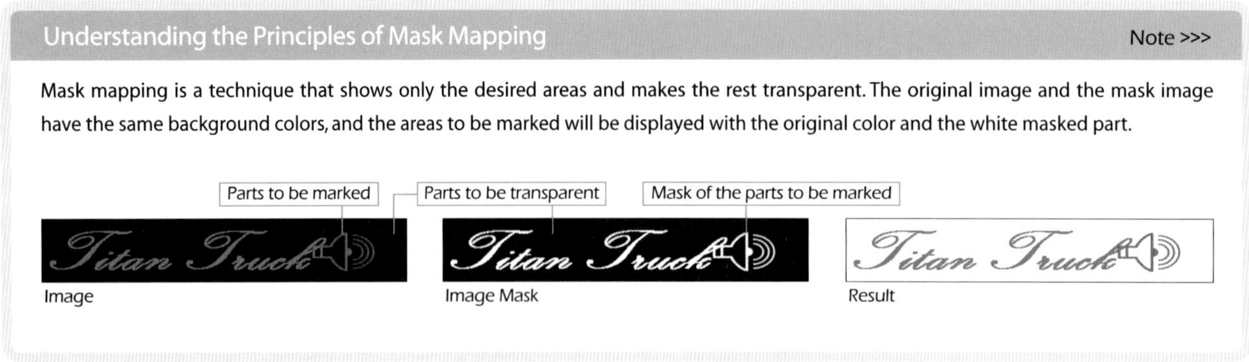

Understanding the Principles of Mask Mapping

Note >>>

Mask mapping is a technique that shows only the desired areas and makes the rest transparent. The original image and the mask image have the same background colors, and the areas to be marked will be displayed with the original color and the white masked part.

Image

Image Mask

Result

Mapping Metal to the Wheel using the Material Library

The collection of pre–made Materials provided with 3ds Max 9 is called the Material Library. Let's discuss how to select metal Materials that can be applied to tire wheels.

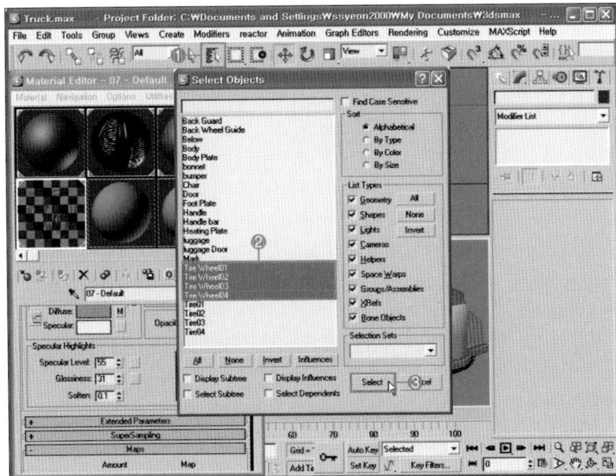

01 Click [Select by Name] on the main toolbar. While pressing <Ctrl>, select the "Tire Wheel" objects in the [Select Objects] dialog box, and click [Select].

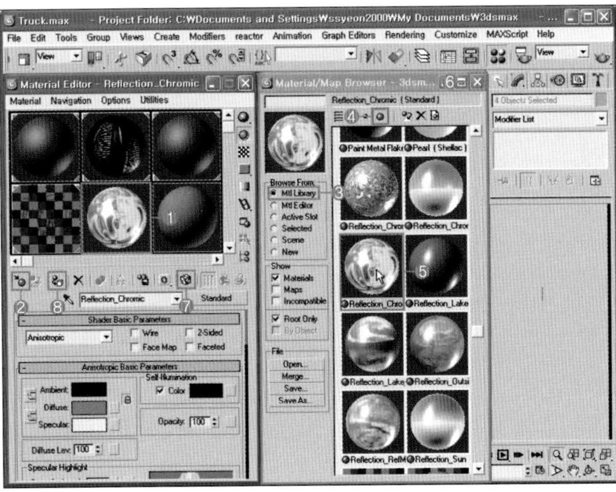

02 Select the fifth Sample Slot in the [Material Editor] dialog box, and activate the [Material/Map Browser] by clicking [Get Material], and click to close. Select [Mtl Library] in the [Material/Map Browser], and click [View Large Icon]. A large image screen appears. Double–click [Reflection_Chrome]. Click [Show Map in Viewport] and [Assign Material to Selection] to apply the Material to the selected object.

Mapping Transparent Glass using the Raytrace Material Type

The truck's glass is hidden in the Viewport. The user can unhide them and map transparent glass with the Raytrace Material type.

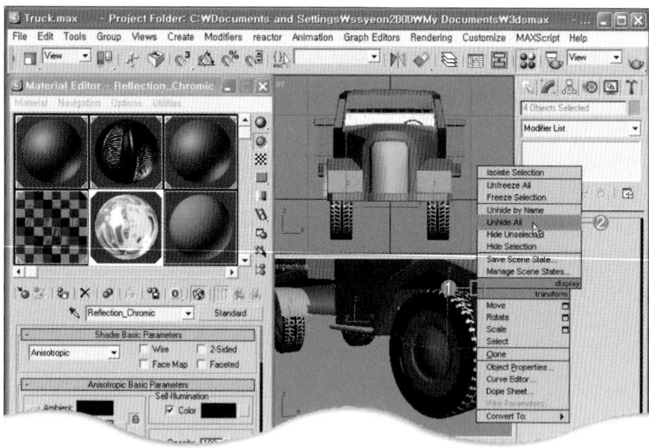

01 To show the hidden "Glass" object, right–click on it, and select [Unhide All] on the quad menu.

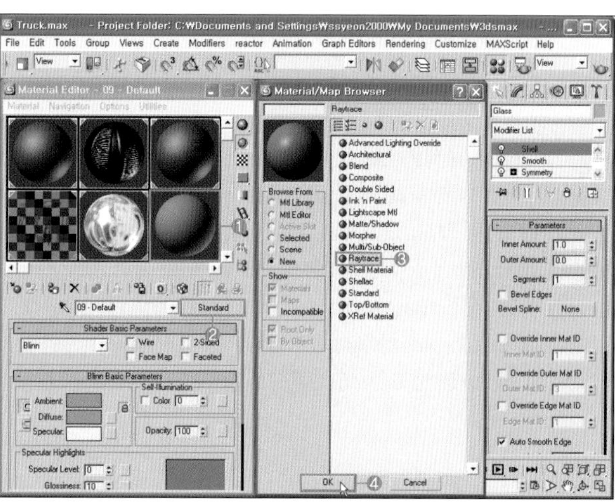

02 Select the sixth Sample Slot in the [Material Editor], and click Standard. Select [Raytrace] in the [Material/Map Browser], and click [OK].

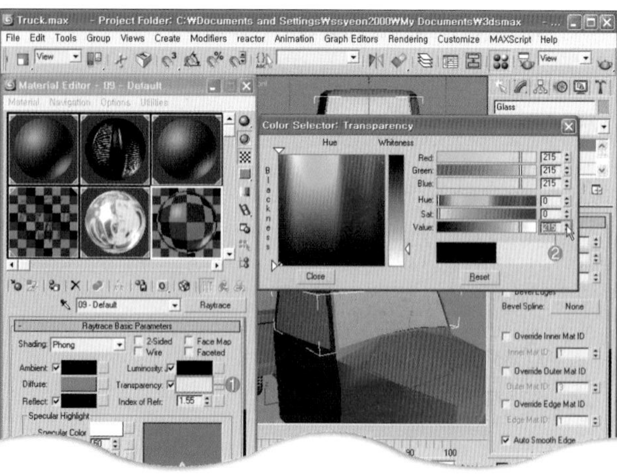

03 Click the color button of [Transparency] in [Raytrace Basic Parameters], and modify to Grey (Value: 215) in the [Color Selector] dialog box.

04 To set the reflection ratio for the objects, click the color button of [Reflect], select black and set the value to [18] in the [Color Selector] dialog box. Click [Show Map in Viewport] and [Assign Material to Selection] to apply the Material to the selected object. Under [Specular Highlight], enter [95] for [Specular Level] and [34] for [Glossiness].

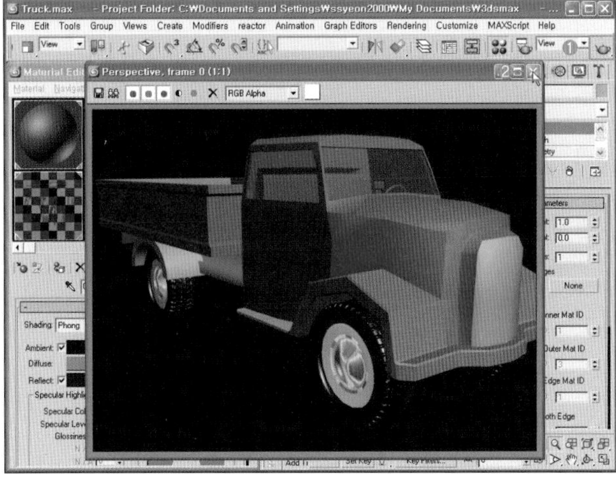

05 Select the Perspective Viewport and click [Quick Render] on the main toolbar to see the rendered scene. Click on the rendered image window to close it.

Modeling Images with the Displace Modifier

Image files can be applied to object surfaces in a similar way as Bump mapping applies Materials.

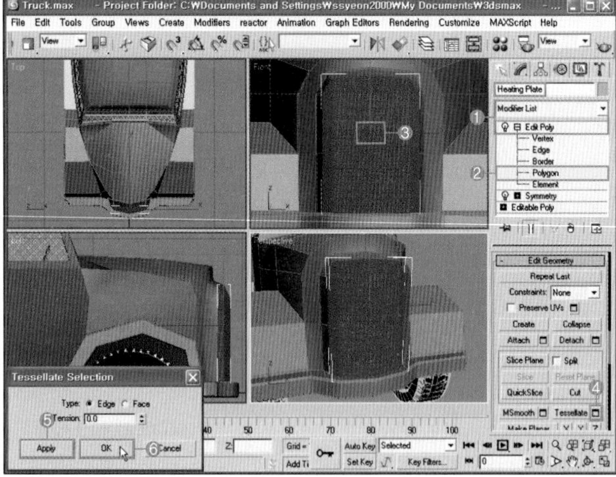

01 Select the "Heating Plate" object and apply the [Edit Poly] Modifier. Select the [Polygon] sub–object and select all of the polygons. Activate the [Tessellate Selection] dialog box by clicking [Tessellate Settings]. Click the [Apply] button twice and [OK] once in the [Tessellate Selection] dialog box to divide the polygons into smaller ones.

tip >>

The Tessellate Feature

Tessellate is a function that increases the number of polygons by dividing the selected polygon in two. It is used to change the form of the polygon into a more complex shape.

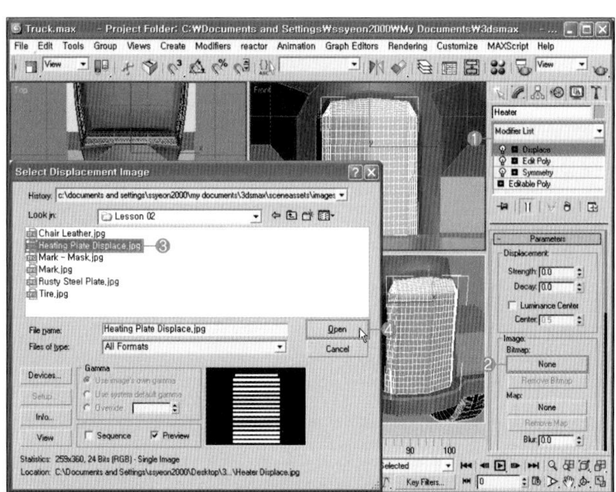

02 Click the [Modifier List] combo box and select the [Displace] Modifier. Click [Parameters]–[Bitmap]– None , select the supplementary CD's "Heating Plate Displace.jpg" file in the [Select Displacement Image] dialog box, and click [Open].

Supplementary CD\Sample\Chapter 4\Exercise 3\Heating Plate Displace.jpg

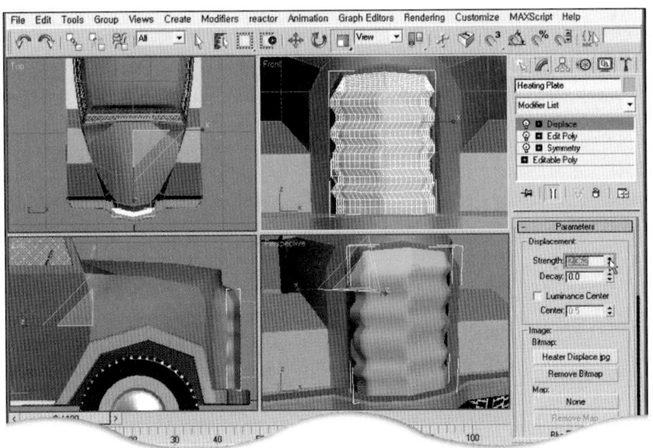

03 Enter [2.3] for [Displacement]–[Strength] to see the changes made to the object.

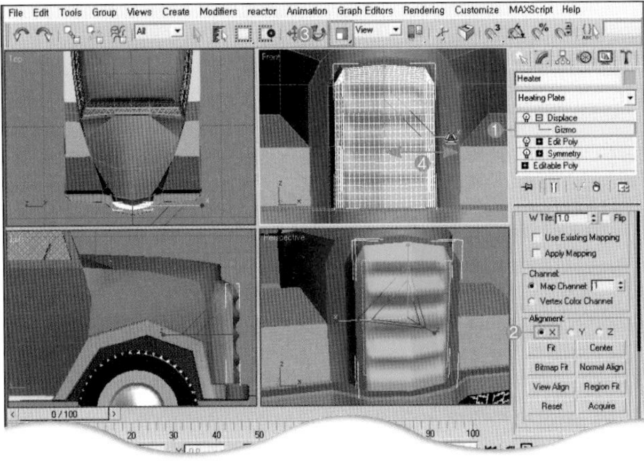

04 Select the [Gizmo] sub–object, select [Alignment]–[X], and adjust the size of the Gizmo with [Select and Scale ].

Mapping the Truck with the Material Library and the Blend Material Type

Materials for car surfaces can be found in the Material Library, applied, and given a rust effect using Blend Material type.

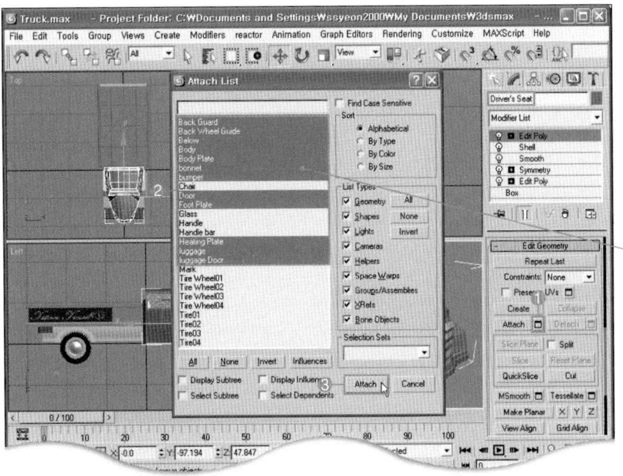

01 Select the “Driver’s Seat” object, and click [Edit Geometry]–[Attach Settings]. Combine the objects related to the body of the car in the [Attach List] dialog box, as shown.

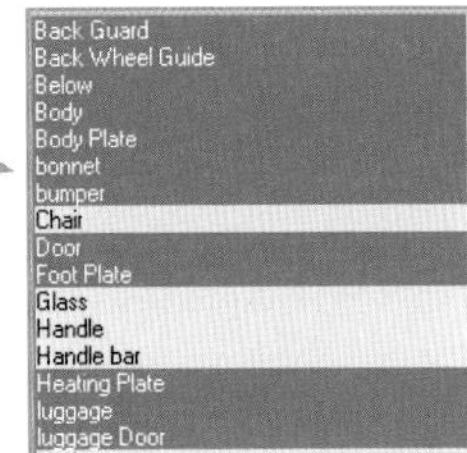

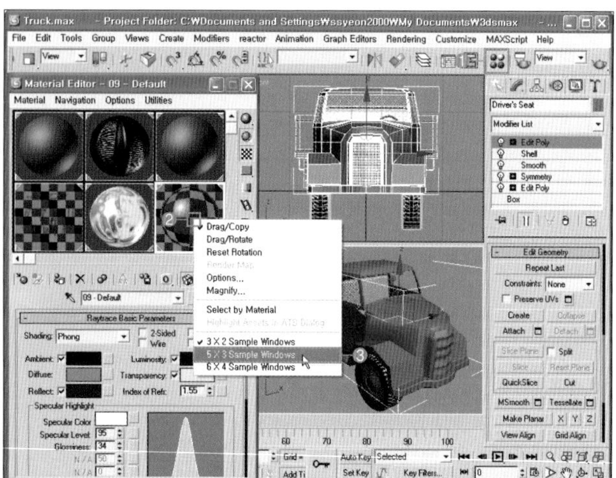

02 Click [Material Editor] on the main toolbar to open the [Material Editor] dialog box. To expand the new Sample Slot, right–click on it and select [5 x 3 Sample Windows] on the menu.

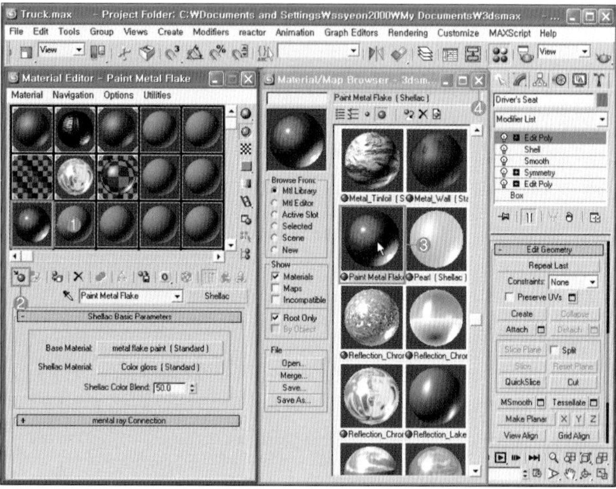

03 Select an empty Sample Slot and click [Get Material] to open the [Material/Map Browser] dialog box. Double–click [Paint Metal Flake] and click to close the [Material/Map Browser].

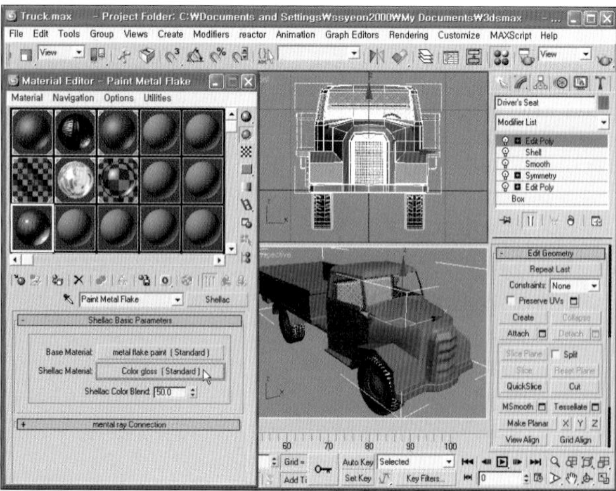

04 To change the color in [Paint Metal Flake]–[Shellac Basic Parameters], click [Color Gloss (Standard)].

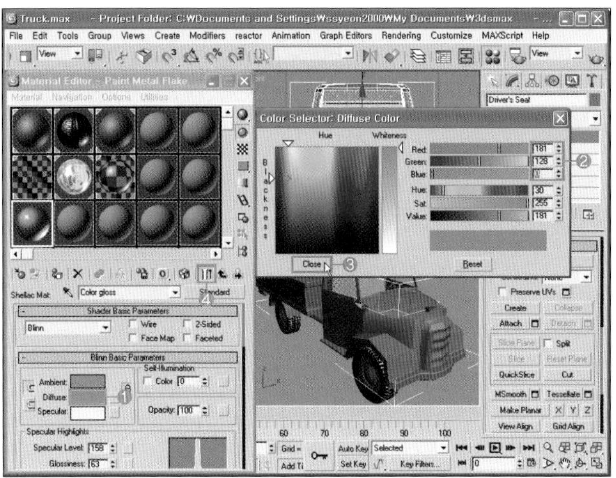

05 Click the color button of [Diffuse] on [Blinn Basic Parameters], and modify to Orange (RGB: 181, 128, 0) in the [Color Selector] dialog box. Click [Go to Parent] to move to the previous screen.

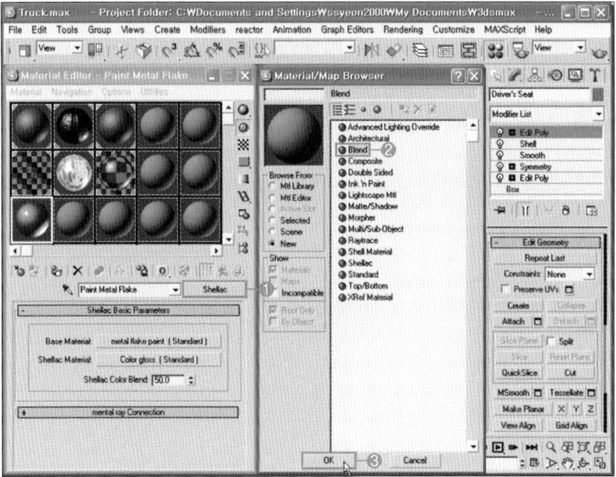

06 To set the [Blend] Material with [Color Gloss (Standard)] Material as the basis, click Shellac and select [Blend] in the [Material/Map Browser], and click [OK].

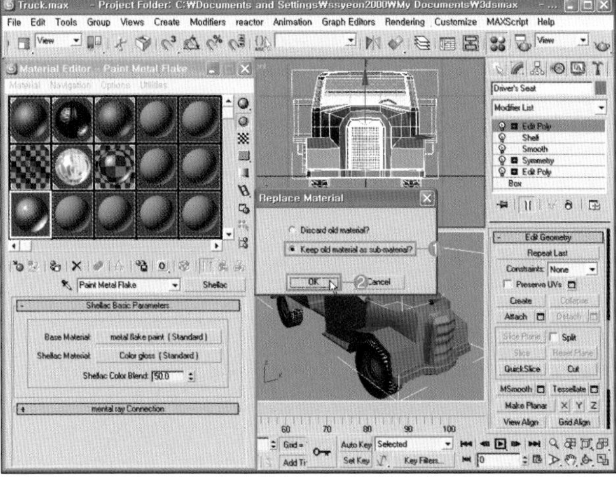

07 When the [Replace Material] dialog box appears, to make [Paint Metal Flake] the basic option, select [Keep old material as sub–material?], and click [OK].

08 Make sure that [Paint Metal Flake (Shellac)] has been applied to the Blend Material type's [Material 1], and click [Material #4 (Standard)] of [Material 2].

09 Click [Maps]–[Diffuse Color]–[None], select [Bitmap] in the [Material/Map Browser], and click [OK].

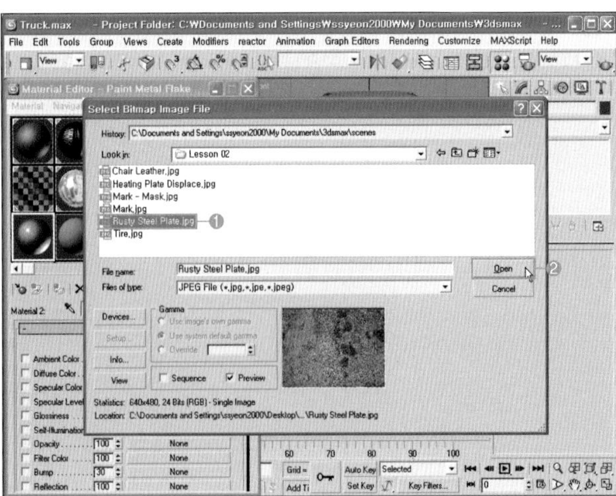

10 Select the supplementary CD's "Rusty Steel Plate.jpg" file in the [Select Bitmap Image File] dialog box, and click [Open].

Supplementary CD\Sample\Chapter 4\Exercise 3\Rusty Steel Plate.jpg

11 Click [Go to Parent] to return to the initial screen.

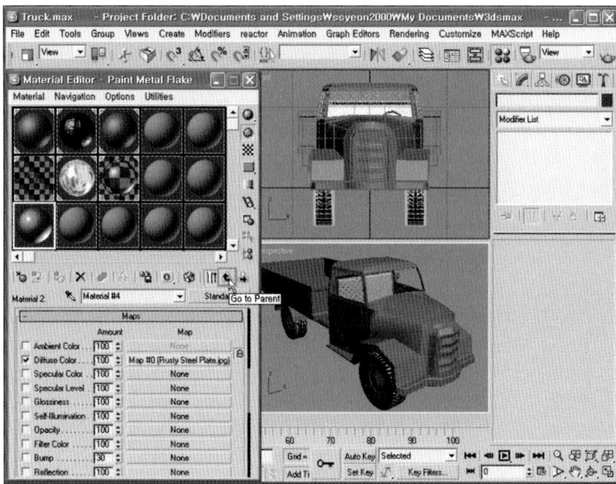

12 Click [Go to Parent] to go up to the top screen.

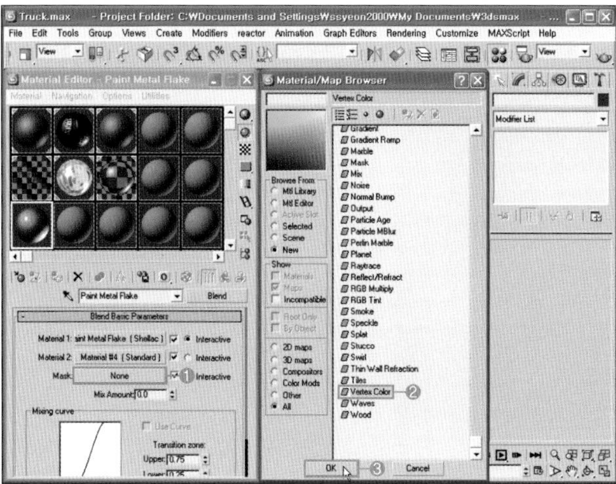

13 For the next process, click [Mask]–None, and select [Vertex Color] in the [Material/Map Browser]. Click [OK].

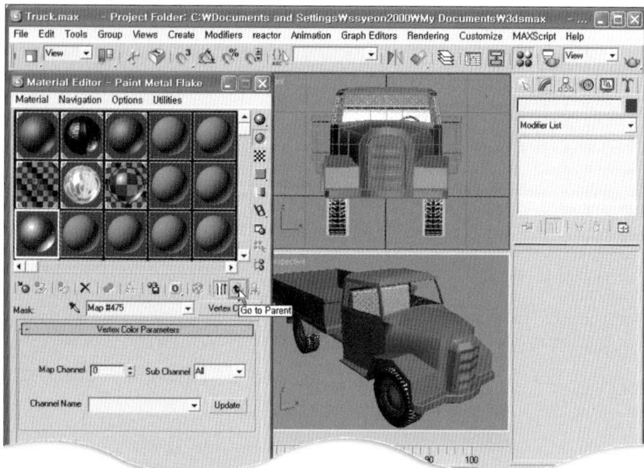

14 When [Vertex Color Parameters] appears, click [Go to Parent] to move to the parent stage screen.

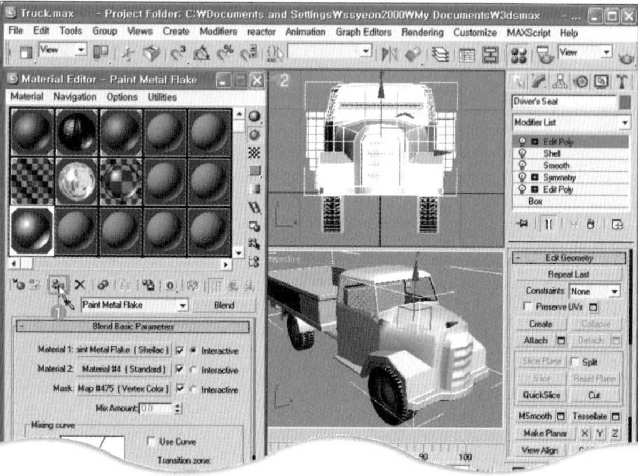

15 Click [Assign Material to Selection] to apply the Material to the "Driver's Seat" object, and click to close it.

Using the Blend Material Type and the Vertex Color Effect

Note >>>

The Blend Material type has the effect of mixing two materials smoothly. If the user does not provide a proper value for [Mix Amount], the effect will be poorly rendered. For the blending to achieve a 1:1 ratio, enter [50] for [Mix Amount]. Refer to the images for examples. To see the effect of the [Vertex Color] map, maintain the value of [Mix Amount] as [0]. By using the Blend Material type, the user can see how batch mixing of the Materials takes effect. However, by using Vertex Color as the mask, the user can only mix the desired parts with the Vertex Paint Modifier.

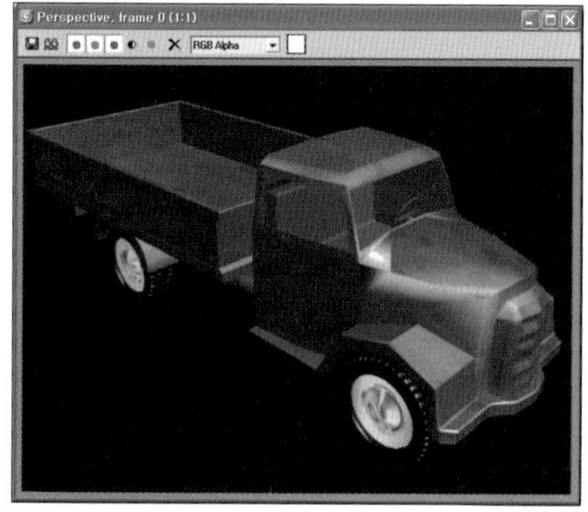

Mix Amount: 50

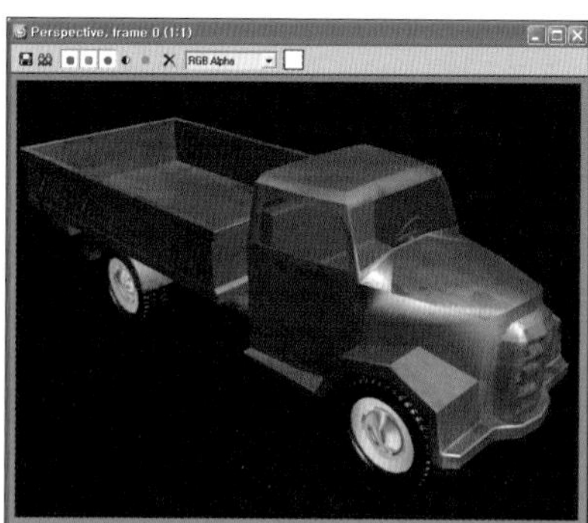

Mix Amount: 0 Vertex Color

Modifying the Blend Material Type with the Vertex Paint Modifier

Next, you can create natural effects for the Blend Material type with the Vertex Paint Modifier and apply the UVW Map Modifier to the applied Material.

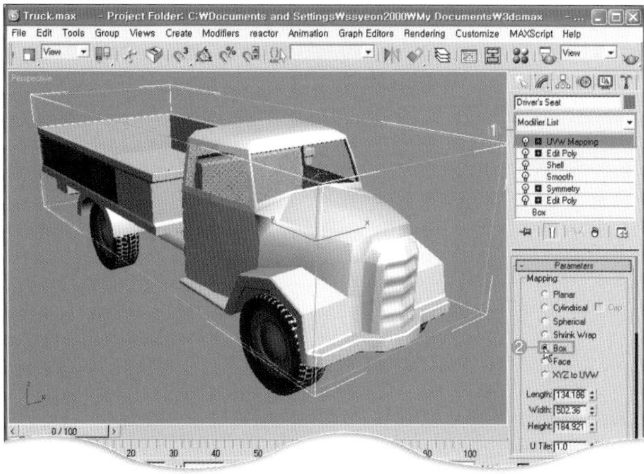

01 With the "Driver's Seat" object selected, click the [Modifier List] combo box and select the [UVW Map] modifier. Select [Parameters]–[Box].

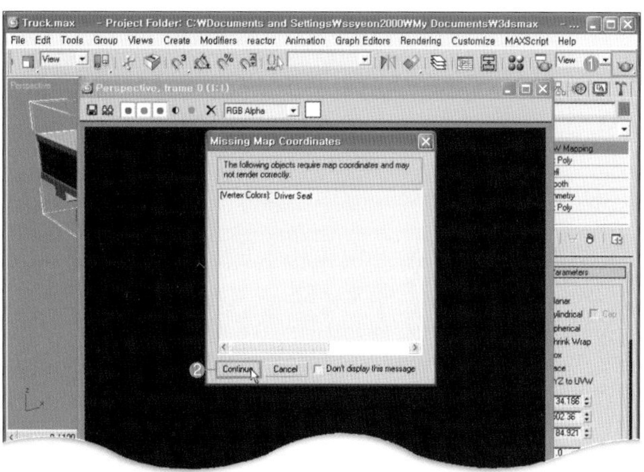

02 Select the Perspective Viewport, and click [Quick Render] on the main toolbar. A dialog box appears, notifying the user that there are some problems in the rendering because of the [Blend] Material's [Vertex Color]. Click [Continue].

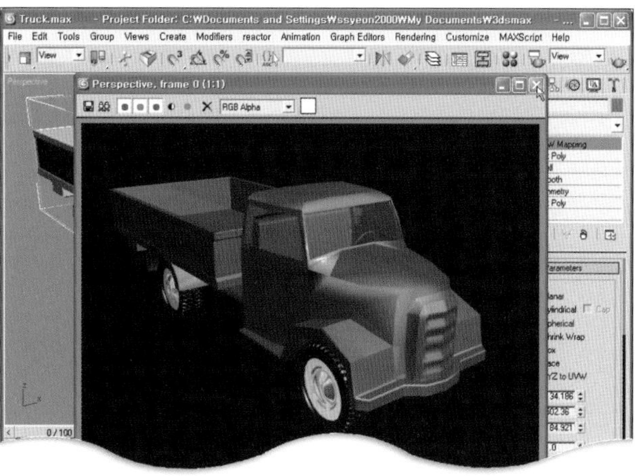

03 The [Mix Amount] value of the [Blend] Material type is set as [0], allowing the user to ensure that the color of [Material 1] is displayed. Click on the rendered image window to close it.

04 With the "Driver's Seat" object selected, click the [Modifier List] combo box and select the [Vertex Paint] modifier. The [Vertex Paint] toolbar appears. The user can hide or show this toolbar with [Edit] in the Parameters.

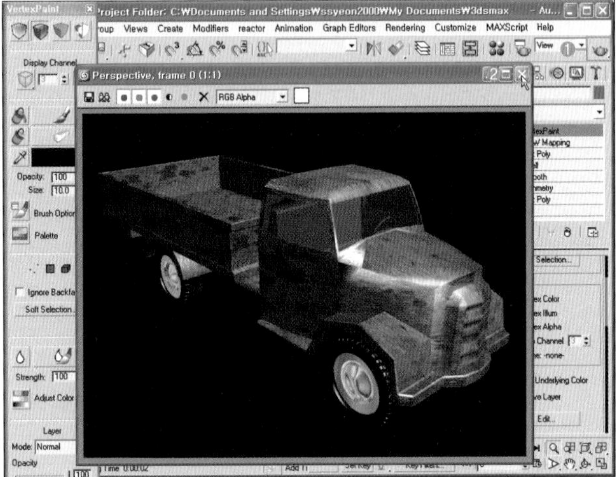

05 Select the Perspective Viewport, and click [Quick Render] on the main toolbar to see the rendered scene. Click [X] on the rendered image window to close it.

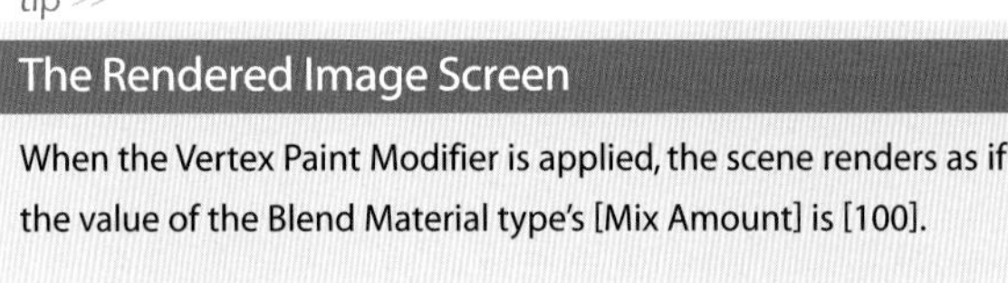

tip >>

The Rendered Image Screen

When the Vertex Paint Modifier is applied, the scene renders as if the value of the Blend Material type's [Mix Amount] is [100].

06 On the [Vertex Paint] toolbar, click [VertexColorDisplay–Shaded] and change the color to black. Click [Paint]. Then click–and–drag in the Viewport to paint it black.

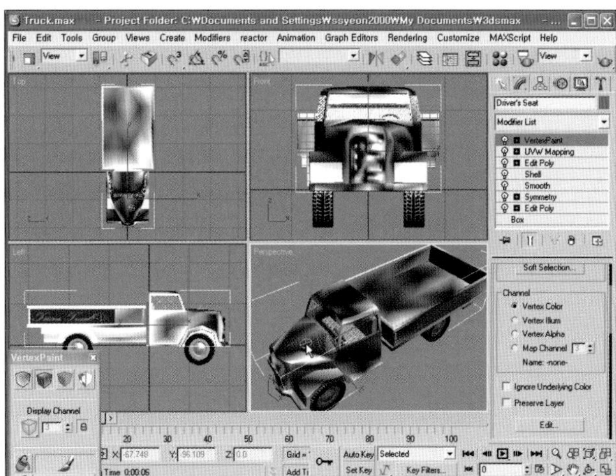

07 With the same method, click–and–drag the other partial polygon to paint it black.

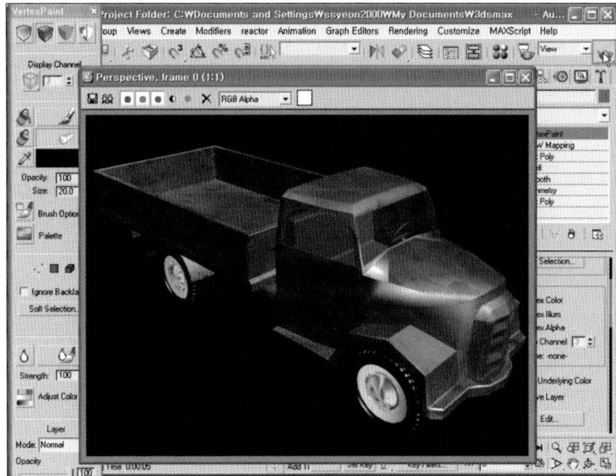

08 Select the Perspective Viewport, and click [Quick Render] on the main toolbar to see the rendered scene. With the black applied, the [Material 1] Material of the Blend Material type appears.

Supplementary CD\Sample\Chapter 4\Exercise 3\Truck–final.max

Chapter 5

Creating a New World in 3ds Max 9

Even with fancy backgrounds and dynamic movements of characters, it is difficult to create a realistic atmosphere without additional effects such as dust or splashing water. To mimic reality, 3ds Max 9 provides features called Particle and Space Warp. Particle expresses natural phenomena, such as snow or rain, and Space Warp is a tool that calculates the effects and strength of a collision. The user can utilize these tools to enhance the quality of an image. Also available is Reactor, a tool that can be used with Particle and Space Warp to make object collisions in a virtual world very realistic.

SECTION 01

Expressing Natural Phenomena

This section will discuss the Particle and Space Warp tools provided in 3ds Max 9 and consider their many uses.

The Particle Feature

If snow, rain, water drops, and whirlwinds were created through traditional modeling, it would not only be time consuming but would also quickly stress system capacity and limitations, because individual particles would have to be created manually. Unlike modeling, the Particle system offers a very effective calculating method that determines the movements of particles through a 2D calculation and connects the particles in the final stage. For this reason, the Particle system is frequently used in game and movie production.

To use the 3ds Max Particle system, select the desired Particle in the Create menu, or click in [Geometry]–[Particle Systems] on the Create panel.

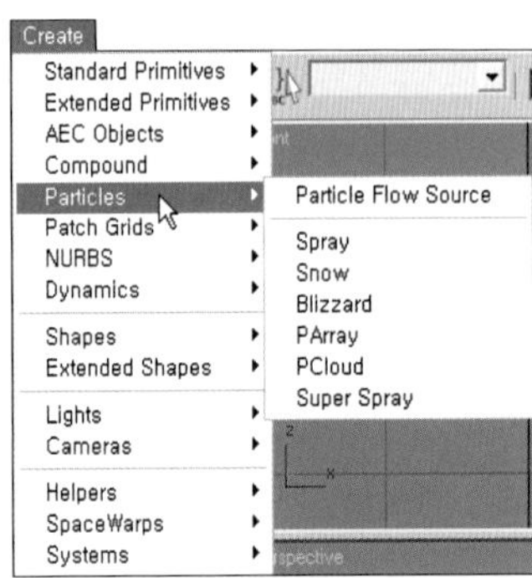

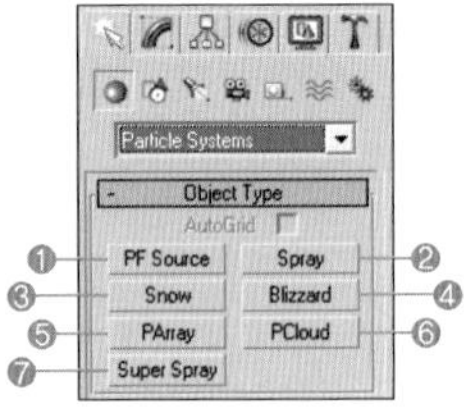

❶ **PF Source**—The Particle Flow that controls the flow of the particles in the event method provides a function that's strong enough to bring the existing Particle object in the shade.

❷ **Spray**—Creates raining or fountain effects.

❸ **Snow**—Creates effects such as snow, snow storms, or colorful flying paper.

❹ **Blizzard**—Creates stronger and more varied snow and blowing effects.

❺ **PArray**—Objects that emit particles can be manipulated separately from the particle objects to create more realistic effects.

❻ **PCloud**—Creates clouds, fumes, stars, and similar effects.

❼ **Super Spray**—Creates stronger rain and fountain effects.

Understanding Particle and Emitter

Particle Objects can be divided into two types. One is the Emitter, which produces the particles, and the other is the Place Holder, which designates another object to be the Emitter.

Characteristics	Particles Emitted
Particles that emits particles	Spray, Snow, Super Spray, Blizzard
Particles that can emit particles only if they are connected to other objects	PArray
Particles that can be used in both forms above	PCloud, PF Source

Emitter

An Emitter could be a faucet pouring water or a sky dropping rain. In the case of the rain, the Particle Object replaces the Emitter, to avoid having to create the entire sky as an Emitter. When the time slider is moved, you will see the flow of the particles from the Emitter.

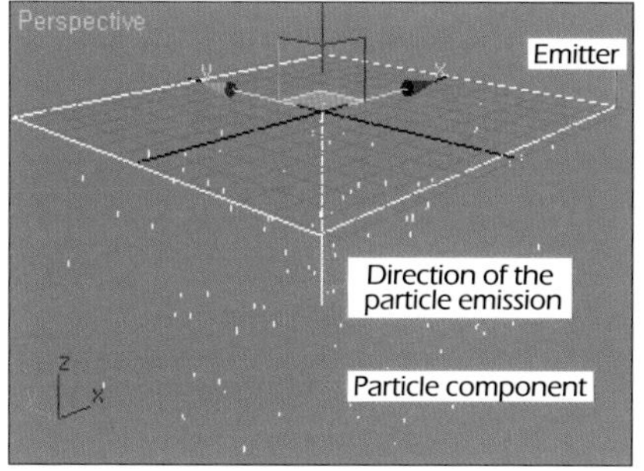

Spray

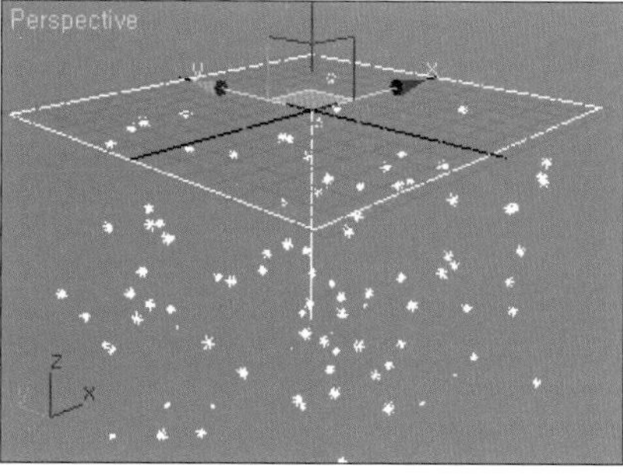

Snow

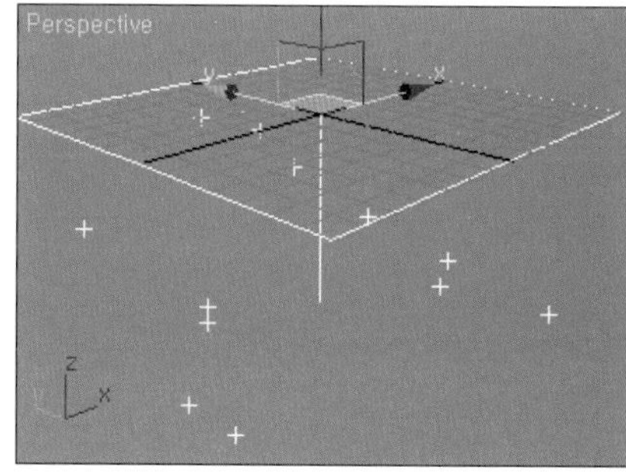

Blizzard

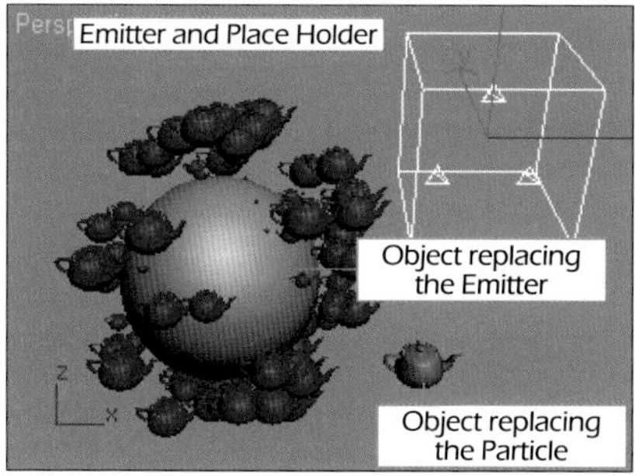

PArray

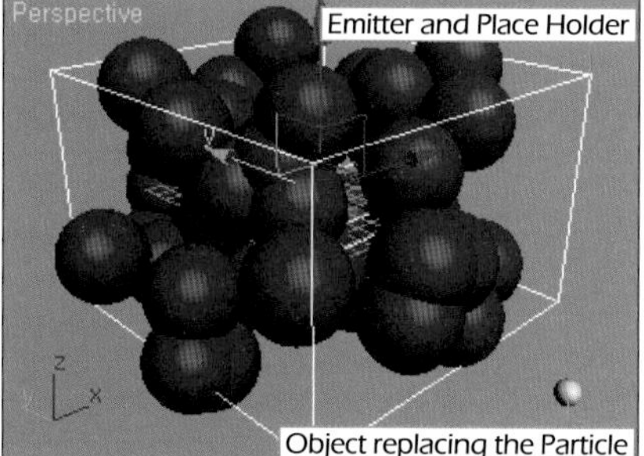

PCloud

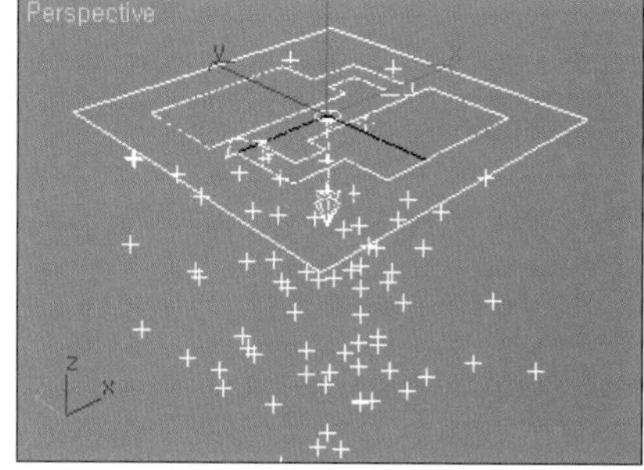

PF Source

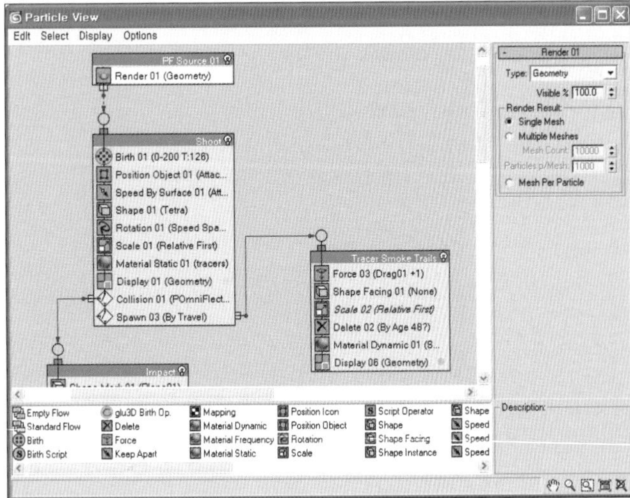

Particle Viewer dialog box for managing the PF Source

Particle Component Mapping

Mapping Particles can be done directly at the Emitter, or mapped onto the object replacing the Particle. In the case of PF Source, the Material Editor can be used to prepare a Map that is to be connected to each event.

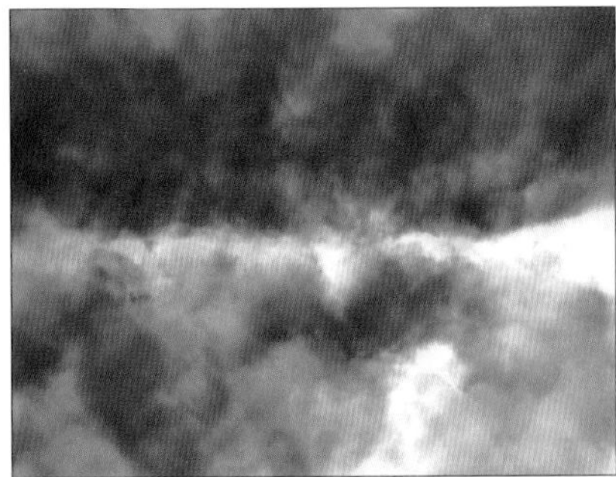

Mapping a cloud to replace an object with PCloud

Mapping examples for each event in PF Source

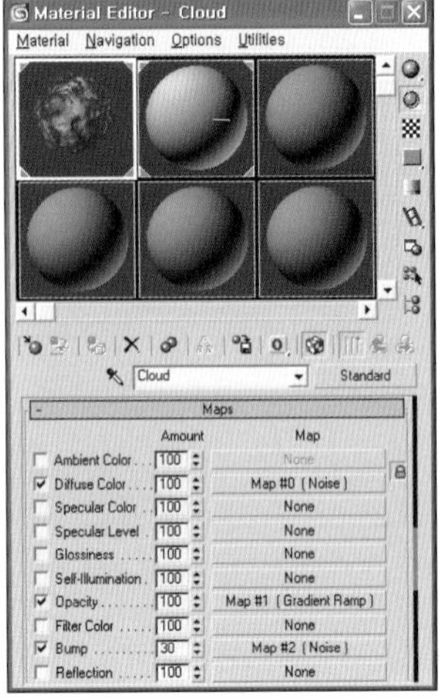

Mapping sources for a cloud

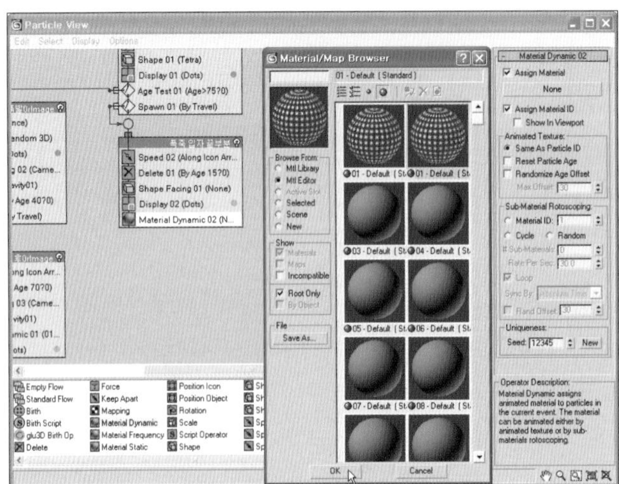

Assigning mapping sources for each PF Source's event

PF Source Event Note >>>

The PF Source feature controls the flow of particles. PF Source Event refers to the actions and reactions this flow takes. When the Particle components are emitted and collide with a specific object, they can instigate another series of Events. PF Source can be used to perfect the way Events are structured and play out.

Using Space Warp to Control the Flow of Particles

Space Warp is a set of tools for controlling the flow of Particles. It can be used to make Particles change direction, or bounce when they hit an object. The Space Warp feature can be used to control an object or designate another object.

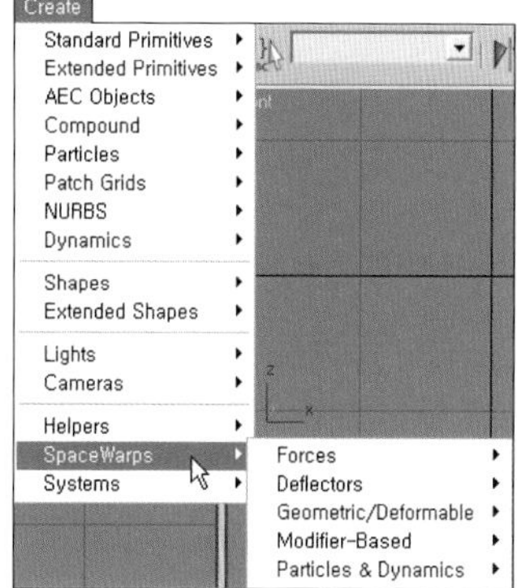

Using Space Warp Forces

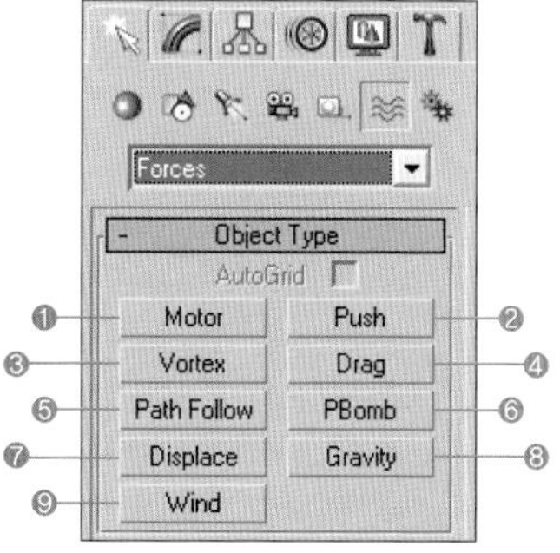

❶ **Motor**—Applies rotating effects to Particle.

❷ **Push**—Pushes Particles with a certain force.

❸ **Vortex**—Generates a whirlwind effect for Particles.

❹ **Drag**—Scatters Particles randomly: used for cigarette smoke, etc.

⑤ **Path Follow**—Causes Particles to follow a set path.
⑥ **PBomb**—Generates explosion effect for Particles.
⑦ **Displace**—Changes Particles into the designated image shape.
⑧ **Gravity**—Applies gravitational fall to Particles.
⑨ **Wind**—Applies wind effects to Particles.

Using Space Warp Deflectors to Calculate a Collision

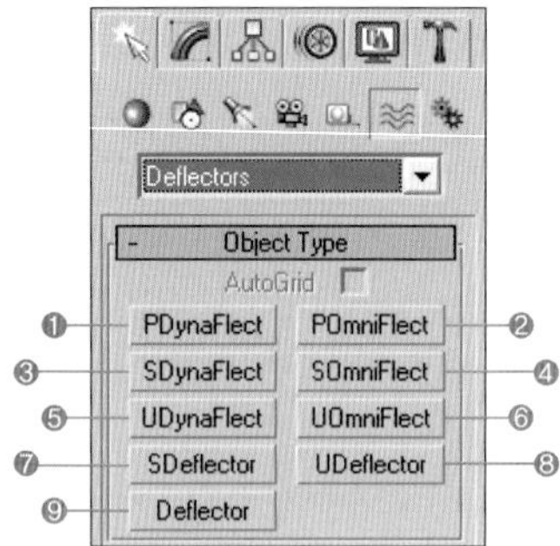

❶ **PDynaFlect**—Calculates collision strength.
❷ **POmniFlect**—Calculates refraction and diffusion, as well as the basic Deflectors.
❸ **SDynaFlect**—Calculates elliptical collisions, which differentiates it from PDynaFlect.
❹ **SOmniFlect**—Calculates elliptical collisions; similar to SDeflector, but with more options.
❺ **UDynaFlect**—Designates specific objects as colliding objects and focuses calculations on polygons.
❻ **UOmniFlect**—Designates specific objects as colliding objects and conducts very elaborate calculations.
❼ **SDeflector**—Calculates elliptical collisions.
❽ **UDeflector**—Designates and uses specific objects as colliding objects.
❾ **Deflector**—Calculates flat collisions.

Let's Go Pro!

Studying Reactor for Simulation

Reactor is a set of tools that expresses various physical phenomena and can be selected in Helpers on the Create panel. The Reactor feature is frequently used with Particle and Space Warp for natural animations. It offers simulation tools that enhance the sense of reality when depicting cloth shaking, objects falling, collisions, and hydromechanics that methods like Space Warp cannot accomplish alone. Reactor in 3ds Max 9 has a new engine called HAVOK 3, which offers more precise functionality.

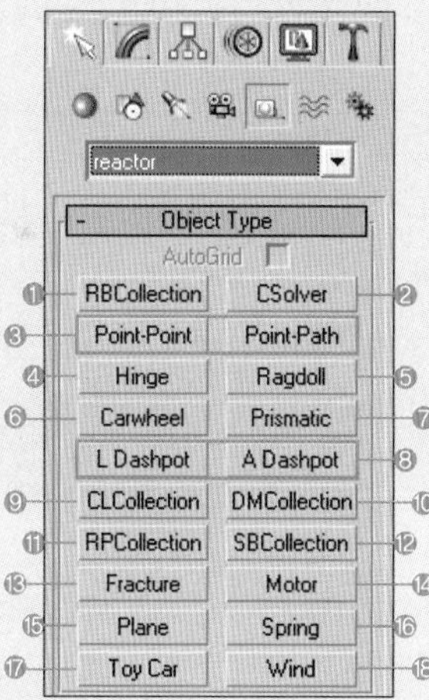

1. **RBCollection**—Creates collision effects occurring among many objects.
2. **CSolver**—Designates a certain object as a limitation for the RBCollection's collision.
3. **Point-Path, Point-Point**—Affixes the object to a specific Path or Point.
4. **Hinge**—Acts as the connection between two objects.
5. **Ragdoll**—Simulates each joint of the human body effectively.
6. **Carwheel**—Useful for attaching an object that acts as a steering wheel for another object.
7. **Prismatic**—Limits movements in a specific direction; used for creating a fork crane.
8. **L Dashpot, A Dashpot**—Creates a spring that is more scalable than a Spring.
9. **CLCollection**—Creates cloth or characteristics of clothing.
10. **DMCollection (Deforming Mesh Collection)**—Creates collision effects for soft objects, such as skin.
11. **RPCollection (Rope Collection)**—Creates effects for ropes.
12. **SBCollection (Soft Body Collection)**—Creates crumpling effects.
13. **Fracture**—Creates shattering or breaking effects.
14. **Motor**—Creates a rotation effect.
15. **Plane**—Makes objects into standard polygons.
16. **Spring**—Creates a springing effect between two objects.
17. **Toy Car**—Makes car wheels move as if swerving on an uneven surface.
18. **Wind**—Creates wind effects.

Exercise 01

Creating a Missile Ejection Effect

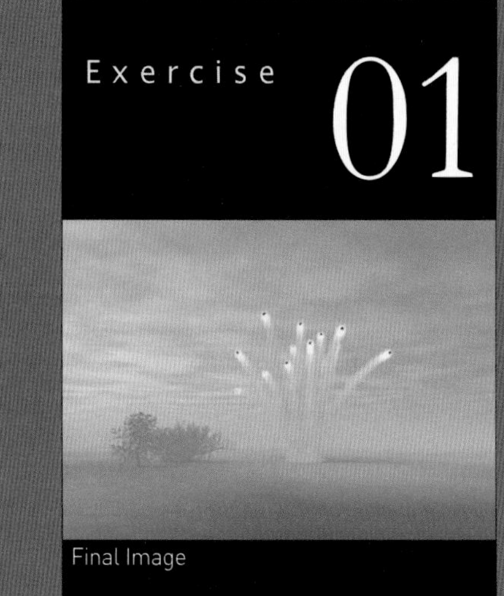
Final Image

PF Source, which controls the movements of Particles with the Event method, is the most versatile of all the Particles engines offered by 3ds Max 9. Because it can express almost any Particle effect to enhance the model's realism, PF Source is a very useful tool. This section will demonstrate how to model a missile effect, with an object soaring and scattering in the air.

Start Files
\Sample\Chapter 5\Exercise 1\
Field.max

Final File
\Sample\Chapter 5\Exercise 1\
Field–final.max
Missle explosion.avi

Allocating Particles

In order to use the PF Source Particles, the first step is to prepare external Space Warp tools that influence the Particles. Gravity, Drag, and Deflector are the most frequently used. Of course, PF Source can be added during construction, but it is recommended to create frequently used factors in the Viewport for convenience.

01 Open the "Field.max" file from the supplementary CD, select the Perspective Viewport, and click [Quick Render] on the main toolbar to see the rendered shape. Click on the rendered image window to close it.

Supplementary CD\Sample\Chapter 5\Exercise 1\Field.max

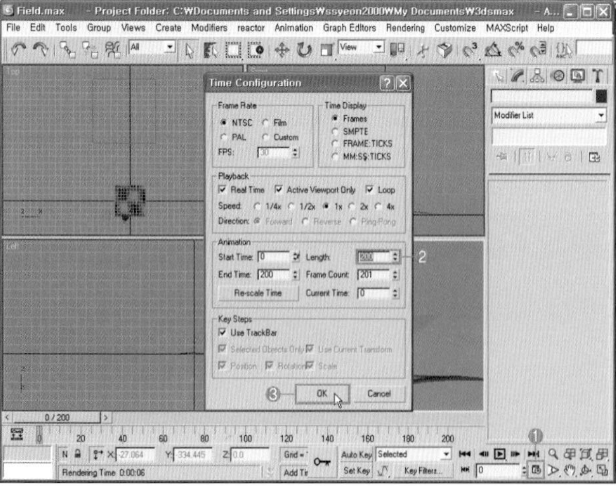

02 To change the processing time of basic frame number 100, click [Time Configuration]. When the Time Configuration dialog box appears, enter [200] for [Animation]–[Length], and click [OK].

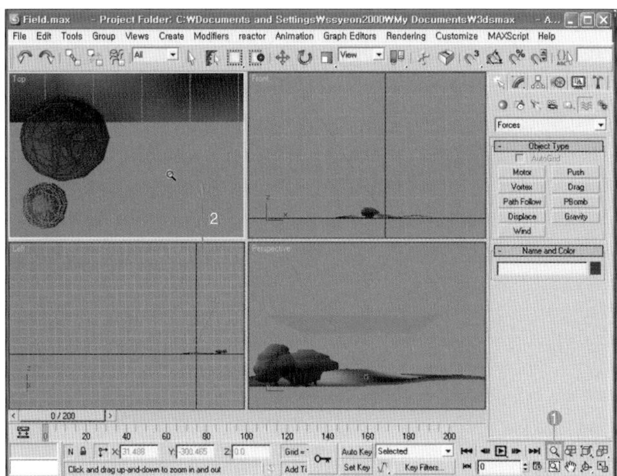

03 Click [Zoom 🔍] in the Viewport, and click–and–drag in the Top Viewport to zoom in on the objects in the Viewport.

04 To apply gravitational effects to the Particles, click [Space Warps]–[Forces]–[Gravity] on the Create panel. Click–and–drag in the Top Viewport to install Gravity.

05 With the "Gravity01" object selected, move to the Modify panel. Set the [Parameters] to apply weak gravity. Enter [0.2] for [Parameters]–[Force Strength].

06 To create a shaking effect for the Particles, click [Geometry]–[Spacewarps]–[Drag] on the Create panel. Click–and–drag in the blank space in the Top Viewport and create a Drag.

07 With the "Drag01" object selected, move on to the Modify panel and set the [Parameters].

② In [Parameters]–[Damping Characteristics]–[Linear Damping], enter [5] for [X Axis], [0] for [Y Axis], and [0] for [Z Axis].

08 To create a wind effect for the Particles, click [Geometry]–[Spacewarps]–[Wind] on the Create panel. Click–and–drag in the blank space in the Top Viewport to create Wind.

09 With the "Wind01" object selected, move to the Modify panel. Enter [1] for [Parameters]–[Strength].

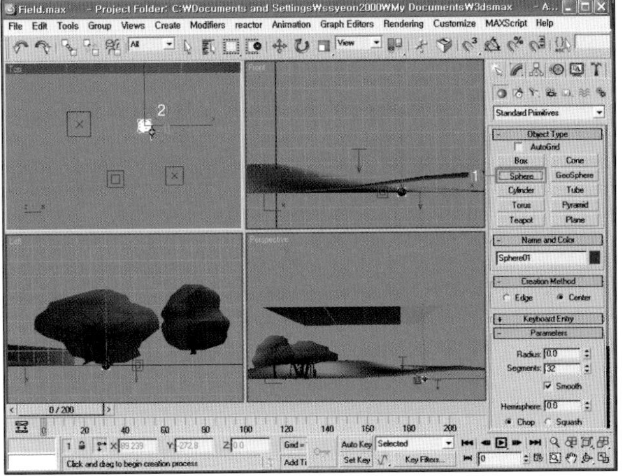

10 On the Create panel, click [Geometry]–[Standard Primitives]–[Sphere]. Click–and–drag in the Top Viewport to create a new Sphere.

tip >>

Size of the 'Sphere' object

The 'Sphere01' should be made slightly small because it will be an alternative object for a particle.

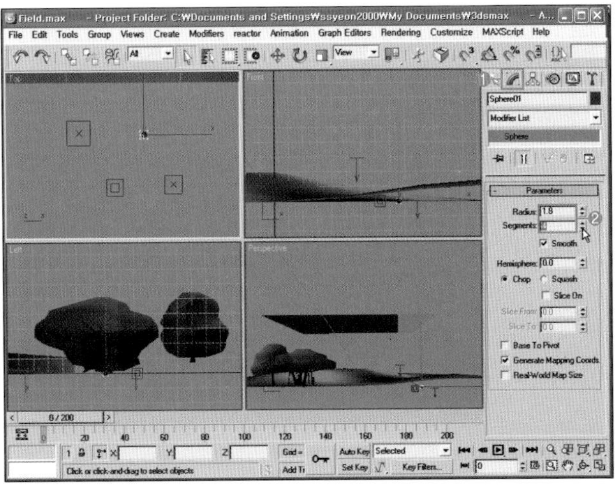

11 With the "Sphere01"object selected, move to the Modify panel and set the [Parameters] to change it into a more angular shape. In [Parameters], enter [1.8] for [Radius] and [4] for [Segments].

Installing PF Sources and Checking Basic Components

This section will discuss how to create PF Source objects and check out the contents of a basic internal event.

01 On the Create panel, click [Geometry]–[Particle Systems]–[PF Source]. Click–and–drag in the Top Viewport and create a PF Source.

02 With the "PF Source01" object selected, move to the Modify panel and set [Emission] to adjust the size of the PF Source. Enter [17] for [Logo Size], [25] for [Length], and [23] for [Width].

03 Click [Select and Move] on the main toolbar, and click–and–drag in the Top Viewport to determine where the Particles will be emitted from.

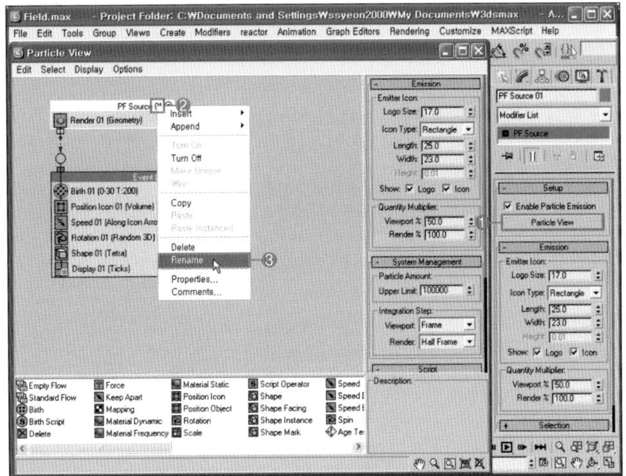

04 To control the flow of the Particles, click Particle View. When the [Particle View] dialog box appears, right–click on the “PF Source01” object and select [Rename] on the menu.

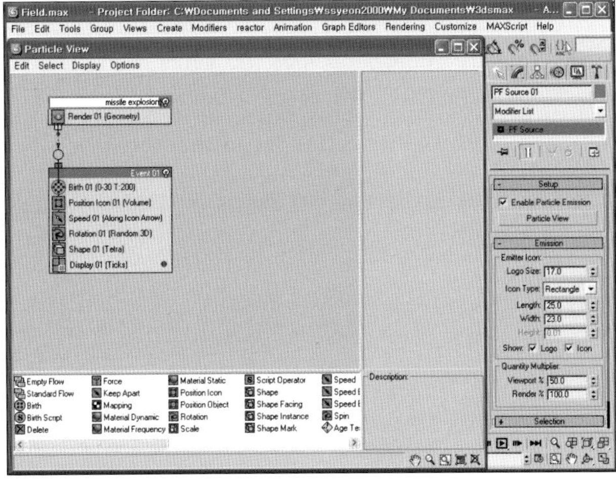

05 Rename the “PF Source01” object as “missile explosion.”

Particle View User Interface

Note >>>

The Particle View dialog box is a tool that can edit the movements of the Particles in the Event method. It is composed of the Event Display, which displays the Events that control the movements of the Particles; the Menu Bar; the Parameter Panel, which controls the parameters of the Event; the Description Panel, which displays explanations for each of the parameters; and the Depot, which is a collection of the pre–made effects that can be registered and used as events.

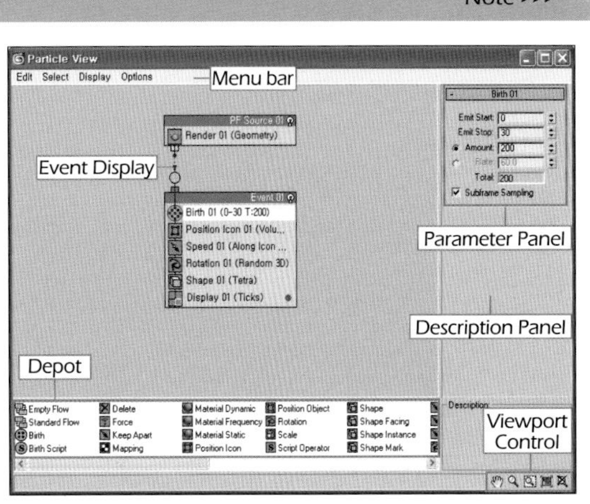

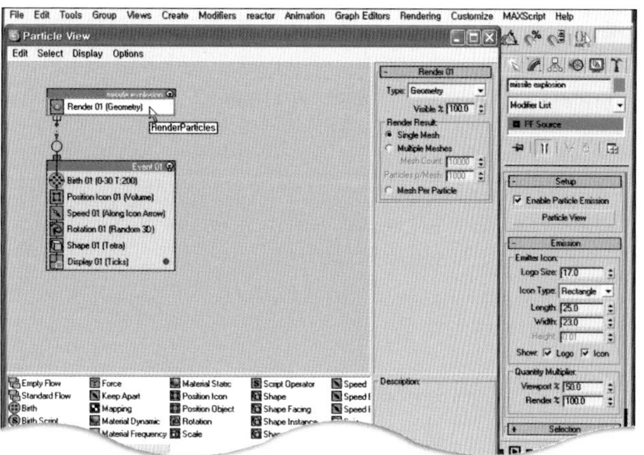

06 Click [Render01] in "missile explosion", and check the parameters' contents, maintaining the default.

Composing Settings and Generating Particles

This is the most important part in the PF Source work. The "Event 01" object decides the generation, basic movement, and shapes of the Particles. This section will discuss the "Event 01" object and how to process this method.

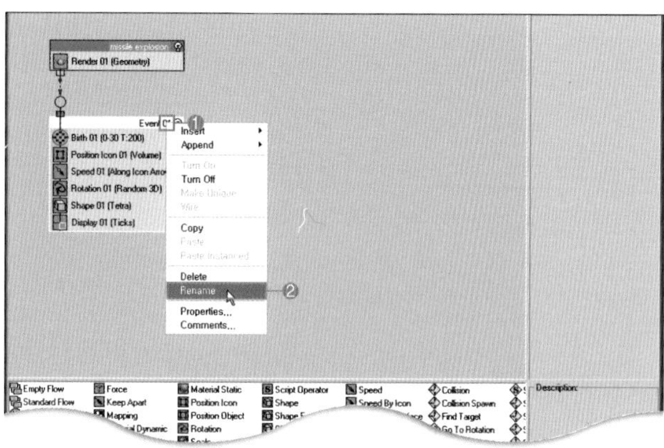

01 Right–click on the "Event01" object and select [Rename] on the menu.

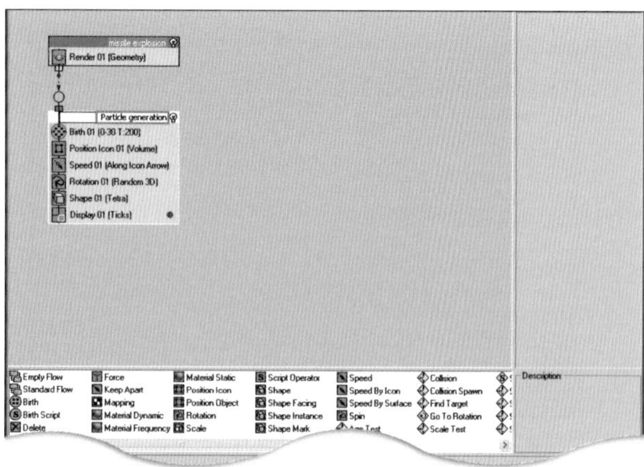

02 Change the name of the "Event01" object to "Particle generation."

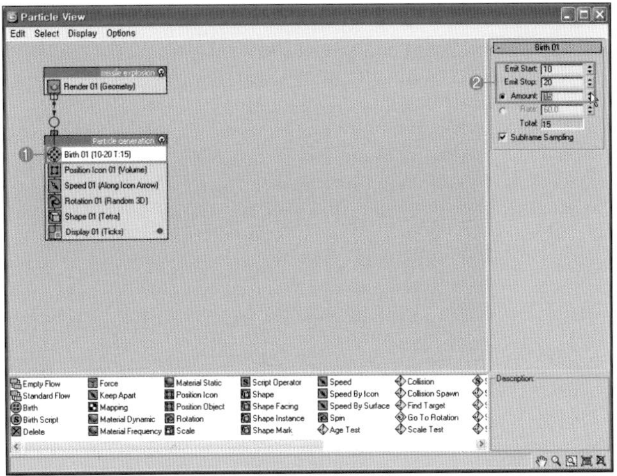

03 Click [Birth01] in the “Particle generation” event, and enter [10] for [Emit Start], [20] for [Emit Stop], and [15] for [Amount]. The new Particle emits fifteen particles between frames 10 and 20.

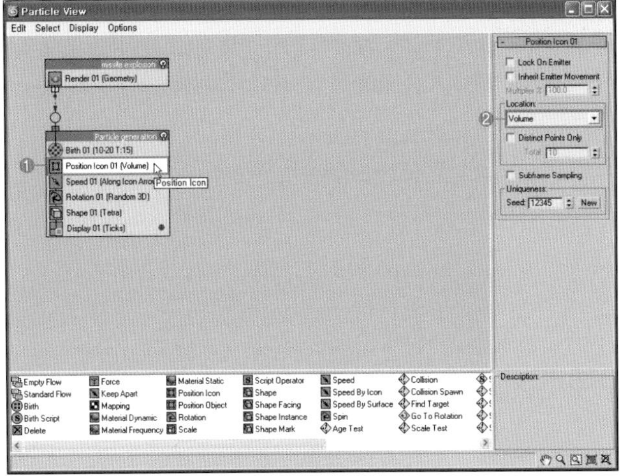

04 Click [Position Icon 01], and check how the Particles are emitted at [Volume] on the [Location] menu.

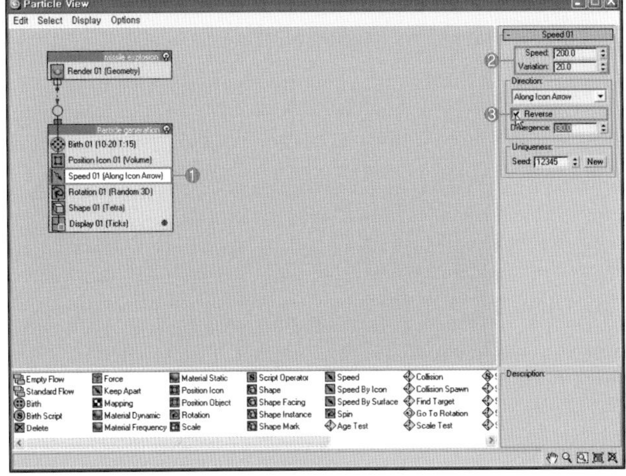

05 Click [Speed 01], enter [200] for [Speed], [20] for [Variation], and check the [Reverse] box for [Direction].

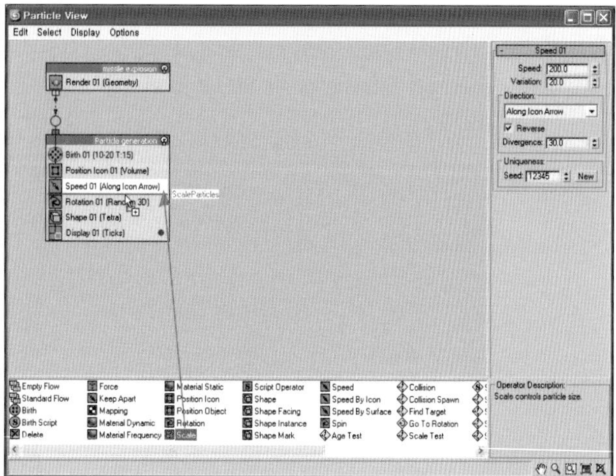

06 Click–and–drag [Scale] below the dialog box to add it under [Speed 01].

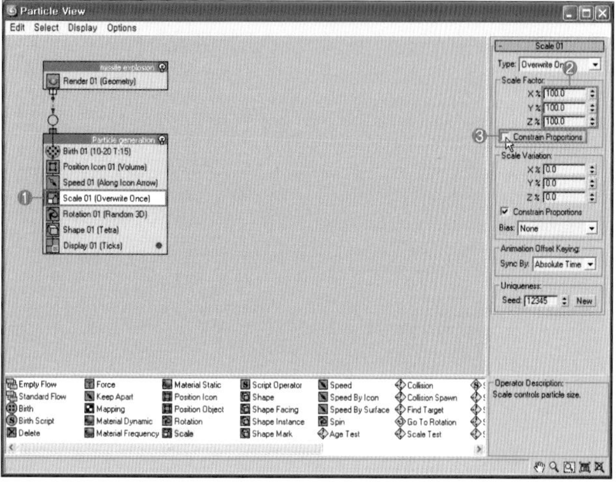

07 Click [Scale 01], maintain the default, and set [Scale Factor]–[Constrain Proportion] so that each change can be activated in the X, Y, and Z–axis directions.

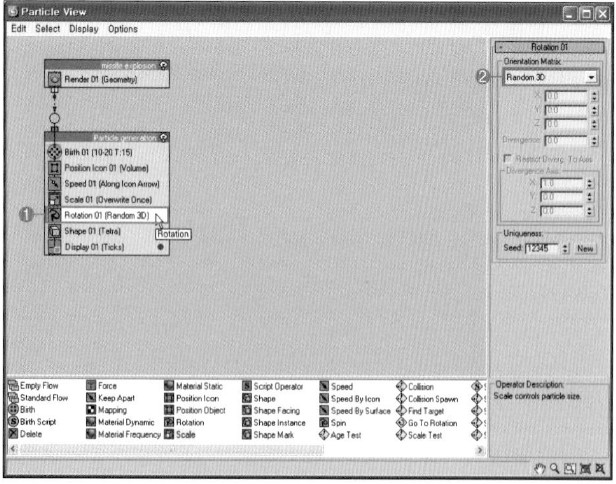

08 Click [Rotation 01] and check if the Particles are set to rotate in all directions (Random 3D).

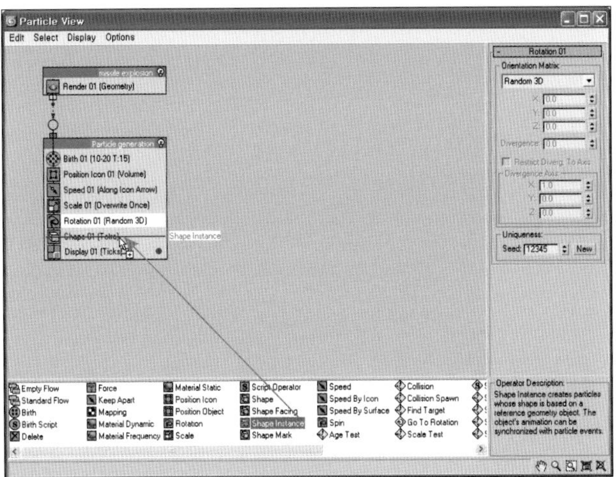

09 Click–and–drag [Shape Instance] below the dialog box to overwrite [Shape 01]. [Shape Instance] replaces [Shape], and makes the separately created [Sphere01] usable as the Particles.

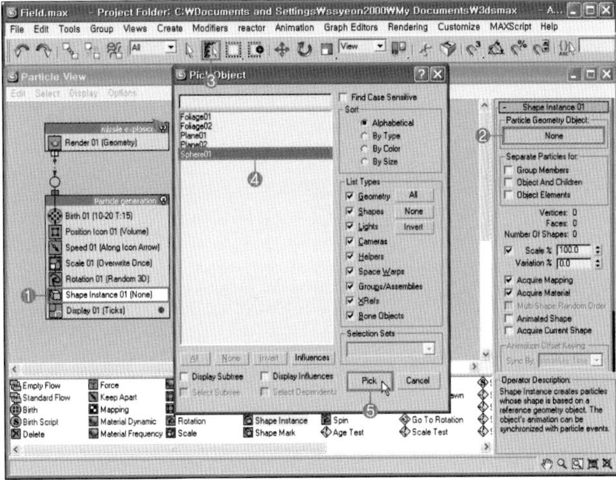

10 Click [Shape Instance 01] and click [Parameters]–[Particle Geometry Object]– None . Click [Select by Name] on the main toolbar, and the Pick Objects dialog box will appear. Select the "Sphere01" object and click [Pick].

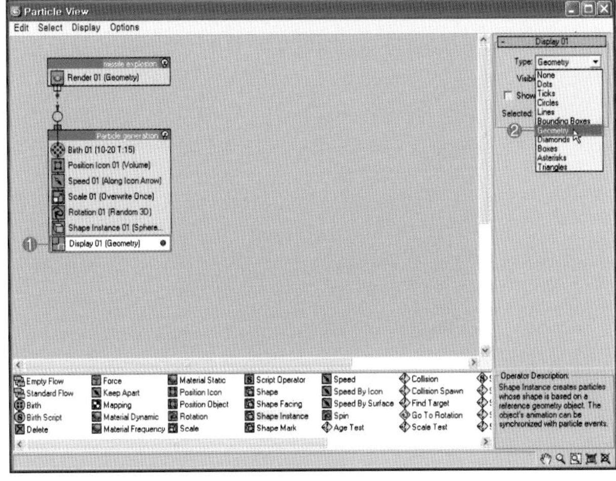

11 Click [Display 01] and select [Geometry] from the [Type] combo box to set the Particles to appear in the shape of [Sphere01] in the Viewport.

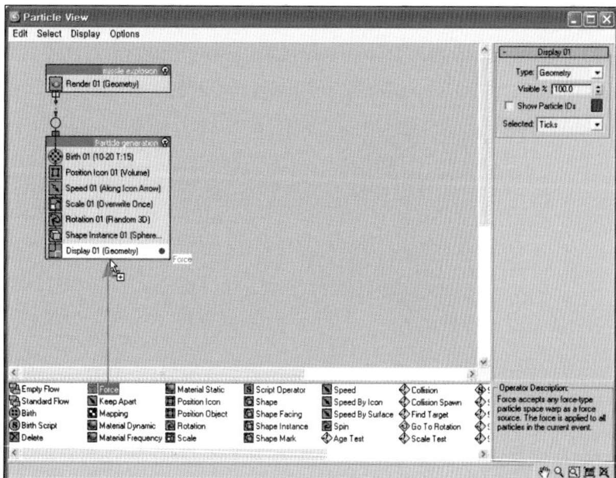

12 Click–and–drag [Force] below [Display 01].

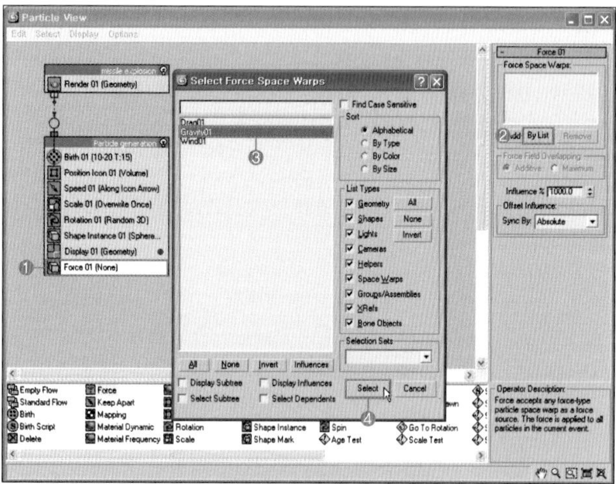

13 Select [Force01], and click By List in the Parameters. When the [Select Force Space Warps] dialog box appears, select “Gravity01” and click [Select].

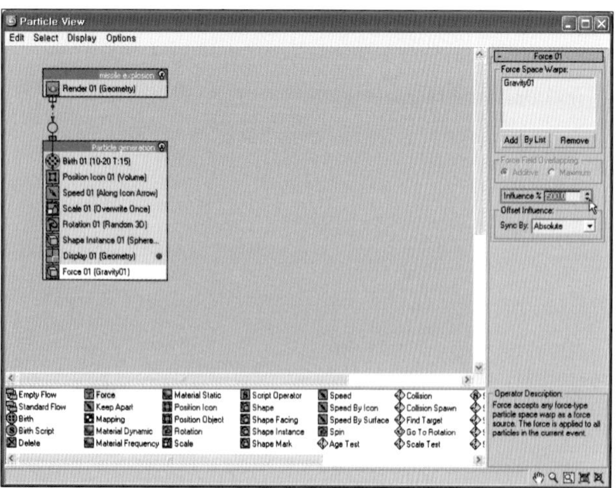

14 Enter [500] for [Influence] in the Parameters to change the amount of gravitational force on the Particles to 500%.

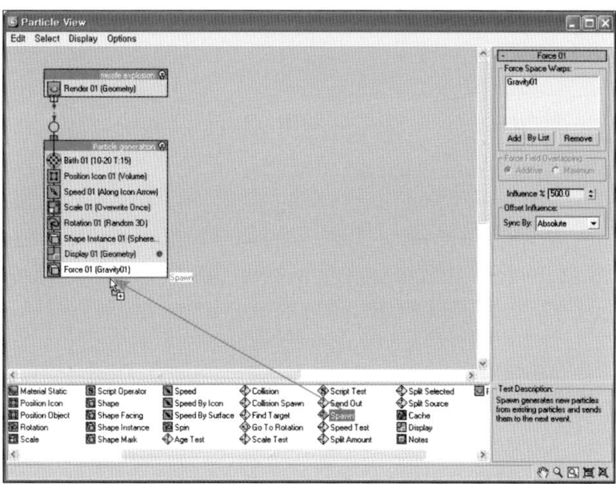

15 Click–and–drag [Spawn] under [Force 01] to add. [Spawn] diffuses the Particles just as an explosion does.

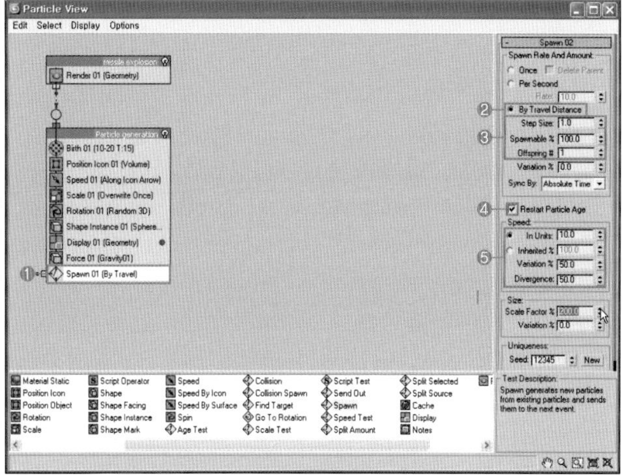

16 Click [Spawn01], and set the Parameters. Click ☒ on the [Particle View] dialog box to close it.

② Click [By Travel Distance] in the Parameters, and enter [1] for [Step Size], [100] for [Spawnable], [1] for [Offspring], and [0] for Variation.

⑤ Then enter [10] for [In Unit], [50] for [Variation], and [50] for [Divergence].

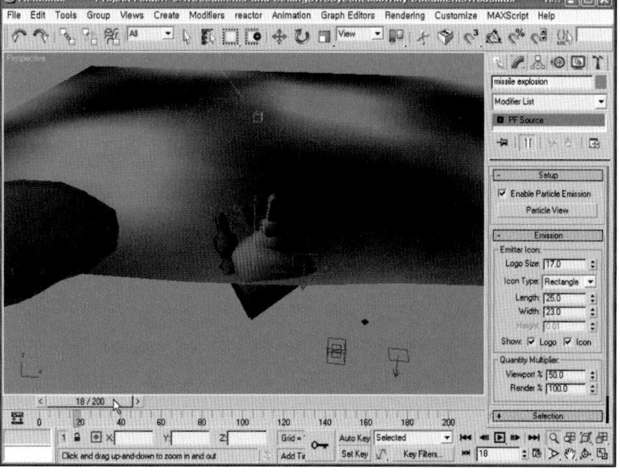

17 By moving the time slider, the user can see that Particles in the shape of Spheres are emitted from the PF Source and gradually diffuse.

Shaping the Fume 

This section will demonstrate how to express the fume around the Particles. The sense of realism can be further enhanced in Particle animations by using Material Map; mapped Particles can change color over time.

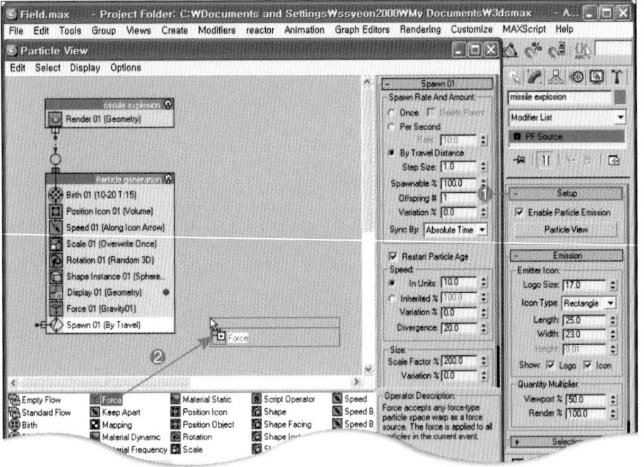

01 Open the [Particle View] dialog box again, click–and–drag [Force] as shown below, and click–and–drag beside the "Particle generation" event to add a new Event.

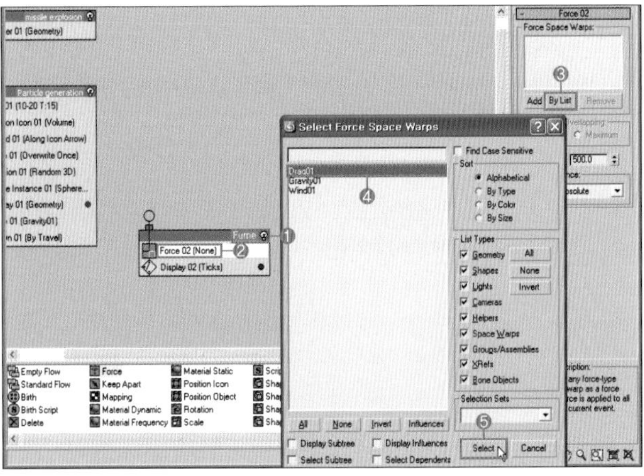

02 Change the name of the "Event01" event to "fume," and click [Force02]. Click By List in the Parameters, and when the Select Force Space Warps dialog box appears, select "Drag01" and click [Select]. The "fume" event makes [Drag] shake the fume emitted by the Particles.

tip >>

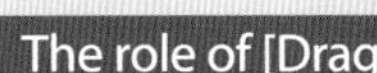

The role of [Drag]

When using the 'Fume' event, the [Drag] will shake the fumes trailing the particle to make it more realistic.

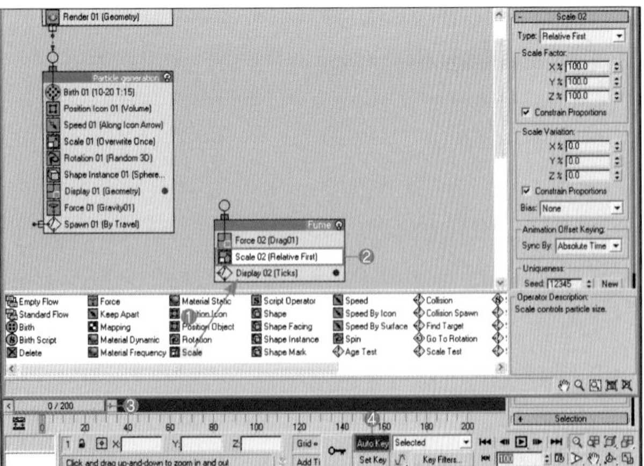

03 Add [Scale] under [Force02], and click [Scale02]. Then, with the time slider at frame 0, click Auto Key to start the animation mode.

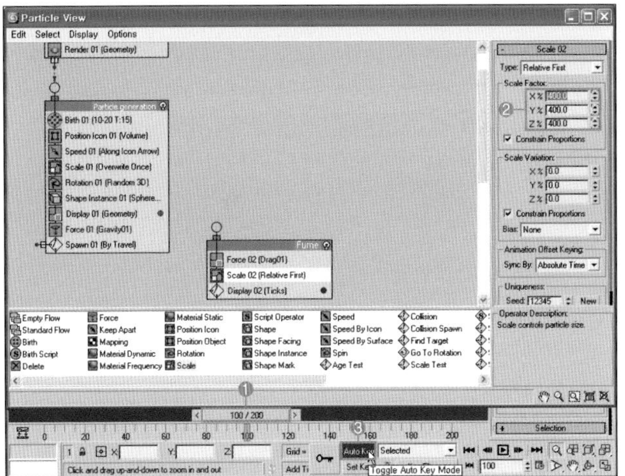

04 Move the time slider to frame 100, and enter [400] for [X] in the Parameters of [Scale 02]. Then click Auto Key to close the animation mode. The fume from each Particle will grow larger gradually.

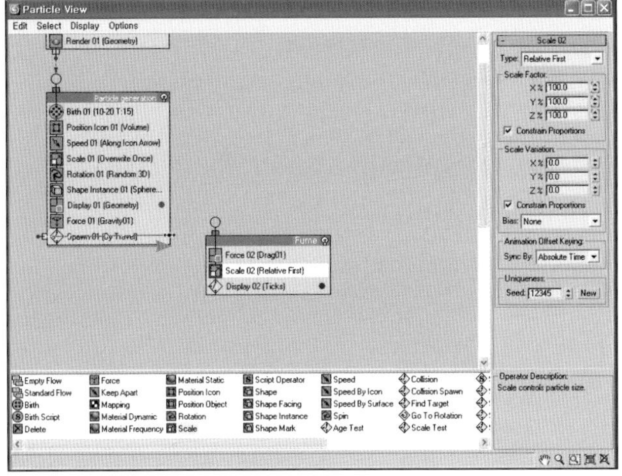

05 Move the bilateral arrow of the "Particle generation" event's [Spawn01] to the right to connect "Particle generation" and "fume" events.

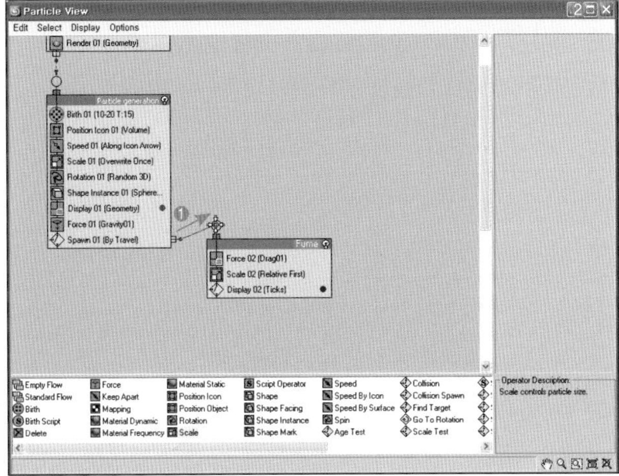

06 Click–and–drag the connection line to the right to the starting point of the "fume" event to connect the two events. Click ☒ to close the dialog box.

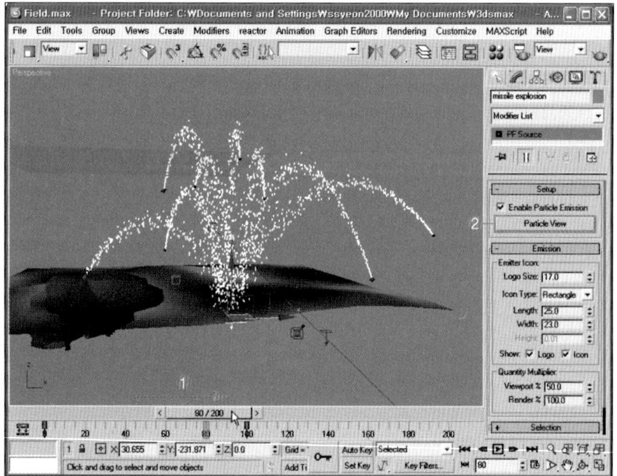

07 When you click–and–drag the time slider, you can see that the fume Particles are being emitted from the end of the Particles as time goes by. To open the. [Particle View] dialog box, click [Particle View] of the "missile" object.

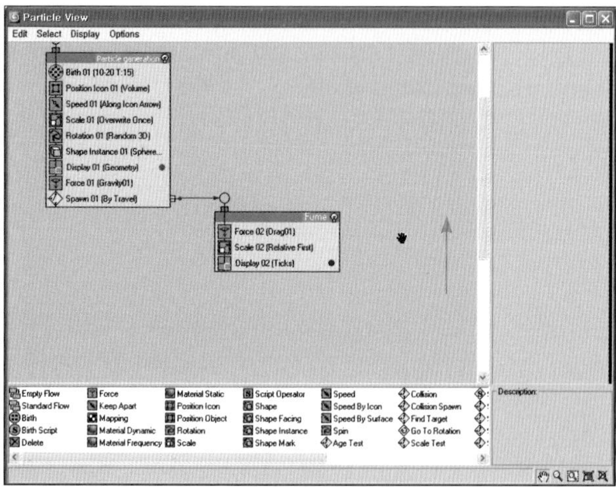

08 Click [Hand] in the [Particle View] dialog box and move the entire screen upwards.

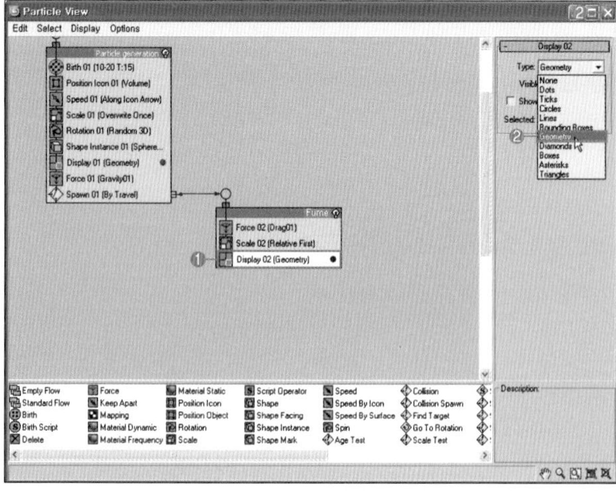

09 Click [Display 02] of the "fume" event, and change the shape of the fume shown in the Viewport by selecting [Geometry] from the Parameters [Type] combo box.

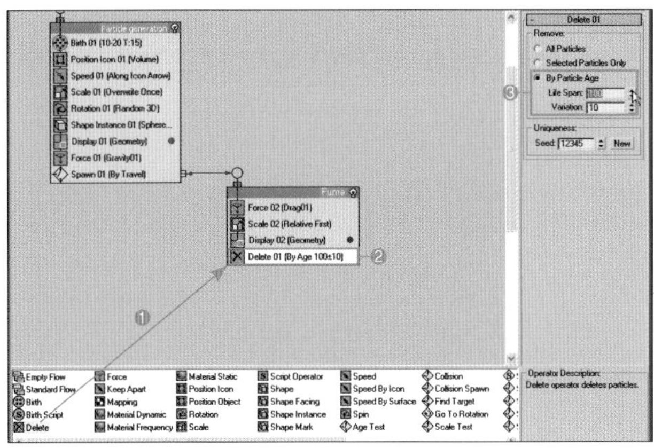

10 Click–and–drag [Delete] as shown below under [Display 02] and add it. Select [Delete 01] and set the parameters. The fume Particles are set to gradually disappear by the pre–set values of [Life Span] and [Variation]. Click ☒ to close the [Particle View] dialog box.

③ Click [By Particle Age] in the Parameters, and enter [100] for [Life Span] and [10] for [Variation].

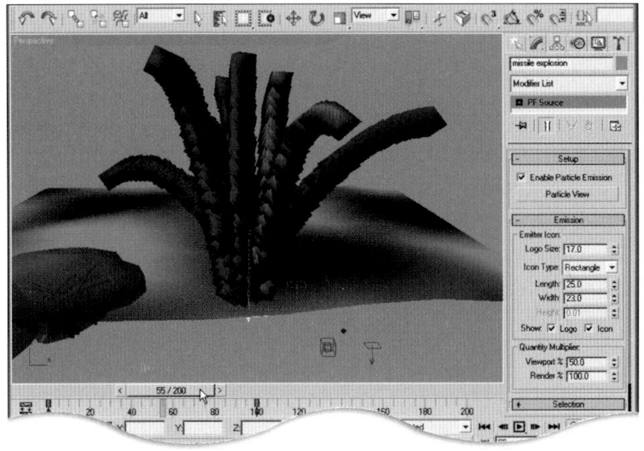

11 By click–and–dragging the time slider, the emitted fumes gradually disappear with time.

Aligning Particles

In many cases, Particles do not appear normal through a camera due to movements like internal rotations. Therefore, we will change the Particles with Shape Facing so that they face the camera.

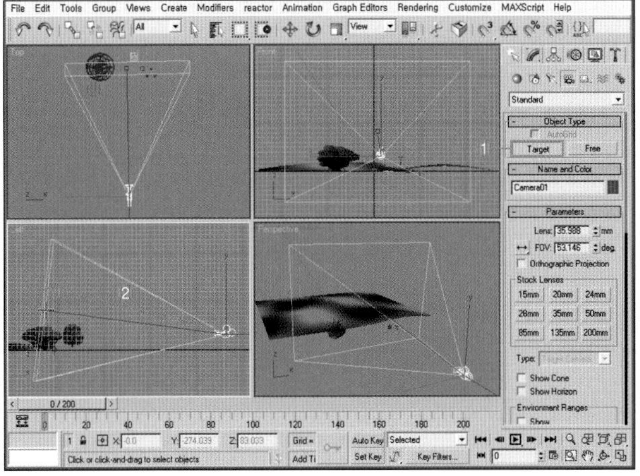

01 On the Create panel, click [Cameras]–[Standard]–

. Click–and–drag in the Left Viewport to install a camera looking toward the field.

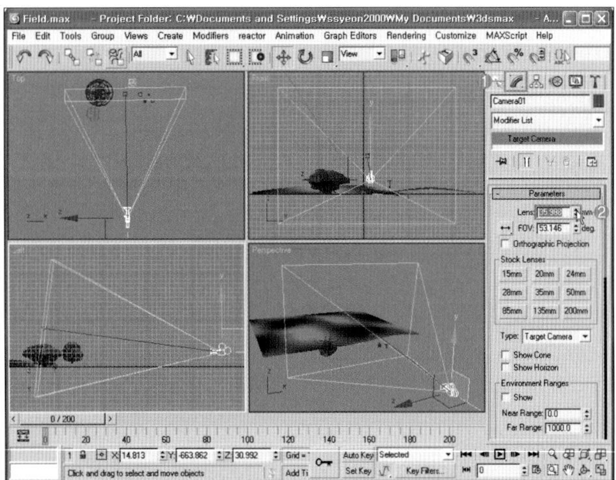

02 With the “Camera01” camera selected, move to the Modify panel. Set the desired view by adjusting the camera’s [Parameters].

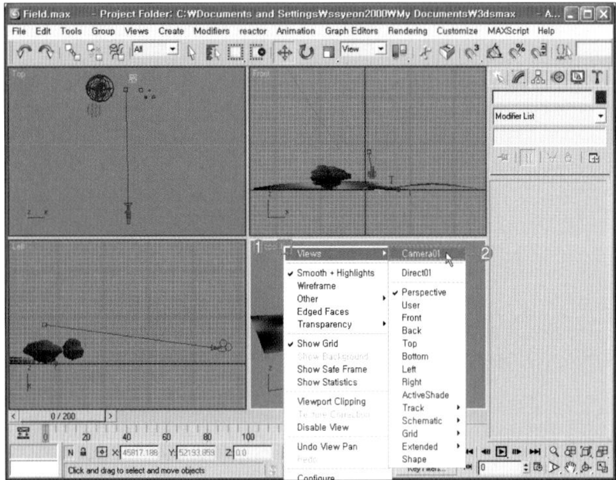

03 Right–click on the text label in the Perspective Viewport, and select [Views]–[Camera01] on the menu. The Perspective Viewport changes to Camera01’s viewpoint.

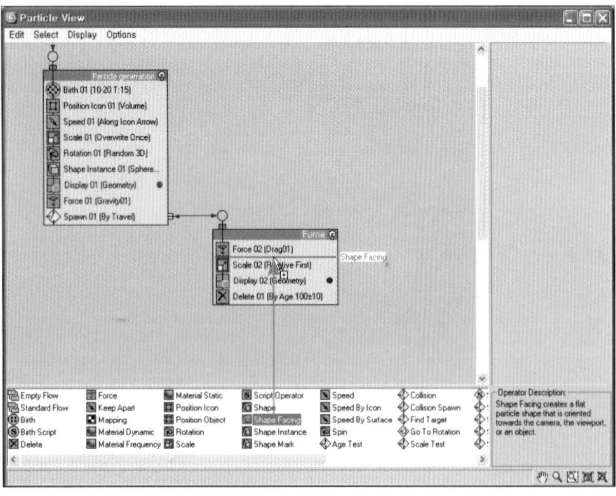

04 Re–open the “missile” object’s [Particle View] dialog box, and click–and–drag to add [Shape Facing] as shown below under “fume” event’s [Force 02]. [Shape Facing] helps to enhance visual clarity by making the Particles face the camera.

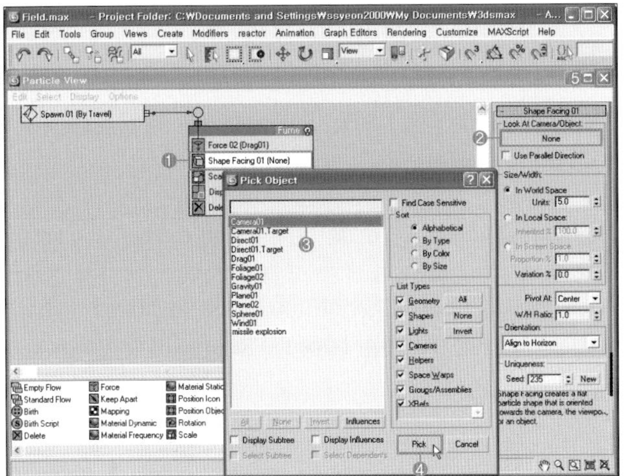

05 Click [Shape Facing 01], click None in the Parameters, and select "Camera01" when the [Pick Object] dialog box appears. Click [Pick]. Click ☒ to close the dialog box.

06 When you click–and–drag the time slider, you can see the fume Particles aligned and facing the camera.

Mapping Realistic Fumes Using Particle Age and Material Dynamic 

You can prepare a Material that changes its color over time using [Particle Age]. This Material can be connected with the fume event using [Material Dynamic] in the [Particle View] dialog box.

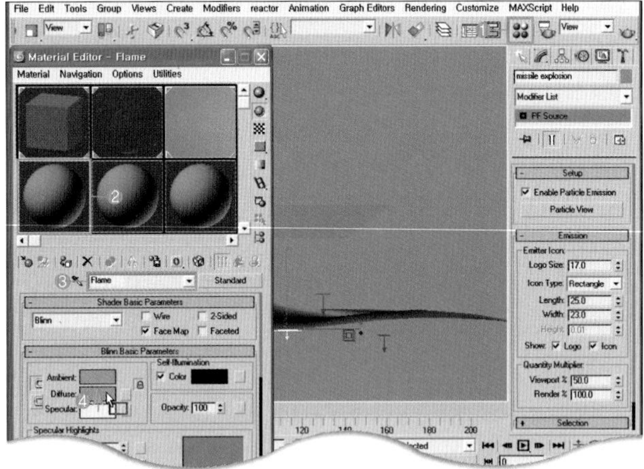

01 Click [Material Editor] on the main toolbar, and select the fourth sample slot of the Material editor in the dialog box that appears. Change the name to "flame." Then, click–and–drag the color button in [Specular] and copy it to [Diffuse].

02 When the [Copy or Swap Colors] dialog box appears, click [Copy].

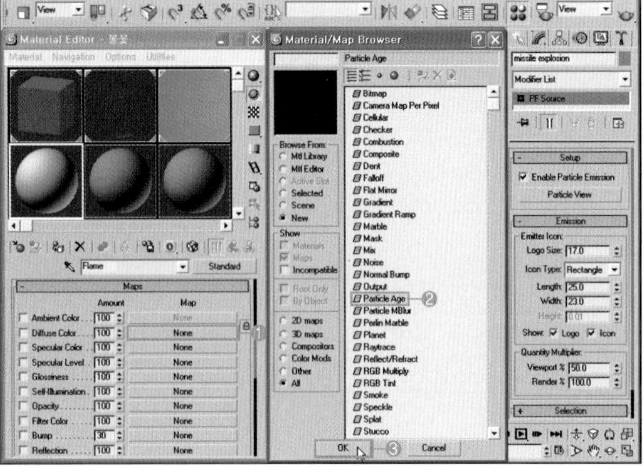

03 Click [Maps]–[Diffuse Color]–None to open the Material/Map Browser dialog box, and select [Particle Age].

tip >>

The Structure of the Material for Fireworks

The mapping source for fireworks, made in a rather complicated way, has the following components:

Standard – Diffuse Color – Particle Age (Yellow, Brown, Gray)
- Self–Illumination – Particle Age (Yellow, Brown, Gray)
- Opacity – Mask – Map – Mask – Map –Gradient (Black, Gray, White)
  Mask – Gradient (Black, Gray, White)
  Mask – Particle Age (White, Gray, Black)

04 Click the color button [Color#1] in [Particle Age Parameters], and change the color to yellow (RGB: 246, 255, 0).

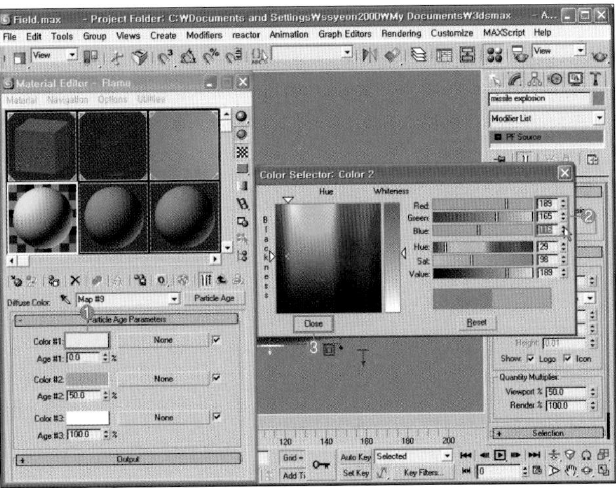

05 Click the color button [Color#2] and change the color to light brown (RGB: 189, 165, 116).

06 Click the color button [Color#3] and change the color to dark gray (RGB: 75, 75, 75).

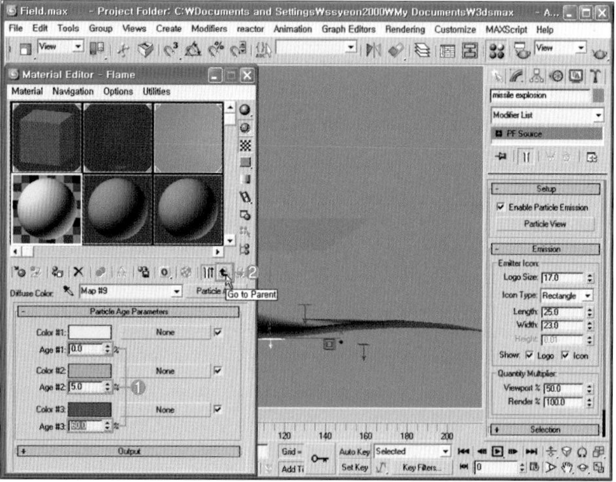

07 To adjust the proportion of the colors, enter [0] for [Age #1], [5] for [Age #2], and [60] for [Age #3], and click [Go to Parent] to return to the initial screen.

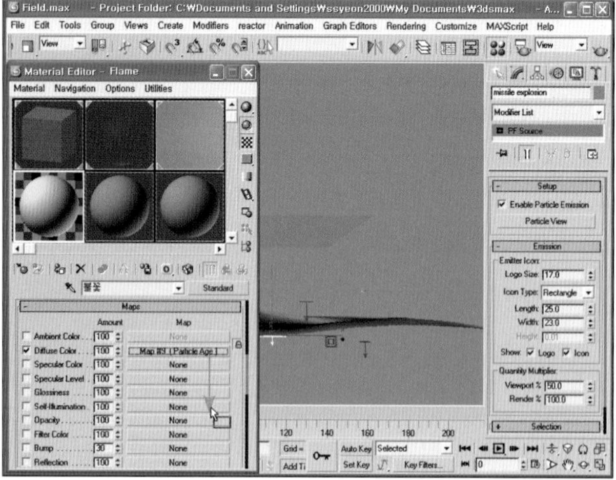

08 Click–and–drag [Map #9 (Particle Age)] in [Diffuse Color] to copy it to [Self Illumination].

09 When the [Copy (Instance)] dialog box appears, select [Instance] to set the value of [Self Illumination] to change according to the changes in [Diffuse Color].

10 Click [Maps]–[Opacity]–None to open the [Material/Map Browser] dialog box, and select [Mask].

11 Click [Mask Parameters]–[Maps]–None to open the [Material/Map Browser] dialog box, and select [Mask].

12 Click [Mask Parameters]–[Maps]–None to open the [Material/Map Browser] dialog box, and select [Gradient].

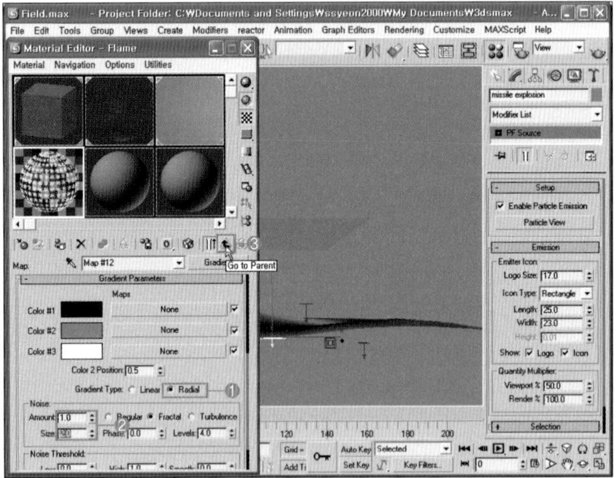

13 When [Gradient Parameters] appears, change [Gradient Type] to [Radial], and enter [1. 2] for [Noise]–[Size] to set the rough, initial gradient effect. Click [Go to Parent] to move to the upper stage.

14 Click [Mask]–None to open the [Material/Map Browser] dialog box, and select [Gradient].

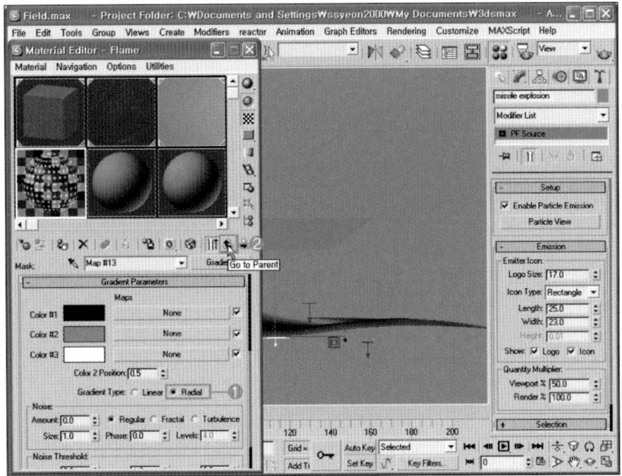

15 When [Gradient Parameters] appears, change [Gradient Type] to [Radial], and click [Go to Parent] to move to the upper stage.

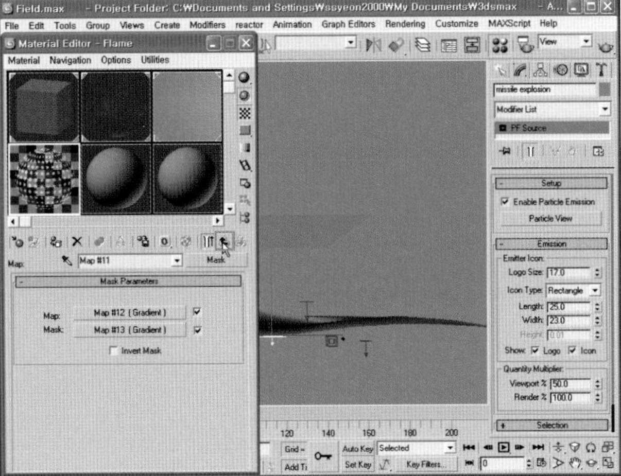

16 Click [Go to Parent] to move to the upper stage.

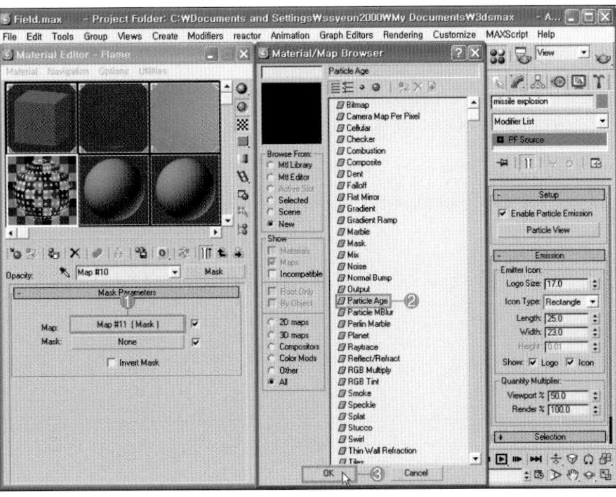

17 Click None in [Mask] to open the [Material/Map Browser] dialog box, select [Particle Age], and click [OK].

18 Click [Go to Parent] while maintaining the default in [Particle Age] to move to the upper stage.

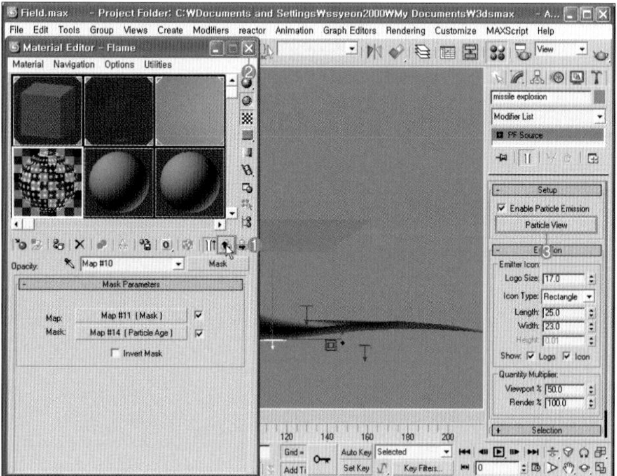

19 Click [Go to Parent] to move to the uppermost stage, and click to close the [Material Editor] dialog box. Click Particle View to open the [Particle View] dialog box of the "missile" object.

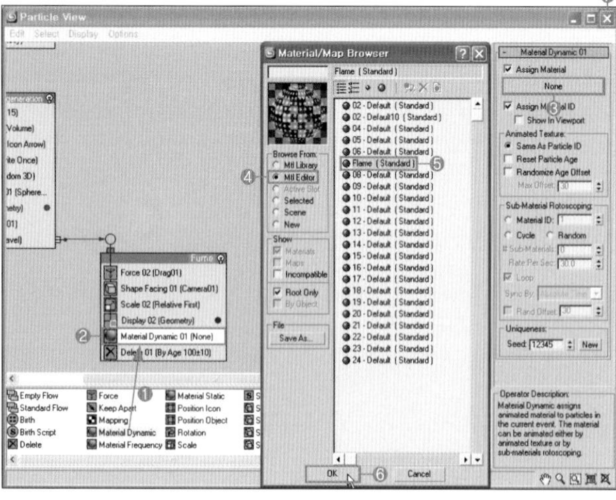

20 Click–and–drag [Material Dynamic] to add it to the spot below "fume" event's [Display 02]. Click [Material Dynamic 01], and click None in the Parameters. Click [Browse From]–[Material Editor] to activate the [Material/Map Browser] dialog box, select the "flame" Material, and click [OK]. Click to close the [Particle View] dialog box.

21 Click–and–drag the time slider to see the fume Particles appear, now mapped with the "flame" Material. But the shape is not shown clearly yet.

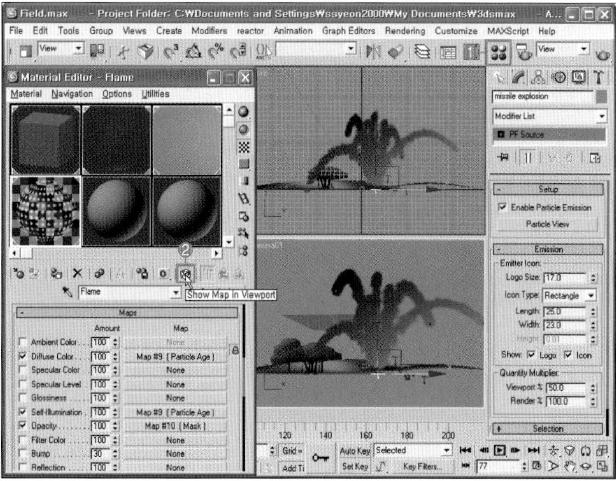

22 Click [Material Editor] on the main toolbar to open the [Material Editor] dialog box, select the "flame" Material, and click [Show Map in Viewport].

23 Select the Perspective Viewport, and click [Quick Render] on the main toolbar to view the rendered scene. Click on the rendering window to close it.

Adding Fog Effect 

You can enhance the sense of reality by adding a fog effect to the field, which looks too clear overall. Since the fog effect makes far–away objects look hazy, it is often used to resolve the unrealistic atmosphere produced in CGs.

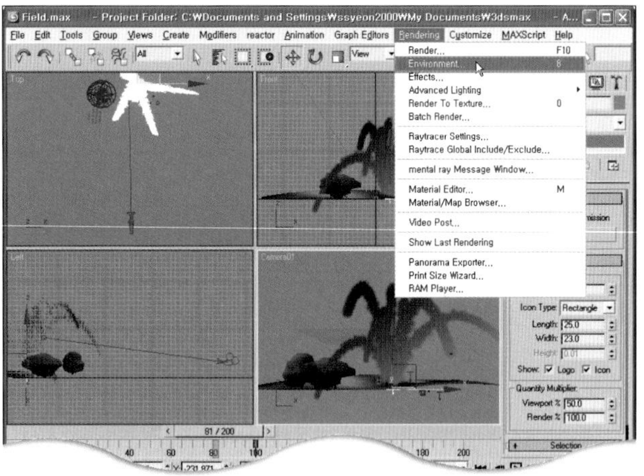

01 To add the fog effect, click [Rendering]–[Environment] on the menu bar.

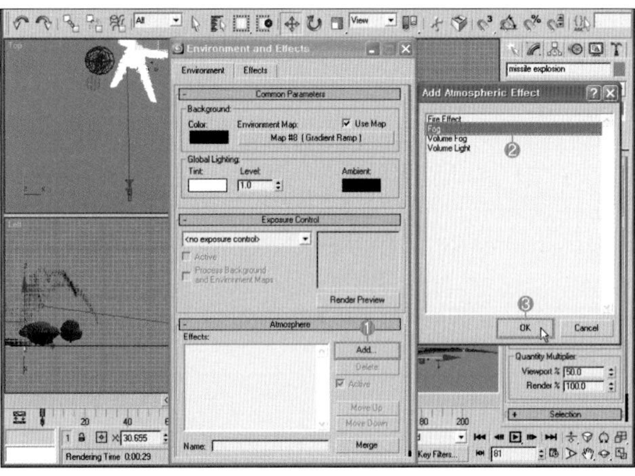

02 Click Add in the [Environment and Effects] dialog box. In the [Add Atmospheric Effect] dialog box, select "Fog", and click [OK].

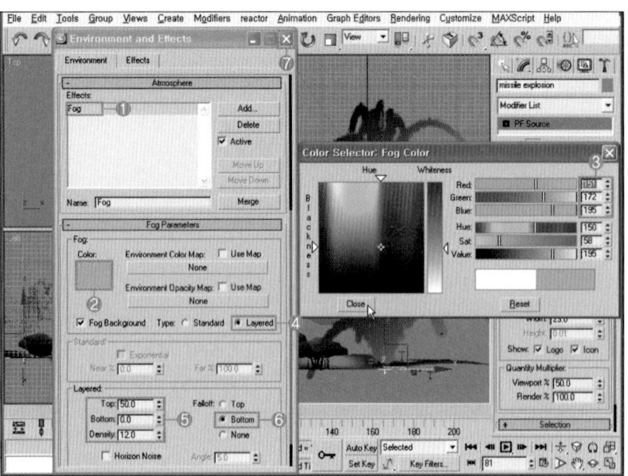

03 Select "Fog", click the color button in [Color], and change the color to sky blue (RGB: 151, 172, 195). Set the [Fog Type] as [Layered], and enter [50] for [Top], [0] for [Bottom], and [12] for [Density], and set [Falloff] as [Bottom]. Click X to close the dialog box.

04 Select the Perspective Viewport, and click [Quick Render] on the main toolbar to view the rendering of the fog. Click on the rendered image window to close it.

Rendering for the Final Video Clip

In this section, we will render the missile animation, which has been the goal of this entire section, and finalize it as a video clip.

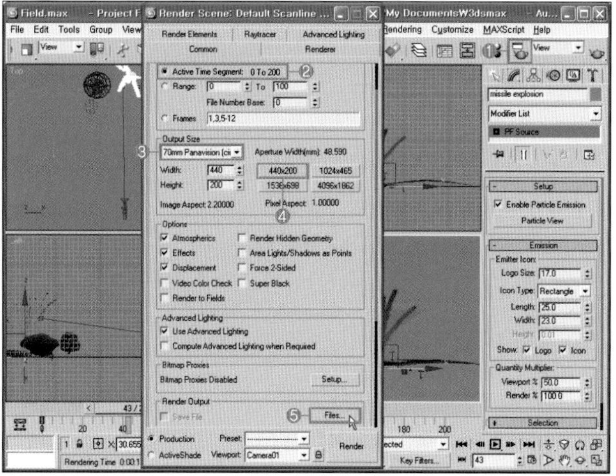

01 To render the final video clip, click [Render Scene] on the main toolbar. When the [Render Scene] dialog box appears, select [Active Time Segment], select [70 mm Panavision (Cine)] for [Output Size], and click [440 x 200]. Click [Render Output]–Files... .

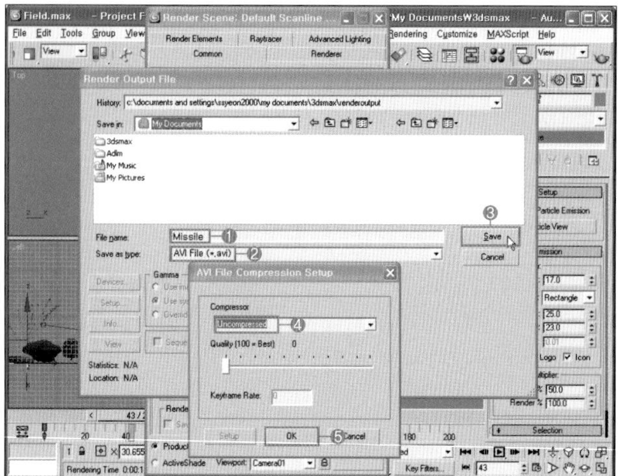

02 When the [Render Output File] dialog box appears, enter "missile" as the file name, and set the file format as an AVI File (*.avi). Click [Setup] to activate the [AVI File Compression Setup] dialog box and click [OK]. Finally, click [Save].

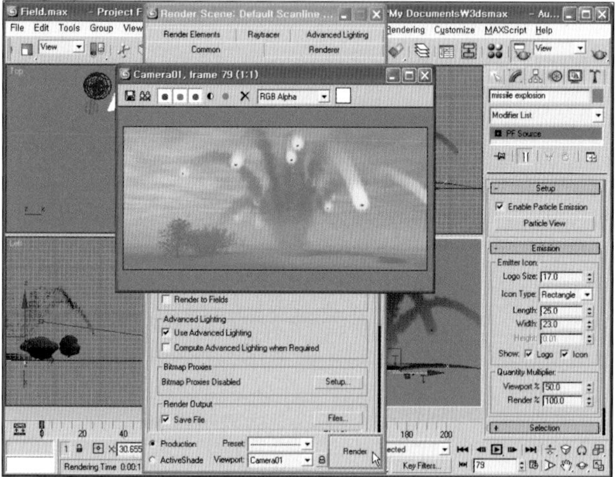

03 Click [Render] in the [Render Scene] dialog box to begin rendering of the final video clip.

Supplementary CD\Sample\Chapter 5\Exercise 1\Field-final.max, Missle explosion.avi

Events for Particle Flow

Let's learn about operators for events, which you need to know to better use the Particle Flow.

Operators to Control Particle Action

Generally, Operators are used to control Particles in the PF Source Particle View dialog box. A total of 26 options are provided. The most important Operators used in controlling the creation and motion of Particles are [Birth], [Delete], [Force], [Position], [Position Object], [Scale], [Shape], [Shape Instance], [Speed], and [Spin].

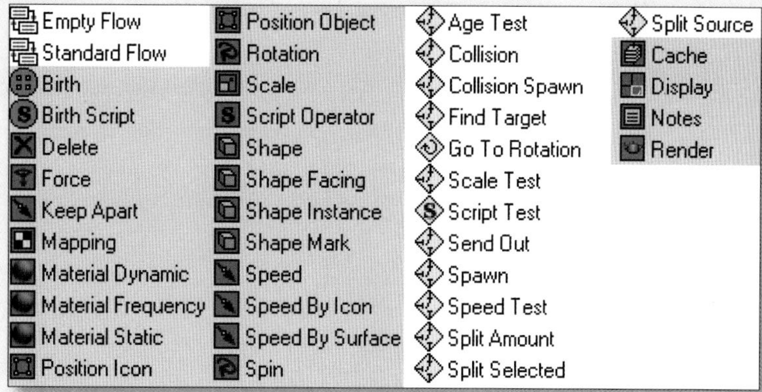

1. **Birth**—Creates a new Particle within the Particle flow.
2. **Birth Scripts**—Creates a Particle with a programming method called Max scripts.
3. **Delete**—Deletes a Particle when desired.
4. **Force**—Computes the collision of Particles with an outside deflector registered.
5. **Keep Apart**—Used to decelerate or separate a fixed selection of Particles.
6. **Mapping**—Adds the UVW Map effect to the whole surface of a Particle.
7. **Material Dynamic**—Maps different materials onto each Event with the material IDs.
8. **Material Frequency**—Adjusts each sub–material ratio of the Material applied to a Particle.
9. **Material Static**—Assigns Materials to an Event.
10. **Position Icon**—Creates a Particle set to the Particle flow icon position.
11. **Position Object**—Uses a separately created object as the Emitter of Particles.
12. **Rotation**—Adjusts the rotation degree of a Particle.
13. **Scale**—Adjust the changes in Particle size.

⑭ **Script Operator**—Controls Particle motion using Max scripts.

⑮ **Shape**—Controls the shape and the size of Particles.

⑯ **Shape Facing**—Forms Particles into a rectangular pattern facing a camera, a direction, or a specific object.

⑰ **Shape Instance**—Replaces a separately created outside object with a Particle.

⑱ **Shape Mark**—Uses part of a mapped outside object as a Particle.

⑲ **Speed**—Adjusts the speed of Particles.

⑳ **Speed By Icon**—Enables Particles to move along an alternate path.

㉑ **Speed By Surface**—Enables a Particle to move on the basis of an alternate object.

㉒ **Spin**—Controls complex rotation of Particles.

㉓ **Cache**—Supports a function that stores Particles in memory to increase computer system speed.

㉔ **Display**—Controls how Particles are shown in the Viewport.

㉕ **Notes**—Allows notes to be inserted into an event.

㉖ **Render**—Controls how Particles look when rendered.

Using Test Operators to Judge States and Instances

The Operator that tests the Age, Collision, and Target of Particles is called the Test Operator. A Test Operator generates natural movement as it computes intermediate stages when a user changes the direction and flow of Particles. This is an important medium that gives the user a connection to each Event.

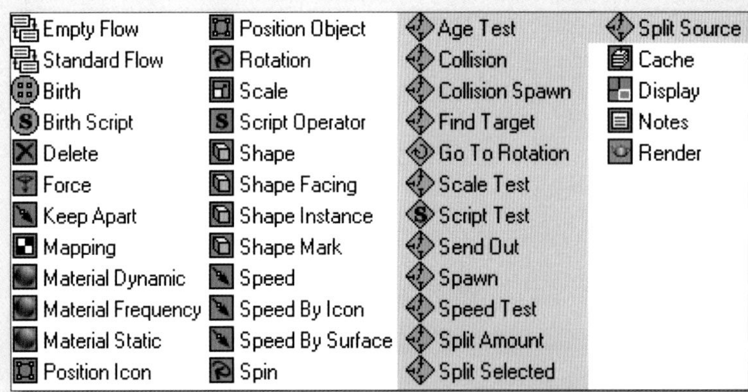

❶ **Age Test**—Tests the age of Particles since their creation.

❷ **Collision**—Tests Particles after they collide with a deflector.

❸ **Collision Spawn**—Creates new Particles after collision with a deflector.

❹ **Find Target**—Enables Particles to trace an outside object.

❺ **Go To Rotation**—Adjusts to enable the rotation of Particles in each specific phase.

❻ **Scale Test**—Tests the size of Particles and causes a change in them.

⑦ **Script Test**—Tests the status of Particles with Max scripts.

⑧ **Send Out**—Passes Particles onto the next event.

⑨ **Spawn**—Generates new Particles from a Particle that experienced a diffusion effect.

⑩ **Speed Test**—Tests the speed and acceleration of Particles.

⑪ **Split Amount**—Splits a specific part of a Particle to pass it onto the next Event.

⑫ **Split Selected**—Splits a selected Particle to pass it onto the next Event.

⑬ **Split Source**—Splits Particles in other Particle flows to pass them onto the next Event.

Controlling Flow

Flow, which refers to the first Event to have Particles, indicates the [PF Source01] Event and the [Event01] event that appears when the [Particle View] dialog box is activated for the first time. The user may keep or erase as many flows within the [Particle View] dialog box as desired. [Empty Flow] indicates the [PF Source01] event with no event included, while [Standard Flow] refers to the [PF Source01] Event and the [Event01] Event.

Exercise 02

Producing Animations

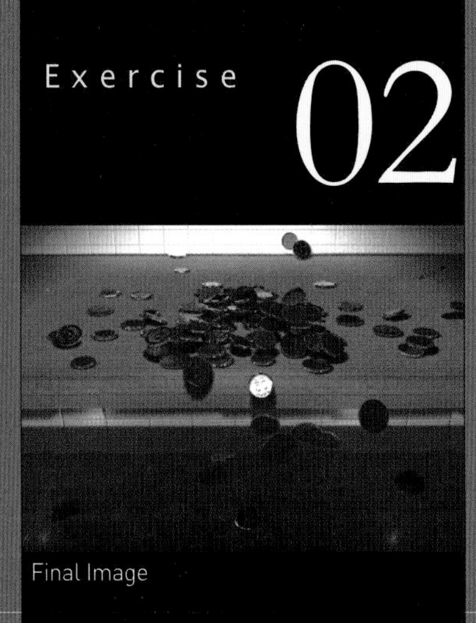
Final Image

The Reactor simulator is a tool that can be used along with Particles and Space Warp. Reactor makes collision effects look very realistic. Reactor refers to all of the tools and key functions used for simulating objects undergoing reactive motion, such as falling objects, springs, jointed limbs, and rustling clothes. This lesson will cover how to use Reactor to create an animated scene in which coins fall on the floor and into water.

Start Files
\Sample\Chapter 5\Exercise 2\Coin.max

Final File
\Sample\Chapter 5\Exercise 2\Coin–final.max

Expressing the Movements of Water Using Water Space Warp

Water Space Warp, available in the Reactor menu, is a tool that precisely expresses the movements of objects moving or floating on the surface of water. It lends a sense of reality when the water's surface is disrupted by the falling coins.

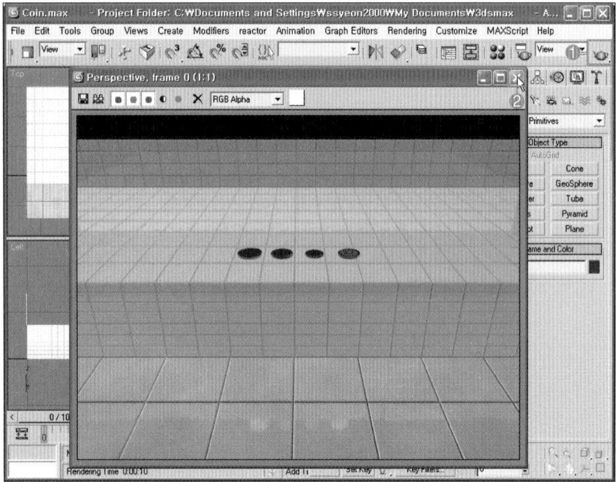

01 Open the "Coin.max" file from the supplementary CD, and select the Perspective Viewport. Click [Quick Render ] on the main toolbar to see the rendered shape of tile floors and the coins. Click ☒ on the rendered image window to close it.

Supplementary CD\Sample\Chapter 5\Exercise 2\Coin.max

tip >>

Render Settings for Sample Files

Prepare the mental ray renderer as the default setting for opening the sample file. The Materials are also all mapped with Arch & Design (mi) Material, and the rendering process follows the mental ray renderer settings. However, for efficiency's sake, the GI and Final Gather options should not be activated.

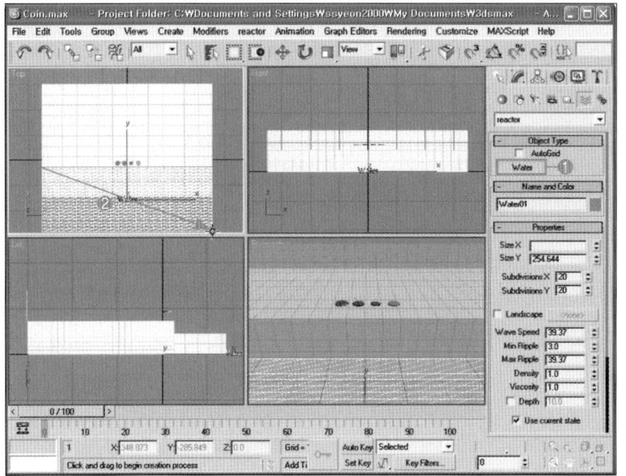

02 On the Create panel, click [Helpers]–[Reactor]–[Water]. Click–and–drag in the Top Viewport from below, as shown, to create the object that will become the water's surface.

tip >>

Water Space Warp

Water Space Warp is a simulation tool that generates the movements of the water's surface. It does not appear during rendering. To resolve this problem, create a separate object for the water's surface, and bind it to the Water Space Warp object. In other words, the object for the water's surface, which appears during rendering, moves according to the motions of Water Space Warp.

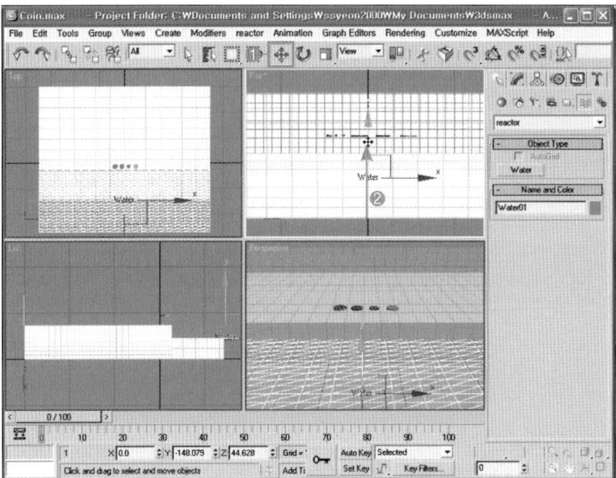

03 Click [Select and Move] on the main toolbar, and move the "Water01" object in the Front Viewport to the end of the "water surface wall" object.

tip >>

Water surface wall Object

After clicking [Select by Name] on the main toolbar and selecting the "water surface wall" object, you can see its location at the end. The "water surface wall" object is used to represent the water when using the Water Space Warp simulation.

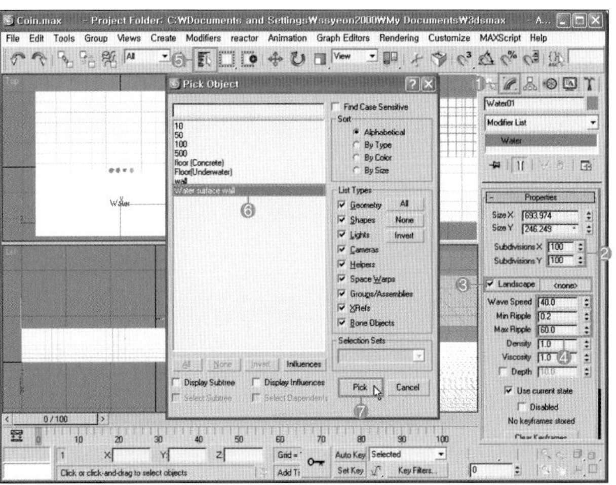

04 With the "Water01" object selected, click [Modify] to move to the Modify panel. In the Parameters, enter [100] for both [Subdivision X] and [Subdivision Y], then enter [50] for [Wave Speed], [0.2] for [Min Ripple], and [60] for [Max Ripple]. Then check the box for [Landscape], and click [None]. Click [Select by Name] on the main toolbar. Click "water surface wall" in the [Pick Object] dialog box, and click [Pick].

Using the Landscape Parameter

Note >>>

The "water surface wall" is set with [Landscape] and the [Water Space Warp] upon executing the Reactor simulation, and is used to generate the water and its surface. If the "water surface wall" object is not set, the water will not be completed.

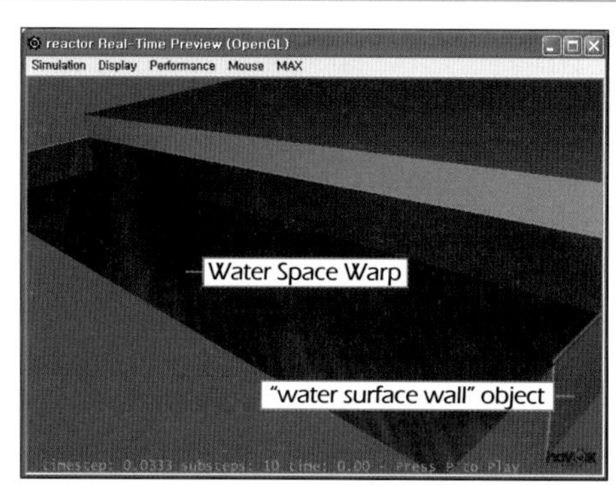

Reacter Simulation Screen

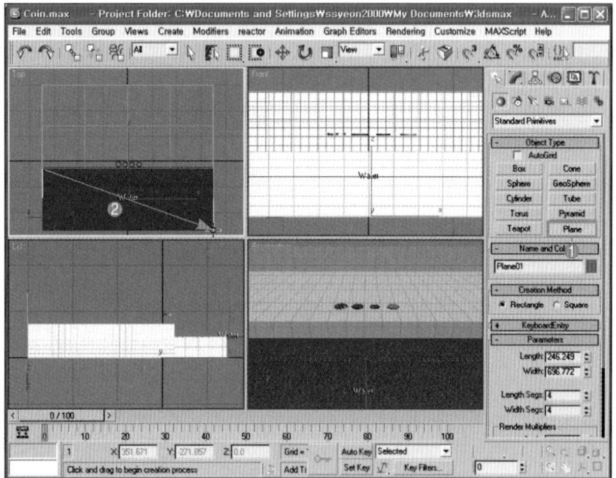

05 To create the water surface object that will be bound to Water Space Warp, click [Geometry]–[Standard Primitives]–[Plane] on the Create panel. Click–and–drag in the Top Viewport to create the new Plane object "Water01."

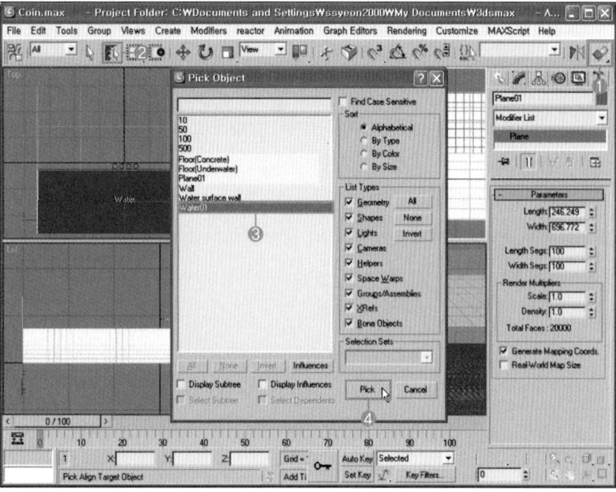

06 To align "Plane01" and "Water01," select "Plane01", and click [icon] on the main toolbar. Click [Select by Name [icon]] on the main toolbar, and click "Water01" in the [Pick Object] dialog box. Click [Pick].

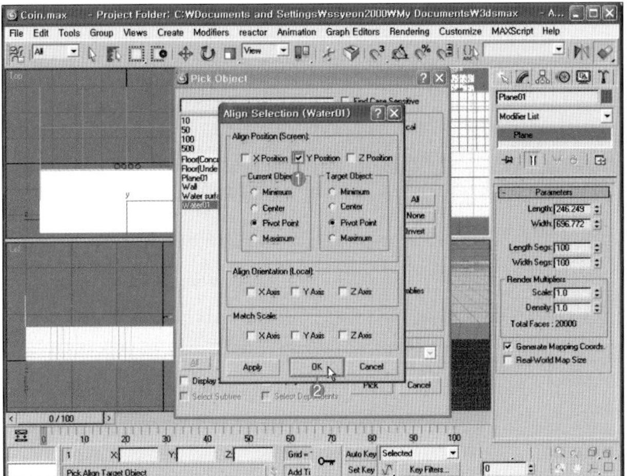

07 When the [Align Selection] dialog box appears, click "polygon Y axis" and select [OK]. The "Plane01" object moves to the location of "Water01."

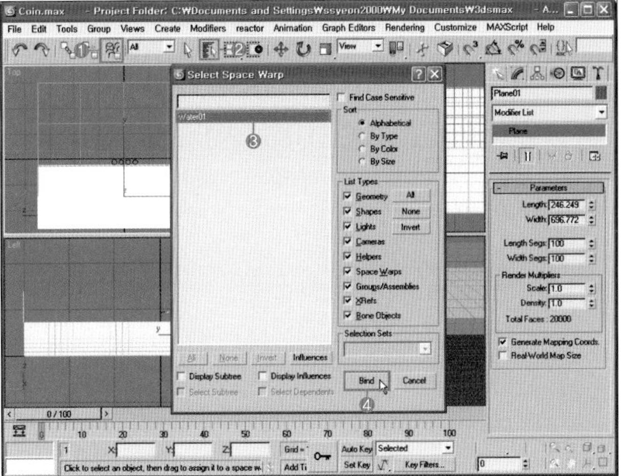

08 To bind "Plane01" to "Water01," click on the main toolbar. Then, click [Select by Name], and click "Water01" in the [Select Space Warp] dialog box. Click [Bind].

tip >>

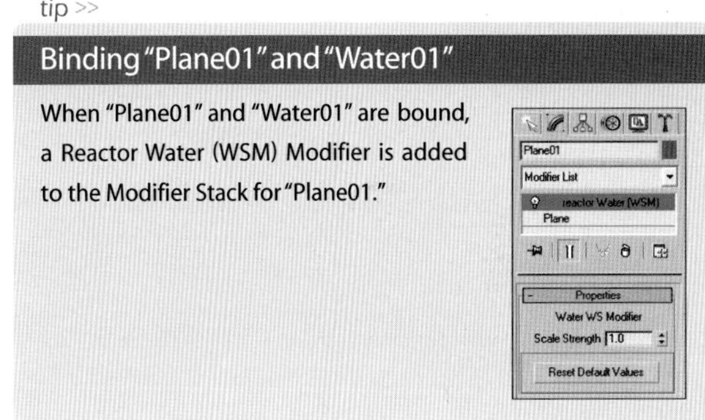

Binding "Plane01" and "Water01"

When "Plane01" and "Water01" are bound, a Reactor Water (WSM) Modifier is added to the Modifier Stack for "Plane01."

Mapping Water Surface Using the Arch & Design (mi) Material

In this section, we will discuss how to map the Arch & Design (mi) Material of mental ray to the Plane object bound to the Water Space Warp, and express the refraction, transparency and waves of water, and the underwater state.

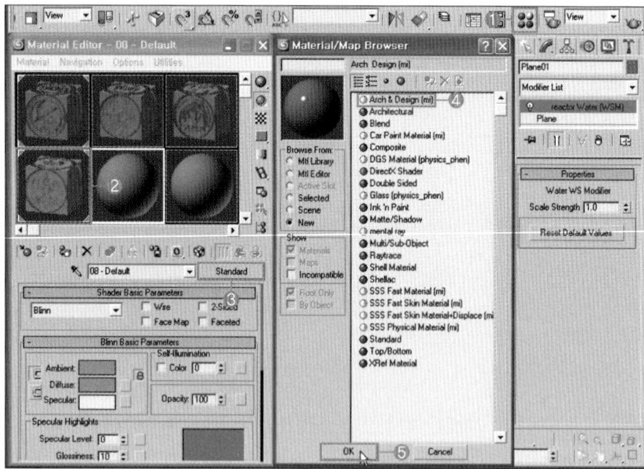

01 Click [Material Editor] on the main toolbar to open the [Material Editor] dialog box. Click the fifth Sample Slot, and click Standard to open the [Material/Map Browser] dialog box. Select [Arch & Design (mi)], and click [OK].

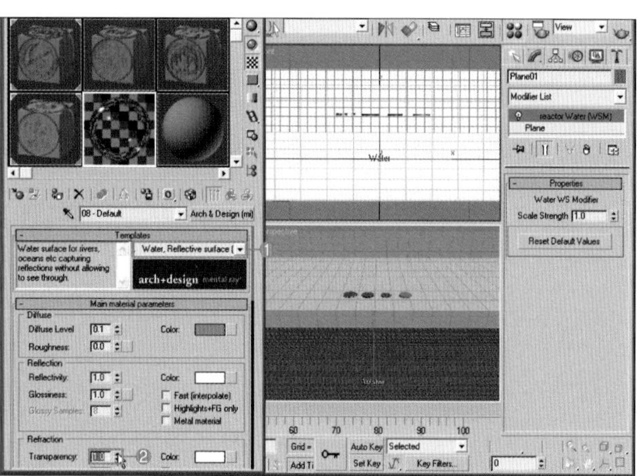

02 Select [Water, Reflective Surface] in [Template], and enter [1] for [Refraction]–[Transparency] to make the water completely transparent.

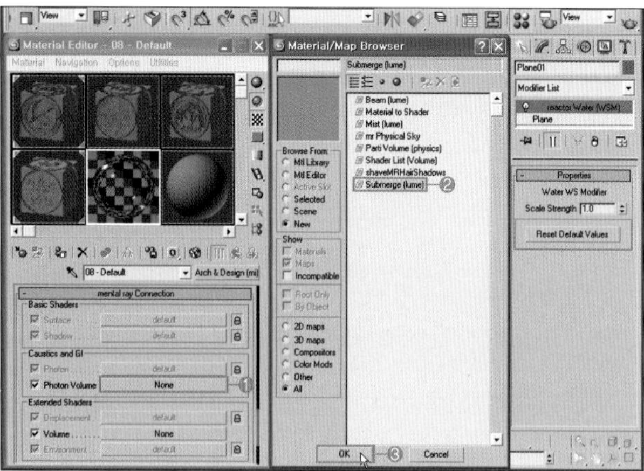

03 Click [mental ray Connection]–[Volume]–None to open the [Material/Map Browser] dialog box. Select [Submerge (lume)], and click [OK].

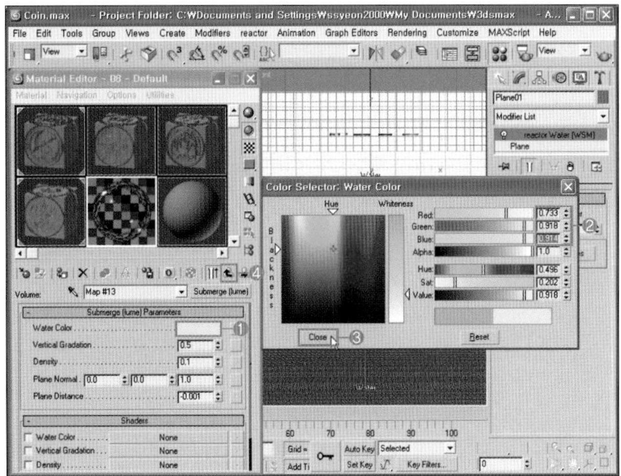

04 Click the [Submerge (lume) Parameters]–[Water Color] color button, and change the color to sky–blue (RGB: 0.733, 0.918, 0.914) in the [Color Selector] dialog box. Click [Go to Parent] to move to the previous screen.

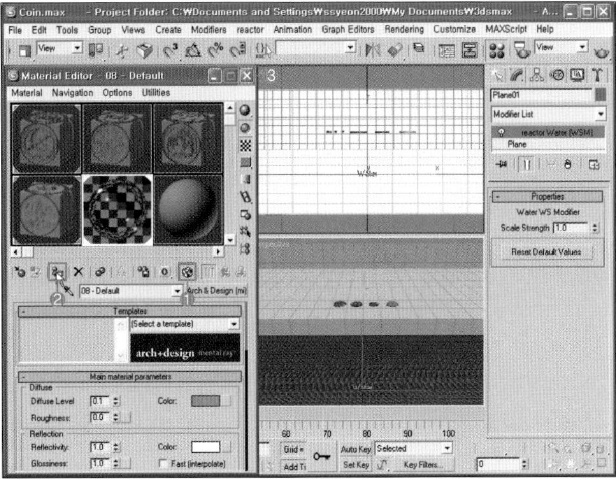

05 Click [Show Map in Viewport] and [Assign Material to Selection] to apply the Material to the "Plane01" object. Click to close the [Material Editor] dialog box.

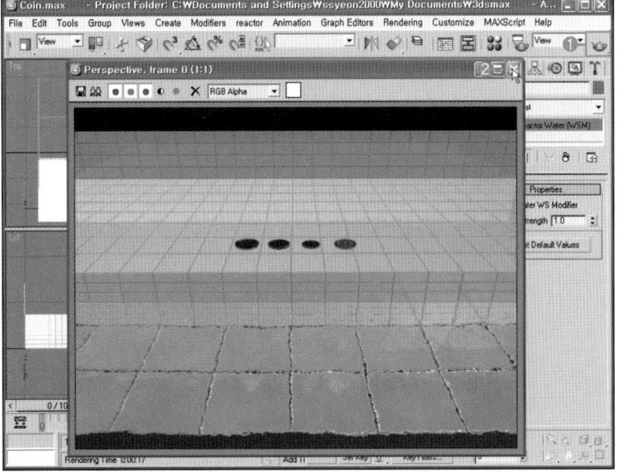

06 Select the Perspective Viewport, then click [Quick Render] on the main toolbar to see the rendering of the water's surface. Click on the rendered image window to close it.

tip >>

Binding Plane to Object

If "Plane01" is not bound to "Water01" by , the water's surface does not appear on the rendered screen.

Depicting Cloth with Reactor Cloth 

In this section, we will discuss how to simulate cloth that wraps the floor polygon using the Cloth Collection in the Reactor tools. Please note that since this process is not to animate the cloth but to display it in a still state, this lesson is not related to the Rigid Body Collection simulation, discussed later.

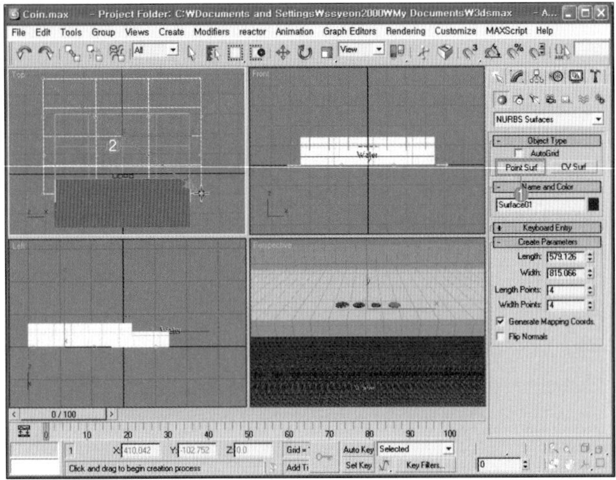

01 To create cloth, click [Geometry]–[NURBS Surface] on the Create panel, and click Point Surf. Click–and–drag in the Top Viewport, as shown, to create the point surf object.

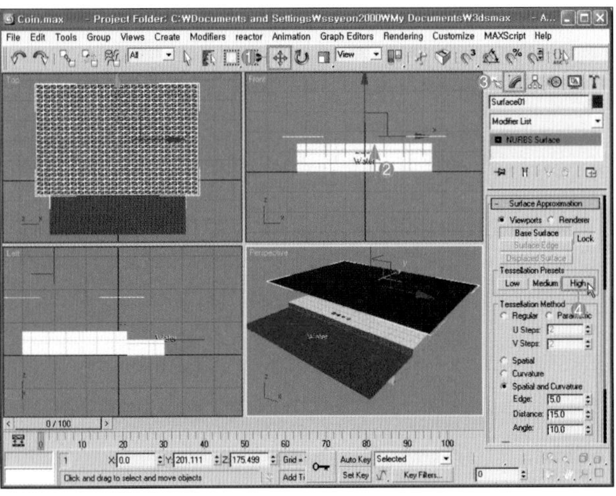

02 Click [Select and Move] on the main toolbar, and move the "Surface01" object upward in the Front Viewport. Select "Surface01" and click [Modify] to move to the Modify panel, and click [Surface Approximation]–[Tessellation Presets]–High to make the polygon composition of the object complicated.

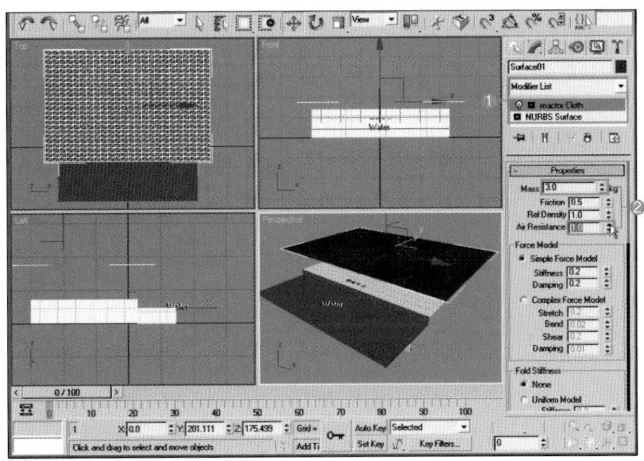

03 With "Surface01" selected, click the [Modifier List] combo box and add the [Reactor Cloth] Modifier. Enter [3] for [Mass] and [1] for Air Resistance.

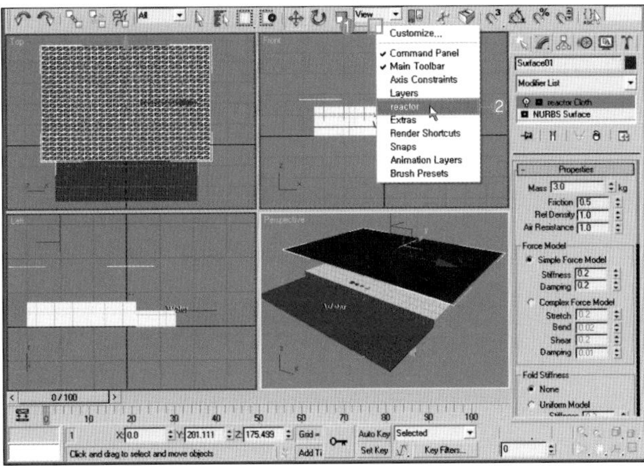

04 When the [icon] icon appears in a blank space on the main toolbar, right-click and select [Reactor] on the menu to display the [Reactor] toolbar.

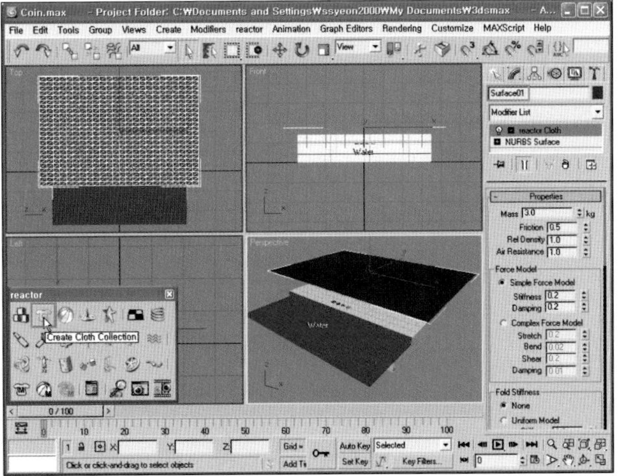

05 With "Surface01" selected, click [Create Cloth Collection [icon]] on the Reactor toolbar to register "Surface01" in the Cloth Collection.

tip >>

Registering Surfaces with Create Cloth Collection

In the Modify stack of the newly created "CLCollection01", the "Surface01" object should be shown as registered. If [Create Cloth Collection] has been clicked without "Surface01" selected, click [Add] in the Modify stack and select "Surface01" to add.

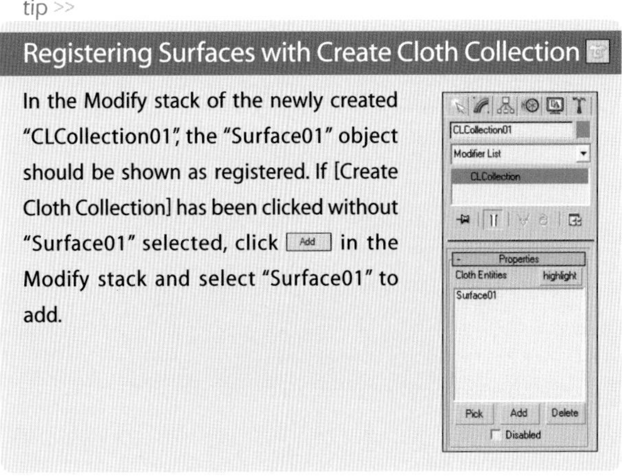

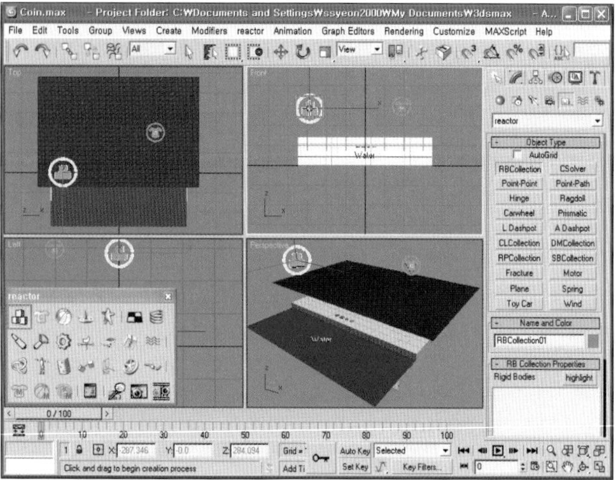

06 To simulate cloth, click [Create Rigid Body Collection] on the [Reactor] toolbar, and click [Viewport] to create a new Rigid Body Collection.

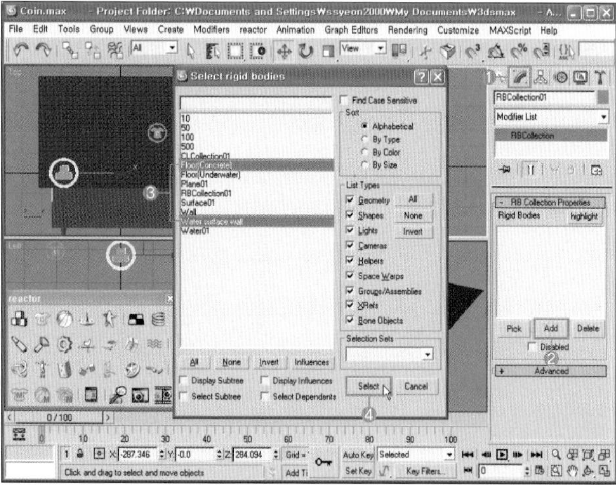

07 With "RBCollection01" selected, click [Modify] to move to the Modify panel. Click Add in the Parameters, click the "Floor(concrete)" and "Water surface wall" objects in the [Select Rigid Objects] dialog box, and click [Select].

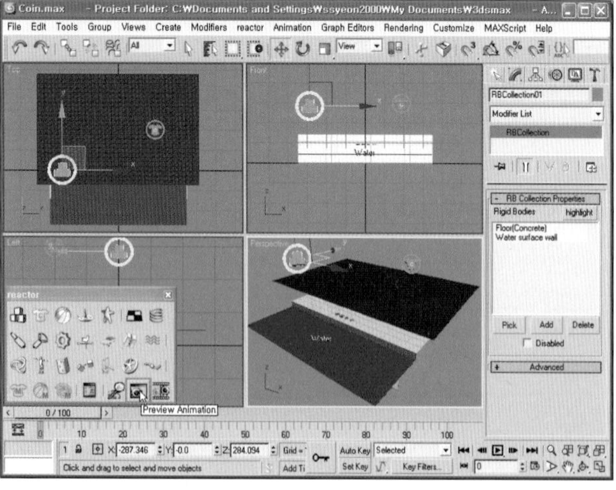

08 On the Reactor toolbar, click [Preview Animation] to open the [Reactor Real–Time Preview] screen.

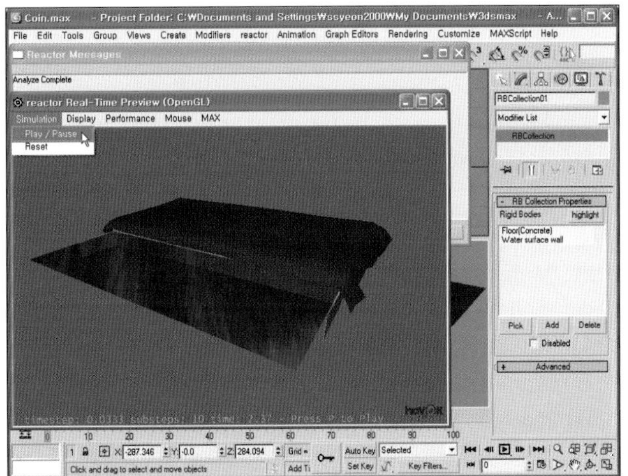

09 Click [Simulation]–[Play/Pause] in [Reactor Real–Time Preview] to watch the simulation. The simulation of a blanket wrapping around a bed plays out.

tip >>

Controlling the Reactor Real–Time Preview

To control the [Reactor Real–Time Preview] display, the three buttons of the mouse can be used; the left button for Rotation, the middle button or scroll wheel button for Pan, and the scroll wheel for Zooming.

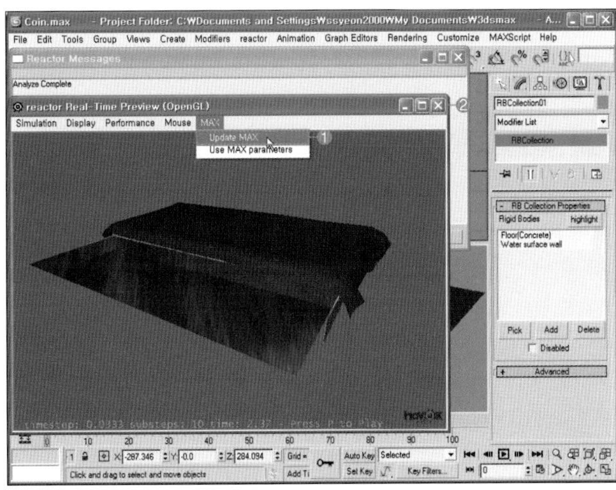

10 When the desired frame appears during the simulation, click [Simulation]–[Play/Pause] to stop the simulation, and renew the current frame's appearance with [Max]–[Update Max]. Click ☒ to close the screen.

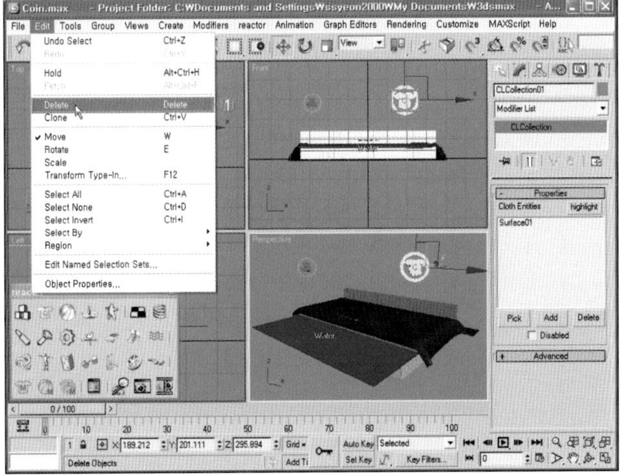

11 When the completed cloth shape is made, select "CLCollection01" to exit the cloth simulation mode, and delete with [Edit]–[Delete].

tip >>

Retain [Reactor Cloth] Modifier

Even after deleting "CLCollection01" to exit the cloth simulation mode, the [Reactor Cloth] modifier applied to "Surface01" must be left as it is. If the [Reactor Cloth] modifier were also deleted, the renewed cloth would become a 2D object.

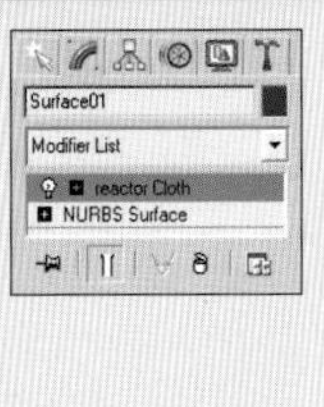

Using the Arch & Design (mi) Material 

Because Arch & Design (mi) Material types do not provide templates for special cloth, you can select Rubber, which is lusterless. In this section, we will discuss how to control the reflection and transparency of the cloth.

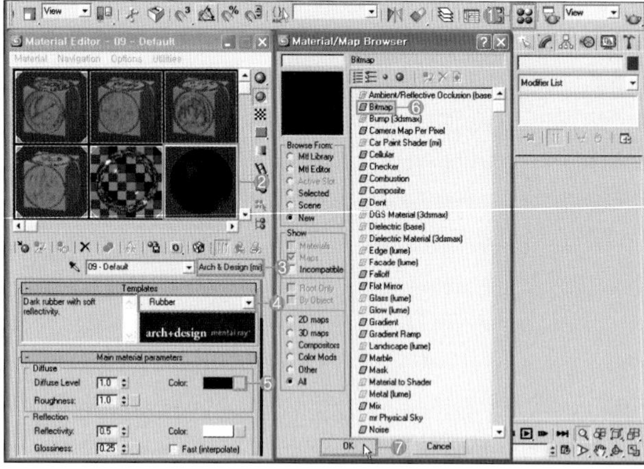

01 Click [Material Editor] on the main toolbar to open the [Material Editor] dialog box. Click the sixth Sample Slot, and click Standard to change to Arch & Design (mi) Material. Select [Rubber] from [Template], click the [Diffuse on Parameter] color button, select the [Bitmap] map in the [Material/Map Browser] dialog box, and click [OK].

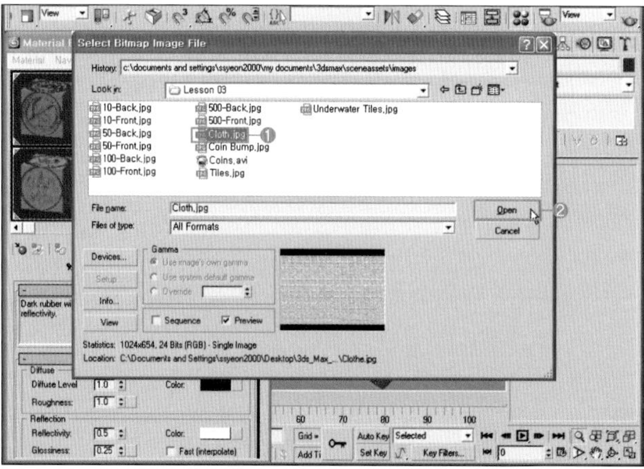

02 Select "Cloth.jpg" in the [Select Bitmap Image File] dialog box, and click [Open]".

Supplementary CD\Sample\Chapter 5\Exercise 2\Cloth.jpg

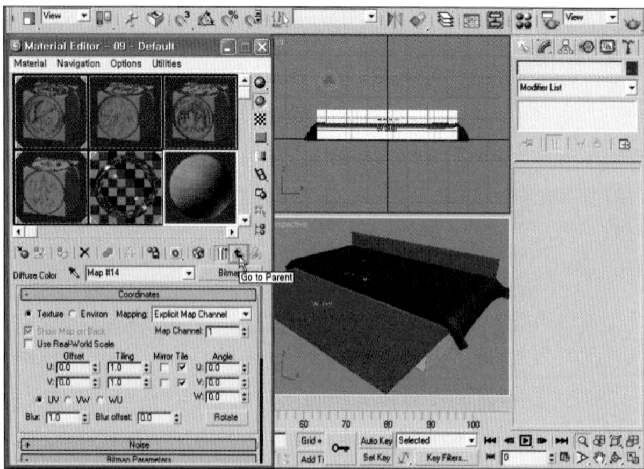

03 Click [Go to Parent] to return to the higher menu level (here, the initial screen).

04 Enter [0.3] for [Refraction]–[Transparency], and right–click on the map button applied to the [Diffused Color]. Select [Copy] on the menu.

05 Check the box for [Special Purpose Maps]–[Bump], enter [1], right–click on None, and select [Paste (Instance)] on the menu.

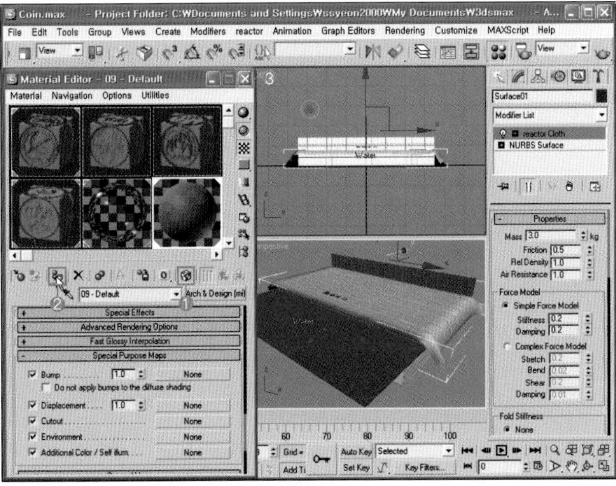

06 Click [Show Map in Viewport] and [Assign Material to Selection] to apply the Material to the “Surface01” object. Click to close the [Material Editor] dialog box.

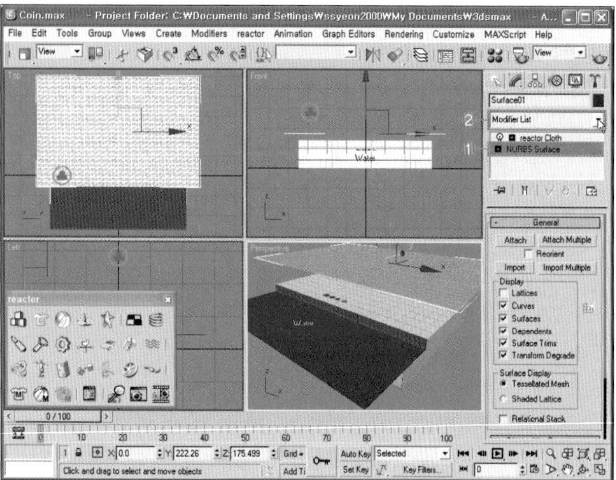

07 With "Surface01" selected, click [NURBS Surface] in the Modify stack, and click the [Modifier List] combo box.

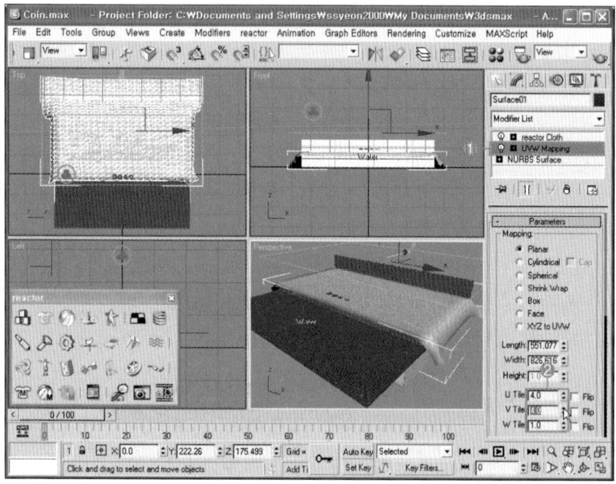

08 Add the [UVW Map] modifier to the [Modifier List], and enter [4] both for [U Tile] and [V Tile] of [Parameters] to have the map tiled repeatedly.

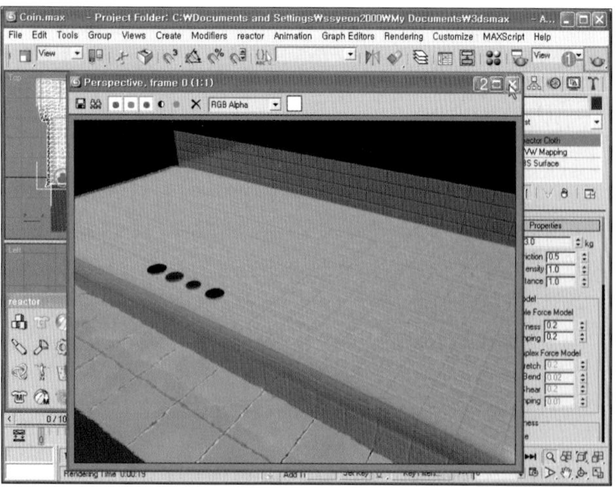

09 Select the Perspective Viewport, and click [Quick Render] on the main toolbar to preview the rendered shape of the cloth. Click ☒ on the rendered image window to close it.

Simulating A Falling Coin with Reactor Rigid Body Collection

This section will discuss how to use the Rigid Body Collection from the Reactor tools to calculate the force of gravity. We will also explore how to apply physical characteristics to objects, how to control the simulator, and how to convert the completed simulation into a max animation.

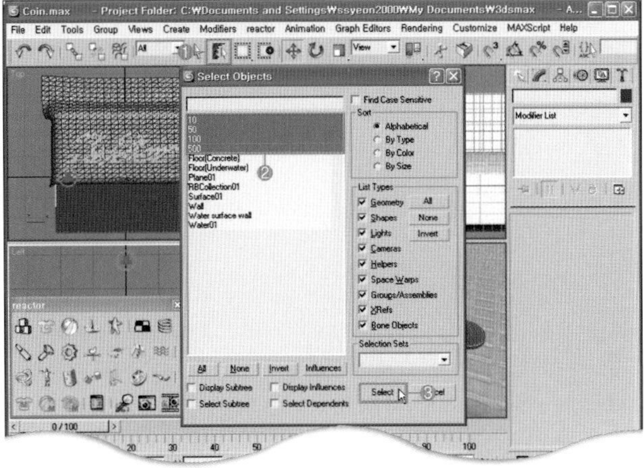

01 Click [Select by Name] on the main toolbar. In the [Select Objects] dialog box, press <Ctrl> and click "10", "50", "100", and "500", and click [Select].

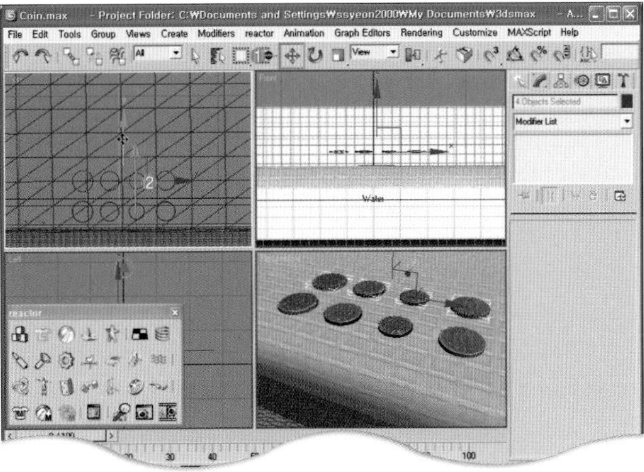

02 Click [Select and Move] on the main toolbar. While pressing <Shift>, copy by click–and–dragging upwards in the Top Viewport.

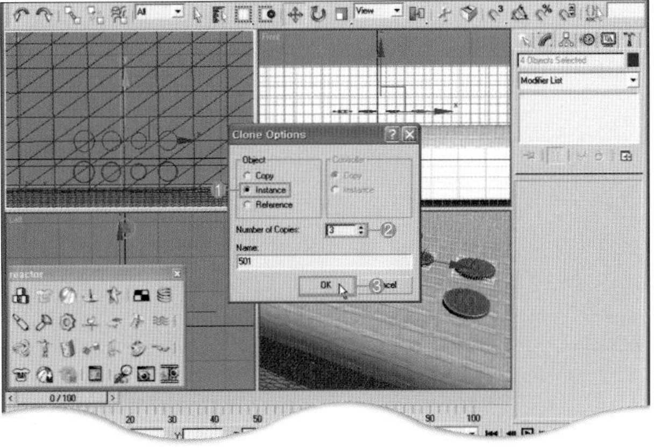

03 When the [Clone Options] dialog box appears, click [Instance] and enter [3] for [Number of Copies]. Click [OK].

tip >>

Clone Options Instances

An Instance made by the Clone Options dialog box is a real–time and reactive copy of the original object. When the original object is modified, all of its Instances are simultaneously modified.
This will allow the user to easily change the Materials of all of the coins for rendering.

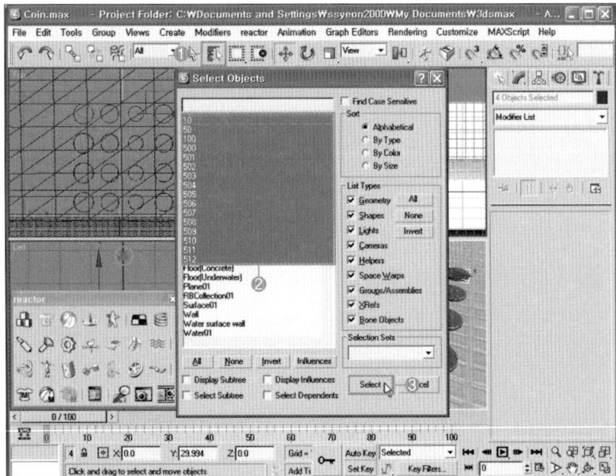

04 Click [Select by Name] on the main toolbar. Click all the coins in the [Select Objects] dialog box as shown in the picture, and click [Select].

tip >>

Simultaneous Selection

To select many coins at the same time, you can speed up the process by clicking the object at the top and then the last object while pressing <Shift>.

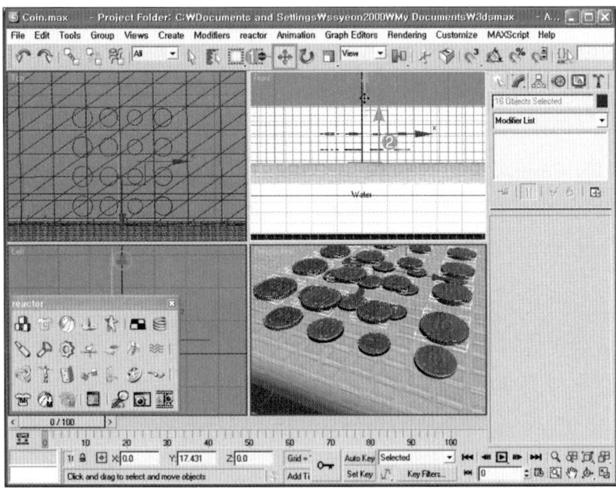

05 Click [Select and Move] on the main toolbar While holding <Shift>, copy the selection in the Front Viewport by click–and–dragging upwards.

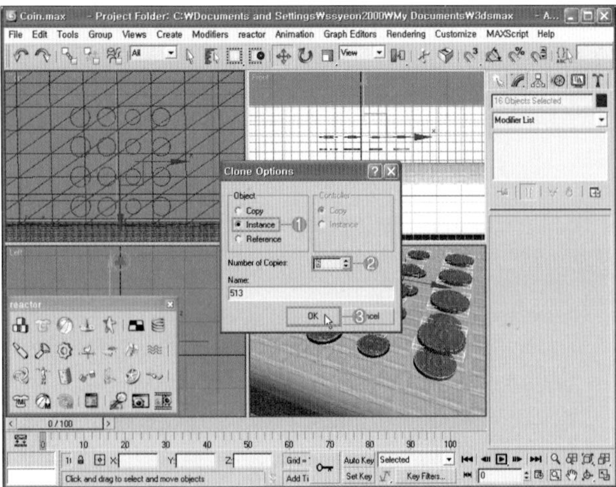

06 When the [Clone Options] dialog box appears, click [Instance], enter [6] for [Number of Copies], and click [OK].

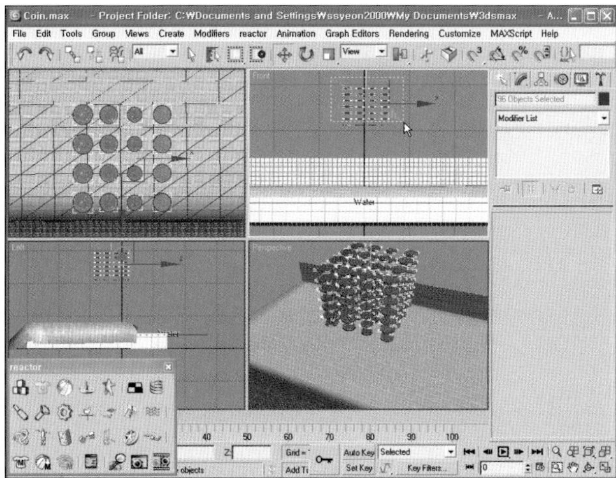

07 Among these copied and aligned coins, click–and–drag to select all of the cloned objects in the Front Viewport.

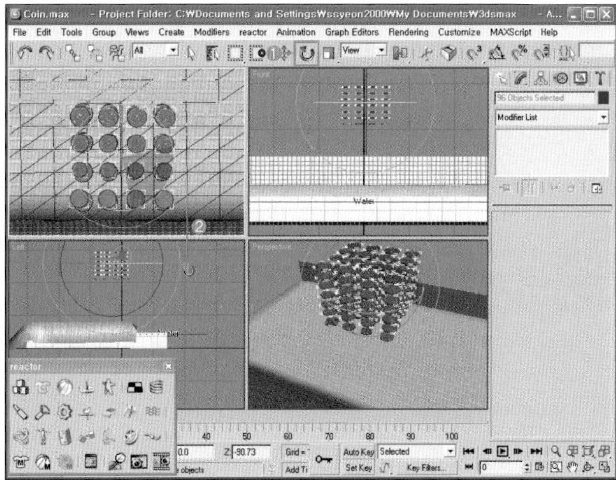

08 Click [Select and Rotate] on the main toolbar, and rotate the object in the Top Viewport to change the location of the coins.

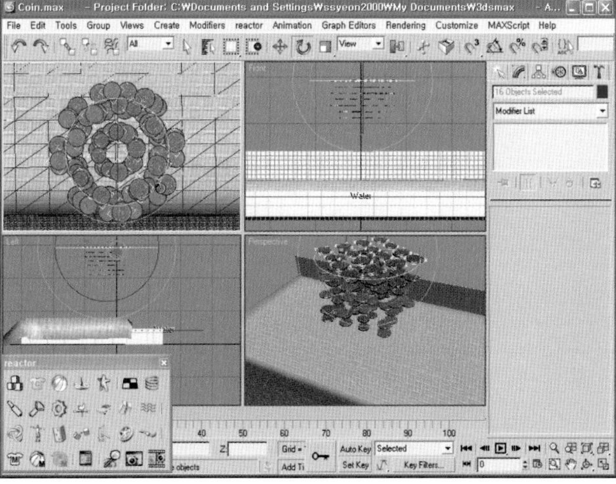

09 Using the same method, select all the coins above the third row and rotate them with [Select and Rotate].

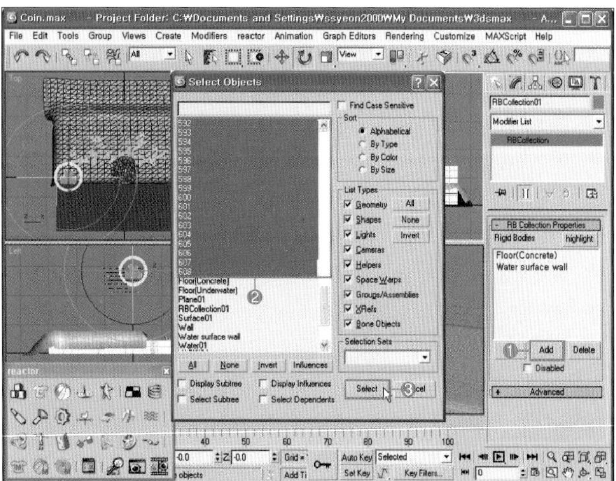

10 Select "RBCollection01," click [Add] in the Parameters, select all the coins in the [Select Rigid Objects] dialog box, and click [Select].

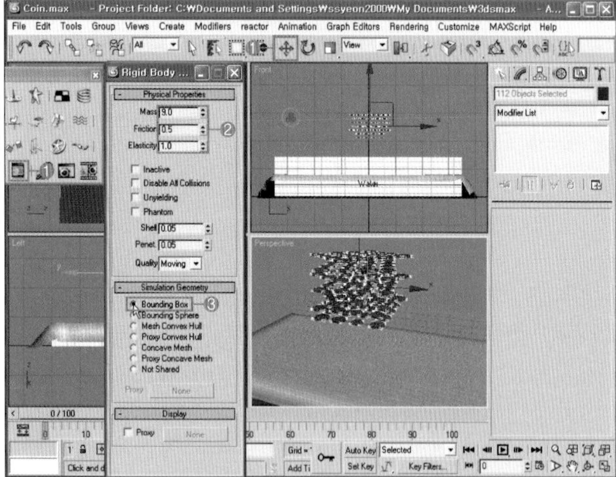

11 To set the physical properties of the selected object, click [Open Property Editor] on the Reactor toolbar. When the [Rigid Body Property Editor] appears, enter [9] for [Mass], [0.5] for [Friction], [1] for [Elasticity], and click [Bounding Box].

tip >>

Mass, Friction, and Elasticity

Mass means the relative weight of the selected object. Friction is the measure of resistance encountered between two objects in motion; objects move easiest at 0 friction. The higher the Elasticity value, the greater the "bounce back" effect from a collision.

Defining an Object's Properties in the Rigid Body Property Editor

Note >>>

Objects used for simulations may be composed of various shapes and polygons. Therefore, careful consideration is required for how to use them in the simulator. There are seven methods for defining an object's bounding properties. The Bounding Box is for treating an object like a box regardless of the actual shape, and Bounding Sphere is for treating it as a sphere. To reflect the shape and polygon structure of the object in more detail, use Mesh Convex Hull, or the even simpler Proxy Convex Hull. To reflect the original shape and the condition of the polygon, use Concave Mesh or Proxy Concave Mesh.

Bounding Box

Bounding Sphere

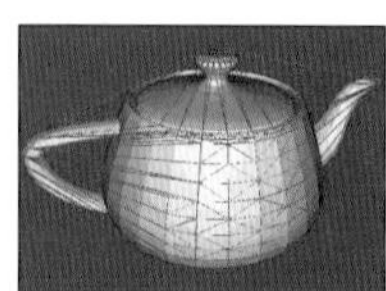

Mesh Convex Hull

Proxy Convex Hull

Concave Mesh

Proxy Concave Mesh

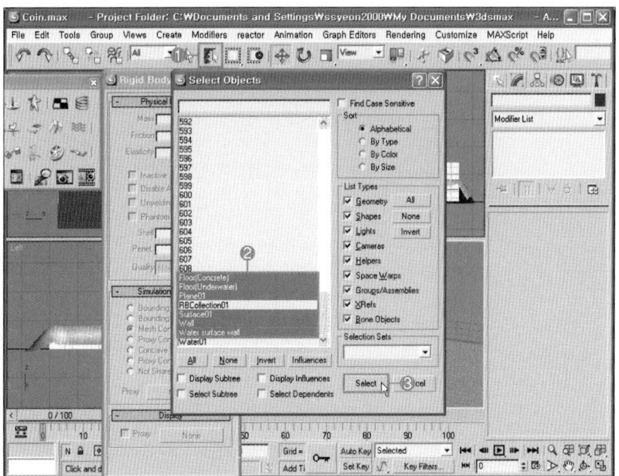

12 Click [Select by Name] on the main toolbar. In the [Select Objects] dialog box, select “Plane01”, “Surface01”, “Floor(underwater)”, “Floor(concrete)”, “Wall”, “Water surface wall”, and click [Select].

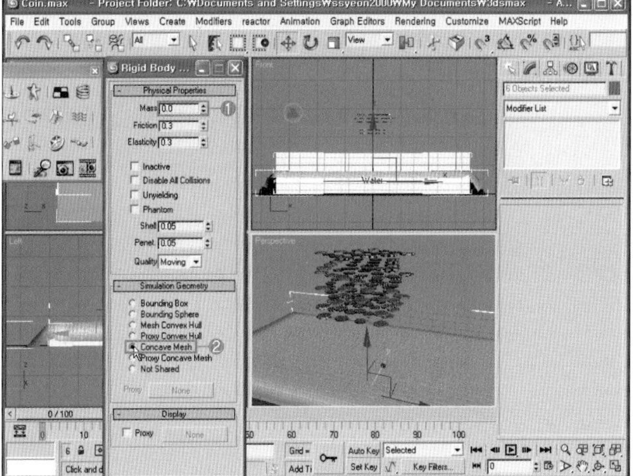

13 Enter [0] for [Mass] in the [Rigid Body Property Editor] dialog box, and change to [Concave Mesh].

tip >>

Controlling Mass Value

Setting the Mass value to 0 isolates an object from the influence of gravity in the simulation, making the object look fixed.

14 Click [Preview Animation] on the Reactor toolbar to open the [Reactor Real–Time Preview] screen. Click [Simulation]–[Play/Pause] in [Reactor Real–Time Preview] to observe the simulation. You will see all the coins falling at once. Click to close the screen.

15 Click [Create Animation] on the Reactor toolbar to convert the Reactor simulation to max key.

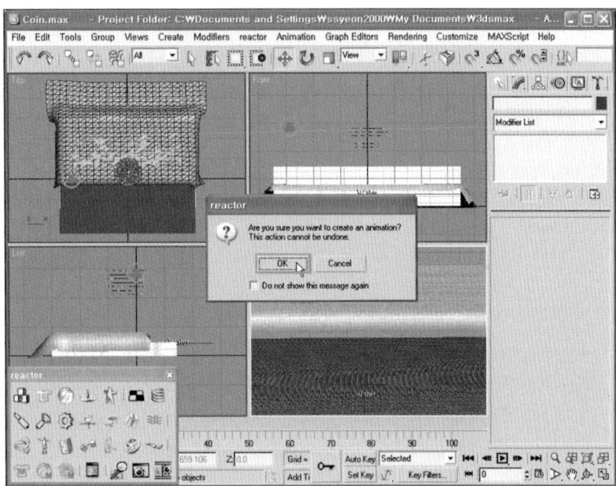

16 When the dialog box appears warning the process cannot be reversed once the simulation is converted to max key animation, click [OK].

17 Move the time slider to see the coins randomly falling from above.

tip >>

Animation Controls

After converting to max key using [Create Animation], animation keys appear that correspond to each coin.

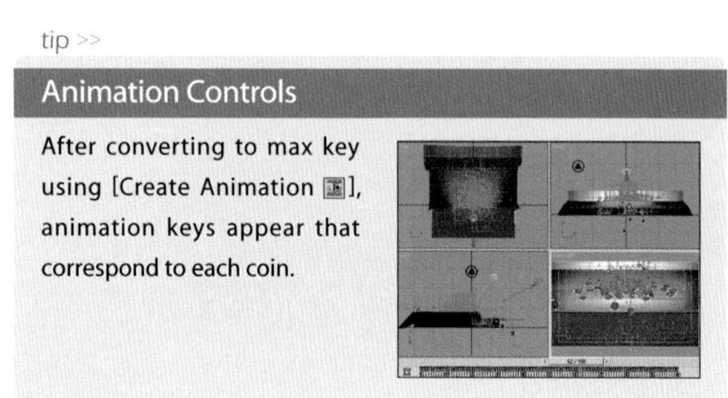

18 Select the Perspective Viewport, and click [Quick Render] on the main toolbar to see the rendered scene. Click on the rendered image window to close it.

Rendering with Mental Ray Renderer and Lights

To enhance the realism of the white and gold coins, you can install lighting using the mental ray renderer's [GI and Final Gather] feature for the rendering.

01 To install the main light, click [Lights]–[Standard]–Target Spot on the Create panel. Click–and–drag in the Left Viewport to install a target spotlight that points downward.

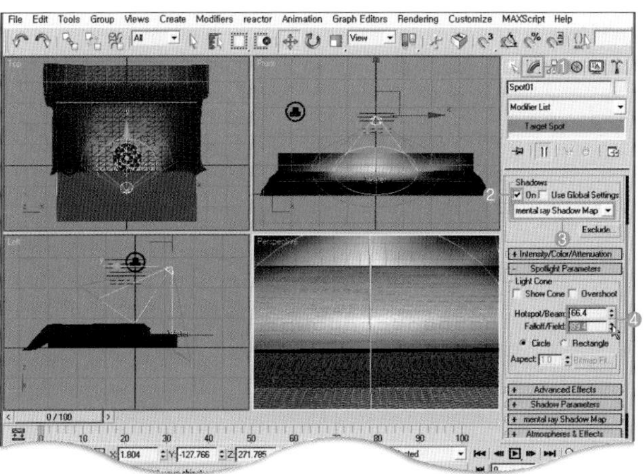

02 With "Spot01" selected, click [Modify] to move to the Modify panel. Check the [Shadows]–[On] box in the Parameters menu, turn the mental ray [Shadow Map] shadow on, and enter [66] for [Hotspot/Beam] and [89] for [Falloff/Field].

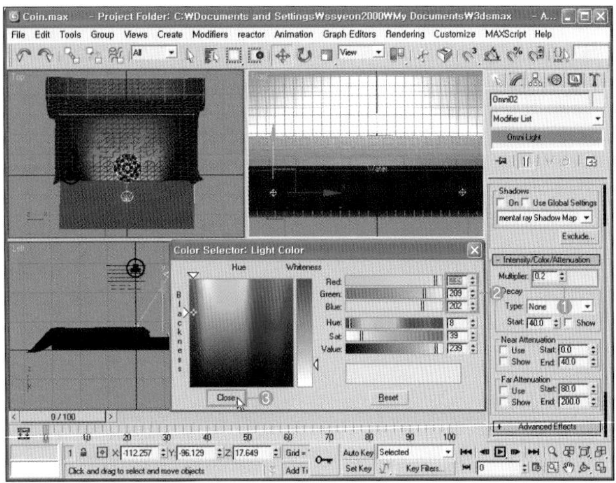

03 Install two Omni lights under the "Water01" object to set the light in the water, and enter [0.2] for the light [Multiplier] and change the color as desired.

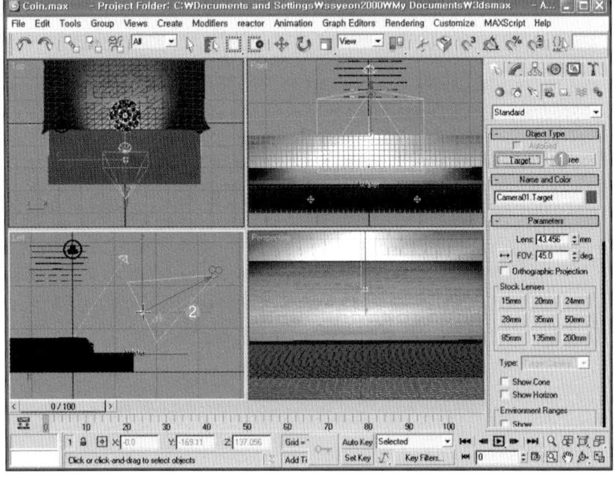

04 To install a camera, click [Cameras]–[Standard]–[Target] on the Create panel. Install a camera that faces forward in the Left Viewport.

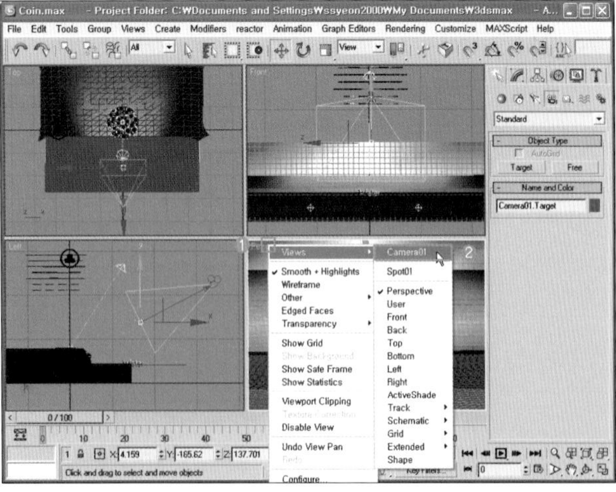

05 Right–click on the Perspective Viewport text label to open the Viewport menu. Select "Camera01" on the menu to change the Viewport view to Camera01's view.

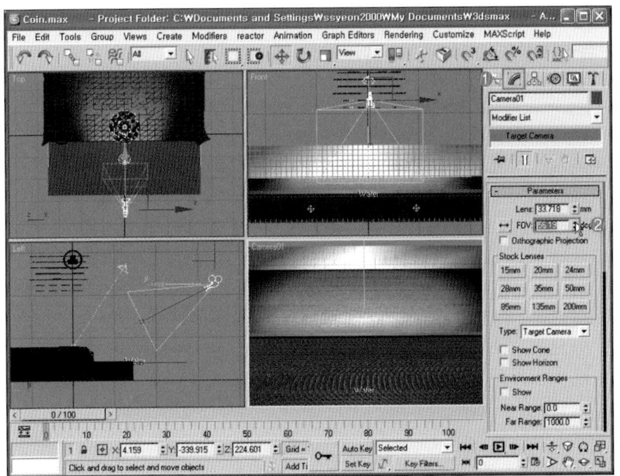

06 Select "Camera01" and click [Modify] to move to the Modify panel. Enter [56] for [Parameters]–[FOV] to widen the photographing angle slightly.

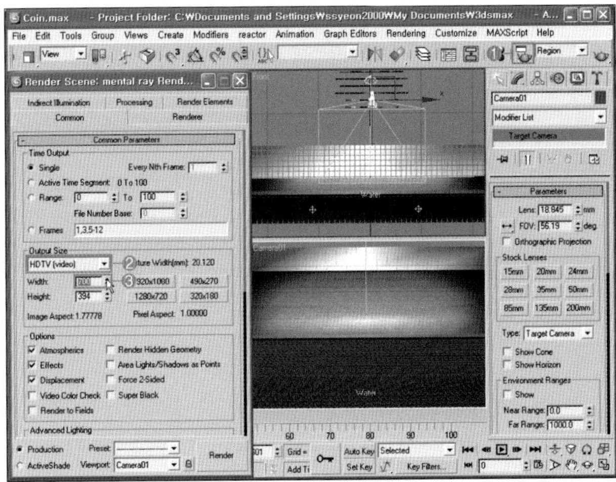

07 Click [Render Scene] on the main toolbar. In the [Render Scene] dialog box, select [HDTV (video)] for the [Output Size], and enter [700] for [Width] to set the rendering size.

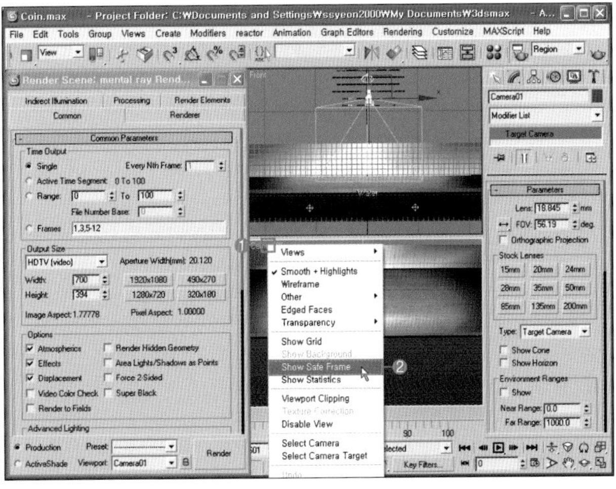

08 On the Viewport menu, select the [Safe Frame] according to the size of the set rendering to make the grid section.

09 Click Render in the [Render Scene] dialog box to confirm the rendering image.

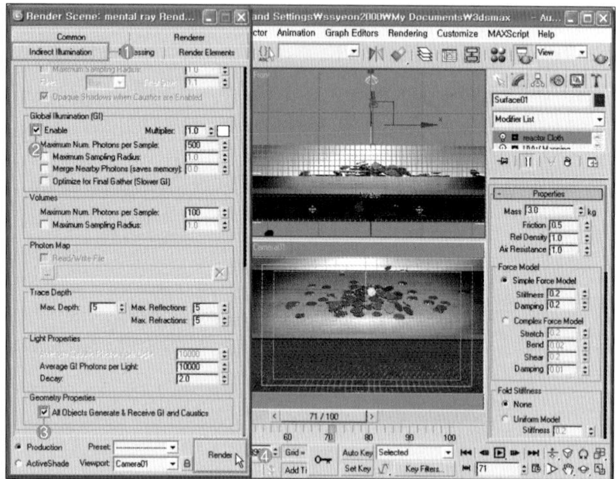

10 To calculate the indirect light in the [Render Scene] dialog box, check [Enable] and [All Objects Generates & Receive GI and Caustics of Global Illumination(GI)], and click Render.

11 After confirming that surrounding lights produce the desired effect, click ☒ to close the image.

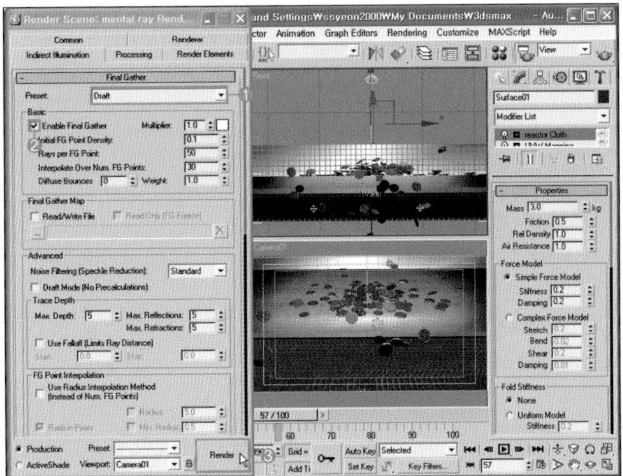

12 Check [Enable Final Gather] in [Final Gather] to correct the contrastive structure of the image in the [Render Scene] dialog box, and click [Draft Render].

13 Verify that the image of the cloth, water's surface, and coins are expressed realistically.

Supplementary CD\Sample\Chapter 5\Exercise 2\Coin–final.max

Index >>>